A Comparative Analysis of Policing Consumer Contracts in China and the EU

Jiangqiu Ge

A Comparative Analysis of Policing Consumer Contracts in China and the EU

Springer

Jiangqiu Ge
School of Law
Fudan University
Shanghai, China

ISBN 978-981-13-2988-3 ISBN 978-981-13-2989-0 (eBook)
https://doi.org/10.1007/978-981-13-2989-0

Library of Congress Control Number: 2018962735

This Springer imprint is published by the registered company Springer Nature Singapore Pte Ltd.
The registered company address is: 152 Beach Road, #21-01/04 Gateway East, Singapore 189721, Singapore

Acknowledgements

This book is based on my PhD dissertation completed at the Maastricht European Private Law Institute, so I would like to dedicate my foremost gratitude to my dear supervisors, Prof. Jan Smits and Dr. Nicole Kornet. Since 2012, they have spent enormous time and energy on guiding me how to write a PhD dissertation. Their encouragement and instructions were always the impetus and the biggest support of my work. Although they were very busy with teaching, writing and other administrative affairs, we kept a routine that we met twice a month. They were always very patient and of great wisdom to make me aware where the problem was and how to fix it. I would never forget the moments when I received the pages that are filled with detailed comments and corrections. Their scrupulous work makes me better understand not only the answers to substantive questions and the importance of readership but also the characters of a true academic, and these characters reveal the orientation to which I should endeavour. Apart from the work, my supervisors also gave me great support in my daily life. They are not only my scholarly supervisors but also life mentors and true friends.

I would like to thank Prof. Michael Faure, Dr. Caroline Cauffman, Prof. Shiyuan Han, Prof. Keke Jin and Dr. Lei Chen, for their insightful comments and valuable feedback. Some comments are very critical, but they definitely made me realise that there are still a lot I can do in my future research. Some special words should be dedicated to Prof. Shiyuan Han. In 2011, when I told him, who was my master thesis supervisor, that I am expecting to become an academic, he introduced me the opportunity that I may conduct a PhD research supervised by Prof. Jan Smits. He said this experience would 'open a window' for me and would be significant to my career. After these years, I become increasingly aware of his considerate intention and always feel grateful.

Writing a PhD dissertation is not easy, which is especially the case when you are doing it abroad. Fortunately, I have a lot of great friends who make me feel that I am at home. My thanks firstly go to my dear friends Mark Kawakami, William Bull, Catalina Goanta and Willem Loof. They are the first colleagues that I met in Maastricht in 2012. Since then, we shared so many great moments in Amsterdam, in Bucharest, in Brasov, in Edinburgh, in Shanghai, in Leuven and of course in

Maastricht. They are always so generous and warm-hearted. They provided me with so much help in my PhD time. I really appreciate it.

The pleasant working environment is another reason why I enjoyed the PhD life in Maastricht. I would like to thank all my friends and colleagues from the faculty, especially from the Maastricht European Private Law Institute. They include Xiahong Chen, Jing Liu, Wenqing Liao, Tianxiang He, Jie Wang, Taotao Yue, Huizhen Chen, Xuesong Li, Jingjing Fu, Xiaowei Yu, Yuan Gao, Guang Shen, Kelly Shang, Liuhu Luo, Ancui Liu, Bo Chen, Mengxing Lü, Xi Chen, Mengmeng Shi, Tian Lü, Yu Zhao, Yingying Jing, Yaojin Peng, Yu Yan, Liang Yu, Chunlei Zhao, Huilan Zhu, Shuo Li, Xiao Wang, Tongle Si, Xi Lin, Junmin Zhang, Zhaofeng Wu, Matteo Bonelli, Daniel On, Frank Nellen, Mieke Olaerts, Anna Berlee, Anna Beckers, Garfias von Fürstenberg Gonzalo, Marieke Hopman, Tobias Jonkers, Thera Dieleman, Katja Zimmermann, Gary Low, Kate O'Reilly, Kim Berg, Caroline Calomme, Gijs van Dijck, Bram Akkermans, Niels Philipsen, Pim Oosterhuis, Agustin Parise, Serban Vacarelu, Adela Ognean, Lars van Vilet, Julieta Marotta, Damla Cavusoglu, Pablo Bravo Hurtado, Christopher Mondschein and Luca Bücken.

When I was preparing the book for publishing, I received great help from the editors, especially Anke Seyfried, Leana Li, Lydia Wang and Fiona Wu, and the production team of Springer. I feel very grateful for their wonderful assistance including patient communication, clear instruction and excellent editing. My thanks also go to my colleagues at Law School of Fudan University for their warm welcome and the pleasant working environment.

I gratefully acknowledge the huge support from my family and my parents-in-law. Special words are dedicated to my parents, Lie Jiang and Fu Meng. Since I was born, they have always encouraged and supported me, mentally and financially, to chase my dream and do whatever I want. They understand me, guide me, lead me while also leave me with much space for designing my own life. No words can describe my appreciation for their endless love and support.

The final 'thank you' goes to my dearest wife Fei Shen (Sophie) and son Yanqing Ge (Sean). They are always the biggest driving force for me to keep working. I am very grateful for all their understanding, support, encouragement and accompanying.

The research for this book was completed on 22 July 2018.

Law School of Fudan University
Shanghai, People's Republic of China
August 2018

Jiangqiu Ge

Contents

Abbreviations

AGBG	*Gesetz zur Regelung des Rechts der Allgemeinen Geschäftsbedingungen* (Act on General Conditions)
B2B	Business to business
B2C	Business to consumer
BGB	*Bürgerliches Gesetzbuch* (German Civil Code)
BMJV	*Bundesministerium der Justiz und für Verbraucherschutz* (Federal Ministry of Justice and Consumer Protection)
CAAC	Civil Aviation Administration of China
CESL	Proposal for a Common European Sales Law
CJEU	Court of Justice of the European Union
CISG	United Nations Convention on Contracts for the International Sale of Goods
CMA	Competition and Markets Authority
CRA	Consumer Rights Act
DCFR	Draft Common Frame of Reference
EU	European Union
EUR	Euros
GDP	Gross Domestic Product
MES	Market Economy Status
NME	Non-market economy
No.	Number
OECD	Organisation for Economic Co-operation and Development
OFT	Office of Fair Trading
PECL	Principles of European Contract Law
PMR	Product Market Regulation
RMB	Renminbi
SASAC	State-owned Assets and Supervision and Administration Commission
SEA	Single European Act
SME	Small and medium enterprise
SOE	State-owned Enterprise

TEC	Treaty establishing the European Community
TEU	Treaty on European Union
TFEU	Treaty on the Functioning of the European Union
TVE	Township and Village Enterprise
UCTA (UK)	Unfair Contract Terms Act (United Kingdom)
UK	United Kingdom
UKlaG	*Gesetz über Unterlassungsklagen bei Verbraucherrechts- und anderen Verstößen* (German Act on Injunctions for the Protection of Consumers' Interests)
US	United States
UTCCR (UK)	Unfair Terms in Consumer Contracts Regulations (United Kingdom)
VZBV	*Verbraucherzentrale Bundesverband* (Federation of German Consumer Organisations)
WTO	World Trade Organization

Chapter 1
Introduction

1.1 Background: Policing Consumer Contracts in a Global Context

Since 2013, the famous Dutch dairy brand Nutrilon has used an online shop on the digital marketplace Tmall, which is a part of the e-commerce giant Alibaba, to retail its dairy products to Chinese consumers.[1] Due to the good reputation of Dutch dairy products,[2] Nutrilon outsells many indigenous producers in China and makes up a sizeable share of the market.[3] As more and more commodities are put on shelve for selling, Chinese consumers will obtain a more direct way to purchase dairy products from Dutch producers.

This is just the epitome of the era of global consumption. Even before Nutrilon's initiative, many Chinese consumers have already experienced purchasing Dutch products from importers and private agents who live in the Netherlands. Similarly, consumers in the Netherlands are also familiar with Chinese products because of their competitive prices. In a word, people's daily consumption has radically changed. In the old days, categories of commodities were rather limited, and

---

[1] The website of this online store is available at: <https://nutrilon.tmall.com/index.htm?spm=a1z10.3-b-s.w5001-14968957225.2.113b1853HImpV4&scene=taobao_shop>, last visited: 2018/7/15. Nutrilon also operates an online store on another big digital marketplace Jingdong, the website of which is available at: <https://mall.jd.com/index-1000002688.html>, last visited: 2018/7/15.

[2] After the '2008 milk scandal', Chinese consumers do not tend to trust the local dairy producers. Consumer confidence decreased significantly. See, for example, Liu, Ye and Yuan (刘建丽、叶树光、原磊), 2010. If affordable, foreign dairy products are much preferable to domestic ones. In terms of '2008 Chinese milk scandal', see Wikipedia, '2008 Chinese milk scandal', available at: <https://en.wikipedia.org/wiki/2008_Chinese_milk_scandal>, last visited: 2015/9/21.

[3] See China Industries Information (中国产业信息网), 'Statistics of Alibaba: Dairy Products Sales Volume 2017' (《2017年全年奶粉母婴在阿里系电商上的销售情况统计》), available at: <http://www.chyxx.com/industry/201803/619274.html>, last visited: 2018/7/15.

J. Ge, *A Comparative Analysis of Policing Consumer Contracts in China and the EU*, https://doi.org/10.1007/978-981-13-2989-0_1

consumption was restricted to affect only domestic producers and consumers. Now, two new characteristics regarding consumption are more and more noticeable.

The first characteristic is 'professionalisation', which refers to the fact that the knowledge and information involved in manufacturing a product become more and more unintelligible to ordinary consumers. For example, it is not necessary for a Chinese consumer to know how Dutch milk powder is produced and packaged. Likewise, Dutch consumers usually do not care about what kind of technology is used to make a Huawei cell phone or how a made-in-China water gun is assembled. This is because the division of labour in society becomes more and more detailed. In addition, traders' professional negotiating and promoting skill is also a part of the 'professionalisation'. As a result, it is believed that consumers' freedom of will is restricted due to the information asymmetry is brought by the expertise possessed only by professional sellers. In many countries, these unbalanced circumstances are supposed to be corrected, and law is believed to be a major approach which should be employed. Legislators tend to regard consumer contracts as a specific category and provide various special contract law rules to protect consumers. Despite some of these rules potentially being at odds with traditional doctrines such as *pacta sunt servanda*, the political orientation and value of consumer protection is considered to be of higher priority. To sum up, rules that seek to police consumer contracts are becoming more and more significant.

The second characteristic is 'internationalisation' (including regionalisation), which refers to the phenomenon that more and more contracts are concluded between a domestic consumer and a foreign trader. This can be easily illustrated with the story related at the beginning of this study. With the help of the development of the Internet and logistics industry, cross-border transactions make it possible for consumers all over the world to enjoy the products manufactured in a different continent.[4] This also brings the phenomenon of 'the internationalisation of consumer law', which focuses on the important role played by international and regional subjects and the efforts that have been made by these supranational rule-makers to protect consumers. Today, consumption is heavily influenced by the activities of international organisations, such as the United Nations and its bodies, the OECD and the World Bank, and regional organisations, such as the European Union (hereinafter 'EU').[5] In brief, the increasing cross-border trade flow raises the need to know more about consumer laws in different jurisdictions.

This study aims to describe the differences and similarities regarding policing consumer contracts in China and the EU and to provide possible explanations for these comparative findings. The remainder of this chapter elaborates the research questions (Sect. 1.2), research hypotheses (Sect. 1.3), research methods and outline

[4] Owing to the character of 'internationalisation', the behaviour of consumers in one country may have a profound influence on the producer or seller in another country. It becomes even possible that consumers can help with reducing instances of labour exploitation in the global supply chain. For further information, see Kawakami 2017.

[5] See Durovic and Micklitz 2017, pp. 1–2.

(Sect. 1.4), academic value and societal relevance (Sect. 1.5) and limits (Sect. 1.6) of this study.

1.2 Research Questions

This study aims to answer two core questions: (1) What are the similarities and differences among the rules on policing consumer contracts in China and the EU? (2) How can we explain these similarities and differences? Obviously, these two questions cannot be answered through a one-step approach but require both description and explanation. The following sub-questions are discussed:

1. In Chinese law and EU law, where can we find the rules regulating consumer contracts? This requires looking at the sources of law.
2. Which legislative rules regulate consumer contracts?
3. How are these rules applied by courts or other authorities? The enforcement of the relevant rules is also important because sometimes the rules themselves are similar but the ways to enforce them in practice are quite different.
4. What are the similarities and differences when we compare these rules and the ways of being enforced?
5. What are the possible reasons for these similarities and differences?

Besides these major research questions, each chapter also has its own sub-questions, which may help readers to be informed about their detailed contents.

1.3 Research Hypotheses

1.3.1 Introduction

As aforementioned, this study aims to answer two categories of research questions: a descriptive category and an explanatory category. For the latter, the explanation of the reasons why the rules for policing contracts in China and the EU are similar or different, this study raises some hypotheses.

Specifically, the reasons why rules of consumer law in different jurisdictions are similar or dissimilar can be explained from multiple perspectives.[6] Among all these perspectives, the one which focuses on the nature of the target economy is worth being considered as the most significant one. Among all the aspects which are

---

[6] For example, it may be explained from a cultural perspective: people in the West usually 'championed a dominion of things that privileged private pleasure and comfort' and 'invested in being a master over things, rather than over other people', while in China, consumption not only satisfies people's daily use but has a much closer link with the possessor's social identity and network. See Trentmann 2016, p. 399.

relevant to the operation of an economy, it is the market to which the most attention should be paid,[7] because, when all is said and done, consumer law is promulgated to regulate transactions between traders and consumers, and the market is exactly the place where these transactions are conducted.[8] Thus, it is to some extent correct to say that the core of consumer law is to serve the market. This means the utility, the orientation and the contents of one jurisdiction's consumer law to a large extent depend on the type of the market. The nature and the features of the market have a profound influence on the design, the expression and the enforcement of the rules of consumer law.[9]

In this section, different types of markets are firstly discussed. The criterion for the distinction adopted by this study and its application to China and the EU is elaborated (Sect. 1.3.2). Subsequently, the impact of the differences of markets on consumer law is elaborated. The features and characteristics of consumer law in different markets are demonstrated, respectively (Sects. 1.3.3 and 1.3.4). Some concluding remarks are given, and the hypotheses to be tested in the following chapters are summarised at the end (Sect. 1.3.5).

1.3.2 Distinctions Between a Competitive Market and a Regulated Market and the Application to China and the EU

1.3.2.1 Different Markets: A Focus on the PMR Indicator

It should be noted that there is not one single type of market.[10] Using various criteria, markets can be categorised into several different sorts. One well-known classification divides all markets into four types: perfect competition, monopolistic competition, oligopoly and monopoly.[11] The distinctions among these four types of markets focus on the following aspects: (1) the amount of firms in the market, (2) the difference among the products provided by these firms, (3) the difficulty to

---

[7] According to Mankiw, 'a market' refers to 'a group of buyers and sellers of a particular good or service'. See Mankiw 2014, p. 66. Some scholars suggest that law may not matter for economic growth and market development. But these comments to a large extent are based on the idea of 'law-then-growth'. It should be noticed that for young markets it could be a 'crash-then-law' mode which shows that the legal change will always follow the economic crashes or problems. See Chen 2003, p. 471.

[8] This is in particular the case in some jurisdictions. For example, since EU consumer law exists to a large extent for the purpose of promoting the establishment of the internal market (for details, see Sect. 2.3.4, Chap. 2 of this study), it is even much more market biased than national contract law. See Micklitz 2005, p. 553.

[9] For a good example that discusses the correlation and interplay between the market and its consumers, see Reisch and Micklitz 2006.

[10] For example, some markets are more organised and some are less. See Mankiw 2014, p. 66.

[11] See Gao (高鸿业) 2014, pp. 154–155.

control the market price by a single firm and (4) the difficulty to enter or exit the market.[12] Thus, in a perfectly competitive market, there are many buyers and sellers in the market; the goods offered by the various sellers are largely the same; and these firms can freely enter or exit the market.[13] Meanwhile, in a monopolistic market, there is only one firm producing and selling products in the market; no substitute goods can be found; and it is extremely difficult or impossible for other firms to enter this market.[14]

In reality, there is no perfectly competitive market or monopolistic market.[15] In most cases, they are two extremes in a theoretical analysis. Monopolistic competition and oligopoly are seen more often.[16] If a market of a national or regional economy is studied from a holistic perspective, it becomes more difficult to identify which type the market (as a whole) falls into, since a national economy may contain some markets that are highly competitive (e.g. ice-cream market)[17] and some other markets that are monopolistic (e.g. public utilities such as water services and electricity).[18]

Nevertheless, there are still some ways to assess the competitiveness of an economy's market. For example, the Economics Department of the Organisation for Economic Co-operation and Development (hereinafter 'OECD') used their 'product market regulation' (hereinafter 'PMR') indicator to measure the regulatory stance and to track reform progress over time of target economies in 1998, and the database was then updated in 2003, 2008 and 2013.[19] To measure the 'regulatory stance', the PMR indicator focuses on the existing laws and regulations and their influence on competition.[20] Three high-level indicators are computed: state control, barriers to entrepreneurship and barriers to trade and investment.[21] These high-level indicators further look into 18 low-level indicators: scope of state-owned enterprises (hereinafter SOEs), government involvement in network sectors, direct control over business enterprises, governance of state-owned enterprises, price controls, command and control regulation, licences and permits system, communication and simplification of rules and procedures, administrative burdens for corporations, administrative burdens for sole proprietor firms, barriers in services sectors, legal barriers to entry,

[12] See Gao (高鸿业) 2014, p. 154.

[13] See Mankiw 2014, p. 280.

[14] See Gao (高鸿业) 2014, p. 186.

[15] See Gao (高鸿业) 2014, p. 187.

[16] See Gao (高鸿业) 2014, p. 195.

[17] See Mankiw 2014, p. 66.

[18] 'Public utilities' are usually seen as a form of 'natural monopoly', which refers to 'a monopoly that arises because a single firm can supply a good or service to an entire market at a smaller cost than could two or more firms'. Mankiw 2014, p. 302

[19] See Koske et al. 2015, p. 7.

[20] This can be observed from the methodology adopted by the OECD. For example, 'The coded information is normalised over a 0 to 6 scale, where a lower value reflects a more competition-friendly regulatory stance'. See Koske et al. 2015, pp. 7–8.

[21] See Koske et al. 2015, p. 9.

antitrust exemptions, barriers in network sectors, barriers to foreign direct investment, tariff barriers, differential treatment of foreign suppliers and barriers to trade facilitation.[22] Through observing the PMR index value (index scale 0 to 6 from least to most restrictive), one may conclude that the regulatory stance of one market (with a lower value) is less restrictive and more competition-friendly, while the regulatory stance of another market (with a higher value) is more restrictive and competition-unfriendly.[23]

The PMR indicator constitutes an important part of the basis of this study's hypotheses. Specifically, in this study, when two jurisdictions' consumer law is described and compared (China and the EU), the market of one jurisdiction is identified as a 'competitive market' if it falls into the aforementioned first type of market (its value of the PMR indicator is low, which means its regulatory stance is less restricted and more competition-friendly), while the market of the other jurisdiction is seen as a 'regulated market'[24] if it is the aforementioned second type of market (its value of the PMR indicator is high, which means its regulatory stance is more restricted and competition-unfriendly).[25]

1.3.2.2 Differences Between a Competitive Market and a Regulated Market

Since the distinction between a competitive market and a regulated market is established on the basis of the PMR indicator value, the focus is placed on the role played by the government of the economy. This can be observed from the 18 low-level indicators, which are computed by the extent to which the government intervenes in the market or the extent to which the government has a negative influence on competition. For example, the 'scope of SOEs' indicator looks into the 'pervasiveness of state ownership across 30 business sectors measured as the share of sectors in which the state controls at least one firm'; the 'direct control over business enterprises' indicator pays attention to the 'existence of special voting rights by the government in privately owned firms and constraints to the sale of government stakes in publicly-controlled firms'; the 'governance of SOEs' indicator focuses on the

---

[22] See Koske et al. 2015, pp. 9–10. For the whole methodology of the PMR, see Koske et al. 2015, pp. 7–15.

[23] For example, based on the PMR indicator, it is pointed out that product market regulations are significantly more competition-friendly than in the average OECD country in the Netherlands and the United Kingdom, while in Poland, Greece, Korea, Mexico, Israel and Turkey, they are significantly less competition-friendly than in the average OECD country. See Koske et al. 2015, p. 19.

[24] The concept of 'regulated market' may be used in many different ways. For example, Hans-W. Micklitz refers 'regulated markets' to 'telecommunication, energy and transport, insurance, capital markets and company law'. See Micklitz 2015, p. 496.

[25] It should be noted that it is difficult to identify a market as a competitive/regulated one without comparison and further elaboration. Thus, the application of this distinction to certain economies is dependent on its score compared with other economies and the substantive analysis given by this study.

'degree of insulation of SOEs from market discipline and degree of political interference in the management of SOEs'; the 'command and control regulation' indicator studies the 'extent to which the government uses coercive (as opposed to incentive-based) regulation, etc.[26]

Indeed, the roles played by the governments in different markets are rather dissimilar. On the basis of the low-level indicators, several major differences can be observed. Firstly, the extent to which the government participates in market transactions is different. In a competitive market, private actors usually play a more central role, while in a regulated market the government is always an unneglectable participant and even sometimes the single trader. This difference also points to the status of SOEs and state shareholding enterprises in the market. In a regulated market, SOEs and state shareholding enterprises are mighty when compared with other private enterprises.[27] Secondly, the extent to which the government controls over the market is different. This is particularly the case with controlling market entry. As aforementioned, competition needs many sellers and producers in the market, so a competitive market usually welcomes new entrants. As a result, burdens on creating firms set by the government are usually less. Inversely, the government in a regulated market usually establishes more burdens on market entry: Administrative burdens on creating firms are more, and it is more difficult to obtain a necessary licence.[28] Thirdly, the tools used by the government to intervene into the market are different. In order to promote competition, the government in a competitive market usually focuses on the incentive-based or market-based tools which may encourage traders and consumers to make more reasonable decisions.[29] In a regulated market, the government inclines to use more coercive tools and relies more on the administrative commands and punishments.[30]

Since China and the EU are selected to be compared, the application of the foregoing distinction is therefore discussed as follows.

---

[26] See Koske et al. 2015, pp. 9–10.

[27] See the indicators of 'scope of state-owned enterprises', 'government involvement in network sectors', 'direct control over business enterprises', 'governance of state-owned enterprises', etc. See Koske et al. 2015, p. 9.

[28] See the indicators 'licences and permits system', 'administrative burdens for corporations', 'administrative burdens for sole proprietor firms', 'barriers in services sectors', 'legal barriers to entry', 'barriers in network sectors', etc., See Koske et al. 2015, pp. 9–10.

[29] For example, the government may take actions to provide consumers with more information. The rationale behind this is that the information asymmetry may undermine sufficient competition. Without obtaining enough information, consumers would be sceptical about whether they have made the right decision, so they might be afraid of investing their money in purchasing commodities of good quality. As a result, these good products might be eliminated, and the producers would lose the incentive of improving the quality of their goods and services. This is well-explained by Akerlof's 'Lemon Theory': in a second-hand car market, because the buyers cannot obtain all necessary information for assessing the quality of the cars, they would only pay the average price. In this case, the sellers who sell good cars cannot gain enough profit, so they would withdraw their cars from the market. In this case, the average quality of the cars in the market would be lower and lower. See Akerlof 1970.

[30] See the indicator 'command and control regulation', etc. See Koske et al. 2015, p. 9.

1.3.2.3 The Application to China and the EU

1.3.2.3.1 A Relatively Regulated Market: The Features of China's Socialist Market Economy

Prior to the reform and opening-up policy,[31] China had a rather regulated market. Even up to this day, it still has some features and characteristics of a regulated market. This can be observed from China's PMR score: China scored 3.17 out of 6 in 2008 and 2.86 in 2013.[32] In comparison, the EU scored 1.53 in 2008[33] and 1.44 in 2013.[34]

In addition to the PMR indicator, this can also be observed from the discussion on whether to grant China the market economy status (hereinafter 'MES') as defined by the World Trade Organization (hereinafter 'WTO'). Although China proclaims in her Constitution that 'The State practices socialist market economy',[35] it is not recognised by all national or regional economies that China should be granted MES. This is not only a problem of designation but also essential to the issues such as tariff and other trading treatments. For example, under Section 15 of China's WTO Accession Protocol,[36] China should be treated as a non-market economy (hereinafter 'NME') in anti-dumping proceedings, which means in determining price comparability, the importing WTO member should use either Chinese prices or costs for the industry under investigation or a methodology that is not based on a strict comparison with domestic prices or costs in China.[37] It is pointed out that NME treatment often leads to the determination of higher anti-dumping duties. However, due to the reason that these provisions 'shall expire 15 years after the date of accession', which is stated in Section 15(d),[38] the correct interpretation of this paragraph has come under debate, as well as whether the latter section stipulates

[31] For a brief introduction, see Wikipedia, 'Chinese economic reform', available at: <https://en.wikipedia.org/wiki/Chinese_economic_reform>, last visited: 2016/10/17.

[32] On the basis of the PMR results of 2008, it is suggested that although the elements of a competitive market-based economy are becoming increasingly well established, the transition is far from complete and the reduction in the extent of government intervention lags behind China's impressive economic development. See Conway et al. 2010, p. 5.

[33] This is computed without the data of Lithuania, Malta, Romania, Bulgaria, Croatia and Cyprus.

[34] For comparison, the OECD countries on average scored 1.48 in 2008 and 1.60 in 2013. Japan scored 1.43 in 2008 and 1.41 in 2013. The United States scored 1.59 in 2008. The complete index can be seen at Koske et al. 2015, p. 29.

[35] The first paragraph of Article 15 of the Chinese Constitution.

[36] World Trade Organization, 'China's WTO Accession Protocol', 11 December 2001, WT/L/432.

[37] Section 15(a) of the China's WTO Accession Protocol.

[38] The whole paragraph reads: 'Once China has established, under the national law of the importing WTO Member, that it is a market economy, the provisions of subparagraph (a) shall be terminated provided that the importing Member's national law contains market economy criteria as of the date of accession. In any event, the provisions of subparagraph (a)(ii) shall expire 15 years after the date of accession. In addition, should China establish, pursuant to the national law of the importing WTO Member, that market economy conditions prevail in a particular industry or sector, the non-market economy provisions of subparagraph (a) shall no longer apply to that industry or sector'.

automatic granting of MES to China after December 2016.[39] As China's biggest trading partner, the EU is wavering over whether to grant China the MES: 'Supporters see MES as a way to win favour in Beijing, while critics argue it will kill industries'.[40] In February 2016, thousands of steel industry workers congregated in Brussels for protesting, trying to press the commission to tackle cheap Chinese steel being 'dumped' across Europe. One of their aims was to persuade the EU not to grant China MES.[41]

Indeed, the hesitation over granting China MES in some senses shows the features of China's socialist economy and reveals the reason why China should be identified as operating a regulated market. This can be firstly demonstrated from the strong position of the 'state sector', including state-owned enterprises and shareholding companies.[42] On the basis of the economic system of China,[43] state-controlled firms, under the protection by barriers to entry of private and foreign firms, can always benefit from substantial monopoly rights and profits in industries ranging from energy, transportation and telecommunication to banking, entertainment, education and health care.[44] Their contribution to the economic growth is huge. It is assumed that the visible state sector, which refers to SOEs and entities directly controlled by SOEs, accounted for more than 40 percent of China's nonagricultural gross domestic product (hereinafter 'GDP') by 2011.[45] 'If the contributions of indirectly controlled entities, urban collectives, and public TVEs are considered, the share of GDP owned and controlled by the state is approximately 50

---

39 See Puccio 2015.

40 Christian Oliver and Michael Pooler, 'Europe split over whether to grant China market economy status', *Financial Times*, 28 December 2015, available at: <http://www.ft.com/cms/s/0/2f581276-a716-11e5-955c-1e1d6de94879.html#axzz40QA5bqxe>, last visited: 2016/2/17.

41 Viktoria Dendrinou, 'Thousands to Protest in Brussels Against China Steel Trading: Calls to stop European Union granting market-economy status to world's largest steel producer', *The Wall Street Journal*, 14 February 2016, available at: <http://www.wsj.com/articles/thousands-to-protest-in-brussels-against-china-steel-trading-1455450843>, last visited: 2016/2/17.

42 In terms of this type of classification, see Zhu 2012, p. 110. Another definition of 'state sector' in China can be found in Szamosszegi and Kyle 2011, p. 1. The latter reads: 'The state sector in China consists of three main components. First, there are enterprises fully owned by the state through the State-owned Assets and Supervision and Administration Commission (hereinafter 'SASAC') of the State Council and by SASACs of provincial, municipal, and county governments. Second, there are SOEs that are majority owners of enterprises that are not officially considered SOEs but are effectively controlled by their SOE owners. Finally, there is a group of entities, owned and controlled indirectly through SOE subsidiaries based inside and outside of China. The actual size of this third group is unknown. Urban collective enterprises and government-owned township and village enterprises (hereinafter 'TVEs') also belong to the state sector but are not considered SOEs'.

43 The first sentence of Article 6 of the Chinese Constitution reads: 'The basis of the socialist economic system of the People's Republic of China is socialist public ownership of the means of production, namely, ownership by the whole people and collective ownership by the working people'.

44 See Zhu 2012, p. 122.

45 See Szamosszegi and Kyle 2011, p. 1.

percent'.[46] Because of the essential role played by the state sector in the Chinese economic development,[47] these firms enjoy the favourable treatment provided by the Chinese government through the approaches including but not limited to preferred access to bank capital, below-market interest rates on loans from state-owned banks, favourable tax treatment, policies that create a favourable competitive environment for SOEs relative to other firms and large capital injections when needed.[48] As a result, these firms are not only rather competitive in the global market competition but also considerably mighty in the domestic market. Due to the far-reaching influence of the state sector in the areas where the entry of private and foreign sectors is restricted, people are always wondering whether the competition in these areas is sufficient enough. Although the WTO accession has to some extent changed the previous situation of monopoly, in the foregoing industries, especially transportation and telecommunication, the market is still under the control of the enterprises which have an obvious characteristic of the state sector.[49] In this sense, when consumers are dealing with the aforementioned traders, they are envisaging not so much the businesses as the state. The foregoing conclusions can also be supported by some low-level PMR indicators. For example, China scored 6 out of 6 in the 'scope of SOEs' indicator. In comparison, the EU scored 3.04.

In terms of the dominant role played by the Chinese government, it also can be observed from the powerful control of the state on the operation of the market. The administrative burdens on market entry are heavy, and various administrative tools are used to supervise the market participants. The government is so powerful that the value orientation and the distribution of resources of the market are all determined by the government but not spontaneously formed by the market. This is because rapid economic growth is very important to the Chinese government.[50]

[46] Szamosszegi and Kyle 2011, p. 1.

[47] It is stated that SOEs constituted 50% of the 500 largest manufacturing companies in China and 61% of the top 500 service sector enterprises. See Geng et al. 2009, p. 155. Furthermore, it is suggested that there were 154,000 SOEs as of 2008, and while these accounted for only 3.1% of all enterprises in China, they held 30% of the value of corporate assets in the manufacturing and services sectors. See Gao Xu, 'State-Owned Enterprises in China: How Big Are They', 19 January 2010, available at: <http://blogs.worldbank.org/eastasiapacific/state-owned-enterprises-in-china-how-big-are-they>, last visited: 2016/7/21.

[48] See Szamosszegi and Kyle, 2011, p. 3.

[49] For example, the telecommunications industry in China is seen as being dominated by three state-run businesses: China Telecom, China Unicom and China Mobile. In November 2011, China's National Development and Reform Commission initiated an investigation into China Telecom and China Unicom over suspected monopoly in the broadband internet market. It is suggested that the government's unusual anti-monopoly probe into its state-owned enterprises may lead to support for bringing in more effective competition to the country's telecommunications sector – one of the Chinese marketplaces still under tight government control. See Vivian Ni, 'China Telecom, China Unicom Face Anti-Monopoly Probe', available at: <http://www.china-briefing.com/news/2011/11/10/china-telecom-china-unicom-face-anti-monopoly-probe.html>, last visited: 2016/2/17.

[50] It is argued that, in China, 'Getting and spending were legitimized in relation to national strength and social solidarity'. Trentmann 2016, pp. 398–399.

Improving aggregate economic performance and raising living standards are of great significance.[51] It is alleged by the government that 'We must adhere to solving problems on the road ahead through promoting development'.[52] As a result, values such as 'fairness', 'sustainability' and 'rule of law' sometimes need to be balanced with the value of 'efficiency', and the process of balancing is under the strict control of the government. For example, in order to pursue greater economic profits, failure to strictly obey the law is sometimes permitted.[53] This is also supported by some low-level PMR indicators. For example, China scored 2.90 of 6 in the 'command and control' indicator, while the EU scored 2.14.

In addition to the strong position of the state sector and the powerful control of the government, another noteworthy feature of China's socialist market economy is related to export as the major driving force of the economy. According to the research by China's National Bureau of Statistics, the rapid economic growth in the first 30 years after the introduction of the reform and opening-up policy was mainly driven by the capital investment and export.[54] As a result, China is now the world's largest manufacturer. The role manufacturing plays in the Chinese economy is considerably more important than the role it plays in the United States and Japan. 'In 2013, China's gross valued added manufacturing was equal to 28.9% of GDP, compared to 12.1% for the United States and 18.7% for Japan'.[55] Compared with consumption, export and the industry of manufacturing are not so relevant to the sound functioning of a competitive product market.[56]

To sum up, China's domestic market is a rather regulated one. It can be observed from the strong position played by the state sectors, the powerful control of the government and the importance of export which is not closely linked with sufficient competition.

---

51 Zhu 2012, p. 110.

52 See Resolutions of the CPC Central Committee on Major Issues regarding the Building of a Harmonious Socialist Society (《中共中央关于构建社会主义和谐社会若干重大问题的决定》), 11 October 2006. It is also recorded in the Communique of the 6th Plenum of the 16th CPC Central Committee (《中国共产党第十六届中央委员会第六次全体会议公报》). An English translation is available at: <http://www.cecc.gov/resources/legal-provisions/communique-of-the-sixth-plenum-of-the-16th-cpc-central-committee-chinese>, last visited: 2016/7/21.

53 For example, it is declared that 'the Chinese government often disregards its own environmental laws in order to promote rapid economic growth'. See Morrison 2015, p. 11.

54 See The Research Group of the Comprehensive Department of the National Bureau of Statistics of the People's Republic of China (国家统计局综合司课题组) 2014, p. 3.

55 Morrison 2015, p. 35.

56 Nevertheless, although in the near future the essence of export for Chinese economic growth should not be underestimated, along with the advance to the new stages of development and the change of global economic situation, the driving force of capital investment and export is receding, while the driving force of consumption is growing. See The Research Group of the Comprehensive Department of the National Bureau of Statistics of the People's Republic of China (国家统计局综合司课题组) 2014, p. 4.

1.3.2.3.2 A Relatively Competitive Market: The Features of the EU Internal Market

The internal market of the European Union, which is also known as the single market, refers to the EU as one territory without any internal borders or other regulatory obstacles to the free movement of goods and services.[57] Compared with China, it has already been shown that the market of the EU is a more competitive one, which is supported by the aforementioned PMR values (1.53 (the EU) vs 3.17 (China)). Some further information on the EU internal market is provided as follows.

Historically speaking, the internal market is a successor to the common market, the creation of which was proposed by the European Economic Community. In the Treaty of Rome (1957), officially the Treaty establishing the European Community (hereinafter 'TEC'), the idea of establishing a market offering free movement of goods, service, persons and capital was already specified.[58] However, the development of the common market envisaged some difficulties, for example, the intangible barriers with mutual recognition of standards and common regulations due to protectionist attitudes. In order to promote the single market, a White Paper was published by the Delors Commission in 1985, in which the issues regarding the removal of physical barriers, technical barriers and fiscal barriers were addressed.[59] At the end of the White Paper, a timetable was put forward, pointing out that the internal market should be completed by 31 December 1992. This document was well-received and followed by the adoption of the Single European Act, which revised the Treaty of Rome and added new momentum to European integration and to complete the internal market. On 1 January 1993, the internal market was finally established. After 20 years, it was affirmed that the development of the internal market had brought a lot of benefits to citizens and companies in the EU.[60] To the European

---

[57] European Commission, 'The European Single Market', available at: <http://ec.europa.eu/growth/single-market/index_en.htm>, last visited: 2016/7/1.

[58] For 'establishing a Common Market', see Article 2 TEC.

[59] See Commission of the European Communities, White Paper from the Commission to the European Council, COM(85) 310 final.

[60] In the Single Market Act II, it is pointed out that a lot has been achieved when the year marks the 20th anniversary of the Single Market: 'From 1992 to 2008 the Single Market has generated an extra 2.77 million jobs in the EU and an additional 2.13% in GDP. For European consumers the Single Market means more choice at lower prices – a 70% reduction in mobile phone costs is but one example. For citizens, the Single Market has given them the capacity to travel freely, to settle and work where they wish. For young people it has opened up the opportunity to study abroad – more than 2.5 million students have seized this opportunity in the last 25 years. For the 23 million companies in the EU the Single Market has opened access to 500 million consumers. The message is clear, the evidence is there: a strong, deep and integrated Single Market creates growth, generates jobs and offers opportunities for European citizens which were not there 20 years ago'. Communication from the Commission to the European Parliament, the Council, the European Economic and Social Committee and the Committee of the Regions, Single Market Act II Together for new growth, COM(2012) 0573 final.

Commission, it has fuelled economic growth and made the everyday life of European businesses and consumers easier.[61]

Apparently, a functioning internal market has a lot of positive influence. For instance, it can stimulate trade, improve efficiency, raise quality of goods and help cut prices. It should be noted that the promotion of competition is always a component part of great significance.[62] Since the aim of the operation of the market is to reduce tariff barriers and non-tariff barriers as much as possible in order to facilitate the free movement of goods, persons, services and capital,[63] one inevitable outcome is that much more freedom will be injected into the market. As a result, competition will be enhanced. Indeed, according to the PMR indicators, the EU internal market is a relatively competitive one, compared with many national or regional markets all over the world, for example, the Chinese domestic market. This is even the case when each single Member State is compared with China: every EU Member State scored a lower PMR value in the 2013 index.[64]

1.3.3 Consumer Law in a Competitive Market

1.3.3.1 The Higher Level of Demand and Concreteness

Consumer law has a close link to market competition. This is not only because it can be observed from a historical perspective: consumer law arose when sufficient competition is impaired by monopoly.[65] They also share a common goal: the aim of promoting competition is to enhance consumer welfare, which is also the goal of consumer law,[66] and consumer law is always seen as an important tool to ensure that consumers gain the benefits of competition.[67] Thus, consumer law is essential to a competitive market. This was true in the past, when people believed that some types

---

[61] European Commission, the European Single Market, available at: http://ec.europa.eu/growth/single-market/index_en.htm, last visited: 2016/7/1.

[62] European Commission, the European Single Market, available at: http://ec.europa.eu/growth/single-market/index_en.htm, last visited: 2016/7/1.

[63] Article 26(2) of the Treaty on the Functioning of the European Union (hereinafter 'TFEU') states: 'The internal market shall comprise an area without internal frontiers in which the free movement of goods, persons, services and capital is ensured in accordance with the provisions of the Treaties'.

[64] Austria: 1.19; Belgium: 1.39; Bulgaria: 1.57; Croatia: 2.08; Cyprus: 1.65; Czech Republic: 1.41; Denmark: 1.21; Estonia: 1.29; Finland: 1.29; France: 1.47; Germany: 1.28; Greece: 1.74; Hungary: 1.33; Ireland: 1.45; Italy: 1.29; Latvia: 1.61; Lithuania: 1.52; Luxembourg: 1.46; Malta: 1.57; Netherlands: 0.92; Poland: 1.65; Portugal: 1.29; Romania: 1.69; Slovak Republic: 1.29; Slovenia: 1.70; Spain: 1.44; Sweden: 1.52; United Kingdom: 1.08. See Koske et al. 2015, p. 29.

[65] See Li and Xu (李昌麒、许明月) 2012, p. 22.

[66] See OECD 2008, p. 8. This OECD document discusses the interplay between competition and consumer policies, the latter including consumer lawmaking.

[67] See OECD 2007, p. 4.

of 'market failure'[68] in a competitive market can be cured by the rules provided in consumer law,[69] such as mandatory information disclosure.[70] Even if behavioural insights are considered and some traditional rules are seen as ineffective, consumer law itself does not lose its significance, because many alternative solutions still can run in the framework of consumer law, such as a more substantive mechanism of controlling standard terms.[71] In this sense, a competitive market has a high level of demand for consumer law.

Furthermore, a higher level of clarity and concreteness of consumer law rules is also demanded. The reason is obvious: as aforementioned, a competitive market usually welcomes new entrants. If a market's consumer law is clear and concrete, traders and consumers will be more willing to enter the market because it is easier to be aware of the law so as to avoid legal risks. It is particularly the case for traders, because consumer law contains a great number of mandatory rules, which may deeply influence their business operation. Furthermore, when the new entrants have become competitors, equal conditions have to be established for them to guarantee effective competition.[72] This also leads to the conclusion that consumer law needs to be transparent and concrete.

1.3.3.2 The Procedure-Oriented Assessment on Misconduct

To further promote sound and sufficient competition, the government of a competitive market needs to crack down on the misconduct of businesses. For example, it regulates misleading advertisements,[73] since false information could entice consumers to make wrong decisions and ultimately cause market failure. In addition, it also refers to the rules regulating product quality, food and pharmaceutical safety, other fraudulent actions and unfair contract terms. However, it should be noted that a functional competitive market is usually seen as being able to efficiently allocate resources, which means the intervention of the government into the substance of transactions, especially the price, is difficult to be justified.[74] Consumer law usually focuses on how the decision is made or how the contract is concluded, but does not care as much about the allocation of substantive rights and obligations. In this

[68] Market failure refers to 'a situation in which the market on its own fails to produce an efficient allocation of resources'. Mankiw 2014, p. 12.

[69] In a market pursuing sufficient competition, consumer protection legislation is seen as an appropriate response to 'market failure'. See Howell and Wilson 2016, p. 150.

[70] See Faure and Luth 2011, p. 338. It was also pointed out that 'Mandatory disclosure is an important instrument in many markets, but policy makers should explore its outcome based on the direct and indirect consequences of consumer behaviour and other factors'. See OECD 2007, p. 5.

[71] See Faure and Luth 2011, pp. 352–354. Nevertheless, this study is not paying much attention to behavioural insights. This is further elaborated in Sect. 1.6 of this chapter.

[72] See Micklitz 2005, p. 567.

[73] See OECD 2008, p. 8.

[74] This also can be seen from the low interest of a competitive market's government in price control in general.

regard, the assessment of fairness usually does not touch upon the substantive contents of a transaction.

1.3.3.3 The Inclination Towards Consumer Information

As mentioned above, information asymmetry is seen as an important type of market failure in a market pursuing sufficient competition.[75] Consumers may suffer detriment when information is withheld, when deceptive information is provided, or when the information is too difficult for them to obtain or evaluate.[76] This, together with consumer behaviour biases, may prevent consumers from making informed and welfare-improving decisions, which may ultimately harm competition. Thus, providing consumers with enough information is another important mission of lawmakers in a competitive market. Consumer law needs to ensure that the consumer is able to exercise intelligently and efficiently the choices that competition provides.[77] Only in this way, the goods and services of good quality would be chosen, producers and sellers would have enough incentive to innovate and the expected sufficient competition would be formed. Therefore, consumer law in a competitive market usually puts more focus on informing consumers rather than other traditional means of consumer protection.[78]

Instead of directly intervening into private relationship, consumer law in a competitive market aims to make the weaker party in the market stronger and let it fight for its own rights and interests. Some scholars point out that the priorities for consumer policy differ greatly between different economies. In a developed market, 'the priorities are, in descending order of importance, consumer information, education and protection'.[79] In less developed economies, the hierarchy is exactly the reverse, 'that is consumer protection, education and information'.[80] This conclusion can be also applied to the distinction between a competitive market and a regulated market. Because of the restricted administrative power in a competitive market, consumer information plays a crucial role in maintaining the order of the market.

[75] See Howell and Wilson 2016, p. 150.

[76] See OECD 2008, p. 9.

[77] See OECD 2008, p. 8.

[78] When the legislator in a specific jurisdiction wants to open up markets or enhance competition, it is possible to adopt a 'protective-instrumental' approach, which is different from the traditional direction of consumer protection at the national level. See Micklitz 2005, pp. 561–562.

[79] Ho 2001, p. 66. For the distinction among consumer education, consumer information and consumer protection, see Swann 1979, p. 267.

[80] Ho 2001, p. 66.

1.3.3.4 The Focus on Private Enforcement

Generally speaking, the availability of rights that benefit consumers is not enough: these rights need to be enforceable.[81] In this sense, the enforcement of consumer law becomes a crucial issue. In this regard, consumer law in a competitive market puts more emphasis on private enforcement compared with consumer law in a regulated market.

Specifically, in a competitive market, consumer law rules usually can be enforced by different actors. For example, there 'may be a single agency charged with enforcing a consumer protection law, but other government bodies – ministries of commerce or industry, sector regulators and in some countries regional and local governments – are also active'.[82] Although public actors are important in enforcing consumer law, compared with a regulated market, there is a stronger need for consumers to help themselves.[83] They are encouraged to claim for their own rights by initiating lawsuits, arbitration, or making use of other dispute resolution mechanism. In a word, 'private enforcement is a powerful instrument to make consumer rights hard and deter future anti-consumer conduct'.[84]

1.3.4 Consumer Law in a Regulated Market

1.3.4.1 The Lower Level of Demand and Concreteness

Compared with its essential role in a competitive market, consumer law is not that important in a regulated market. This is because the functions of market itself are rather limited in a regulated market. Even law is not indispensable. Instead, government bears a great amount of obligations and responsibilities to ensure the daily operation of the market.

Besides, for a regulated market, consumer law does not need to be concrete and precise, because there is a lack of incentive. Compared with a competitive market, the government of a regulated market is described as less competition-friendly. An important aspect is that it is not that interested in attracting more traders to participate in the market competition. As aforementioned, administrative burdens are heavy, and it is more difficult to obtain a necessary licence. In this regard, the government of a regulated market usually does not have the incentive to provide more precise rules which may help new entrants to reduce costs. Furthermore, this also can be explained from the perspective of the government's powerful control over the market. Since the government's intervention is more frequent and various in the tools its uses in a regulated market, it usually has more prompt and efficient

[81] See Micklitz 2005, pp. 577–578.

[82] See OECD 2008, p. 9.

[83] See Swann 1979, pp. 266–267.

[84] Cseres 2008, p. 87.

approaches to react to new developments in the market. The lawmaker sometimes deliberately leaves gaps in legislation to allow administrative bodies to take further action.

1.3.4.2 The Substance-Oriented Assessment on Misconduct

The consumer law in a regulated market also focuses on cracking down on misconduct, but the assessment on 'misconduct' is more substantive.

This can be observed from the perspectives of state sector and the extent to which the government controls the market. Specifically, when the government itself is involved in market transactions, it has its own benefits. Even if acting as a market supervisor, it has a stronger incentive to control the market and ensure that the developing direction of the market meets its own plan. As aforementioned, the extent of price control in a regulated market is higher than in a competitive market, and price in most cases can be seen as the most important part of the substance of a contract. Thus, it is not difficult to infer that the consumer law in a regulated market is more likely to intervene into the substance of a transaction, which means it needs to decide what is 'good' or 'fair' in a substantive way.

1.3.4.3 The Inclination Towards Consumer Protection

The consumer law in a regulated market usually inclines to lay its focus on consumer protection rather than consumer information. This is because, if the market is controlled by government or some other monopolistic entities, consumers usually do not have many options, so granting them information for them to make choices is not that conducive. In addition, producers' innovation and the development of the market do not rely on consumers' choices. On the contrary, consumer law usually puts more efforts into protecting consumers from being actually harmed, in a property or personal sense, by the monopolistic price and quality.

1.3.4.4 The Focus on Public Enforcement

For the matter of enforcement, compared with a competitive market, the consumer law in a regulated market usually puts more focus on public enforcement rather than private enforcement. The reason for this is that the market participants of a regulated market usually include state-owned or state-involved enterprises. A single consumer or even a consumer organisation usually does not have the incentive or ability to struggle against these large enterprises if their misconduct infringed his rights or interests. Thus, the government takes this role. Since the government of a regulated market is more powerful and more inclined to intervene in the market, it might perform a better role in detecting violations and enforcing consumer law in general.[85]

1.3.5 Summaries and Research Hypotheses

On the grounds of the foregoing analysis, some conclusions can be achieved as follows.

First of all, by using the OECD PMR indicator, markets can be categorised into two sorts: markets which are more competitive and markets which are comparatively regulated. The major difference emphasised by this study is the role of government. This can be observed from three perspectives: the extent to which the government participates in market transactions, which refers to the status of the state sector; the extent to which the government control over the market, which mentions the administrative burdens for market entry; and the tools generally used by the government. If we use a sports game as an analogy, the government of a competitive market plays a role as referee mainly. Its aim is to ensure that the players are playing under the well-accepted rules and maintain the order of the game. In contrast, the government of a regulated market is not only the referee. Sometimes it is the player, the coach or even sometimes the organiser of the game. It not only oversees the game but also participates in the game and sometimes guides the direction of the game. It plays the roles of participant, regulator and dominator.

If this distinction is applied to assess the markets of China and the EU, it is not difficult to find out China's domestic market is a relatively regulated one, because in many core industries the state-controlled market participants play an essential role and the government frequently intervenes into the operation of the market. Inversely, the EU internal market is a relatively competitive one, because the running of the market is mostly left to the market participants and the barriers to the market entry is comparatively fewer.

The prominent distinction between a regulated market and a competitive market causes consumer law in these two different types of market to be rather dissimilar. To be specific, consumer law in a competitive market has the following features and characteristics. Firstly, it has a higher level of demand for consumer law and it requires that consumer law should be concrete and unequivocal. Secondly, although consumer law has the function of cracking down on misconduct in businesses, it usually does not touch upon the substantive contents of transactions in the market. Thirdly, the provision of information occupies a position of great significance. Fourthly, the private enforcement of consumer law is seen as an important way to realise the legislative objectives in practice.

In contrast, a regulated market usually does not have a high demand for consumer law because the administrative approaches are more efficient and effective.

---

[85] For a comparison among private law, administrative law and criminal law enforcement from a law and economics perspective, see Weber and Faure 2015.

Even if there are consumer law rules, they do not have to be relatively clear and concrete because gaps and vagueness permit further interpretation and administrative reaction. Secondly, the government of a regulated market usually has its own interests in the market. It causes the assessment of misconduct to be a more substantive one. Thirdly, the focus of consumer law in a regulated market is usually laid on consumer protection. Fourthly, compared with the emphasis on private enforcement in a competitive market, the enforcement of consumer law in a regulated market to a large extent depends on the administrative power.[86]

Therefore, the following hypotheses are to be verified by the further research:

1. With a more regulated market, China has a lower level of demand for consumer law rules, and the level of requirement for the clarity and concreteness of these rules is also lower. On the contrary, the demand for consumer law rules and their clarity and concreteness in the EU, which has a more competitive market, should be much higher.
2. The criteria employed by Chinese consumer law on assessing misconduct are more substantive. In comparison, the assessment of misconduct in the EU context is a more procedural one.
3. Chinese consumer law puts more emphasis on consumer protection in order to safeguard the property and personal rights and interests of consumers, whereas EU consumer law inclines to provide consumers with sufficient information in order to facilitate consumers to exert their party autonomy.
4. The public enforcement of consumer law rules is more important in China than in the EU. The latter focuses more on private enforcement.

1.4 Methodology and Outline

1.4.1 Introduction

Compared with the natural science disciplines like physics and chemistry, there is not a very solid consensus on the methodologies employed by researchers of legal science. Even whether it is science or to what extent it has an academic nature remains controversial. To set a starting point, this study adopts the classification proposed by Jan Smits in his 'The Mind and Method of the Legal Academic'[87] that

[86] In addition, some other differences may be found as well. For example, it is argued that, in a market that pursues sufficient competition, consumer law may not be interested in tying the parties together beyond what is necessary for effective competition. This is the reason why consumers are granted the rights enabling them to get out of a contract, such as the right to rescission in case the product or the service is defective and the right of withdrawal. See Micklitz 2005, pp. 574–577. This could lead to a hypothesis that the consumer law in a competitive market provides more tools for the consumer to escape from the contract while the consumer law in a regulated market provides less. Nevertheless, this study leaves this hypothesis to the future research.

[87] See Smits 2012b. This book has been translated into Chinese, see Smits (斯密茨) 2017.

the methodologies of legal research can be categorised into four types: the descriptive one which answers the question 'how does the law read', the normative one which advises solving the problem with 'how ought the law to read', the empirical one which aims to find out 'what are the consequences of applying a certain legal rule' and the theoretical one which researches the fundamental question 'what is law'.[88] From the introduction of the background and the research questions, it is not difficult to discover that multiple methodologies should be adopted to answer the corresponding research questions raised by this study. In essence, however, this research is a descriptive one.

Specifically, to answer the question 'Where can we find the rules regulating consumer contracts in China and the EU', it needs to use the descriptive approach to elaborate the sources of law. Subsequently, in order to introduce and discuss the specific legal rules on the topic in Chinese law and her European counterpart, a descriptive approach has to be adopted to unscramble the legal rules systematically, to provide the whole picture in an orderly way and to sum up the essential points on the basis of the previous work. Even to the question of 'How are these rules applied by courts or other authorities', this study mainly provides an introduction from a descriptive perspective. Not too much empirical data is provided. As the core outcome of the research, the similarities and differences are also the outcome of the aforementioned descriptive work. Besides, empirical data or purely theoretical arguments are still not the primary contents when the explanatory analyses are provided. Furthermore, although normative choices are inevitable when describing the rules, especially when interpreting them, the normative approach is not a major methodology applied by this study either.

Nevertheless, among all descriptive legal studies, the comparative ones have their own characteristics. In the rest of this section, several subjects which are relevant to this methodological underpinning are introduced. To be specific, the explanation of why the comparative approach is adopted as the methodology is shown first (Sect. 1.4.2.1). After that, the reasons why Chinese law and EU law are chosen as research objectives are provided (Sect. 1.4.2.2). There is also a brief discussion of how the methodology of comparative law works in this study (Sect. 1.4.2.3). At the end, the outline of this study is presented (Sect. 1.4.3).

1.4.2 The Comparative Approach as the Major Methodology

1.4.2.1 The Incentives to Adopt the Comparative Approach

In terms of the reasons why this study adopts a comparative approach, it can be demonstrated by two aspects. Two adjectives could be used here to describe them: the first one is 'helpful'; the second one is 'valuable'.

---

[88] See Smits 2012b, p. 9.

Regarding the reason for 'helpful', it can be firstly observed that it will save time and money because people can find a solution to a specific condition in foreign law when they cannot find it in national law. Put differently, where national law does not provide a solution to a specific case or the applicable rule is unclear or because there is no rule available at all, foreign materials could probably be considered to help the judge with making a decision. The second reason is that countries are always forced to meet some requirements in order to enter international organisations or join international treaties. Besides, the global economy will also affect legal transplants; for example, a country would attract more foreign investments with the law that the investors are used to. In this case, as Jan Smits states: 'in today's world, political and economic pressure and commercial dominance are far more important explanations for legal transplants than the mandatory adoption of foreign institutions'.[89] In addition, continuing Europeanisation and globalisation will lead to a further increase of comparative reasoning in the years to come.[90] As a result, 'the store of legal arguments to be considered in deciding hard cases, or in drafting new legislation, will become more and more similar across the world'.[91] Therefore, a comparative study will also contribute to this tendency.[92]

Indeed, these arguments suit the contents of this study very well. For example, the new Chinese Consumer Protection Law 2013[93] came into force in 2014. A brand new type of withdrawal right, which is primarily applicable to distance consumer contracts, has been introduced in this legislation. However, the wording of the relevant article is so concise that for many details it needs further interpretation. In this regard, the European Union and its Member States have a long history of regulating and enforcing statutory withdrawal rights. Even in the book published by those who preside over China's legislative work, it is admitted that the European rules, such as the ones with regard to the length of the period, were referred to when the law was made.[94] Thus, in order to find the best interpretation as a solution for the current vagueness, the method of comparative study is definitely 'helpful'.[95]

Regarding the reason of 'valuable', it is believed that most legal systems share the common goal of finding and applying the best possible legal rules.[96] However, even if the ultimate goal is similar, the approaches to realise it are sometimes different. In different jurisdictions, legislators can always find an approach which to a great extent suits the domestic or regional specific circumstance. In this regard, the

---

89 Smits 2006, p. 531.

90 See Durovic and Micklitz 2017.

91 Smits 2006, p. 537.

92 It is widely recognised that one of the main aims of study of comparative law is to contribute to legal harmonisation. Thus, if harmonisation is a trend, comparative law is very 'useful' in this sense. See Zweigert and Kötz 1998, p. 24 ff.

93 Law of the People's Republic of China on the Protection of Consumer Rights and Interests (2013 Amendment) (《中华人民共和国消费者权益保护法(2013修正)》).

94 See Jia (贾东明) 2013, p. 106.

95 See Chap. 5.

96 See Smits 2006, p. 528.

methodology of comparative study actually shows the potential and possibilities of human being, particularly when they deal with collective sophisticated social issues, through manifesting the difference. The value of comparative study does not depend on finding commonalities. Instead, 'it helps us to fully realise what law is by uncovering its many varieties in the form of diverging solutions to similar problems'.[97]

In this study, it is also the case that the comparative study will help the legislators to build a 'toolbox' even if the legal institution in the jurisdiction is already quite mature. For instance, the rules on policing unfair terms have existed in both Chinese law and EU law for a long period, but in some certain points, the legislators hold different ideas. Some different approaches are adopted to regulate this specific area.[98] In this context, although the rules in the other jurisdiction may not be 'helpful', it is still 'valuable' to be aware of them. The underlying reasons and arguments of different approaches may help people to acquire a broader and deeper understanding of the relevant issues.

1.4.2.2 Why China and the EU?

The major reason why this study chooses China and the EU, as the target jurisdictions to make the comparison, lies in the size of the two economies.

To be specific, the EU has become the largest economy in the world since 2007 and China is also on her way to becoming the largest economy as a country. The rapid growth of e-commerce in both the EU and China shows the new direction of economic development. Apart from the demand that they have to understand each other well due to the more frequent economic and trade contact, the experiences and problems that one jurisdiction has suffered may also inspire or help the other. Furthermore, it is pointed out that the aim of this study is to test several hypotheses on the relationship between the different types of markets and their consumer law. China and the EU are just the representatives of a rather regulated market and a comparatively competitive market, respectively. Thus, choosing them as the comparative targets fits in with the research aim very well.

However, the economic relevance is not the sole reason why China and the EU are chosen.[99] There are at least two other reasons.

The first one could be observed from a historical perspective. To the world of law, Germany, France and England are the cradles and representatives of two major legal systems. Since China began to transplant a modern legal system in late *Qing* Dynasty, these western countries have already become the jurisdictions from which China learns mostly. Along with the integration of Europe, the legal knowledge of these countries has been concentrated and contributed to establish a new European Union private law. On the other hand, based on the contents learned from Europe, China as the student has also developed a lot which fits its own national conditions.

---

[97] Smits 2012a, p. 178.

[98] See Chap. 4.

[99] This is further addressed in the following text. See Sect. 1.5.2 of this chapter.

Considering the strong link that these two jurisdictions have in the history, it would be interesting to see how they resemble or differ today. Furthermore, due to the fact that some legislation in both China and the EU has been deeply influenced by the international conventions and model law,[100] the observation on this influence in two legal contexts could also be meaningful.

Secondly, the reason for choosing China and the EU could be seen from a cultural perspective. As mentioned above, one of the reasons why the comparative approach is adopted is to seek the potential, the possibilities and the common wisdom of mankind in social governance.[101] Both China and the EU have long histories and both of their cultures have raised influencing thoughts and ideas. Up to this day, this accumulation of wisdom is still reflected in the lawmaking process, legal practice and academic works. For example, the Chinese legal rules may reflect the philosophy of Confucius, which could be still an important philosophic doctrine in the world and interesting to a western audience.[102] Chinese consumer law may also manifest the cultural characteristic, which is rather different from the EU, that consumption not only meets the requirements of people's daily use but is closely linked with their social class and network.[103] In addition, from discovering and observing the similarities of rules in different jurisdictions, we may find some common ideas which are applicable to a broader range of human beings.

Nevertheless, it should be noted that, when making the comparison, this study only looks into the legislation at the EU level. In addition, German law and English law are touched upon for observing how EU rules are implemented on the national level. Nevertheless, German law and English law rules themselves are not the research target. Since this study also addresses two preliminary issues to set the scope of discussion, sources of law and the concept of consumer contract, it needs to be clarified that how EU law is implemented in Germany and England under these two topics is not discussed. German law and English law are only looked into, as illustrations, when the substantive rules on unfair contract terms and withdrawal rights are compared.

1.4.2.3 How This Comparative Study Works

In this study, the methodology of comparative approach is composed of two parts: a descriptive one and an explanatory one. Specifically, most of the comparative study is carried through on a descriptive basis, which means the descriptive study that shows 'what is the existing law in different jurisdictions' and 'what are the differences and similarities' is the major part of the research. Apart from the description,

---

[100] For example, regarding the influence of CISG on China, see Han (韩世远) 2011, pp. 7–13. For the influence on the EU, see Smits 2007, p. 1187.

[101] See Sect. 1.4.2.1 of this chapter.

[102] Simona Novaretti's article is a good example which shows the philosophy behind the contractual legal rules and practice. See Novaretti 2010.

[103] See Trentmann 2016, p. 399.

on each topic an explanation is provided of the possible reasons why they are similar or different.

As to description, a functional approach is applied. This means, in most substantive chapters of this study, the separate functional questions which are relevant to the topic are enumerated. As to explanation, this study aims to explain legal differences from the distinction between a competitive market and a regulated market. It is suggested that the factors such as the economic system, the political system and ideology, religion, history and geography, demographic factors, co-influence of other means of control and accidental and unknown factors could also be involved in a comparative study.[104] However, this study puts its emphasis on the differences in the markets. At the end of every substantive chapter, the comparative remarks achieved from the descriptive work are used to test the hypotheses. Some explanation on whether the hypotheses can be verified or not is given.

1.4.3 Outline

This study is composed of six chapters: Chap. 1, Introduction; Chap. 2, Sources of Consumer Contract Law; Chap. 3, The Concept of Consumer Contract; Chap. 4, Unfair Terms; Chap. 5, Withdrawal Rights; and Chap. 6, Conclusion.

Apart from the current Chap. 1, Chap. 2 intends to answer the preliminary question of what are the sources of law in China and the EU. Put differently, the discussion of what kind of instrument can be recognised as 'law' in the Chinese and EU contexts is the major content. Chapter 3 provides the definition and the requirements of 'a consumer contract', to which the specifically designed consumer protection rules are applicable, in order to set the scope of the type of contract under scrutiny in this study. Chapters 4 and 5 are the chapters in which two major legal mechanisms for policing consumer contracts are discussed separately. The legal rules and their enforcement on unfair terms and withdrawal rights in the context of Chinese law and EU law are described. Chapter 6 concludes by testing the aforementioned four hypotheses.

1.5 Academic Value and Societal Relevance

1.5.1 Academic Value

The most significant academic value of this study is its novelty. Based on the fact that it is written in English, the novelty can be seen in the following aspects.

[104] See Bogdan 2013, pp. 57–62.

Firstly, it is novel because it is the first elaborate description of Chinese consumer contract law in English.[105] The studies available so far focus on general aspects of contract law. For example, the general rules on policing contracts and the legal consequences when a contract is policed to be not binding are demonstrated in the book *Chinese Contract Law: Theory and Practice* written by Mo Zhang.[106] Rules and their interpretation on unfair contract terms are also mentioned in this book. Bing Ling's 'Contract Law in China' provides another general introduction of Chinese Contract Law 1999,[107] where the relevant rules, for example the rules on unfair contract terms, are included.[108] However, these books have not touched upon consumer law.[109] The special rules and legal institutions applied to consumer contracts are not covered. In journal articles, Jörg Binding's 'Consumer Protection Law in the People's Republic of China' is an important piece but the newly adopted institutions in the new Chinese Consumer Protection Law 2013 are not introduced meticulously, which means the new articles on withdrawal rights are not included.[110]

Secondly, the novelty is based on the fact that there is scarcely English language literature which compares Chinese consumer law rules with European rules. Although some books and journal articles have already provided a comparison of Chinese law and EU law in other domains, for example the book written by Jun-wei Fu on comparative contract law principles,[111] the domain of consumer law has been left unconsidered. The book *Comparative Consumer Sales Law* only contains one short article which introduces Chinese consumer law in general, where not much detailed information is provided.[112] This study fills the vacuum. Furthermore, regarding the specific approach of the comparison, this study refers to many court judgements to show how the rules are interpreted in practice. Besides the legal rules, social mechanisms such as media supervision and administrative intervention are also referred to in this study.

Thirdly, and more substantively, this study analyses consumer law in China and the EU on basis of hypotheses about the influence of different types of economies on consumer law. Although some studies which address the interplay between consumer law (or consumer policy) and the market have already been conducted, they rarely establish their findings on a comparative study, which means the focus is

---

[105] Although much attention is paid to China's economic growth, the focus is usually on the side of production but not consumption. See Trentmann 2016, p. 355. Indeed, not too much research on Chinese consumer law has been conducted.

[106] See Zhang 2006.

[107] Contract Law of the People's Republic of China (《中华人民共和国合同法》).

[108] See Ling 2002. See also Bu 2013, pp. 81–86.

[109] Another book addressing Chinese contract law that should be mentioned is 'Chinese Contract Law: Civil and Common Law Perspectives'. See DiMatteo and Chen 2017.

[110] See Binding 2014.

[111] See Fu 2011.

[112] See Han 2017.

usually on only one jurisdiction.[113] In this sense, this study provides a new perspective.

1.5.2 Societal Relevance

2015 was the 40th anniversary of the establishment of diplomatic relations between the European Union and the People's Republic of China. To Hans Dietmar Schweisgut, who is the Ambassador of the EU to China, 'this is an important milestone in an ever closer and more important relationship between our union of 28 Member States and the country which may soon be the biggest economy in the world'.[114] Indeed, this is not surprising because the EU has already become China's biggest trading partner while China is the EU's second biggest one. According to the statistics given by the Delegation of the European Union to China, in 2014, the EU imports from China were worth € 302.5 billion, while the EU exports to China reached € 165 billion.[115] Consumers in both China and the EU have been more and more influenced by this increasing commercial intercourse. On this occasion, if an ordinary EU consumer wants to purchase a Chinese product, the corresponding party in most cases is not the Chinese company as the producer but usually a European agent or a European company which is selling Chinese products and vice versa.[116] Nevertheless, there are at least two phenomena which may lead to EU/Chinese consumers engaging directly with Chinese/EU companies more often in the near future.

The first one is about the fact that more and more European companies set up a branch in China and more and more Chinese companies set up a branch in the EU. This makes this study useful for these companies to know about the other jurisdiction's law.

The second one is related to the development of new business modes, especially the ones which are relevant to e-commerce and the logistics industry. It should be noted that the number of transactions which have a cross-border feature is rapidly increasing. With Internet access, consumers do not have to go abroad in order to purchase foreign products. The geographical location of shops is not a problem anymore. Bluntly speaking, even if a Chinese company does not set up a branch in the EU, it can still sell products to EU consumers via its e-platform. In this case, EU

---

[113] See, for example, Micklitz 2005, Reisch and Micklitz 2006, Cseres 2008.

[114] Hans Dietmar Schweisgut, 'A word from the EU Ambassador', available at: <http://eeas.europa.eu/delegations/china/eu_china/40th_anniversary_of_eu_china_relations/index_en.htm>, last visited: 2016/7/22.

[115] 'The EU represents 14% of China's external trade. EU-China bilateral trade in goods reached € 467.5 billion in 2014 and increased of 9.1% from the previous year'. 'EU_China Trade (11/03/2015)', available at: <http://eeas.europa.eu/delegations/china/press_corner/all_news/news/2015/20150311_en.htm>, last visited: 2016/7/22.

[116] For some illustrations, see Sect. 1.1 of this chapter.

law applies.[117] This also applies to EU companies. Thus, this also raises the demands for the EU and Chinese traders and lawyers to know about the other jurisdiction's legal rules.

1.6 Limits

The research carried out in this study is limited in four different ways.

Firstly, not the whole of consumer contract law is covered in this study. Both in the EU and China, there are many legal rules regulating the policing of consumer contracts, such as the rules requiring the true and accurate declaration of intention; this means there is no space for concluding a contract by fraud or coercion, banning the sale of specific commodities according to administrative reasons or regulating that a contract is only valid when concluded by a private actor with full capacity. However, this study merely deals with unfair terms and withdrawal rights.

Secondly, although this study provides a comparative study between China and the EU, it does not mean that all EU Member States are covered. The main focus is on the EU level, which means the relevant EU directives are discussed. It has to be noted that the EU is not one monolithic block. Even if the EU directives provide some unified rules, their implementation, interpretation and enforcement may widely differ in the Member States level, let alone the social effect brought by these rules, which is deeply influenced by each Member State's historical and cultural environment. Nevertheless, this study's aim is only to compare the Chinese rules and the rules regulated at the EU level. Only when researching the implementation of EU legislation, this study chooses English law and German law as two representative jurisdictions.

Thirdly, as aforementioned in Sect. 1.4.1 of this chapter, this study does not pay much attention to the theoretical foundations of the rules on consumer protection or the relevant empirical evidence. This needs clarification, since nowadays the traditional descriptive (doctrinal) approach is not the only way to study consumer contract law. Other legal and interdisciplinary methodologies have great influence. For example, behavioural economics plays an increasingly important role in today's consumer law research.[118] Abundant studies have been conducted and have explained why some types of consumer law mechanisms (e.g. mandatory information duties) do not work[119] and whether and how consumer law can be inspired by behavioural

[117] This is on the basis of Article 6 of the Regulation 593/2008 of the European Parliament and of the Council of 17 June 2008 on the law applicable to contractual obligations (Rome I).

[118] For a summary of literature, see Sibony and Helleringer 2015, FN no. 1, pp. 209–210.

[119] For example, Oren Bar-Gill and Omri Ben-Shahar use the CESL as an example to show that four regulatory techniques (mandatory pro-consumer agreements, mandated disclosure, regulation of entry to and withdrawal from contracts and pro-consumer default rules and contract interpretation) used by European consumer contract law may be ineffective – and perhaps worse – inefficient and harmful to consumers. See Bar-Gill and Ben-Shahar 2013.

insights.[120] In the fields of unfair terms and withdrawal rights, which are the two substantive topics addressed by this study, this is also the case.[121] This study does not address these aspects of consumer law research. Instead, this study focuses on the description of the research objects. Since English language literature on Chinese consumer law, especially the new rules on withdrawal rights, is generally lacking, as well as literature comparing Chinese and EU consumer law, this study undertakes the essential first step of presenting the rules, to see how they are regulated and interpreted and to summarise the similarities and differences. The work on this 'first step' comprises most of this study.

Fourthly, a normative approach which aims to find out which rule is better is not adopted. The discussion on 'what is the best solution' is not included when the comparative remarks are made, because it is believed that the design and the enforcement of legal rules always have their cultural and economic context. The premise for searching a 'one-fit-all' solution is that there is a universal solution, which may not be the case in many circumstances. Thus, instead of setting a benchmark to evaluate the rules in different jurisdictions, this study focuses more on explaining the differences.

References

(Akerlof 1970) George A. Akerlof, 'The Market for "Lemons": Quality Uncertainty and the Market Mechanism', 84 *The Quarterly Journal of Economics* 3, 1970, p. 488–500.

(Bar-Gill & Ben-Shahar 2013) Oren Bar-Gill & Omri Ben-Shahar, 'Regulatory Techniques in Consumer Protection: A Critique of European Consumer Contract Law', 50 *Common Market Law Review*, 2013, p. 109–126.

(Binding 2014) Jörg Binding, 'Consumer Protection Law in the People's Republic of China', *China-EU Law Journal* 3, 2014, p. 223–252.

(Bogdan 2013) Michael Bogdan, *Concise Introduction to Comparative Law*, Groningen: Europa Law Publishing, 2013.

(Bu 2013) Yuanshi Bu (ed.), *Chinese Civil Law: A Handbook*, München: Beck, 2013.

(Chen 2003) Zhiwu Chen, 'Capital Markets and Legal Development: The China case', 14 *China Economic Review* 4, 2003, p. 451– 472.

(Cseres 2008) KJ Cseres, 'What Has Competition Done for Consumers in Liberalised Markets?', 4 *The Competition Law Review* 2, p. 77–121.

(Dimatteo & Chen 2017) Larry A. DiMatteo and Lei Chen (eds.), *Chinese Contract Law: Civil and Common Law Perspectives*, Cambridge: Cambridge University Press, 2017.

(Durovic & Micklitz 2017) Mateja Durovic & Hans-W. Micklitz, *Internationalization of Consumer Law: A Game Changer*, Cham: Springer, 2017.

(Faure & Luth 2011) Michael G. Faure & Hanneke A. Luth, 'Behavioural Economics in Unfair Contract Terms: Cautions and Considerations', 34 *Journal of Consumer Policy* 3, 2011, p. 337–358.

[120] See, for example, Helleringer and Sibony 2017 and OECD 2017.

[121] As aforementioned, Michael Faure and Hanneke Luth's research shows that behavioural economics may lead to a call for more substantive control of standard terms and may argue for a more limited dependence upon information disclosure and consumer vigilance in standard terms in consumer policy. See Faure and Luth 2011.

(Fu 2011) Junwei Fu, *Modern European and Chinese Contract Law: A Comparative Study of Party Autonomy*, Alphen aan den Rijn: Kluwer Law International, 2011.

(Gao (高鸿业) 2014) 高鸿业主编[Hongye Gao (ed.)]:《西方经济学(微观部分)》[Western Economics: Microeconomics],中国人民大学出版社2014年第6版[China Renmin University Press, 6th edition]。

(Geng, Yang & Janus 2009) Xiao Geng, Xiuke Yang & Anna Janus, 'State-owned Enterprises in China: Reform dynamics and impacts', in Ross Garnaut, Ligang Song & Wing Thye Woo (eds.), *China's New Place in a World in Crisis: Economic, Geopolitical and Environmental Dimensions*, Canberra: ANU E Press, 2009, p. 155–178.

(Han (韩世远) 2011) 韩世远[Shiyuan Han]:"中国合同法与CISG"[Chinese Contract Law and the CISG],《暨南学报》2011年第2期[Journal of Jinan University (Philosophy and Social Sciences), 2011(2)],第7—13页[pp. 7–13]。

(Han 2017) Shiyuan Han, Consumer Sales Law in People's Republic of China, in Geraint Howells, Christian Twigg-Flesner, Hans-W. Micklitz, Chen Lei (eds.), *Comparative Consumer Sales Law*, Abingdon: Routledge, 2017.

(Helleringer & Sibony 2017) Geneviève Helleringer & Anne-Lise Sibony, 'European Consumer Protection Through the Behavioral Lens', 23 *Columbia Journal of European Law* 3, 2017, p. 607–646.

(Ho 2001) Suk-ching Ho, 'Growing Consumer Power in China: Some Lessons for Managers', 9 *Journal of International Marketing* 1, 2001, p. 64-83.

(Howell & Wilson 2016) Nicola Howell & Therese Wilson, 'The Limits of Competition: Reasserting a Role for Consumer Protection and Fair Trading Regulation in Competitive Markets', in Deborah Parry, Annette Nordhausen, Geraint Howells & Christian Twigg-Flesner (eds.), *The Yearbook of Consumer Law 2009*, New York: Routledge, 2016, p. 147–174.

(Jia (贾东明) 2013) 贾东明主编[Dongming Jia (ed.)]:《中华人民共和国消费者权益保护法解读》[Understanding on the Law of the People's Republic of China on the Protection of Consumer Rights and Interests],中国法制出版社2013年版[China Legal Publishing House, 2013]。

(Kawakami 2017) Mark T. Kawakami, *Flawed Strategies to Reducing Labor Exploitations: Reassessing the Role of Private Actors in the Global Supply Chain*, Maastricht: Universitaire Pers Maastricht, 2017.

(Li & Xu (李昌麒、许明月) 2012) 李昌麒、许明月[Changqi Li, Mingyue Xu]:《消费者保护法》[Consumer Protection Law],法律出版社2012年第3版[Law Press, 2012, 3rd edition]。

(Ling 2002) Bing Ling, *Contract Law in China*, Hongkong: Sweet & Maxwell Asia, 2002.

(Liu, Ye & Yuan (刘建丽、叶树光、原磊) 2010) 刘建丽、叶树光、原磊[Jianli Liu, Shuguang Ye & Lei Yuan]:"'三鹿奶粉事件'对乳制品消费及食品安全控制的影响"[Sanlu Milk Powder Scandal's Impact on Dairy Consumption and Food Safety Control],《经济与管理研究》2010年第6期[Research on Economics and Management, 2010(6)],第26-31页[p. 26–31]。

(Mankiw 2014) N. Gregory Mankiw, *Principles of Microeconomics*, 7th edition, Stamford: Cengage Learning, 2014.

(Micklitz 2005) Hans-W. Micklitz, 'The Concept of Competitive Contract Law', 23 *Penn State International Law Review* 3, p. 549–585.

(Micklitz 2015) Hans-W. Micklitz, 'The Transformation of Enforcement in European Private Law: Preliminary Considerations', 23 *European Review of Private Law* 4, 2015, p. 491–524.

(Novaretti 2010) Simona Novaretti, 'General Clauses and Practice: The Use of the Principle of Good Faith in Decisions of Chinese Courts', 18 *European Review of Private Law* 5, 2010, p. 953–981.

(Reisch & Micklitz 2006) Lucia A. Reisch & Hans-W. Micklitz, Consumers and Deregulation of the Electricity Market in Germany, 29 *Journal of Consumer Policy* 4, 2006, p. 399–415.

(Sibony & Helleringer 2015) Anne-Lise Sibony & Geneviève Helleringer, 'EU Consumer Protection and Behavioural Sciences: Revolution or Reform?', in Alberto Alemanno & Anne-Lise Sibony (eds.), *Nudge and the Law: A European Perspective*, Oxford: Hart Publishing, 2015, p. 209–233.

(Smits 2006) Jan Smits, 'Comparative Law and Its Influence on National Legal System', in Mathias Reimann & Reinhard Zimmermann (eds.), *The Oxford Handbook of Comparative Law*, Oxford: Oxford University Press, 2006, p. 477–512.

(Smits 2007) Jan Smits, 'Law Making in the European Union: On Globalization and Contract Law in Divergent Legal Cultures', 67 *Louisiana Law Review*, 2007, p. 1181–1203.

(Smits 2012a) Jan Smits, 'Rethinking Methods in European Private Law', in Maurice Adams & Jacco Bomhoff (eds.), *Practice and Theory in Comparative Law*, Cambridge: Cambridge University Press, 2012, p. 170–185.

(Smits 2012b) Jan M. Smits, *The Mind and Method of the Legal Academic*, Cheltenham: Edward Elgar Publishing, 2012.

(Smits (斯密茨) 2017) 【荷】扬·斯密茨[Jan Smits]:《法学的观念与方法》[The Mind and Method of the Legal Academic],魏磊杰、吴雅婷译[Translated by Leijie Wei and Yating Wu], 法律出版社2017年版[Law Press, 2017]。

(Swann 1979) Dennis Swann, *Competition and Consumer Protection*, New York: Penguin Books, 1979.

(The Research Group of the Comprehensive Department of the National Bureau of Statistics of the People's Republic of China(国家统计局综合司课题组) 2014) 国家统计局综合司课题组[The Research Group of the Comprehensive Department of the National Bureau of Statistics of the People's Republic of China]:"我国经济增长动力及其转换"[The Driving Forces of the Domestic Economic Growth and Its Transformation],《调研世界》2014年第12期[The World of Survey and Research, 2014(12)],第3—8页[p. 3–8]。

(Trentmann 2016) Frank Trentmann, *Empire of Things: How We Became a World of Consumers, Fifteenth Century to the Twenty-First*, New York: HarperCollins, 2016.

(Weber & Faure 2015) Franziska Weber & Michael Faure, 'The Interplay between Public and Private Enforcement in European Private Law: Law and Economics Perspective', 23 European Review of Private Law 4, 2015, p. 525–549.

(Zhang 2006) Zhang Mo, *Chinese Contract Law*, Leiden: Koninklijke Brill NV, 2006.

(Zhu 2012) Xiaodong Zhu, 'Understanding China's Growth: Past, Present, and Future', 26 *Journal of Economic Perspectives* 4, 2012, p. 103–124.

(Zweigert & Kötz 1998) Konrad Zweigert and Hein Kötz, *An Introduction to Comparative Law*, Translated by Tony Weir, Oxford: Oxford University Press, 1998.

Research Services, Working Papers, Etc

(Conway et al. 2010) Paul Conway et al., 'Product Market Regulation and Competition in China', OECD Economics Department Working Papers, No. 823, OECD Publishing, 2010, available at: <https://doi.org/10.1787/5km32vmgmfbx-en>.

(Koske et al. 2015) Isabell Koske et al., 'The 2013 update of the OECD's database on product market regulation: Policy insights for OECD and non-OECD countries', OECD Economics Department Working Papers, No. 1200, OECD Publishing, 2015, available at: <https://doi.org/10.1787/5js3f5d3n2vl-en>.

(OECD 2007) OECD: 'Roundtable on Economics for Consumer Policy', DSTI/CP(2007)1/FINAL, available at: < www.oecd.org/sti/consumer/39015963.pdf>.

(OECD 2008) OECD: 'The Interface between Competition and Consumer Policies', DAF/COMP/GF(2008)10, available at: <www.oecd.org/regreform/sectors/40898016.pdf>.

(OECD 2017) OECD: 'Use of Behaviour Insights in Consumer Policy', OECD Science, Technology and Innovation Policy Papers, No. 36, 2017, available at: <http://www.oecd-ilibrary.org/docserver/download/c2203c35-en.pdf?expires=1501141760&id=id&accname=guest&checksum=8B3B166E107839DBEEDCCF933EECD022>.

(Puccio 2015) Laura Puccio, 'Granting Market Economy Status to China: An Analysis of WTO Law and of Selected WTO Members' Policy', European Parliamentary Research Service, November 2015 – PE 571.325, available at: <http://www.europarl.europa.eu/RegData/etudes/IDAN/2015/571325/EPRS_IDA%282015%29571325_EN.pdf>.

(Morrison 2015) Wayne Morrison, 'China's Economic Rise: History, Trends, Challenges, and Implications for the United States', Congressional Research Service, 7-5700, www.crs.gov, RL 33534, 21 October 2015, available at: <https://www.fas.org/sgp/crs/row/RL33534.pdf>.

(Szamosszegi & Kyle 2011) Andrew Szamosszegi & Cole Kyle, 'An Analysis of State-owned Enterprises and State Capitalism in China', 26 October 2011, available at: <http://www.uscc.gov/sites/default/files/Research/10_26_11_CapitalTradeSOEStudy.pdf>.

Chapter 2
Sources of Consumer Contract Law

2.1 Introduction

Many types of rules can influence the behaviour of a trader who is dealing with a consumer. Within all these rules, some are binding because they are legislated in statutes or decided in precedents. The legitimacy of these rules usually derives from the institutions that enact them. In most cases, if the trader does not obey these rules, the consumer may go to the court or other public institutions for enforcement. These rules are usually qualified as 'legal rules'. However, it is noteworthy that the answer to 'who creates legal rules' is rather different in diverse jurisdictions. For instance, in civil law countries the rules contained in the statutory law are relatively more important, while in common law countries, case law plays a more significant role. In contrast, some other rules are self-regulated, and traders follow them only because they are willing to attract consumers by providing a higher level of protection. In this category, some of the rules can also be relied upon by consumers because they are explicitly recorded in the contract.

Limited by the research scope, this study only focuses on the aforementioned first type of binding rules. Specifically, the aim of this study is to compare the rules which set rights and obligations of the parties to a consumer contract in target jurisdictions, but not to examine the rules which are only designed for one single transaction by the parties or the moral rules which do not create any legal rights or obligations. Thus, the first step is to find these rules. In law, the question 'where do we find legal rules' can be converted to 'what are the sources of law', and this is exactly the question which this chapter discusses.

In the Chinese context, it is not possible to understand what are the sources of consumer contract law without a basic comprehension of the sources of law in general. Thus, this chapter firstly offers a brief introduction of several rules which are seen as law, including 'the Constitution',[1] 'legislation', 'documents published

[1] The Constitution in this study refers to the Constitution of the People's Republic of China (2004 Amendment) (《中华人民共和国宪法(2004修正)》).

J. Ge, *A Comparative Analysis of Policing Consumer Contracts in China and the EU*, https://doi.org/10.1007/978-981-13-2989-0_2

by the Supreme People's Court', 'doctrines', 'policies', etc. Subsequently, the instruments that should be seen as the sources of Chinese consumer contract law are provided on the basis of the introduction above.

To the EU counterpart, the emphasis laid on rules which set rights and obligations of the parties to a consumer contract has to be considered together with the EU's peculiarity of being a 'multilevel system of governance'. In EU law, it is important to find out the level on which the rule is regulated and how it binds. In this sense, merely describing the traditional sources of law in the Member States' domestic legal system is not enough.

In order to compare the legal rules in China and the EU, it is noteworthy that figuring out where to find these rules can only contribute to the description of similarities and differences. As to the possible explanation of why they are similar/different, it is necessary to see the reasons why legislators adopt these rules as well. To be specific, legal rules are in many circumstances enacted in order to achieve some concrete economic or political goals or to reflect some certain value which is widely accepted by community. Thus, legislators in different jurisdictions make different choices, and the result of this will be manifested by distinct rules.

Thus, in this chapter, the contents that may contribute to answer the questions 'where do we find the rules which set the rights and obligations of the parties to a consumer contract' and 'why are they regulated' are focused upon. The description of Chinese law and EU law is provided in sequence (Sects. 2.2 and 2.3). At the end of the chapter, a comparison between China and the EU and a possible explanation of differences among Chinese and EU law are provided (Sect. 2.4).

2.2 Chinese Law

2.2.1 Introduction

As mentioned, if one wants to know which instruments set rights and obligations of the parties to a consumer contract in China, one has to at least acquire some elementary understanding of China's legal system: what is seen as 'law' and who makes it.

Indeed, the topic of sources of law in general has already been richly discussed by legal theory scholars in their textbooks. However, their opinions are widely divergent because they apply different criteria to define the concept of 'law'. Sometimes whether a specific instrument can be seen as a source is relatively controversial. In this section, this discussion is presented firstly (Sect. 2.2.2.1): it shows the general understanding of 'what are the sources of law' in Chinese academia. Based on all existing opinions, some comments are made so as to contribute to this debate.

Secondly, official documents, such as the statutes enacted by the National People's Congress,[2] the administrative regulations promulgated by the State Council,[3] the judicial interpretations and cases published by the Supreme People's Court,[4] the policies made by the state government and the Chinese Communist Party[5] and some other objects which could be seen as the sources of law, such as the doctrines and customary law, are separately investigated (Sect 2.2.2.2, 2.2.2.3, 2.2.2.4, 2.2.2.5, 2.2.2.6, and 2.2.2.7). In order to obtain a more comprehensive picture of the legal system in China, some basic information regarding legal education is provided. This section also provides a summary of legal sources in the field of consumer protection (Sect. 2.2.3) and the motives for adopting legal rules on consumer protection (Sect. 2.2.4).

2.2.2 *Sources of Law in General*

2.2.2.1 Discussion on 'Sources of Law'

2.2.2.1.1 Opinions and Arguments

To define and talk about the sources of law, Chinese scholars generally use the concept of *yuanyuan* ('渊源'), which is exactly the translation of 'source' in English. It refers to the place where something (originally the water) begins. The use of this word can be traced back to the *Han* Dynasty.[6] Although the compound word *falü yuanyuan* ('法律渊源', which literally means 'sources of law') seems like indigenous parlance in Chinese language, which is different from some other legal terms imported from Japanese legal terminology,[7] Chinese scholars suggest that this Chinese phrase was taken from the translation of *Fontes Juris* in the late *Qing* Dynasty (late nineteenth century and early twentieth century).[8] Since Chinese legal scholars and legislative activities at that time were deeply influenced by Japanese scholars, while Japanese scholars were deeply influenced by European law (including German law, French law and Dutch law), it is not difficult to deduce that the

[2] National People's Congress of the People's Republic of China (中华人民共和国全国人民代表大会).

[3] State Council of the People's Republic of China (中华人民共和国国务院).

[4] Supreme People's Court of the People's Republic of China (中华人民共和国最高人民法院).

[5] Communist Party of China (中国共产党).

[6] The original Chinese text is: '然考其师友渊源所渐,犹未及乎游、夏,而曰管、晏及,伊、吕不加,过矣。' See Biography of Dong Zhong-shu, in History of the Han Dynasty (《汉书·董仲舒传赞》). The content of this ancient book is about the history of China from 202 B.C. to 23 A.D. and it was finished at about 109 A.D.

[7] The concept of 'quanli' ('权利', the Chinese translation of 'right') is a good example. For more examples, see Qu (屈文生) 2012.

[8] See Zhang (张文显) 2011, p. 52.

Chinese discussion on sources of law has had a European brand from the very beginning.

As a result of the literal interpretation of this term, 'sources of law' refers to all the things which could become a part of law in their original places. However, the scholars in China differ considerably about the meaning of this term, especially between the scholars of jurisprudence and the scholars of private law. In a word, it is hard to say there is a generally accepted definition of 'sources of law'. Compared with the emphasis of it in Taiwan,[9] the relevant problems of 'sources of law' have been ignored in Mainland China for a long period.

To introduce the development of the sources of law in Chinese history, Zongling Shen, a leading authority in Chinese jurisprudence, starts with the transformation from customary law to statute law in 536 B.C. It is believed that the promulgation of the punishment called *Xing Shu* by Zi Chan, an official of *Zheng* State,[10] was the symbol of this significant change.[11] It is not difficult to find that he implies legislation contributed most to the sources of law in China. In the third edition of another authoritative textbook of jurisprudence edited by Wenxian Zhang, Wangsheng Zhou tries to define the sources of law in a particular way: 'The forming process of law is always based on some kinds of motivations and approaches, and some resources will be abstracted to actualise the institutional configuration of authorities and rights. Therefore, these motivations, approaches and the resources are the sources of law in China'.[12] Although this definition is rather vague and obscure, a list of sources is provided: it includes legislation, decisions and policies of administration, cases and interpretations of people's courts, policies of the state and the relevant organisation, international law, customary law, ethics and conception of justice, articles of incorporation and contracts, comparative law and legal theory.[13]

Nevertheless, in the fourth edition of Wenxian Zhang's book, the definition of 'sources of law' has been simplified and materialised, and some standpoints have been changed. The new author of this part, Long Li, suggests that there are two indispensable elements in 'sources of law', and they are 'the direct relation with the efficacy of law' and 'the specific pattern of manifestation of the existing legal documents'.[14] This is also different from the previous edition, in which the sources of law are only composed of the Constitution, legislation, administrative regulations, local regulations, autonomous regulations, separate regulations and international

[9] Article 1 of Taiwan Civil Code states: 'If there is no applicable act for a civil case, the case shall be decided according to customs. If there is no such custom, the case shall be decided according to the jurisprudence'. Translated by www.lawbank.com.tw, available at: <http://db.lawbank.com.tw/Eng/FLAW/FLAWDAT0201.asp>, last visited: 2012/11/11.

[10] See Zuo Zhuan, noted by Du Yu (《左传·昭公六年》,杜预注).

[11] See Shen (沈宗灵) 2004, p. 310.

[12] The original Chinese text is: '我们认为,法的形成过程总是基于某种动因和进路,选择和提炼一定的资源,以实现权力和权利的制度性配置的过程。这种使法得以形成的资源、进路和动因,就是法的渊源。' Zhang (张文显) 2007, p. 89.

[13] See Zhang (张文显) 2007, pp. 92–94.

[14] See Zhang (张文显) 2011, p. 53.

treaties; customs, policies and cases are 'informal' sources.[15] In Long Li's other article, he suggests that 'sources of law' refers to the patterns of the manifestation of legal norms that can be cited by judges, can influence or can have binding force.[16] According to this viewpoint, the Constitution, statutes and regulations, legal interpretations, customary law, contracts, international treaties and international practice are the sources of law in China.[17] In other words, case law, comparative law and legal theory are not sources of law, and sources of law only consist of the sources which can be cited by people's courts.

From the perspective of private law, some leading scholars also have their particular proposition which may differ from other scholars' opinions. For instance, Kaixiang Liu suggests that the state policies are sources of law on the grounds of Article 6 of the General Principles of the Civil Law 1987,[18] which may support the idea held by Zongling Shen mentioned above.[19] Besides, he alleges that customs as customary law are also sources of law even if they were not adopted by legislation.[20] In contrast, with regard to customary law, Liming Wang, another leading author in civil law, states that only the customs which had been approved by the state could become sources of law.[21] Another leading scholar, Shiyuan Han, attempts to explain this topic from a comparative perspective. He indicates that the term *Rechtsquellen* has two meanings in German, which are the sources of right and the sources of law, but it points to two different words in Chinese, which are *quan yuan* ('权源', which literally means 'sources of right') and *fa yuan* ('法源', which literally means 'sources of law').[22] The former relates to the binding force based on the agreement of the parties in juridical acts, and the latter directs to the legal instruments where all civil subjects can find the unified rules. Hence, Shiyuan Han holds the opposite opinion to Long Li that it is inaccurate to say that contracts are also sources of law.

Compared with the opinions suggested by the scholars of jurisprudence, most scholars of private law address this topic in a pragmatic way. They rarely give a criterion to distinguish which kinds of legal documents can be qualified as sources and which cannot. Shiyuan Han, however, is exceptional, and he proposes his own classification: the sources of contract law can be distinguished into two parts – the sources which have 'absolute effects' and the sources which have 'relative effects'. The former refers to the legislation which should be unequivocally cited by judges when they make judgments, including statutes and their interpretations,

[15] See Zhang (张文显) 2011, pp. 56–58.

[16] See Li and Liu (李龙、刘诚) 2005, p. 4.

[17] See Li and Liu (李龙、刘诚) 2005, pp. 4–6.

[18] General Principles of the Civil Law of the People's Republic of China (《中华人民共和国民法通则》).

[19] See Liu (刘凯湘) 2008, p. 32. Article 6 of the General Principles of the Civil Law 1987 reads: 'Civil activities must be in compliance with the law; where there are no relevant provisions in the law, they shall be in compliance with state policies'.

[20] See Liu (刘凯湘) 2008, p. 35.

[21] See Wang et al. (王利明等) 2011, p. 17.

[22] See Han (韩世远) 2011, p. 16.

administrative regulations, local regulations, autonomous regulations, separate regulations, judicial interpretations and international treaties. The latter refers to the legal instruments which can become the grounds of reasoning in judgments. They should be followed, which may help enhance judges' confidence and the extent to which court decisions are convincing, but they should not be cited as the basis for making judgments. They are composed of the orders, directives and regulations of the ministries and commissions under the State Council; decisions and resolutions adopted by the People's Congress of the cities/countries; orders, directives and regulations of local people's governments; guiding opinions for making judgments of the Supreme People's Court; and guiding cases of the Supreme People's Court, international practice and customary law.[23]

2.2.2.1.2 Some Comments

As mentioned above, most academic discussion on the sources of law lacks practical relevance. In contrast to the criteria given by other scholars, Long Li and Shiyuan Han's criterion focusing on 'whether it can be cited by judges' is more practical: it can contribute to instruct the judges on where they can find law and which legal documents should be cited whereas the others should not be. This can be further explained from the two following perspectives.

Firstly, this criterion clearly shows the fact that judges can cite legal instruments other than those recognised as 'legislation' as legal basis. Specifically, in the Chinese context, the concept of 'law' has at least three levels of meaning: a broad one, a medium one and a narrow one.[24] The broad one refers to all legal sources. In comparison, when 'law' is discussed on the medium level, it refers to 'legislation' contained in the Legislation Law 2015.[25] Its Article 2 clarifies that Chinese legislation contains laws, administrative regulations, local regulations, autonomous regulations and separate regulations.[26] It should be noted that when the concept of 'laws' is employed together with 'regulations', it refers to the statutes made by the National People's Congress.[27] Here the concept of 'law' is employed in the narrow sense. As aforementioned, it is noteworthy that the Legislation Law 2015 fails to mention some other legal instruments apart from legislation. For instance, Chinese law also contains judicial interpretations. An important judicial interpretation should be mentioned here: the Provisions of the Supreme People's Court on Citation of Such Normative Legal Documents as Laws and Regulations in the Judgments (hereinafter

---

[23] See Han (韩世远) 2011, pp. 16–21.

[24] In some cases, there is one more level which can be seen as 'the broadest one'. To this layer, not only the rules of positive law but also the ones of customary law or even natural law can be recognised as law.

[25] Legislation Law of the People's Republic of China (2015 Amendment) (《中华人民共和国立法法(2015修正)》).

[26] This is further discussed in Sect. 2.2.2.3 of this chapter.

[27] Article 7 of the Legislation Law 2015.

'Interpretation No. 14 [2009] of the Supreme People's Court').[28] It regulates: 'A judgment made by the people's court shall cite relevant laws, regulations and other normative legal documents in accordance with law as a ruling basis'.[29] In the area of civil law, Interpretation No. 14 [2009] further provides that 'A civil judgment shall cite laws, legal interpretations or judicial interpretations, and may directly cite the administrative regulations, local regulations, or regulations on the exercise of autonomy and separate regulations that should be applied'.[30] From this instrument, it can be observed that the status of judicial interpretations in practice is just the same as the aforementioned legislation. On the basis of Long Li and Shiyuan Han's criterion, they are legal sources as well.

Secondly, this criterion particularly points out the fact that not all documents produced by the legislature are legal sources, while not all legal sources are produced by the legislature. Only the instruments that can be seen as law can set legal rights and obligations, otherwise no binding force is granted.[31] For instance, administrative regulations promulgated by the State Council are sources of law, whereas another type of official documents called 'regulatory documents' ('规范性文件'), which is also produced by the State Council, are not legal sources.[32] In contrast, legal sources can also sometimes grant to other instruments the status of law, even if they are not produced by the national legislature. Just as Shiyuan Han suggests, international treaties are sources of Chinese law as well.[33] It is regulated by Article 142 of the General Principles of Civil Law 1987 that international treaties even have priority over national statutes.[34]

The aim of this study is to investigate the rules which set rights and obligations of the parties to a consumer contract. Thus, it is necessary to observe the instruments

---

[28] Provisions of the Supreme People's Court on Citation of Such Normative Legal Documents as Laws and Regulations in the Judgments (《最高人民法院关于裁判文书引用法律、法规等规范性法律文件的规定》), Interpretation No. 14 [2009] of the Supreme People's Court (法释[2009]第14号).

[29] See Article 1 of the Interpretation No. 14 [2009] of the Supreme People's Court.

[30] See Article 4 of the Interpretation No. 14 [2009] of the Supreme People's Court. In comparison, the list containing legislation that can be cited in the field of criminal law is shorter: only statutes, legal interpretations or judicial interpretations are mentioned. In the field of administrative law, the list is longer: the interpretations of administrative regulations or administrative rules promulgated by the State Council or the departments authorised by the State Council can also be cited. See Articles 3 and 5 of the Interpretation No. 14 [2009] of the Supreme People's Court.

[31] For instance, it is argued that the rule regulated in the official documents made up by the departments of the State Council cannot be applied to decide whether a contract term violates the law (in which case it becomes void and null) or not. See Han (韩世远) 2015.

[32] With regard to the analysis on regulatory documents, see Huang (黄金荣) 2014, p. 13.

[33] See Han (韩世远) 2011, pp. 19–20.

[34] It states: 'If any international treaty concluded or acceded to by the People's Republic of China contains provisions differing from those in the civil laws of the People's Republic of China, the provisions of the international treaty shall apply, unless the provisions are ones on which the People's Republic of China has announced reservations./International practice may be applied on matters for which neither the law of the People's Republic of China nor any international treaty concluded or acceded to by the People's Republic of China has any provisions'.

from a closer view, in order to find out whether they set rights and obligations and how they influence the parties. As six important topics in the debate on the sources of law in China, the Constitution, legislation including statutes and regulations, the legal documents made up by the Supreme People's Court, doctrines, policies and customary law are discussed.

2.2.2.2 The Constitution

The Constitution of the People's Republic of China is the fundamental law of the State, so it should have been a source of law beyond all doubt. Besides, since the legitimacy of all the legislation is derived from the Constitution, judges must follow the principles and rules regulated by the Constitution.[35] However, although the status of the Constitution could have made it a rather significant or even the most significant source in the Chinese legal system, it is noteworthy that it has not become an instrument that can be cited in judgments, which makes it different from the other sources.

In practice, there used to be some judges who cited articles of the Constitution or argued that the right entitled by the Constitution to a party was infringed. The most famous case is 'Yuling Qi v Xiaoqi Chen et al.'.[36] In this case, the Supreme People's Court suggested: 'Based on the given facts, the right of Yuling Qi which has been infringed by Xiaoqi Chen is the right to receive education, which is given by the Constitution, and the infringement is realised by means of infringing the right of name, so the defendant should bear the civil liability'.[37] However, this decision was repealed later.[38] The feature of the Constitution of People's Republic of China that it cannot be applied or cited by people's courts is confirmed. Besides, constitutional review is not allowed. Thus, in Long Li or Shiyuan Han's definition, it is more appropriate to say that the Constitution guides the legislation and judicial activities but is not a source of law itself.

---

[35] See Li and Liu (李龙、刘诚) 2005, p. 4.

[36] For the facts and the judgment, see Yuling Qi v Xiaoqi Chen et al. See also, pkulaw.cn, 'Dispute over Infringement of a Citizen's Basic Right to Receive Education Protected by Constitution Through Infringement of Right of Name', available at: en.pkulaw.cn, Reference Code of pkulaw.cn: CLI.C.66950(EN).

[37] See the Official Reply of the Supreme People's Court on Whether the Civil Liabilities Shall Be Borne for the Infringement upon a Citizen's Basic Right of Receiving Education (《最高人民法院关于以侵犯姓名权的手段侵犯宪法保护的公民受教育的基本权利是否应承担民事责任的批复》), Interpretation No. 25 [2001] of the Supreme People's Court (法释[2001]25号).

[38] The aforementioned Interpretation No. 25 [2001] of the Supreme People's Court lost its efficacy due to the Interpretation No. 15 [2008] of the Supreme People's Court. See the Decision of the Supreme People's Court on Abolishing the Relevant Judicial Interpretations (the Seventh Batch) Promulgated before the End of 2007 (《最高人民法院关于废止2007年底以前发布的有关司法解释(第七批)的决定》), Interpretation No. 15 [2008] of the Supreme People's Court (法释[2008]15号).

The question of constitutionality can be raised during the process of legislation. For instance, the promulgation of the Property Law 2007[39] had been delayed before taking effect in 2007 because of an open letter which stated that the principles of the draft of Property Law had deviated from the principle of socialism on the basis of the Constitution.[40] In addition, there was a heated discussion in academia on how to use constitutionality as an approach to interpret the law.[41] Nevertheless, few judges apply this approach in reality.

In this study's context, it should be noted that although the Constitution does mention the word 'consumption',[42] it does not provide any specific rule regarding the rights and obligations of a consumer contract. Therefore, not too much attention is paid to the Constitution in the following description of the substantive rules.

2.2.2.3 Legislation

No matter what criterion we adopt, there is no doubt that legislation composes the most important part of Chinese law. As previously mentioned, legislation in China can be divided into several different types, which are 'laws', 'administrative regulations', 'local regulations', 'autonomous regulations' and 'separate regulations'. They are all legal sources that can be cited in judgments on the basis of Interpretation No. 14 [2009]. They are explained in detail in the Legislation Law 2015.[43]

In terms of the definitive meaning of legislation, on the grounds of the Legislation Law 2015, 'laws' ('法律') refer to the legal documents which are enacted and amended by the National People's Congress and its Standing Committee, governing criminal offences, civil affairs, the State organs and other matters.[44] 'Administrative regulations' ('行政法规') refer to the legal documents which are formulated by the State Council, governing the matters requiring the formulation of administrative regulations in order to implement the provisions of law and matters within the administrative functions and powers of the State Council as provided for in Article 89 of the Constitution.[45] 'Local regulations' ('地方性法规') refer to the legal documents which are formulated by the people's congresses or their standing committees of the provinces, autonomous regions and municipalities directly under the

[39] Property Law of the People's Republic of China (《中华人民共和国物权法》).

[40] See Chen 2010, pp. 989–990. For the relevant news and comments, see Eva Cheng, 'New Chinese property law protects robber barons', available at: <http://www.greenleft.org.au/node/37269>, last visited: 2012/12/2.

[41] For the recent discussion, see Wang (王书成) 2012; Liu (柳建龙) 2011.

[42] For example, Article 14 of the Constitution states: 'The State properly apportions accumulation and consumption, concerns itself with the interests of the collective and the individual as well as of the State…'

[43] See Article 2 of the Legislation Law 2015.

[44] See Article 7 of the Legislation Law 2015. Considering the language habit of legal English, the term of 'law' is substituted by the term of 'statute' hereinafter if it is not cited directly.

[45] See Article 65 of the Legislation Law 2015.

Central Government.[46] 'Autonomous regulations and Separate regulations' ('自治条例和单行条例') refer to the legal documents which are formulated by the people's congresses of the national autonomous areas.[47]

In the area of consumer law, China did not have any specific legislation. Until 1993, no general legislation on consumer protection had been promulgated, although some regional consumer organisations had come into existence in the mid-1980s,[48] and several items of national legislation which are relevant to the protection of consumer, for example, the laws on pharmaceutical administration[49] and standardisation,[50] were introduced. This situation fundamentally changed in 1993, when the Chinese Consumer Protection Law 1993[51] was enacted. Up to this day, there are numerous laws and regulations setting rights and obligations to traders and consumers so legislation forms a most important legal source in this area. Examples are provided in Sect. 2.2.3 of this chapter.

2.2.2.4 Legal Documents Created by the Supreme People's Court

2.2.2.4.1 Judicial Interpretations

Judicial interpretations are the legal documents promulgated by the Supreme People's Court on specific issues.[52] Interpretation No. 14 [2009] mentioned before is a good example. In most cases, judicial interpretations are designed to interpret

[46] See Article 72 of the Legislation Law 2015.

[47] See Article 75 of the Legislation Law 2015.

[48] The first consumer organisation was spontaneously set up by some retired veteran in Hebei province in 1983. They used the criminal law rules and some administrative regulations to protect their consumer rights. See Yang (杨琴) 2011, p. 25.

[49] The Pharmaceutical Administration Law was first promulgated in 1984, and the latest amendment was published in 2015. See the Pharmaceutical Administration Law of the People's Republic of China (2015 Amendment) (《中华人民共和国药品管理法(2015修正)》).

[50] See the Standardization Law of the People's Republic of China (《中华人民共和国标准化法》), which has come into force since 1989. Its Article 8 states: 'The formulation of standards shall be conducive to ensuring safety and the people's health, safeguarding consumer interests and protecting the environment'.

[51] Law of the People's Republic of China on the Protection of Consumer Rights and Interests (《中华人民共和国消费者权益保护法》).

[52] It is noteworthy that judicial interpretations are not the only legal documents made by the Supreme People's Court. The Supreme People's Court also publishes official documents for other issues (e.g. management, daily operation, etc.) regarding the people's court system. Different types of documents use different serial numbers. Judicial interpretations usually use 'fashi' ('法释', which means interpretations made by the Supreme People's Court), while other official documents usually use 'fafa' ('法发', which means instruments published by the Supreme People's Court) or simply 'fa' ('法', which refers to the Supreme People's Court). However, this is not always the case, since in early years some judicial interpretations also used 'fafa [year] No. xxx' as their serial number. One good example is the Opinions of the Supreme People's Court on Several Issues concerning the Implementation of the General Principles of the Civil Law of the People's Republic of

the laws. In order to improve legal certainty and ensure that similar cases are treated equally, the Supreme People's Court finds that publishing judicial interpretations is an appropriate approach which may help obtain a uniform interpretation.

The status of judicial interpretations, however, is always a problem in the context of Chinese law. The reason is apparent: compared with statutes and regulations, judicial interpretations are not products of lawmaking processes, which are mostly regulated in the Legislation Law 2015, and this may lead to the consequence that there is an obvious lack of legitimacy. In addition, due to the reason that judicial interpretations are made by the Supreme People's Court, it may deprive the party's right to appeal. Nevertheless, in practice judges always cite judicial interpretations.[53] Since the ratio of first instance judgments being overruled is an important benchmark to assess the quality of their work,[54] it is risky to give decisions which contradict judicial interpretations. Taking this into account, most scholars hold a positive attitude on whether it can be recognised as a legal source.[55]

For the purposes of this work, judicial interpretations are sources of law.

China (For Trial Implementation). This document is no doubt a judicial interpretation, but its serial number is 'fafa [1998] No. 6'. This study translates 'fashi' into 'interpretation of the Supreme People's Court' and translates 'fafa' or 'fa' into 'instrument of the Supreme Peoples' Court'.

[53] See Article 4 of the Interpretation No. 14 [2009] of the Supreme People's Court. However, it is dubious why a judicial interpretation can regulate that judicial interpretations should be cited. According to Shiyuan Han, this seems a kind of 'self-coronation'('自我加封'). See Han (韩世远) 2011, p. 17.

[54] In the Notice of the Supreme People's Court on Issuing the Guiding Opinion of the Supreme People's Court on Carrying out the Case Quality Evaluation Work (for Trial Implementation) (《最高人民法院印发〈最高人民法院关于开展案件质量评估工作的指导意见(试行)〉的通知》) (Instrument No.6 [2008] of the Supreme People's Court (法发[2008]6号)), the quality of trial work is supposed to be assessed in three aspects: justice, efficiency and effects. Its Article 8 firstly points out the 'ratio of cases whose first judgment is changed in appeal' is an important index to evaluate the quality of trial work from the perspective of justice. It reads: 'The index of justice in trial work is composed of 11 grade III indices, namely, ratio of cases the jurisdiction over which is changed, ratio of cases under trial by jury in the first instance, ratio of cases whose first judgment is changed in appeal, ratio of cases remanded by the appeal court to the court of the first instance for new trial, ratio of cases whose effective judgment is changed, ratio of effective cases remanded for new trial, ratio of cases subject to the second instance, ratio of cases with discontinuation or termination of enforcement, ratio of cases under illegal trial, ratio of cases under illegal enforcement, and ruling paper quality index'. Furthermore, Article 10 of the Instrument No. 6 [2008] of the Supreme People's Court mentions that the ratio of appeal cases is the first criterion to assess the effect in trial work. It reads: 'The index of effects in trial work is composed of 11 grade III indices, namely, ratio of appeal cases, ratio of petition cases, ratio of cases concluded through mediation, ratio of cases withdrawn, ratio of complaints by letters and visits, ratio of repeated complaints by letters and visits, ratio of cases actually enforced, ratio of cases whose execution objects are realised, ratio of cases whose judgment is voluntarily executed, ratio of cases whose complaints are settled by the first judgment, and index of public satisfaction level'.

[55] Besides the opinions that regard judicial interpretations as legal sources, there is another opinion which suggest that judicial interpretations should be considered as customary law as one of the informal sources so as to be cited by judges legally. See Cao (曹士兵) 2006, pp. 178–181.

2.2.2.4.2 Cases Published by the Supreme People's Court

In Chinese legal history, judicial cases have always had an unclear status. On the one hand, they constituted an important part of the legal system as they supplemented the statutory law. The phenomenon called 'Li yi fu lü' ('例以辅律', which means cases are the auxiliary sources supporting the statutory law) is believed to have existed for a long time.[56] On the other hand, 'case law' ('判例法', which is generally used to describe the legal system in the common law countries) did not have a good reputation because the phenomenon called 'yi li po lü' ('以例破律',which refers to the fact that judges would break the statutory law if they follow the precedent) also existed, and this was not considered to be permitted.[57] Nowadays, scholars still suggest that the system of case law does not fit in well with China's national conditions. Long Li gives three reasons: (1) case law does not conform to China's reality, and it does not meet the requirements of the National People's Congress system; (2) our judges are untrained in case law, and the procedure of case law is very complicated, which also costs too much time, and the result cannot be delivered to the parties promptly; and (3) case law pays too much attention to the specific circumstances of the case, which makes it obviously biased.[58]

Although China is not a case law country, it does not mean that cases are insignificant in China. Furthermore, change has come with the introduction of the official case guidance system in 2010. Nowadays, there are two major types of cases which are published by the Supreme People's Court. The first one is 'gazette cases'; the second one is 'guiding cases'. These two types are introduced as follows.

Since 1985, the Supreme People's Court has selected significant judgments from all over the country to publish them in the 'Gazette of the Supreme People's Court of the People's Republic of China' every month. It was required that the judgments published must have been determined based on discussion by the Judicial Committee of the Supreme People's Court. Therefore, some people regard 1985 as the date of birth of the case guidance system.

The official case guidance system established by the Supreme People's Court came into effect in 2010. In order to distinguish the new system from the case law system in common law countries, the Chinese word *an li* ('案例', which only refers to the English word 'case') but not *pan li* ('判例', which is always used to describe the cases which have binding forces or are seen as law) is employed.[59]

The concrete function of guiding cases is that Chinese judges will refer to guiding cases when they make judgments, if the case being tried by a people's court at

---

[56] See Hu and Yu (胡云腾、于同志) 2008, p. 3.

[57] See Shen (沈宗灵) 2004, p. 321.

[58] See Zhang (张文显) 2011, p. 53.

[59] See Hu and Yu (胡云腾、于同志) 2008, p. 7. It is pointed out the fundamental difference between the Chinese Case Guidance System and the case law system of common law countries is that it only has the effect of guidance but not binding force.

any level is similar to a guiding case in terms of basic facts and application of law.[60] Specifically, a civil law judge, for example, will refer to a guiding case when the pending case share the same cause of action, similar factual backgrounds, and the same disputed issues with the guiding case. Disputed issues should include not only factual disputes but also legal disputes.[61] Furthermore, in contrast to the gazette cases system,[62] the new system requires the judges to *canzhao* ('参照') guiding cases.[63] The word *canzhao* here literally means 'refer to'. For the meaning of every single character, *can* means 'consult' and *zhao* means 'follow'. Indeed, the use of *canzhao* here not only implies that Chinese judges should follow guiding cases but also leaves the space for interpretation that judges may cite these guiding cases in their judgments.[64] In the newly published *Detailed Rules for the Implementation of the Provisions of the Supreme People's Court on Case Guidance*, it is further confirmed that 'Where a people's court at any level refers to a guiding case in the trial of a similar case, it shall quote the guiding case as the judgment's reasoning, instead of citing it as the basis for the judgment'.[65]

For the specific criteria regarding how guiding cases are selected, it is pointed out that a guiding case refers to a judgment which has already come into effect and meets the following requirements: (1) the judgment attracts wide attention from society; (2) the legal provisions are, to a greater degree, on the principles of law; (3) the judgment is representative in nature; and (4) the judgment is difficult, complicated or novel.[66] Although it is apparently the Supreme People's Court that is in charge of

[60] See Article 9 of the Detailed Rules for the Implementation of the Provisions of the Supreme People's Court on Case Guidance (《〈最高人民法院关于案例指导工作的规定〉实施细则》), Instrument No. 130 [2015] of the Supreme People's Court (法[2015]130号).

[61] See Chen Kui, 'How to Apply the Guiding Cases of the Supreme People's Court in Judicial Practice', China Guiding Cases Project, 22 April 2012, available at: <https://cgc.law.stanford.edu/commentaries/3-judge-chen>, last visited: 2016/10/20.

[62] In an interview, the judge who is in charge of the Chinese Case Guidance System gives several differences between guiding cases and the cases published before, which can be elaborated in three aspects: (1) name, only the cases published through the procedure regulated by 'the Provisions' can be named 'guiding cases'; (2) procedure, guiding cases have to be selected through the strict procedure which is explicit in 'the Provisions'; and (3) effect, the judges should refer to guiding cases and they could cite them while the other cases should not be cited. See The Supreme People's Court of the People's Republic of China (中华人民共和国最高人民法院), 'The Director of the Research Office of the Supreme People's Court Meets the Press on the Case Guidance System' (《最高人民法院研究室负责人就案例指导制度答记者问》), available at: <http://www.court.gov.cn/xwzx/jdjd/sdjd/201112/t20111220_168539.htm>, last visited: 2013/2/15.

[63] See Article 7 of Notice of the Supreme People's Court on Issuing the Provisions on Case Guidance (《最高人民法院印发〈关于案例指导工作的规定〉的通知》) (Instrument No. 51 [2010] of the Supreme People's Court (法发[2010]51号)). It reads: 'When trying similar cases, people's courts at all levels shall use the guiding cases issued by the Supreme People's Court as a reference'.

[64] There is a heated debate on how to understand the phrase 'yingdang canzhao'. See, for example, Lei (雷磊) 2015, p. 273.

[65] See Article 10 of the Instrument No. 130 [2015] of the Supreme People's Court.

[66] See Article 2 of the Instrument No. 51 [2010] of the Supreme People's Court. Its point (5) mentions that other cases that have a guiding function can also become guiding cases.

the selection, examination and reporting for approval of guiding cases,[67] it should be noted that the judges from people's courts of all levels and even scholars and lawyers are entitled to recommend a judgment to be selected if they deem it complies with the aforementioned criteria.[68]

So far, 18 batches of guiding cases have been published.[69] Although some leading scholars such as Liming Wang deny that guiding cases are now sources of law in China,[70] it is still a great change that guiding cases can be cited in judgments. Considering that some judges of local courts argue that guiding cases should not be cited because they are not law and they do not have binding force,[71] the opinion of Shiyuan Han that the cases should be treated as a source with relative effect, which means the guiding cases could become the grounds of reasoning in judgments, makes sense.[72] In any case, it should be noticed that only the guiding cases promulgated by the Supreme People's Court could be sources of law in China.

2.2.2.5 Legal Doctrine

2.2.2.5.1 What Is 'Doctrine' in China?

In China, 'doctrine' refers to the academic points of view on legal issues proposed by scholars. If legislators adopt some academic points to enact legal rules, or judges accept some academic points and use them to make judgments, these points can set rights and obligations in fact. Thus, legal doctrine can be qualified as a legal source. In order to influence legislators and judges, scholars can spread their academic points through the books they write. Giving lectures is also an effective way. In addition, legal education is important, because most judges used to be law school students, so the education they received usually has a deep impact on the court decisions they make.

2.2.2.5.1.1 Books

Legal books in China can be divided into various types: textbooks, monographs and 'books guiding the practice'.

---

[67] See Article 3 of the Instrument No. 51 [2010] of the Supreme People's Court.

[68] See Article 5 of the Instrument No. 51 [2010] of the Supreme People's Court.

[69] For the English translation of the first ten batches of guiding cases, see Stanford Law School | China Guiding Cases Project, 'Guiding Cases in Perspective', available at: <https://cgc.law.stanford.edu/guiding-cases/>, last visited: 2016/10/20.

[70] See Wang (王利明) 2012, p. 71.

[71] See Zhao Ji (赵霁), 'Discussion on the Binding Force of the Guiding Cases' (《指导性案例的拘束力问题探讨》), available at: <http://www.gy.yn.gov.cn/Article/spyf/dlq2010/fglt/201104/22595.html>, last visited: 2016/7/25.

[72] See Han (韩世远) 2011, p. 20. For 'relative effect', see Sect. 2.2.2.1.1 of this chapter.

Before and in the early twenty-first century, legal research of Chinese mainland scholars was still rather weak. In 1990, there was a popular saying that 'When Chinese scholars are doing research, they are just plagiarising foreign scholars. Scholars in Beijing are plagiarising scholars in Taiwan. Scholars in other places are plagiarising scholars in Beijing'.[73]

Indeed, because of the same language, the books written by scholars in Taiwan were used for reference frequently. According to research by Suli, from 2000 to 2006, the most cited Chinese legal academic book was *Civil Law Theories and Case Studies* ('民法学说与判例研究') written by Tez-chien Wang, an authority on civil law in Taiwan who received his doctorate degree from the University of Munich. His doctoral dissertation was supervised by Karl Larenz. The inclination to cite translated works and introductions to foreign law is also revealed through research on the articles published on CSSCI – 'Chinese Social Sciences Citation Index' – journals from 1998–2007.[74] The legal work that had been cited most was *General Principles of German Civil Law* ('德国民法总论', the original German title is *Allgemeiner Teil des BGB* by Dieter Medicus) translated by Jiandong Shao. The second most cited legal work was *Modern German Property Law* ('德国当代物权法') written by Xianzhong Sun.[75]

Up to this day, the phenomenon mentioned above is still common in Chinese legal academia,[76] but along with the maturity of Chinese mainland scholars who received legal education after 1977, the level of the textbooks written by Chinese mainland scholars has become higher – there are now more footnotes, more reasonable arguments and more references in these books. For example, the textbook *Criminal Law* ('刑法学') written by Mingkai Zhang,[77] one of the top authors in criminal law, is much used by criminal judges and inquisitors. It is even honoured as 'The Bible with a yellow cover in criminal law'. However, there is still a criterion which distinguishes top textbooks from ordinary ones: how the author applies the legal methodology, especially comparative study. Besides the rigorous logic and convincing argument, the discussion of the Japanese criminal law system is also a highlight in Mingkai Zhang's *Criminal Law*.

Apart from the textbooks, there is also a kind of popular books named 'books guiding the practice'. Sometimes the textbooks concentrating on theoretical controversies

[73] See Suli (苏力) 2006, p. 10. See also Suli (苏力) 2004, p. 65.

[74] CSSCI journals are recognised as the top journals in Chinese legal academia. See Sect. 2.2.2.5.1.2 of this chapter.

[75] See Luan and Luo (栾春娟、罗海山) 2009, p. 71.

[76] In addition, scholars suggest that civil law research in China is far from perfect because (1) comparative research only stops at the description of the positive law but fails to touch upon legislative reasons, background, legal practice, etc.; (2) little emphasis has been put on institutional history and theoretical history; and (3) as to the research on judicial decisions, analysing typical cases is the mainstream, while empirical methods are rarely used to provide materials for doctrinal legal research. See Jin (金可可) 2012, p. 50.

[77] See Zhang (张明楷) 2011.

are too difficult for judges to read.[78] Instead, the books merely telling judges how to make judgments are seen as welcome. Some scholars, who are good at writing this kind of books even if they are not able to write good textbooks, are thus influential in practice.

2.2.2.5.1.2 Journal Articles

Although some people criticise Chinese legal scholars for quoting books too much,[79] the articles published in journals still play a crucial role, because these articles, especially the ones published in CSSCI journals, usually reflect the academic frontiers. When judges are confronted with difficult situations which they have never faced, they may turn to these journals for instruction.

CSSCI, the Chinese Social Sciences Citation Index, is a project which Nanjing University handpicks the top journals with high academic quality from thousands of journals in China. The journals selected are determined by quantitative indicators like the factor of influence and the rate of quoting, along with the opinions of some experts. Good authors in China prefer to publish their articles in CSSCI journals, generally speaking, because of the higher quality of the journal. Moreover, the promotion of lecturers and associate professors depends on the quantity of the articles published in CSSCI journals as well. According to the latest 2017–2018 version, there are 23 CSSCI law journals.[80]

[78] By the end of 2005, there were only 51.6% of all judges in China who obtained bachelor degrees. See Zhu (朱景文) 2007, pp. 197–198.

[79] The top 26 literatures which were cited more than 30 times are all books but no articles. See Luan and Luo (栾春娟、罗海山) 2009, p. 71.

[80] The full list is *Journal of Comparative Law* (《比较法研究》), *Contemporary Law Review* (《当代法学》), *Science of Law* (Journal of Northwest University of Political Science and Law) (《法律科学(西北政法大学学报)》), *Studies in Law and Business* (《法商研究》), *Law Science* (《法学》), *Jurists Review* (《法学家》), *Legal Forum* (《法学论坛》), *Law Review* (《法学评论》), *Chinese Journal of Law* (《法学研究》), *Law Science Magazine* (《法学杂志》), *Law and Social Development* (《法制与社会发展》), *Journal of East China University of Political Science and Law* (《华东政法大学学报》), *Global Law Review* (《环球法律评论》), *Tsinghua University Law Journal* (《清华法学》), *Modern Law Science* (《现代法学》), *Journal of Political Science and Law* (《政法论丛》), *Tribune of Political Science and Law* (《政法论坛》), *Political Science and Law* (《政治与法律》), *China Legal Science* (《中国法学》), *Peking University Law Journal* (《中外法学》), *Administrative Law Review* (《行政法学研究》), *Criminal Science* (《中国刑事法杂志》) and *Oriental Law* (《东方法学》). See Institute for Chinese Social Sciences Research and Assessment of Nanjing University (南京大学中国社会科学研究评价中心), 'Public Notification Regarding Journals Selected by the Chinese Social Sciences Citation Index (2017–2018)' (《关于〈中文社会科学引文索引(CSSCI)来源期刊和收录集刊(2017–2018)目录〉的公示》), available at: <http://cssrac.nju.edu.cn/a/xwdt/zxdt/20170116/2805.html>, last visited: 2017/5/1.

2.2.2.5.1.3 Lectures and Training Courses for Judges

Some law schools in China create training courses for judges. These training courses are sometimes set up for judges who come from undeveloped areas. In some cases, courts also invite scholars of authority to give lectures to judges in order to enhance the ability of judges to deal with difficult cases.[81]

2.2.2.5.2 How Legal Doctrine Sets Rights and Obligations

Pursuant to Interpretation No. 14 [2009] of the Supreme People's Court, it is not permissible to cite a scholar's doctrine in judgments. Therefore, most people do not consider doctrine as a source of law. However, according to the criterion mentioned in the introduction of this chapter, doctrine sometimes does create rights and obligations for the parties to a contract.

Indeed, although it is not permissible to cite doctrine, judges sometimes apply doctrine without citing it when they make arguments. This makes doctrine still influential in practice.[82] For example, 'transferring guarantee' is not recorded or mentioned in the Chinese Property Law 2007 so there will not be a real right occurring according to the principle of *numerus clausus*, even if the parties of a contract have agreement on this.[83] However, when judges are dealing with relevant cases, the legal reasoning usually starts from the concept of 'transferring guarantee', and this is generally provided by doctrine. Put differently, the precondition or the prior standard of whether the agreement will lead to a change of real right will be decided based on doctrine. This can be illustrated with the following case.

---

[81] 'The 2007 Initial Training Class for the Xinjiang Political and Legal Cadres Held by Tsinghua University'(首期清华大学新疆政法干部高级培训班) is a good example. It is reported that experts from the Supreme People's Court, Supreme People's Procuratorate, Tsinghua University and Peking University gave lectures to the trainees. See Nianci Sheng (盛念慈), 'The Initial Training Class for the Xinjiang Political and Legal Cadres Held by Tsinghua University is Brought to a Successful Close' (《首期清华大学新疆政法干部高级培训班圆满结束》), available at: <http://www.xjkunlun.cn/zzgz/gbgz/gbjy/2007/197331.htm>, last visited: 2016/7/25.

[82] Many judges try to apply the views of academic authorities to help themselves deal with the intractable cases. The best example is the 'Chongqing Cable Case': without precise illustration, the major part of the judgment's reasoning is exactly the same as one article written by the aforementioned authority Tez-chien Wang. This is well described in Zhu (朱晓喆) 2015, p. 157.

[83] In this study, 'transferring guarantee' refers to the Chinese concept '让与担保'. However, since it is not recorded by the Chinese Property Law 2007, there is a dispute about the meaning of this concept. Furthermore, when dealing with the relevant cases, Chinese judges differ considerably: It is not clear whether the agreement on 'transferring guarantee' between the parties should be valid. It is also not clear whether the creditor's priority right for claim should be supported. For a summary, see Gaoshan Legal (高杉Legal), 'A Collection of Judicial Viewpoints in Typical Cases on Transferring Guarantee' (让与担保典型案例裁判观点集成), available at: http://www.360doc.com/content/15/0616/20/22513831_478599531.shtml, last visited: 2017/7/13.

Chunlin He v Kaiming Luo[84]

Judgment: 'Transferring guarantee' refers to a kind of non-typical guarantee that guarantees the creditor's right by transferring a guaranty's right of the debtor or the third party, usually the ownership, to the creditor previously. As a result of the liquidation of liabilities, the creditor should return the guarantee to the debtor or the third party and he has the priority right for a claim with regard to the receipts resulting from the disposal of the guarantee in case the debtor cannot fulfil his obligation. In this case, Kaiming Luo and Mingzhen Wang had provided the housing involved as a guaranty for the loan but the form of guarantee the parties adopted was transferring the ownership to Chunlin He. The parties agreed with that the debtor would regain the housing in the case where all the obligations are settled by repaying the capital and interest. The above-described behaviour meets the requirements of transferring guarantee but violates the rules confirmed by the Property Law that the mortgagee may not enter into an agreement with the mortgagor that the mortgaged property should come under the ownership of the creditor when the debtor defaults. Therefore, the essence of selling the housing is to provide a transferring guarantee so it is invalid because of violating the law.

In the area of consumer contracts, it is also possible to observe this phenomenon especially where the law shows gaps. A book *Understanding on Law of the People's Republic of China on the Protection of Consumer Rights and Interests* (hereinafter 'the Understanding of authority') has great influence in practice because it is written by the officials who were in charge of the process of lawmaking: it is presented by the Civil Law Office of the Legislative Affairs Commission of the Standing Committee of the National People's Congress.[85] Although the opinions it expresses cannot be seen as legislative interpretation, the opinions given by this study are still believed to be of relatively high authority.[86]

Thus, in the following chapters regarding specific issues, doctrine is seen as an important perspective when the law is described and interpreted.[87]

---

[84] Chunlin He v Kaiming Luo (何春霖与罗开明等房屋买卖合同纠纷上诉案), Civil Judgment (2008) Cheng-Min-Zhong-Zi No. 2318 of the Chengdu Intermediate People's Court in Sichuan Province (四川省成都市中级人民法院(2008)成民终字第2318号民事判决书)

[85] The original Chinese name of this department is '全国人大常委会法制工作委员会民法室'. On the grounds of its authority given by the Constitution and law, 'the NPC and its Standing Committee jointly exercise the power to enact laws in China. The Standing Committee enacts and amends all laws except laws that should be enacted and amended by the NPC. When the NPC is not in session, its Standing Committee may partially supplement and amend laws it enacted, provided that the changes do not contravene the laws' basic principles. The Standing Committee also has the power to interpret the Constitution and other laws'. See the National People's Congress of the People's Republic of China, 'Functions and Powers of the Standing Committee', available at: <http://www.npc.gov.cn/englishnpc/Organization/2007-11/15/content_1373018.htm>, last visited: 2016/9/8.

[86] See Jia (贾东明) 2013.

[87] In this sense, a 'doctrinal approach' is utilised to describe the law.

2.2.2.5.3 Legal Education in China

Apart from the approach that judges could acquire the propositions of academic by reading books and attending lectures or training courses, there is another significant approach that makes doctrine play an important role in legal practice, that is, legal education, because more and more judges are graduates of law schools so what they have learned in law schools can deeply influence their judgments.[88]

Modern Chinese legal education began along with China's economic reform, which was also the era of reform and opening up in the late 1970s. Because of the demand for the rule of law and a market economy, it needed more professionals who know law well to maintain the order of the new market and society. But during the Great Cultural Revolution (1966–1976), only two law schools were not eliminated. The law students who had been educated before 1977 were in great shortage.[89] In addition, the law professionals trained from 1949–1977 were deeply affected by many political movements and ideology. As a result, the legal training for them might not be enough.[90]

Legal education has been rapidly developing since then. Nowadays, most universities in China have established law schools. Considering the fact that more and more law students have joined the civil service based on the demand that the government needs good lawyers to serve the state, the universities are encouraging their students to join China's massive bureaucracy. If students enter the peak of the leadership of China, it will be directly related to a higher reputation and more resources of money and people, which can be definitely conducive to the university.[91]

Whatever the reasons are, by 2008, there were 604 universities which had established a law faculty and 287,000 undergraduate law students. There were 333

---

[88] This is regulated by Article 9 of the Judges Law of the People's Republic of China (2001 Amendment) (《中华人民共和国法官法(2001修正)》): A judge must possess the following qualifications: … (6)to have engaged in the legal work for at least 2 years in the case of graduates of law major of colleges or universities or from non-law majors of colleges or universities but possessing professional knowledge of law, and among whom those to assume the posts of judges of superior people's courts and of the Supreme People's Court shall have engaged in legal work for at least 3 years; or to have engaged in legal work for at least 1 year in the case of those who have a master's degree of law or doctor's degree of law, or those who have master's degree or doctor's degree of non-law majors but possess the professional knowledge of law, and among whom those to assume the posts of judges of superior people's courts and of the Supreme People's Court shall have engaged in legal work for at least 2 years.

[89] Taking 10 years of the Great Cultural Revolution as an example, there were 8 law schools in China during 1966–1970, and the number of students who graduated from these 8 law schools was only 833. During 1971–1977, there were only 2 law schools left, and there were only 46 law students graduated per year. See Fang (方流芳) 1996, p. 128.

[90] See Suli (苏力) 2006, p. 4.

[91] For example, Keqiang Li (李克强), the prime minister and also a member of Politburo Standing Committee, graduated from Peking University and one of his teachers is Xiangrui Gong (龚祥瑞), a very famous administrative law professor. It is suggested that his education received from Peking University may affect his policies on the management of the state. See Chris Buckley, 'Insight: China premier-in-waiting schooled in era of dissent', 28 October 2011, available at: <http://www.reuters.com/article/us-china-politcs-li-idUSTRE79R09O20111028>, last visited: 2017/5/5.

universities which were qualified to recruit graduate students and 29 universities providing courses for a doctor's degree in law. There were 80,000 graduates in total.[92] With regard to the careers or destinations of these law students, diversity is a main feature. For instance, in 2006, 62% of the students who graduated from the law school of Peking University entered corporations, law firms and financial institutions, while 38% of the students entered state organs and administrative institutions including judicial organs like people's courts and people's procuratorates. These two percentages in postgraduate students were 48% and 52%.[93] In another good law school, which is the 26th in the 2012 QS Law School Ranking,[94] the law school of Tsinghua University, 35 of 77 undergraduate students chose to pursue a master's degree in China after their graduation, and 19 of them went abroad for pursuing an LLM degree or a master's degree in 2011. The destinations included Harvard University, New York University, Cornell University, Columbia University, University of Michigan, Oxford University and Kyoto University. Besides, two of them entered the state organs, six of them went to state-owned companies and five of them became lawyers.[95]

Scholars usually have an optimistic view of Chinese legal education. Some of them, Xiangde Ji, for instance, even claim that 'Legal education in China constitutes a part of the architecture with three pillars of which the other two are legal education in the United States representing the professional education mode and legal education in German representing the quality education mode'.[96] However, there are still many problems coming with the rapid expansion of legal education. For example, Xiangde Ji suggests that legal education nowadays is primarily driven by economic profits. Not only general universities but also universities of science and engineering set up faculties of law. Not only undergraduate students but also students of technical secondary schools, junior colleges, higher vocational colleges and adult education take courses on law. All this leads to confusion about training level, reduction of the level of enrolment and a lack of qualified teaching staff.[97] In addition, the rate of employment of law students was the tailender in all liberal arts majors in 2007.[98]

---

[92] See Xu (徐卫东) 2008, p. 3.

[93] See Suli (苏力) 2006, p. 7.

[94] See QS Top Universities, 'QS World University Rankings by Subject 2012: Law', available at: <www.topuniversities.com/university-rankings/world-university-rankings/2012/subject-rankings/social-science/law?page=1>, last visited: 2013/1/11.

[95] See Sina Education (新浪教育), 'The Report of the Employment of the Undergraduate Students of Tsinghua Law School' (《清华大学法学院就业情况》), available at: <http://edu.sina.com.cn/gaokao/2012-06-07/2118341709.shtml, last visited: 2012/12/17>. For more information about the courses that Tsinghua Law School students take, see Jiangqiu Ge, 'The Comparative Contract Law Course in Maastricht seen through Chinese Eyes', available at: <http://www.mepli.eu/2013/01/the-comparative-contract-law-course-in-maastricht-seen-through-chinese-eyes>, last visited: 2013/2/15.

[96] See Ji (冀祥德) 2010, p. 50.

[97] See Ji (冀祥德) 2010, p. 51.

[98] See Ji (冀祥德) 2010, p. 53.

2.2.2.6 Policies

In most scholars' opinion, the state's or the Chinese Communist Party's policies are not sources of law. Zongling Shen, however, considers that policies of the party in power are legal sources because policies of the party could become policies of the state, and policies of the state may transform the law.[99] Within the context of private law, Kaixiang Liu also suggests that state policies are sources of law. His argument is based on Article 6 of the General Principles of the Civil Law 1987.[100]

Apart from academic opinions, the 11th and 12th 5-year plan (a series of social and economic development initiatives shaped by the Communist Party of China through the plenary sessions of the Central Committee and national congresses)[101] also declare that these documents have 'legal effects', for example, in the area of environmental mandatory targets.[102] However, it should be noticed that the declaration of 'legal effects' does not bring any real legal effects to this important policy instrument. Firstly, no matter how strict or complicated the procedure to make a 5-year plan, it is not a product of the aforementioned legislatures. It also cannot be cited or applied in judicial decisions.

Generally speaking, most policies do not create any rights and obligations for the parties to a consumer contract. Although sometimes the national policies may have a deep influence on the lawmaking process, this type of influence is rather indirect to the transactions in the market. Even if compared with doctrine, policies are more abstract and usually cannot help with judges' reasoning and interpretation. Therefore, only if a policy is accepted and unequivocally recorded by law, does it become a legal rule. This study does not put much emphasis on policies.

2.2.2.7 Customary Law and Transaction Practices

2.2.2.7.1 Customary Law

With regard to the question when a custom could become 'customary law' as a legal source in China, scholars' opinions focus on the criterion of recognition by the state. For example, Huixing Liang, a leading scholar in the area of Chinese civil law, provides the requirements for a custom to become customary law: (1) the custom exists; (2) everybody in the community should confirm its status as law; (3) the custom has

[99] See Shen (沈宗灵) 2004, p. 322.

[100] See Liu (刘凯湘) 2008, p. 32. Article 6 reads: 'Civil activities must be in compliance with the law; where there are no relevant provisions in the law, they shall be in compliance with state policies'.

[101] For a brief introduction of the significance of the 'five-year-plan', see S. R., 'Why China's Five-year Plans are so Important', The Economist, 26 October 2015, available at: <http://www.economist.com/blogs/economist-explains/2015/10/economist-explains-24>, last visited: 2016/7/27.

[102] See Book 14, Chapter 48 of the 11th Five-Year-Plan ('十一五'规划) and Book 16 of the 12th Five-Year-Plan ('十二五'规划).

not been recorded by official legal documents; (4) it should not violate the principle of public order and social ethics; and (5) it should be recognised, expressly or by implication, by the state.[103] Liming Wang also suggests that only the customs recognised by the state are sources of law.[104] Although there is an opposite opinion that the customs recognised by the state are simply statute law, which implies that they are not 'customs' anymore,[105] most scholars agree that the customs that meet the above requirements can be recognised as sources of law. On the statutory level, it is clearly regulated by the General Provisions of the Civil Law 2017[106] that 'Civil disputes shall be resolved in accordance with the law; or if the law is silent, customs may apply, but not contrary to public order and good morals'.[107]

Nevertheless, customary law is believed to exist only in some remote places and among minorities in China, and it is to a large extent related to the laws on marriage and succession. It can rarely be found in the field of consumer contracts. Although it is prescribed in Article 14 of the Consumer Protection Law 2013[108] that consumers are entitled to human dignity and respect for their ethnic mores and customs, this article does not create rights and obligations for parties. Thus, this study does not pay much attention to customary law.

2.2.2.7.2 Transaction Practices

Customary law is not the only way to use the Chinese word *xiguan* ('习惯', which literally means 'custom') in the context of law. In the Contract Law 1999,[109] *xiguan* is also used as a word combination, *jiaoyi xiguan* ('交易习惯', which literally means 'transaction custom'), to regulate transaction practices. This is introduced as follows.

Jiaoyi xiguan is mentioned in several places of the Contract Law 1999. For example, Article 60(2) provides that 'The parties shall abide by the principle of good faith, and perform obligations of notification, assistance, and confidentiality, etc. in accordance with the nature and purpose of the contract and the transaction practice'.[110] Although the same word *xiguan* is employed, scholars do not recognise 'transaction practices' as a type of customary law. This is based on three reasons: (1) these practices do not have to be recognised by the state; (2) these practices are not always legally binding; and (3) these practices require judges to decide and

[103] See Liang (梁慧星) 2007, p. 28.

[104] See Wang et al. (王利明等) 2011, p. 17.

[105] See Liu (刘凯湘) 2008, p. 35.

[106] General Provisions of the Civil Law of the People's Republic of China (《中华人民共和国民法总则》).

[107] Article 10 of the General Provisions of the Civil Law 2017.

[108] Law of the People's Republic of China on the Protection of Consumer Rights and Interests (2013 Amendment) (《中华人民共和国消费者权益保护法(2013修正)》).

[109] Contract Law of the People's Republic of China (《中华人民共和国合同法》).

[110] It also can be found in Articles 22, 26, 61, 92, 125(1), 136, 293, 368 of the Contract Law 1999.

explain before being applied to court decisions.[111] In the case of Article 60(2) of the Contract Law, if a judge wants to identify a type of accessory obligation through transaction practice, he needs to substantively investigate the practice and provide a reasonable explanation on why it applies first.[112]

Transaction practices do have an impact on consumer contracts. In many circumstances, judges need to assess whether a certain transaction practice, usually a business one, is applied to a consumer contract. Sometimes it determines the answer to whether a standard term is unfair or not. For instance, in the '10 Major Measures to Safeguard Consumers' Rights 2009'[113] published by the China Consumers' Association,[114] to challenge the hotel industry's practice that a 'consumer needs to check out before 12.00, otherwise the fee for another half day is charged' is one of the ten measures.[115] In a typical case of this kind, the hotel as the defendant used 'transaction practice' to defend itself. The people's court pointed out that the standard term mentioning this practice is valid because it does not violate the rules on standard terms.[116] Scholars suggest that this is a good example to show how transaction practices influence consumer contracts.[117] However, as previously mentioned, transaction practices are not always approved by courts. In a Gazette case 'Yanhui Yang v China Southern Airlines Co Ltd and Minhui Company', the people's court denied the application of a transaction practice of the civil aviation industry that 'only the codes but no Chinese name of the airport is printed on plane tickets'. The relevant part of the judgment is presented as follows.

Yanhui Yan v China Southern Airlines Co Ltd and Minhui Company[118]

Facts and Claims: Yanhui Yang (hereinafter 'the plaintiff') purchased a plane ticket from Shanghai to Xiamen of China Southern Airlines at a discount of 10% off. It was specified in the plane ticket that the departure place was Shanghai PVG. When the plaintiff showed this air ticket at Shanghai Hongqiao Airport, the staff members in the airport informed her that she should take the plane at Shanghai Pudong Airport. Because there was not enough time for her to hurry up to Pudong Airport, she purchased a new plane ticket at full price from Shanghai to Xiamen. After the plaintiff returned to Shanghai, she claimed for refunding the money for the ticket in full amount. The defendants pleaded that the air ticket was marked with the name of the airport as represented by the code PVG, which was operated strictly in accordance with the provisions of the Civil Aviation Administration of China (CAAC). Besides, the plaintiff was a local resident of Shanghai, she should have known that there were two airports in

---

[111] See Mi (米新丽) 2016, p. 32.

[112] See Mi (米新丽) 2016, p. 32.

[113] For the details of '10 Major Measures to Safeguard Consumers 2009' (2009年十大消费维权举措), see Ren (任震宇) 2009.

[114] China Consumers' Association (中国消费者协会).

[115] See Yang (杨兆敏) 2009; Ren (任震宇) 2009.

[116] See Li (李华斌) 2008, p. 96.

[117] See Mi (米新丽) 2016, p. 36.

[118] Yanhui Yan v China Southern Airlines Co Ltd. and Minhui Company (杨艳辉诉南方航空公司、民惠公司客运合同纠纷案), Gazette of the Supreme People's Court of the People's Republic of China, 2003(5) (《中华人民共和国最高人民法院公报》2003年第5期).

Shanghai, and there were distinctions of PVG and SHA on the ticket. Even if she did not know which airport PVG and SHA represented, she could have made an inquiry by telephone. Also, the plaintiff failed to prove that there was causation between the facts 'she missed the flight' and 'there was no full Chinese name of the airport in the ticket'.

Judgment: There are two big airports in Shanghai – Hongqiao Airport and Pudong Airport. This is well known to Shanghai residents. However, the special codes of SHA and PVG for the two airports were not known to all Shanghai people. The defendant China Southern Airlines, as a carrier, should clearly mark the name of the airport on the plane tickets it sells with the generally used characters of our country, or with other ways that are sufficient to ensure the passengers' full understanding. The defendant only marked Shanghai Pudong Airport with 'Shanghai PVG' on the plane ticket, which resulted in the plaintiff's failure to take the agreed aviation flight at the scheduled time. Therefore, it should accept the negligent liability for not properly performing the accessory obligations.

In addition, the people's court dealing with this case issued a judicial proposal to the CAAC and suggested that 'Where there are two or more civilian airports in the same city, the aviation companies and the aviation passenger transport sales agents shall, when filling in and issuing tickets marking with the place of departure, and using special code of the airport, use the generally used characters of our country in other proper ways, so as to ensure the correct understanding of the passenger transport contract, and improve the good image of the service of the civil aviation industry of our country'. This proposal was accepted by the CAAC[119] and widely praised by scholars.[120]

Although transaction practices could have a deep impact on consumer contracts and determine the contents of rights and obligations, they are usually rather concrete, which requires judges to make assessment in every single case. Thus, this study does not look into these practices unless it is necessary.

2.2.3 Sources of Chinese Consumer Contract Law

On the basis of the introduction above, in order to find where we can find the legal rules on policing consumer contracts, the emphasis is on statutes, regulations and judicial interpretations. Besides, when describing the rules contained in legislation and interpretations, the guiding cases published by the Supreme People's Court and the leading scholars' opinions on interpretation have a special role to play. Specifically, in the area of consumer contract law, the following legal documents have a central role in this study.

Regarding legislation, it is beyond doubt that the Contract Law 1999 and the Consumer Protection Law 2013 are of the most significance, because the former provides the general rules on policing contracts, most of which are applicable to consumer contracts, and the latter offers special rules on consumer protection. In this regard, the interpretations of these laws are as important as the laws themselves.

[119] See Workers' Daily (工人日报) 2003.

[120] See Mi (米新丽) 2016, p. 36.

There are also two judicial interpretations to the Contract Law 1999.[121] They also play an important role in contract law practice. In addition, some statutes such as the Insurance Law 2009,[122] the Product Quality Law 2009[123] and the Food Safety Law 2015[124] are also sources of Chinese consumer contract law because some articles contained in these statutes regulate the traders' obligations when they deal with the consumer. Of the administrative regulations, some of them also touch upon the topic of policing consumer contracts. For instance, the Regulation on Direct Selling Administration 2005[125] regulates the consumer's withdrawal right.[126] For the local regulations, regulations of each province on the protection of consumer rights and interests are noteworthy, because they are implementing the national statute at the provincial level and sometimes they provide more detailed rules.

As already mentioned, apart from legislation and judicial interpretations, guiding cases and doctrines should not be neglected. For example, Guiding Case No. 1 mentions the rule on how to determine whether a contractual standard term is an unfair term.[127] As to doctrine, the Understanding of authority is of great essence. When the introduction is made to demonstrate the consumer contract legal rules, doctrine always contributes to better understand underlying legislative considerations.

2.2.4 Motives for Adopting Legal Rules on Consumer Protection

According to the legislator, there are three major reasons to adopt legal rules on consumer protection. They are mentioned in Article 1 of the Consumer Protection Law 2013: the first one is to protect the lawful rights and interests of consumers; the

---

[121] They are the Interpretation I of the Supreme People's Court of Several Issues concerning the Application of the Contract Law of the People's Republic of China (《最高人民法院关于适用〈中华人民共和国合同法〉若干问题的解释(一)》) (Interpretation No. 19 [1999] of the Supreme People's Court (法释[1999]19号)) and the Interpretation II of the Supreme People's Court of Several Issues concerning the Application of the Contract Law of the People's Republic of China (《最高人民法院关于适用〈中华人民共和国合同法〉若干问题的解释(二)》) (Interpretation No. 5 [2009] of the Supreme People's Court (法释[2009]5号)).

[122] Insurance Law of the People's Republic of China (2009 Revision) (《中华人民共和国保险法(2009修订)》).

[123] Product Quality Law of the People's Republic of China (2009 Amendment) (《中华人民共和国产品质量法(2009修正)》).

[124] Food Safety Law of the People's Republic of China (2015 Revision) (《中华人民共和国食品安全法(2015修订)》).

[125] Regulations on Direct Selling Administration (《直销管理条例》), Order of the State Council, No.443 (国务院令第443号).

[126] See Chap. 5 of this study.

[127] Shanghai Zhongyuan Property Consultancy Co Ltd. v Dehua Tao (上海中原物业顾问有限公司诉陶德华居间合同纠纷案), Gazette of the Supreme People's Court of the People's Republic of China, 2012(2) (《最高人民法院公报》2012年第2期).

second one is to maintain the order of society and economy; and the third one is to promote the sound development of the socialist market economy.

Among all these three motives, the first one is recognised as the one of the most important. It is described as the 'core and foundation' of the Consumer Protection Law 2013 by the Understanding of authority. It is declared that many chapters in the Consumer Protection Law 2013 are designed to protect consumers' rights. In comparison, the expectation that the law may maintain the economic order is also one of the motivations. It is believed that through protecting the lawful rights and interests of the consumer and maintaining the economic order, it enhances the confidence of consumers in the whole society, expanding the demand of consumption, and gives the businesses who provide a higher level of consumer protection more opportunities for growing and developing. As a result, the consumer protection law is considered to strengthen the healthy development of the socialist market economy.[128]

2.3 EU Law

2.3.1 Introduction

In order to describe the instruments which set rights and obligations of the parties to a consumer contract, the EU's peculiarity of 'multilevel governance' should be taken into account. Unlike China, the EU does not have a central government in charge of all affairs. There is not a legislature with 'all-encompassing competence'[129] inside the EU. On the contrary, legislative competence is allocated to several levels. Rules that may impact upon the rights and obligations of the parties are not only regulated in the domestic laws of the Member States but also provided in the EU legislation and case law.

In this section, this multilevel system is briefly introduced (Sect. 2.3.2). However, since the EU level is chosen to compare with Chinese law, most attention is paid to this level. This means that the focus lies on harmonising measures of the EU (Sect. 2.3.3). Besides, the motives for adopting legal rules on consumer protection is also provided (Sect. 2.3.4).

[128] Jia (贾东明) 2013, p. 3.

[129] See Twigg-Flesner 2010, p. 1. See also Smits 2007, p. 1182. 'There is at present no highest European authority to provide binding contract law rules outside of the (rather limited) competence of the European Union'.

2.3.2 *Sources of Private Law in the EU*

2.3.2.1 Introduction

As mentioned above, the European Union has a multilevel system of private law, which means competences lie with both the European Union and the Member States.[130] In this regard, 'private law in the EU' and 'EU private law' have a different connotation. The former has a broader meaning. It consists not only of EU legislation but also of national law and conventions adopted by the Member States. In comparison, EU private law is only one of the levels contained in the whole private law system in the EU. It merely consists of measures and case law at the EU level. Its measures are mainly based on Article 114 TFEU.[131] In addition, there is a third level that consists of international treaty law, in particular the CISG.[132]

In this section, private law in the EU is described at the national level (Sect. 2.3.2.2), EU level (Sect. 2.3.2.3) and international level (Sect. 2.3.2.4).

2.3.2.2 National Level

The starting point in describing private law in the EU is the legal diversity inherent to 28 different national jurisdictions. The current EU consists of civil law and common law jurisdictions, as well as mixed jurisdictions.[133] Within these legal families, individual jurisdictions can widely differ.[134] For example, contract law in Germany differs from that in France and the Netherlands. The formal communist countries in Central and Eastern Europe also have their own characteristics. This study considers in particular German law and English law wherever useful to illustrate the European approach.

---

[130] See Van den Bergh 2010, p. 57.

[131] It states: 'Save where otherwise provided in the Treaties, the following provisions shall apply for the achievement of the objectives set out in Article 26. The European Parliament and the Council shall, acting in accordance with the ordinary legislative procedure and after consulting the Economic and Social Committee, adopt the measures for the approximation of the provisions laid down by law, regulation or administrative action in Member States which have as their object the establishment and functioning of the internal market'.

[132] For an introduction of these levels, see Smits 2007, p. 1182.

[133] See Smits 2007, p. 1183.

[134] For a detailed introduction, see Zweigert and Kötz 1998, pp. 277–285.

2.3.2.3 EU Level

2.3.2.3.1 Sources of EU Law in General

Generally speaking, EU law consists of three categories of sources: primary law, secondary law and supplementary law.[135]

Within these three categories, primary law refers to the treaties establishing the European Union and its predecessors. These treaties are of great significance because they set out the distribution of competences between the Union and the Member States. The powers of the European institutions are also established or confirmed by the treaties. The treaties thus contain the whole framework and operation system of the European Union.

The secondary sources of EU law are legal instruments based on the treaties including unilateral secondary law and conventions and agreements. Unilateral acts can be divided into different categories, enumerated in Article 288 TFEU – regulations, directives, decisions, opinions and recommendations – whereas some 'atypical' acts are not.

As can be observed from the word 'supplementary', the foremost function of the supplementary law is to fill the gaps left by primary and secondary law. It is the Court of Justice of the European Union (hereinafter 'CJEU') which takes the responsibility to fulfil this duty.

Besides the aforementioned three categories of sources, it is noteworthy that legal scholarship plays an important role in the context of EU private law. It is even suggested that, in the whole European private law debate, legal scholarship plays a central role.[136] European private law is to a large extent an academic venture, reflecting on the need for and methods of harmonisation and drafting model rules for future legislation.

2.3.2.3.2 EU Private Law: Harmonisation and Its Instruments

In the area of EU private law, the motive of establishing an internal market grants the EU legislator the competence to introduce measures. The two most important measures are regulations and directives. To the former, a 'regulation' is directly applicable and does not, generally speaking, require specific steps to be taken at national level for it to become fully effective. If a regulation conflicts with existing national law, any such national rules need to be amended or repealed.[137] However, 'directives' issued by the EU are more important legal instruments for private law.

---

[135] These three categories can be also described as three major sources, which refer to the founding treaties, EU legislation and the general legal principles shaped by the Court of Justice of the European Union. See Weatherill 2010a, p. 27.

[136] See Twigg-Flesner 2010, p. 12.

[137] See Twigg-Flesner 2010, p. 4. Article 288(2) TFEU reads: 'A regulation shall have general application. It shall be binding in its entirety and directly applicable in all Member States'.

Directives require a specific result, but leave it up to individual Member States to choose the 'form and methods'[138] as to how this result can be achieved in national law.[139] The major aim of directives is to deal with barriers to the internal market by divergences in national legislation of the Member States. The directives that are looked into by this study are described in Sect. 2.3.3 below.

Directives of the EU are still the preferred way of achieving a higher degree of harmonisation for the EU legislator.[140] As a matter of fact, the demand for more common private law rules in the EU seems to increase as the scope of the freedom to conclude border-crossing contracts is extended.[141] However, from an opposite perspective, it is also argued that the importance of EU private law in the integration process of the EU has been overrated. Indeed, besides private law, tax law and procedural law may be more crucial to overcome existing barriers for cross-border trade.[142]

As a whole, at the current stage, the EU directives provide the majority of the rules which set rights and obligations of the parties to a consumer contract on the EU level.

2.3.2.3.3 The Level of Harmonisation

Directives can set two different levels of harmonisation.

The first one is called 'minimum harmonisation'. This means the EU only sets a minimum level of protection. The individual Member State can go beyond this level and offer more protection if they wish to do so.[143] For example, if the directive specifies that the period for a consumer to withdraw from a contract is 7 days as the minimum, the Member States can regulate the period to be at least 7 days or longer.[144] However, minimum harmonisation is often criticised for its lack of harmonising effect. If one individual Member State law can still go further than required, companies are still being faced with legislation that is divergent and may still be deterred from doing business elsewhere.[145] Therefore, it is quite difficult to say that directives at a 'minimum level' have already met the purposes and goals of the EU. This is why this so-called 'minimum' harmonisation has often been criticised.[146]

---

[138] See Article 288(3) TFEU.

[139] See Twigg-Flesner 2010, p. 3.

[140] See Müller-Graff 2004, p. 78.

[141] See Müller-Graff 2004, p. 77.

[142] See Smits 2007, 1193.

[143] See Craig and Búrca 2011, p. 600.

[144] For example, Germany made use of this minimum harmonisation approach when the Doorstep Selling Directive was implemented. The time limit for withdrawal right regulated by the directive was extended to 14 calendar days, where the directive only requires 7.

[145] See Smits 2007, pp. 1185–1186.

[146] For example, Twigg-Flesner states: 'Minimum harmonisation does not eliminate the diversity in the laws and regulations between the Member States, but merely serves to reduce its breadth. Differences remain, and may continue to pose a barrier to the functioning of single market' (Twigg-Flesner 2013, p. 44).

Maximum harmonisation requires that Member States should not maintain or introduce provisions diverging from those laid down in a piece of EU legislation when implementing it.[147] For example, if a time span is regulated as '14 days', it has to be regulated as '14 days' in all Member States' domestic legislation. According to EU legislator, maximum harmonisation is the only way to eliminate the barriers stemming from the fragmentation of the rules. It will enhance legal certainty for consumers and businesses and contribute to a high level of consumer protection and a better functioning internal market.[148] Thus, it is now preferred by EU legislator and used in multiple recent EU directives. For instance, the Unfair Commercial Practices Directive[149] adopts a maximum harmonisation approach. Its Annex I contains a full list of all practices which can be deemed as unfair without a case-by-case assessment. This list can only be modified by the revision of the directive.[150] In addition, the full harmonisation of consumer information and the right of withdrawal in distance and off-premises contracts can be seen in the Consumer Rights Directive.[151]

2.3.2.3.4 Enforcement

This part discusses the role of the CJEU. The CJEU, composed of the Court of Justice, the General Court and specialised courts,[152] was established to ensure that EU law is applied in the same way in all EU Member States and to settle legal disputes between national governments and EU institutions. In some circumstances, if the rights of a private actor, including an individual, a company and an organisation in the EU, are infringed by action or inaction by a EU institution or its staff, the private actor can take action through the CJEU, besides taking action through national courts.

Regarding the specific work engaged by the CJEU, it usually gives rulings on cases brought before it. The most common types of cases are interpreting the law

[147] See, for example, Article 4 of the Consumer Rights Directive. It states: 'Member States shall not maintain or introduce, in their national law, provisions diverging from those laid down in this Directive, including more or less stringent provisions to ensure a different level of consumer protection, unless otherwise provided for in this Directive'.

[148] See Recital 3 of the Timeshare Directive and Recitals 5 and 7 of the Consumer Rights Directive.

[149] Directive 2005/29/EC of the European Parliament and of the Council of 11 May 2005 concerning unfair business-to-consumer commercial practices in the internal market and amending Council Directive 84/450/EEC, Directives 97/7/EC, 98/27/EC and 2002/65/EC of the European Parliament and of the Council and Regulation (EC) No 2006/2004 of the European Parliament and of the Council [2005] OJ L149/22.

[150] See Recital 17 of the Unfair Commercial Practices Directive.

[151] Directive 2011/83/EU of the European Parliament and of the Council of 25 October 2011 on consumer rights, amending Council Directive 93/13/EEC and Directive 1999/44/EC of the European Parliament and of the Council and repealing Council Directive 85/577/EEC and Directive 97/7/EC of the European Parliament and of the Council [2011] OJ L304/64.

[152] For a detailed introduction of these three bodies, see Craig and Búrca 2011, pp. 58–61.

(preliminary rulings), enforcing the law (infringement proceedings), annulling EU legal acts (actions for annulment), ensuring the EU take action (actions for failure to act) and sanctioning EU institutions (actions for damages).[153]

To be specific, the function of interpreting the law is to ensure the unified application of EU law in all Member States, because different domestic courts might interpret EU law differently. If a national court is in doubt about the interpretation or the validity of a rule, or whether a national law or practice is compatible with EU law or not, it can consult the CJEU for clarification.[154] If a national government fails to comply with EU law, an action can be started by the European Commission or another EU country. Annulling EU legal acts concerns the situation that an EU act is believed to violate EU treaties or fundamental rights. For example, in its *Tobacco* judgment of 2000, the CJEU held that Article 95 of the EC treaty (now Article 114 TFEU) does not grant a general power to regulate the internal market.[155] Instead, there must be actual – or at least probable – obstacles to the functioning of the internal market if Article 95 is to be used as a basis for lawmaking. If these requirements are not met, the directive lacks a legal basis and can be set aside by the CJEU.[156] In addition, ensuring the EU takes action requires the Parliament, Council and Commission to make certain decisions under certain circumstances, and sanctioning EU institutions directs to the function of taking action when the private actors' rights and interests are infringed by the action or inaction of the EU or its staff.

2.3.2.3.5 Academic Achievements and Optional Instruments

Legal scholars play an important role in discussing European private law. Their efforts are often directed at finding commonalities and differences among jurisdictions and at drafting model rules.[157]

Indeed, the idea behind these academic researches sometimes is the promotion of an exhaustive regulation of private, contract or consumer law on the European level or, to make it clearer, a European civil code. In 1989, the European Parliament passed a resolution calling for the preparation of a European civil code.[158] This call led to some academic enthusiasm.[159] However, the European Commission did not

---

153 For these functions and their legal basis, see Weatherill 2010a, pp. 205–206.

154 See Article 267 TFEU.

155 See Case 376/98 [2000] ECR I-08419.

156 See Smits 2006, p. 68.

157 Twigg-Flesner states: 'The objective of such work is not only to identify the extent to which there are differences between the national private law systems, but also to consider whether the approach adopted in one particular legal system might offer a template for reform or development elsewhere – including, potentially, harmonisation pursued at the EU level' Twigg-Flesner 2010, p. 2.

158 See Resolution of the European Parliament of May 26, 1989 on action to bring into line the private law of the Member States [1989] OJ C158/400.

159 For example, the first edition of the book *Towards a European Civil Code* was published in 1994. The latest version is Hartkamp et al. 2011.

answer these calls. It was clarified in the 'European Contract Law and the revision of the acquis: the way forward' that the Commission does not intend to propose a 'European civil code' which would harmonise contract laws of Member States.[160]

This did not stand in the way of several academic initiatives aimed at drafting rules. The first one which should be mentioned is the Principles of European Contract Law (PECL).[161] It is a set of model contract law rules drafted by some leading scholars in the EU. Based on the work of PECL, the Draft Common Frame of Reference (DCFR) was presented in 2009.[162] It is a draft for the codification of the whole European contract law and related fields of law. It was described as 'a European Civil Code in all but name'.[163]

Instead of introducing these rules as a replacement of national law, the European Commission decided to work on a so-called optional instrument, which is a European contract law system parallel to the Member States' domestic private law.[164] When the parties, primarily those wishing to operate in the internal market, engage in a cross-border transaction, they would be provided with an alternative set of rules. The parties can choose the instrument as the law to regulate their contract. This is the reason why it is 'optional'.[165] It should be noticed that although the 'Green Paper from the Commission of 1 July 2010 on policy options for progress towards a European Contract Law for consumers and businesses' is the first official document in which the phrase of 'optional instrument' is mentioned, this type of legislative instrument has long existed in the context of EU law.[166] In the area of consumer contracts, the Proposal for a Common European Sales Law (CESL) is the first and only EU optional instrument to have been formally proposed.[167] However,

---

[160] The whole clarification reads: 'Although it is premature to speculate about the possible outcome of the reflection, it is important to explain that it is neither the Commission's intention to propose a 'European civil code' which would harmonise contract laws of Member States, nor should the reflections be seen as in any way calling into question the current approaches to promoting free circulation on the basis of flexible and efficient solutions'. Communication from the Commission to the European Parliament and the Council, European Contract Law and the revision of the acquis: the way forward, COM(2004) 651 final.

[161] For Parts I and II, see Lando and Beale 2000; for Part III, see Lando et al. 2003.

[162] For an outline edition, see Bar et al. 2009.

[163] See Jansen and Zimmermann 2010.

[164] It should be noted that the legal basis for adopting optional instruments remains controversial. For example, CJEU claims that Article 114 TFEU could not provide a legal basis for a measure which leaves unchanged the different national laws already in existence, but instead creates an additional system, since that measure cannot be regarded as being aimed at approximate the laws of the Member States. See Case C-436/03 [2006] ECR I-03733, para. 44.

[165] See Green Paper from the Commission of 1 July 2010 on policy options for progress towards a European Contract Law for consumers and businesses, COM(2010) 348 final, p. 9.

[166] The first official proposal can be traced back to 1970. See Proposal for a Council Regulation embodying a Statute for European Company, COM(70) 600 final. For a comprehensive analysis of EU optional instruments, see Bull 2016.

[167] See Proposal for a Regulation of the European Parliament and of the Council on a Common European Sales Law, COM(2011) 635 final.

it was withdrawn at the end of 2014.[168] Since then, the Commission has published two legislative proposals by the end of 2015 to harmonise Member States' contract laws governing online sales and the supply of digital content.[169] This suggests that the European Commission has abandoned the idea of an optional instrument.

This study does not put much focus on the various academic efforts as they did not lead to concrete legislative action on the part of the European Union.

2.3.2.4 International Level

Due to the fact that 24 EU Member States are parties to the United Nations Convention on Contracts for the International Sale of Goods (CISG),[170] the CISG forms a third level in the multilevel system of European private law. Although the field of application of the CISG is limited to the international sale of movable goods between professional parties,[171] it still exerts a profound influence on private law in the EU because the rules of the Convention apply unless the parties have opted out of it.[172]

However, the suggestion that the CISG is an important regime in practice is only true to the extent that the CISG is not excluded by the parties. More relevant in the context of consumer contracts is that there is no room for application of the CISG in business-to-consumer contracts.[173]

---

[168] See Annex II, item 60 of the Communication from the Commission to the European Parliament, the Council, the European Economic and Social Committee and the Committee of the Regions, Commission Work Programme 2015: A New Start, COM(2014) 910 final. The reason of withdrawing the proposal is to modify it in order to 'fully unleash the potential of ecommerce in the Digital Single Market'.

[169] They are the Proposal for a Directive of the European Parliament and of the Council on certain aspects concerning contracts for the supply of digital contents (COM(2015) 634 final) and the Proposal for a Directive of the European Parliament and of the Council on certain aspects concerning contracts for the online and other distance sales of goods (COM(2015) 635 final). Further on these proposals, see Smits 2016.

[170] With the exception of Ireland, Malta, Portugal and the United Kingdom.

[171] See Articles 1–2 CISG.

[172] See Article 6 CISG.

[173] Unless the seller, at any time before or at the conclusion of the contract, neither knew nor ought to have known that the goods were bought for personal, family or household use. (See Article 2(a) CISG.)

2.3.3 *Sources of EU Consumer Contract Law*

The main source of EU consumer contract law consists of a number of EU directives. These are the following[174]: the Product Liability Directive,[175] the Commercial Agents Directive,[176] the Unfair Contract Terms Directive,[177] the Consumer Sales Directive,[178] the Electronic Signatures Directive,[179] the Electronic Commerce Directive,[180] the General Product Safety Directive,[181] the Distance Marketing Directive,[182] the Unfair Commercial Practices Directive, the Misleading and Comparative Advertising Directive,[183] the Consumer Credit Directive,[184] the Timeshare Directive,[185] the Injunctions Directive,[186] the Consumer Rights Directive and the Package Travel Directive.[187]

As mentioned, the phrase 'legal sources' used in this chapter refers to the legal instruments containing rules which set rights and obligations of the parties to a

---

[174] See Smits 2014.

[175] Council Directive 85/374/EEC of 25 July 1985 on the approximation of the laws, regulations and administrative provisions of the Member States concerning liability for defective products [1985] OJ L210/29.

[176] Council Directive 86/653/EEC of 18 December 1986 on the coordination of the laws of the Member States relating to self-employed commercial agents [1986] OJ L382/17.

[177] Council Directive 93/13/EEC of 5 April 1993 on unfair terms in consumer contracts [1993] OJ L95/29.

[178] Directive 1999/44/EC of the European Parliament and of the Council of 25 May 1999 on certain aspects of the sale of consumer goods and associated guarantees [1999] OJ L171/12.

[179] Directive 1999/93/EC of the European Parliament and of the Council of 13 December 1999 on a Community framework for electronic signatures [2000] OJ L13/12.

[180] Directive 2000/31/EC of the European Parliament and of the Council of 8 June 2000 on certain legal aspects of information society services, in particular electronic commerce, in the Internal Market [2000] OJ L178/1.

[181] Directive 2001/95/EC of the European Parliament and of the Council of 3 December 2001 on general product safety [2002] OJ L11/4.

[182] Directive 2002/65/EC of the European Parliament and of the Council of 23 September 2002 concerning the distance marketing of consumer financial services and amending Council Directive 90/619/EEC and Directives 97/7/EC and 98/27/EC [2002] OJ L271/16.

[183] Directive 2006/114/EC of the European Parliament and of the Council of 12 December 2006 concerning misleading and comparative advertising [2006] OJ L376/21.

[184] Directive 2008/48/EC of the European Parliament and of the Council of 23 April 2008 on credit agreements for consumers and repealing Council Directive 87/102/EEC [2008] OJ L133/66.

[185] Directive 2008/122/EC of the European Parliament and of the Council of 14 January 2009 on the protection of consumers in respect of certain aspects of timeshare, long-term holiday product, resale and exchange contracts [2009] OJ L33/10.

[186] Directive 2009/22/EC of the European Parliament and of the Council of 23 April 2009 on injunctions for the protection of consumers' interests [2009] OJ L110/30.

[187] Directive (EU) 2015/2302 of the European Parliament and of the Council of 25 November 2015 on Package Travel and Linked Travel Arrangements, amending Regulation (EC) No 2006/2004 and Directive 2011/83/EU of the European Parliament and of the Council and Repealing Council Directive 90/314/EEC [2015] OJ L326/1.

consumer contract. Thus, the main focus is laid on the EU directives, because they provide most of the substantive rules where the statutory rights and obligation are prescribed. These rules have profound influence on the consumers' daily activities due to the reason that they need to be implemented on the national level.

The most important directives on consumer protection are part of a programme run by the European Commission called 'Regulatory Fitness and Performance Programme (REFIT)'.[188] These directives are the Unfair Commercial Practices Directive, the Consumer Sales Directive, the Unfair Contract Terms Directive, the Misleading and Comparative Advertising Directive and the Injunctions Directive. Besides, the Consumer Rights Directive is mentioned as well.[189]

In this study, the Unfair Contract Terms Directive and the Consumer Rights Directive are the most relevant to the topics of unfair terms and withdrawal rights. In order to obtain a better understanding of the rules, this research also looks into the directives repealed by the Consumer Rights Directive, which are the Doorstep Selling Directive[190] and the Distance Selling Directive.[191] In addition, some other directives, which regulate some specific types of consumer contracts but do not provide the rules in general, are studied as well, such as the Timeshare Directive, the Package Travel Directive, the Insurance and Reinsurance Directive[192] and the Consumer Credit Directive.

As aforementioned, the case law of the CJEU plays an important role since it interprets the law to ensure the unified application of EU law in all Member States. It sometimes provides substantive rules which may have a profound impact on parties' rights and obligations. Nevertheless, in this study the focus lies on the directives, since in the Chinese counterpart the emphasis is also on the selected national statutes. Thus, the CJEU cases are mentioned only when they help to understand the interpretation of the statutory law.

---

[188] See Evaluation and Fitness Check (FC) Roadmap 2015, pp. 1–2.

[189] It will be evaluated separately by the Commission in accordance with its Article 30. See Evaluation and Fitness Check (FC) Roadmap 2015, p. 2.

[190] Council Directive of 20 December 1985 to protect the consumer in respect of contracts negotiated away from business premises (85/577/EEC) [1985] OJ L 372/31.

[191] Directive 97/7/EC of the European Parliament and of the Council of 20 May 1997 on the protection of consumers in respect of distance contracts [1997] OJ L144/19.

[192] Directive 2009/138/EC of the European Parliament and of the Council of 25 November 2009 on the taking-up and pursuit of the business of Insurance and Reinsurance (Solvency II) [2009] OJ L 335/1.

2.3.4 *Motives for Adopting Legal Rules on Consumer Protection*

Article 114 TFEU is the legal basis for most measures adopted in the field of European private law.[193] This article was introduced by the Single European Act 1986 (SEA) with an intention of accelerating the creation of the internal market using the procedure of qualified majority voting in the European Council.[194] According to Article 114 TFEU, these measures have an aim to help with the establishment and functioning of the EU internal market.[195] Thus, this aim becomes the primary motive for adopting legal rules on consumer protection.

Indeed, 'this internal market is the core of the EU'.[196] An internal market contains the free movement of goods, persons, services and capital.[197] Many instruments of EU law, no matter whether they concern public law or private law, are to achieve the internal market objective.[198] In the Communication from the Commission to the Council and the European Parliament on Contract Law of 2001, the reasons why the EU should seek the harmonisation of contract law have been stated again: if the co-existence of national contract laws obstructs the functioning of the internal market, the European Institutions may be called upon to take appropriate action.[199] Apparently, the reason for harmonisation is mainly an economic one. It is believed that the diversity in the EU may distort the functioning of the European economy.

However, Article 114 TFEU does not contain a general authorisation. It is limited by Article 5(2) TEU that 'the Union shall act only within the limits of the competences conferred upon it by the Member States in the Treaties to attain the objectives set out therein'.[200] In other words, Article 114 TFEU is only applied to reduce or remove the competitive disadvantages which are the result of higher costs

---

[193] See Twigg-Flesner 2013, p. 30.

[194] The predecessor of Article 114 TFEU is Article 95 TEC. Prior to the SEA, harmonisation measures had to be adopted on the basis of Article 94 TEC. But Article 94 TEC requires the unanimity within the European Council and only involves the European Parliament by way of consultation. To Twigg-Flesner, Article 95 TEC (now Article 114 TFEU) introduced a more efficient procedure, allowing for harmonisation measures to be adopted by qualified majority voting. Furthermore, the co-decision procedure, giving the Parliament greater involvement and the power to block the adoption of legislation, must be followed. See Twigg-Flesner 2013, pp. 30–31.

[195] See Article 114(1) TFEU. It is just as Twigg-Flesner states: 'The bulk of European Union private law is the result of the legislative harmonisation agenda pursued by the EU, primarily in pursuit of its objective of creating an internal market' Twigg-Flesner 2010, p. 2.

[196] Smits 2006, p. 57.

[197] See aforementioned Chap. 1, Sect. 1.3.2.3.2.

[198] See Schmid 2005, pp. 215–216.

[199] Communication from the Commission to the Council and the European Parliament on Contract Law, COM(2001) 398 final, para. 23.

[200] See Weatherill 2010b, p. 58. See also Müller-Graff 2004, p. 78. The latter reads: 'In the present state of development of primary Community law no express power is vested in the Community to issue a directive that would oblige the Member States to adopt a Civil Code or a coherent net of rules which constitute the core and system of private law'.

of having to obey the rules which are stricter in some Member States than in others.[201] It does not provide a wide competence that allows the adoption of broad legislation which only has a tenuous link to the internal market objective.[202]

In this respect, it should be emphasised again that, although the legislation on consumer protection composes an important part of EU private law, the primary motive is not to protect consumers.[203] In spite of the fact that Article 169 TFEU does provide that the Union may adopt measures which pursue the interests of consumers and to ensure a high level of consumer protection,[204] this article and its predecessor, Article 153 TEC, were hardly ever used as a basis for European legislation. It only supports the internal market provision. It leads to the result that the protection of the consumer is made dependent on the question whether harmonisation promotes the internal market.[205]

Nevertheless, the importance of consumer protection as an indirect motive should not be underestimated, because consumer law is seen as closely related to the internal market.[206] The European Commission believes that 'Empowered and confident consumers can drive forward the European economy'.[207] The argument which suggests that disparities in the rules protecting consumers in different Member States will undermine consumers' confidence so they will also harm the internal market is the dominant justification for action in the field of consumer law.[208] This argument is used for adopting several EU directives, such as the Unfair Commercial Practices Directive and the Consumer Rights Directive.[209] Furthermore, compared with the questionable conclusion on whether harmonisation really promotes the internal market, EU legislation is indeed a success on consumer protection: 'If consumer protection had been left to the Member States, the uniform minimum level of protection that we have now would probably not have been attained'.[210]

---

[201] See Twigg-Flesner 2013, p. 31.

[202] See C-376/98 [2000] ECR I-08419.

[203] See Smits 2007, p. 1189. To quote Hans-W. Micklitz, EC consumer law 'is no longer social protection that legitimates market regulation to fight down imbalance of power, but economic instrumentalisation to establish the Internal Market'. Micklitz 2005, p. 553.

[204] Article 169(1) TFEU reads: 'In order to promote the interests of consumers and to ensure a high level of consumer protection, the Union shall contribute to protecting the health, safety and economic interests of consumers, as well as to promoting their right to information, education and to organise themselves in order to safeguard their interests'.

[205] See Smits 2006, p. 73.

[206] See Zimmermann 2009, p. 481.

[207] Communication from the Commission to the European Parliament, the Council, the Economic and Social Committee and the Committee of the Regions, A European Consumer Agenda – Boosting confidence and growth, COM(2012) 225 final.

[208] See Twigg-Flesner 2013, pp. 34–35.

[209] See Recital 4 of the Unfair Commercial Practices Directive and Recital 6 of the Consumer Rights Directive.

[210] Smits 2006, p. 73.

2.4 Comparison Between China and the EU

The aim of this section is to provide a brief comparison of the sources of Chinese and European consumer law. Several conclusions can be made on the basis of this comparison.

Firstly, in terms of the sources of law in general, to compare China and the EU is rather difficult because the former is a country with full legislative competence of one national lawmaker, whereas the latter is a union of sovereign countries. The majority of Chinese legal sources are statutes and regulations guaranteed by the national power. When a rule is considered as 'creating legal rights and obligations', it is usually made up by the legislature of the National People's Congress, the State Council, the Supreme People's Court or the local people's congresses. Besides, it usually can be unequivocally cited or applied in judgments. In comparison, private law in Europe is a mix of rules made at both the national and European level. EU directives have to be implemented on the national level. Even if the directives also provide rules on setting legal rights and obligations to the parties, the binding force here mostly applies to the legal effects which influence the Member States. In this sense, understanding how the Member States introduce directives into their domestic law is just as important as the rules contained in directives.

Secondly, courts and scholars play an essential role in both China and the EU. As to the former, although in the traditional understanding courts should not be recognised as lawmakers, the Supreme People's Court in China produces a great number of legal rules which set substantial rights and obligations through promulgating judicial interpretations and guiding cases, while in the EU, the case law of the CJEU also constitutes a source of law. However, it is noteworthy that Chinese and EU courts take action at different stages. The judicial interpretations produced by the Chinese Supreme People's Court usually come into force at the end of a considerably long period after the introduction of the laws they interpret. The Supreme People's Court picks up the essence from the local courts all around the country and makes it guidance which can be applied in the whole nation. The contents of judicial interpretations always reflect the experience gained in the judicial practice. By contrast, in the light of its functions, the CJEU in many circumstances is addressed in an early stage because the national courts are dependent on its clarification. The work of the judges is not to collect and enact the feasible rules to envisage the complex practice but to make sure that EU law is applied in a consistent way. As to academics, both in China and the EU scholars are involved in the lawmaking process and sometimes even provide the first draft of the legislation which will come into effect in the future.

Thirdly, with regard to the sources of consumer contract law, in China statutes, regulations and their interpretations are the major sources, while in the EU, the focus lies on directives and the national laws of the Member States. Nevertheless, although the nature of these legal instruments is different, the substance of the rules could of course be similar.

At last, an apparent difference is to be found in motivations for adopting consumer protection rules. In the Chinese context, there are three motivations of introducing consumer law rules. There is a progressive relationship between them: the ultimate goal is to promote the socialist market economy, and the approach to realise it is protecting the consumer's lawful rights and interests and maintaining the order of society and economy. It should be noted that, although promoting the socialist market economy is the goal, the protection of the weaker party in the market – consumer – is the practical result. In contrast, the motivation in the EU is much more an economic one: to promote an internal market. However, the practical result is also a set of rules aimed at protecting consumers.

References

(Bar, Clive, Schulte-Nölke, Beale, Herre, Huet, Storme, Swann, Varul, Veneziano & Zoll 2009) Christian von Bar, Eric Clive, Hans Schulte-Nölke, Hugh Beale, Johnny Herre, Jérôme Huet, Matthias Storme, Stephen Swann, Paul Varul, Anna Veneziano and Fryderyk Zoll (eds.), *Principles, Definitions and Model Rules of European Private Law: Draft Common Frame of Reference (DCFR)*, Outline Edition, prepared by the Study Group on a European Civil Code and the Research Group on EC Private Law (Acquis Group) based in part on a revised version of the Principles of European Contract Law, Munich: sellier. european law publishers, 2009.

(Van den Bergh 2010) Roger Van den Bergh, 'Private Law in a Globalizing World: Economic Criteria for Choosing the Optimal Regulatory Level in a Multilevel Government System', in Michael Faure & André van der Walt (eds.), *Globalization and Private Law: The Way Forward*, Cheltenham: Edward Elgar Publishing, 2010, p. 57–96.

(Bull 2016) William A. Bull, *Optional Instruments of the European Union: A Definitional, Normative and Explanatory Study*, Cambridge: Intersentia, 2016.

(Cao (曹士兵) 2006) 曹士兵[Shibing Cao]:《最高人民法院裁判、司法解释的法律地位》[The Status of Decisions and Judicial Interpretations of the Supreme People's Court],《中国法学》2006年第3期[China Legal Science, 2006(3)],第175—181页[p. 175–181]。

(Chen 2010) Lei Chen, 'Private Property with Chinese Characteristics: A Critical Analysis of the Chinese Law on Property of 2007', 18 *European Review of Private Law* 5, 2010, p. 983–1004.

(Craig & Búrca 2011) Paul Craig & Gráinne de Búrca, *EU Law: Texts, Cases, and Materials*, 5th edition, Oxford: Oxford University Press, 2011.

(Han (韩世远) 2011) 韩世远[Shiyuan Han]:《合同法总论》[The Law of Contract],法律出版社2011年第3版[Law Press, 2011, 3rd Edition]。

(Han (韩世远) 2015) 韩世远[Shiyuan Han]:"消费者合同三题:知假买假、惩罚性赔偿与合同终了"[Three Problematic Issues in Consumer Contracts: Buying Fake on Purpose, Punitive Damage and the End of Contract],《法律适用》2015年第10期[Journal of Law Application, 2015(10)],第87—92页[p. 87–92]。

(Hartkamp, Hesselink, Hondius, Mak & Perron 2011) Arthu Hartkamp, Martijn Hesselink, Ewoud Hondius, Chantal Mak, Edgar du Perron (eds.), *Towards a European Civil Code*, Fourth revised and expanded edition, Alphen aan den Rijn: Kluwer Law International, 2011.

(Hu & Yu (胡云腾、于同志) 2008) 胡云腾、于同志[Yunteng Hu & Tongzhi Yu]:"案例指导制度若干重大疑难争议问题研究"[On Several Significant and Difficult Issues Regarding the Case Guidance System],《法学研究》2008年第6期[Chinese Journal of Law, 2008(6)],第3—24页[p. 3–24]。

(Huang (黄金荣) 2014) 黄金荣[Jinrong Huang]:"'规范性文件'的法律界定及其效力"[The Definition of 'Regulatory Documents' and Its Legal Effects],《法学》2014年第7期[Law Science, 2014(7)],第10-20页[p. 10–20]。

(Jansen & Zimmermann 2010) Nils Jansen & Reinhard Zimmermann, 'A European Civil Code in All But Name: Discussing the Nature and Purposes of the Draft Common Frame of Reference', 69 *The Cambridge Law Journal* 1, 2010, p. 98–112.

(Ji (冀祥德) 2010) 冀祥德[Xiangde Ji]:"对中国法学教育全面反思与展望"[The Difficulties and Prospects of the Current Legal Education in China],《中国政法大学学报》2010年第4期[Journal of CUPL, 2010(4)],第50—58页。

(Jia (贾东明) 2013) 贾东明主编[Dongming Jia (ed.)]:《中华人民共和国消费者权益保护法解读》[Understanding on the Law of the People's Republic of China on the Protection of Consumer Rights and Interests],中国法制出版社2013年版[China Legal Publishing House, 2013]。

(Jin (金可可) 2012) 金可可[Keke Jin]:"民法实证研究方法与民法教义学"[On Empirical Approach of Civil Law and Doctrinal Approcah of Civil Law],《法学研究》2012年第1期[Chinese Journal of Law],第48—50页[p. 48–50]。

(Lando & Beale 2000) Ole Lando & Hugh Beale (eds.), *Principles of European Contract Law, Parts I and II (Combined and Revised)*, prepared by the Commission of European Contract Law, the Hague: Kluwer Law International, 2000.

(Lando, Clive, Prüm & Zimmermann 2003) Ole Lando, Eric Clive, André Prüm & Reinhard Zimmermann (eds.), *Principles of European Contract Law, Part III*, prepared by the Commission on European Contract Law, the Hague: Kluwer Law International, 2003.

(Lei (雷磊) 2015) 雷磊[Lei Lei]:"指导性案例法源地位再反思"[Rethinking the Guiding Cases' Status of Legal Sources],《中国法学》2015年第1期[China Legal Science, 2015(1)],第272—290页[p. 272–290]。

(Li & Liu (李龙、刘诚) 2005) 李龙、刘诚[Long Li & Cheng Liu]:"论法律渊源——以法学方法和法律方法为视角"[On Sources of Law – From the Perspective of Legal and Jurisprudence Methodologies],《法律科学》2005年第2期[Law Science (Journal of Northwest University of Politics and Law), 2005(2)],第3-8页[p. 3–8]。

(Li (李华斌) 2008) 李华斌[Huabin Li]:"12点后退房,宾馆多收半天房费合法吗?"[Is It Lawful for Hotels to Charge Half Day's Fee When Check-out After 12.00?],《中国审判》2008年第8期[China Trial, 2008(8)],第94—98页[p. 94–98]。

(Liang (梁慧星) 2007) 梁慧星[Huixing Liang]:《民法总论》[General Introduction to Civil Law],法律出版社2007年第3版[Law Press, 2007, 3rd Edition]。

(Liu (刘凯湘) 2008) 刘凯湘主编[Kaixiang Liu (ed.)]:《民法学》[Civil Law],中国法制出版社2008年第三版[China Legal Publishing House, 2008, 3rd Edition]。

(Liu (柳建龙) 2011) 柳建龙[Jianlong Liu]:"合宪性原则的本相与争论"[The Truth and Discussion of the Principle of Constitutionality],《清华法学》2011年第1期[Tsinghua University Law Journal, 2011(1)],第108—124页[p. 108–124]。

(Luan & Luo (栾春娟、罗海山) 2009) 栾春娟、罗海山[Chunjuan Luan, Haishan Luo]:"中国民事法学研究现状的考察"[A Study on Chinese Civil Law Research],《哈尔滨工业大学学报(社会科学版)》2009年第4期[Journal of Harbin Institute of Technology(Social Sciences Edition), 2009(4)],第67—72页[p. 67–72]。

(Mi (米新丽) 2016) 米新丽[Xinli Mi]:"关于交易习惯的几点思考"[Several Thoughts About Transaction Customs],《政法论丛》2016年第2期[Journal of Political Science and Law, 2016(2)],第31—37页[p. 31–37]。

(Micklitz 2005) Hans-W. Micklitz, 'The Concept of Competitive Contract Law', 23 *Penn State International Law Review* 3, p. 549–585.

(Müller-Graff 2004) Peter-Christian Müller-Graff, 'EC Directives as a Means of Private Law Unification', in Arthur Hartkamp, Martijn Hesselink, Ewoud Hondius, Carla Joustra, Edgar du Perron & Muriel Veldman (eds.), *Towards a European Civil Code*, 3rd fully revised and expanded edition, Nijmegen: Kluwer Law International, 2004, p. 77–100.

(Qu (屈文生) 2012) 屈文生[Wensheng Qu]:"和制汉语法律新名词在近代中国的翻译与传播——以清末民初若干法律辞书收录的词条为例"[The Translation and Dissemination of Modern Chinese Legal Concepts Coined in Japan – The Research on Entries Included by

Several Legal Dictionaries in Late Qing and Early Republic],《学术研究》2012年第11期[Academic Research, 2012(11)],第122—129页[p. 122–129]。

(Ren (任震宇) 2009) 任震宇[Zhenyu Ren]:"中消协公布2009年消费维权十大举措"[The China Consumers' Association Publishes 10 Major Measures to Safeguard Consumers' Rights 2009],《中国消费者报》2009年3月20日第A02版[China Consumer News, 2009/3/20, Page A02]。

(Schmid 2005) Christoph U. Schmid, 'The Instrumentalist Conception of the Acquis Communautaire in Consumer Law and Its Implications on a European Contract Law Code', 1 *European Review of Contract Law* 2, 2005, p. 211–227.

(Shen (沈宗灵) 2004) 沈宗灵[Zongling Shen]:《法理学》[Jurisprudence],高等教育出版社2004年第2版[Higher Education Press, 2004, 3rd Edition]。

(Smits 2006) Jan M. Smits, 'European Private Law: A Plea for A Spontaneous Legal Order', in Deirdre M. Curtin, Jan M. Smits, André Klip, Joseph A. McCahery, *European Integration and Law: Four Contributions on the Interplay between European Integration and European and National Law to Celebrate the 25th Anniversary of Maastricht University's Faculty of Law*, Antwerpen: Intersentia, 2006, p. 55–107.

(Smits 2007) Jan Smits, 'Law Making in the European Union: On Globalization and Contract Law in Divergent Legal Cultures', 67 *Louisiana Law Review*, 2007, p. 1181–1203.

(Smits 2014) Jan M. Smits, William Bull, Catalina Goanta & Mark Kawakami (eds.), *European Private Law(2014–2016)*, 4th Edition, Nijmegen: Ars Aequi Libri, 2014.

(Smits 2016) Jan M. Smits, 'New European Union Proposals for Distance Sales and Digital Contents Contracts: Fit for Purpose?', *Zeitschrift für europäisches Privatrecht* 2, 2016, p. 319–324.

(Suli (苏力) 2004) 苏力[Suli]:《也许正在发生——转型中国的法学》[Maybe It is Happening – The Transformation of China's Legal Scholarship],法律出版社2004年版[Law Press, 2004]。

(Suli (苏力) 2006) 苏力[Suli]:"当代中国法学教育的挑战与机遇"[The Challenges and Opportunities of Chinese Modern Legal Education],《法学》2006年第2期[Law Science, 2006(2)],第3—21页[p. 3–21]。

(Twigg-Flesner 2010) Christian Twigg-Flesner, 'Introduction: Key Features of European Union Private Law', in Christian Twigg-Flesner (ed.), *The Cambridge Companion to European Union Private Law*, New York: Cambridge University Press, 2010, p. 1–19.

(Twigg-Flesner 2013) Christian Twigg- Flesner, *The Europeanisation of Contract Law: Current Controversies in Law*, 2nd edition, Abingdon: Routledge, 2013.

(Wang et al. (王利明等) 2011) 王利明等[Liming Wang et al.]:《民法学》[Civil Law],法律出版社2011年第3版[Law Press, 2011, 3rd Edition]。

(Wang (王利明) 2012) 王利明[Liming Wang]:"我国案例指导制度若干问题研究"[On Chinese Case Guidance System],《法学》2012年第1期[Law Science, 2012(1)],第71—80页[p. 71–80]。

(Wang (王书成) 2012) 王书成[Shucheng Wang]:"论合宪性解释方法"[On the Interpretation of Constitutionality],《法学研究》2012年第5期[Chinese Journal of Law, 2012(5)],第50—68页[p. 50–68]。

(Weatherill 2010a) Stephen Weatherill, *Cases and Materials on EU Law*, 9th edition, Oxford: Oxford University Press, 2010.

(Weatherill 2010b) Stephen Weatherill, 'Competence and European Private Law', in Christian Twigg-Flesner (ed.), *The Cambridge Companion to European Union Private Law*, Cambridge: Cambridge University Press, 2010, p. 58–69.

(Workers' Daily (工人日报) 2003) 工人日报[Workers' Daily]:"一场诉讼改变了民航规定"[A Lawsuit Change CAAC's Regulation],《工人日报》2003年6月14日[Workers' Daily, 2003/6/14]。

(Xu (徐卫东) 2008) 徐卫东[Weidong Xu]:"中国高等法学教育三十年发展回顾"[Thirty Years of Legal Education in Main Land of China],《当代法学》2008年第1期[Contemporary Law Review, 2008(1)],第3—10页[p. 3–10]。

(Yang (杨琴) 2011) 杨琴[Qin Yang]:"中日经济发展与消费者法制"[Sino-Japanese Economic Development and Consumer Law],《贵州大学学报(社会科学版)》2011年第6期[Journal of Guizhou University(Social Sciences), 2011(6)],第24—31页[p. 24–31]。

(Yang (杨兆敏) 2009) 杨兆敏[Zhaomin Yang]:"只要损害了利益,就要挑战行规权威"[Industry's Authority Should be Challenged When Consumers' Interests Are Infringed],《工人日报》2009年9月9日第5版[Workers' Daily, 2009/09/09, Page 5]。

(Zhang (张文显) 2007) 张文显主编[Wenxian Zhang (ed.)]:《法理学》[Jurisprudence],高等教育出版社2007年第3版[Higher Education Press, 2007, 3rd Edition]。

(Zhang (张文显) 2011) 张文显主编[Wenxian Zhang (ed.)]:《法理学》[Jurisprudence],高等教育出版社2011年第4版[Higher Education Press, 2011, 4th Edition]。

(Zhang (张明楷) 2011) 张明楷[Mingkai Zhang]:《刑法学》[Criminal Law],法律出版社2011年第四版[Law Press, 2011, 4th Edition]。

(Zhu (朱景文) 2007) 朱景文[Jingwen Zhu]:《中国法律发展报告》[Report on the Chinese Legal Development],中国人民大学出版社2007年版[China Renmin University Press, 2007]。

(Zhu (朱晓喆) 2015) 朱晓喆[Xiaozhe Zhu]:"比较民法与判例研究的立场和使命"[The Standpoints and Aims of Comparative Civil Law and Case Study],《华东政法大学学报》2015年第2期[ECUPL Journal, 2015(2)],第149— 160页[p. 149-160]。

(Zimmermann 2009) Reinhard Zimmermann, 'The Present State of European Private Law', 57 *American Journal of Comparative Law* 2, 2009, p. 479–512.

(Zweigert & Kötz 1998) Konrad Zweigert and Hein Kötz, *An Introduction to Comparative Law*, Translated by Tony Weir, Oxford: Oxford University Press, 1998.

Research Services, Working Papers, Etc

(Evaluation and Fitness Check (FC) Roadmap 2015) European Commission, 'Evaluation and Fitness Check (FC) Roadmap', 12/2015, available at: <http://ec.europa.eu/smart-regulation/roadmaps/docs/2016_just_023_evaluation_consumer_law_en.pdf>.

Chapter 3
The Concept of Consumer Contract

3.1 Introduction

In many jurisdictions, the idea that consumers need special protection due to their lack of sufficient knowledge, information and bargaining power is widely accepted.[1] The special rules aimed at protecting consumers are believed to be a good cure to deal with the disparity between the parties of a consumer contract. However, because these provisions are only regulated for a given purpose, not all private actors in the whole market can invoke them. Prior to the discussion on the substantive contents of the consumer contract rules, it is necessary to make explicit who is protected and against whom these provisions will be enforced.

In Chinese law, the rules in the Contract Law 1999[2] are applicable to all contracts. In contrast, special rules regulated by the Consumer Protection Law 2013[3] can be claimed only when the contracting party is recognised as a 'consumer' and the counterparty is recognised as a 'business operator'. Taking into account that it is usually the special rule which provides a higher level of protection,[4] whether the private actor involved is granted, the status of consumer becomes a crucial issue. Because the definitions given by Articles 2 and 3 of the Consumer Protection Law 2013 are rather vague, they need further interpretation, especially where the contract is concluded by a legal person or for medical treatment and education. Considering that consumers may enjoy additional compensation other than the general compensation regulated by the Contract Law, there exists a type of consumer

[1] For the discussion on whether a disparity of bargaining power can be identified as a justification for consumer protection measures, see Howell and Wilson 2016, p. 153.

[2] Contract Law of the People's Republic of China (《中华人民共和国合同法》).

[3] Law of the People's Republic of China on the Protection of Consumer Rights and Interests (2013 Amendment) (《中华人民共和国消费者权益保护法(2013修正)》).

[4] For example, the remedy for a fraudulent act is rather advantageous to the consumer in the context of the Consumer Protection Law 2013 than in the context of the Contract Law 1999.

J. Ge, *A Comparative Analysis of Policing Consumer Contracts in China and the EU*, https://doi.org/10.1007/978-981-13-2989-0_3

who intentionally buys defective goods to seek benefit. Whether these actors can be granted, the identity of consumer is also worth discussing.

In EU law, each directive has its own provision to define the 'consumer' and 'trader', but most of the provisions are exactly the same in wording: they all refer to any natural person who is acting for purposes which are outside his trade, business or profession, and a trader should be any natural or legal person who is acting for purposes relating to his trade, business, craft or profession. Nevertheless, it does not mean that there is no dispute on these definitions. For example, the first question that might be asked is, in the situation where a businessman buys goods which are totally irrelevant to his business, whether he can be regarded as a consumer. The second question is whether a legal person, particularly a small- or medium-sized one, can be treated as a consumer. These questions are connected with the reasons on introducing EU private law instruments and the legitimacy of the rules on consumer protection. It is not only scholars who are writing about these issues, but case law of the CJEU has also touched upon them several times.

In this chapter, the following questions are addressed on the basis of the introduction of Chinese law and EU law: (1) How does the legislator define the concepts of 'consumer' and 'business operator/trader'? (2) How should these rules be interpreted in practice? (Sects. 3.2.1 and 3.3.1). After answering these two questions, two topics which are widely discussed in China and the EU are introduced separately. The first one is to deal with a phenomenon in China, in which a private actor is trying to achieve additional benefit by means of applying special rules for consumer protection (Sect. 3.2.2). The second one is about whether legal persons, especially the small businessman as well as small- and medium-sized enterprises ('SMEs'), can be granted the identity of consumer, which is heatedly debated in the EU (Sect. 3.3.2). At the end of the chapter, a comparative review and a possible explanation of differences among Chinese law and EU law are provided (Sect. 3.4).

3.2 Chinese Law

3.2.1 Definitions of Consumer and Business Operator

3.2.1.1 Legislative Expression and Its Interpretation

Article 2 of the Chinese Consumer Protection Law 2013 is the provision which provides the definition of 'consumer'. It states: 'The rights and interests of consumers in purchasing and using commodities or receiving services for daily consumption shall be under the protection of the present Law, or under the protection of other relevant laws and regulations in the absence of stipulations in this Law'. Besides, Article 3 provides the definition of 'business operator': 'In providing commodities produced or sold by them or services to consumers, business operators shall comply with this Law; or comply with other relevant laws and regulations if this law is silent'. In order to provide farmers with the equivalent protection because they also lack the specialised knowledge and the power of negotiation, Article 62 provides a special rule: 'This Law shall apply, by reference, to farmers' purchase and use of means of production directly for agricultural production'.

From the wording of Article 2, it is apparent that the interpretation of 'daily consumption' ('生活消费', which literally means 'consumption for daily life') is the core to evaluate whether a private actor is a consumer. In the Understanding of authority, it is introduced that, during the process of the amendment of the law, it was suggested that the currently used wording had brought confusion to legal practice, so it should be revised. The legislator, however, subsequent to a serious discussion, decided to keep the formulation of 'daily consumption' to define the consumer.[5] It is further explained that the connotation of 'daily consumption' is so broad that all types of consumption can be included: living consumption such as buying clothes, food, accommodation and transportation services, developing consumption such as career training and spiritual consumption such as tourism. The concept of 'daily consumption' is also developing along with the development of the society that one type of consumption which is not a daily one nowadays may become a daily one in the future, such as space exploration.[6] Thus, it is still believed to be the optimal approach to define 'consumer'. Scholars also agree that the concept of 'daily consumption' could be extensively interpreted.[7]

With respect to the definition of 'business operator', the article itself only states that a business operator should be someone who provides the commodities produced or sold by himself or services to consumers, but there is no further elaboration. Only the Understanding of authority demonstrates that it is not appropriate to treat a natural person as a business operator if he only sells goods or provides services once in a while. Two examples are provided: (1) a man who is selling his second-hand bicycle on Taobao.com ('淘宝网') and (2) a housewife who is selling her unwanted clothes to her neighbour.[8] In these cases, due to the reason that the seller is not a business operator, there is no consumer contract, which means the specific rules such as the right of withdrawal cannot be invoked by the purchaser.

Nevertheless, compared with the old definition provided by the Consumer Protection Law 1993,[9] no big change can be found. It leads to the result that some old problems have not been solved. Scholars criticise that the legislator did not respond to the suggestion that the definitions of 'consumer' and 'business operator' should be amended by the Consumer Protection Law 2013. For example, Jingming Wu considers it as a pity that the second draft does not make any change with regard

[5] See Jia (贾东明) 2013, pp. 6–7.

[6] See Jia (贾东明) 2013, p. 7.

[7] For example, Liming Wang mentions that 'daily consumption' refers to not only the purchase with regard to the buyer's living demands but also the purchase for collection, storage or present. Even a person who purchases for his friend's or family's living consumption is also a consumer. See Wang (王利明) 2002, p. 3.

[8] See Jia (贾东明) 2013, p. 7.

[9] Law of the People's Republic of China on the Protection of Consumer Rights and Interests (《中华人民共和国消费者权益保护法》).

to the definitions of consumer and business operator.[10] Lixin Yang also suggests that Article 2 of the Consumer Protection Law 1993 should be amended so that some groups, such as cafeterias of the organs of Chinese Communist Party or government, can be granted the identity of consumer.[11]

In the following sections, several more controversial issues are addressed.

3.2.1.2 Several Specific Issues

3.2.1.2.1 Legal Persons

The first issue to be discussed is whether a legal person can be treated as a consumer.

It firstly should be noted that the Consumer Protection Law 2013 does not provide a clear answer for this question. However, some other national instruments can be referred to. Specifically, apart from the Consumer Protection Law 2013, a national standard, the Introduction for Use of Products of Consumer Interest (《消费品使用说明》), also provides some terminologies and definitions, such as the concept of consumer, although it is not law. In its first version of 1985 and the 1997 amendment, a consumer was identified as an individual member of society who purchases and uses goods or accepts service for the purpose of individual or family's daily demands.[12] But in its latest version which came into effect in 2014, the word 'individual' is deleted. The definition of consumer is simplified as a member of society who purchases and uses goods or accepts service for the purpose of daily demands.[13]

Although most scholars suggest that 'consumer' only refers to individuals,[14] some local regulations still provide that legal persons can also be granted the status of consumer. For example, Article 2 of the Measures of Guangdong Province for

[10] See Jingming Wu (吴景明), 'Regrets in the Amendatory Progress of Consumer Protection Law' (《中国政法大学副教授:消法修改遗憾》), available at: <http://finance.sina.com.cn/review/mspl/20131008/112116920314.shtml>, last visited: 2013/10/23.

[11] See Yang (杨立新) 2013, p. 25.

[12] Introduction for Use of Products of Consumer Interest – General Principles, GB 5296.1–1997 (《消费品使用说明——总则》,中华人民共和国国家标准:GB 5296.1—1997)

[13] Introduction for Use of Products of Consumer Interest – Part 1: General Principles, GB 5296.1–2012 (《消费品使用说明——第一部分:总则》,中华人民共和国国家标准:GB 5296.1—2012)

[14] As Liming Wang states, there are at least three reasons why only individuals could be granted the status of consumer. Firstly, the legislative intention of consumer protection law is to protect the weaker party in modern society. This special protection is regulated because consumers are weaker party and limiting the scope of consumer to individuals is the precondition of this presumption. Secondly, the rights protected by consumer protection law are always related to basic human rights and these human rights are only granted to individuals. Thirdly, it is impossible for legal persons to consume or utilise goods or accept services for the purpose of 'daily demands'. See Wang (王利明) 2002, pp. 6–7. It is also clarified by Huixing Liang that consumer refers to a natural person. See Liang (梁慧星) 2001.

Implementing the Law of the People's Republic of China on the Protection of Consumer Rights and Interests (Amended in 2012)[15] provides: '"Consumer" in this local regulation refers to individuals and legal persons who purchase and use commodities or accept services for the purpose of daily demands'. Although the mainstream of scholars does not agree that legal persons can be treated as consumers, there are also some journal articles arguing that legal persons can be identified as consumers, because it is very common for legal persons to purchase goods or services and distribute them to their employees.[16]

According to the Understanding of authority, a consumer must be a natural person. The arguments are rather traditional. Firstly, the special protection is awarded because the consumer is believed to be a weaker party, but the legal person is never a weaker party in the light of its status of negotiation and economic power. It can always claim its rights and interests on the basis of the Product Liability Law 2009[17] and the Contract Law 1999; secondly, this is in accordance with the international trend because most jurisdictions in the world limit the scope of consumers to individuals; and thirdly, even if a legal person is purchasing for its employees' welfare and the consumption itself is not relevant to its business, the ultimate actor who bears the consequences is a natural person. If he suffers damage, he can directly initiate a lawsuit and claim damage from the seller.[18]

It can be argued that the Chinese Consumer Protection Law 2013 should only be enforced by natural persons. In addition to the arguments provided by the Understanding of authority, some articles of the law also imply that a consumer refers to a natural person. For example, Article 14 regulates that 'consumers shall be entitled to human dignity, respect for their ethnic mores and customs, and legal protection of personal information'. Obviously, human dignity is only applicable to natural persons, and only natural persons have ethnic mores and customs. Besides, other consumers' rights regulated by Chap. 2 of the Consumer Protection Law 2013, e.g. 'the right to be free from damage to personal and property safety',[19] 'the right to obtain true information',[20] 'the right to independently choose commodities and services',[21] 'the right to fair dealing',[22] 'the right to form social organisations'[23] and 'the right to gain knowledge regarding the consumption and protection of consumer

---

[15] Measures of Guangdong Province for Implementing the Law of the People's Republic of China on the Protection of Consumer Rights and Interests (Amended in 2012) (《广东省实施〈中华人民共和国消费者权益保护法〉办法)

[16] See Qian (钱玉文) 2006, p. 137.

[17] Product Quality Law of the People's Republic of China (2009 Amendment) (《中华人民共和国产品质量法(2009修正)》).

[18] See Jia (贾东明) 2013, p. 11.

[19] See Article 7 of the Consumer Protection Law 2013.

[20] See Article 8 of the Consumer Protection Law 2013.

[21] See Article 9 of the Consumer Protection Law 2013.

[22] See Article 10 of the Consumer Protection Law 2013.

[23] See Article 12 of the Consumer Protection Law 2013.

rights and interests',[24] are also the rights which natural persons are entitled to in most cases. However, it should be emphasised again that although the Understanding of authority adopts a negative answer, the law itself does not provide a clear answer.

3.2.1.2.2 Patients and Students

The second issue is whether patients and students can be treated as consumers.

Some scholars consider that the patient cannot apply the provisions regulated by the Consumer Protection Law 2013, because in China most hospitals are funded by the government, so these hospitals are run with a non-for-profit aim. This argument can also be applied to the contract for education. Thus, hospitals and schools should not be deemed 'business operators'.[25] The opposite view suggests that there are still a great number of private hospitals/schools in China, and patients/students would not experience any difference when they receive medical/educational services from public hospitals/schools. Furthermore, the disproportion of information and knowledge and the disparity of bargaining power, which are emphasised by the Consumer Protection Law and make up the groundwork of consumer protection, also emerge in medical treatment contracts.[26] In practice, different courts hold different ideas.[27] Even in one case, the court of first instance and the court of second instance can come to completely opposite conclusions.[28]

The Understanding of authority admits that the circumstances of medical and educational contracts are 'rather complicated'. It is pointed out that some medical treatment is a result of statutory obligation, such as compulsory treatment and emergency rescue, which does not belong to 'transaction'. In the context of educational contract, the '9-year compulsory education system'[29] also makes education a public welfare undertaking but not a transaction. However, the nature of

[24] See Article 13 of the Consumer Protection Law 2013.

[25] See Gao and He (高虹、何忠正) 1998, pp. 645–646.

[26] See Han (韩世远) 2011, pp. 734–737. The information problems in the context of medical malpractice are also touched upon by Yu 2017, p. 307.

[27] For example, in a gazette case, the court held that services that are regulated by the Consumer Protection Law needs to the commercial services which seek for profits. The People's Hospital is not an organisation who seeks for profits, so it is not a 'trader' in the sense of consumer law. See Guofeng Zheng, Guoqing Chen v Jiangsu People's Hospital (郑雪峰、陈国青诉江苏省人民医院医疗服务合同纠纷二审案), Gazette of the Supreme People's Court of the People's Republic of China, 2004(8) (《中华人民共和国最高人民法院公报》2004年第8期).

[28] See He (何春雷) 2009. Quoted in Jiang (强美英) 2010, p. 29.

[29] The Chinese title of this system is '九年制义务教育'. It refers to a compulsory education system adopted in China, which requires all children of the appropriate age to accept education provided by the nation. On the grounds of Article 2 of Compulsory Education Law of the People's Republic of China (2015Amendment) (《中华人民共和国义务教育法(2015修正)》), 'The State implements a system of nine-year compulsory education. /Compulsory education means education which is uniformly provided by the State and which all the school-age children and adolescents must receive, and constitutes a public welfare undertaking which must be guaranteed by the State. /No tuition or miscellaneous fees shall be charged for provision of compulsory education'.

providing medical beauty services and career training is completely different from what is mentioned previously. Thus, using a single criterion to evaluate, it is not possible. Considering there is still a lack of consensus, it is not clarified by the law whether the Consumer Protection Law is applicable to medical/educational service contracts. The courts should be aware of the specific facts and, still, decide on the basis of the interpretation of daily consumption.[30]

3.2.1.2.3 Financial Investors

The third issue is the status of 'financial consumers'.

Since 2002, more and more Chinese scholars have started researching on a new concept: 'financial consumer'.[31] Based on comparative studies,[32] some scholars suggest that the purchasers of financial product, who were deemed 'financial investors', should also be granted the status of consumer. In early 2010, scholars suggested that 'financial consumer' would become a legal category and relevant legislation to protect them would be introduced.[33] Nevertheless, some scholars consider that enacting a unitary statute to regulate all financial domains is not realistic. This is because the 'divided supervision mode' that the Chinese financial market is supervised by a central bank (the People's Bank of China)[34] and three commissions (the China Insurance Regulatory Commission, the China Securities Regulatory Commission and the China Banking Regulatory Commission)[35] separately has already resulted in different viewpoints on whether the special protection of consumer should be awarded. In the foreseeable future, this divided mode will not be fundamentally changed. Furthermore, the borderline between the protection of financial consumer and financial investor is rather vague, because the rationale of financial investor protection is also on the basis of unbalanced status concerning information, knowledge and bargaining power. If the supervisor of financial market could provide enough protection for financial investors, it would not be necessary to adopt a new financial protection law or regulation.[36]

In the context of the amended Consumer Protection Law 2013, although the core concept 'daily consumption' has not been changed, it confirms that the financial

[30] Jia (贾东明) 2013, p. 10.

[31] It is suggested that the concept of 'financial consumer' was first put forward in Weiling Wang's article in 2002. See Wang (王伟玲) 2002, pp. 34–36.

[32] For example, the introduction of US law and Japanese law can be found in Jin Zeng's article. See Zeng (曾锦) 2013, p. 33. A more specific introduction of UK law and US law could be found in Fan Liao's article. See Liao (廖凡) 2012, pp. 95–104.

[33] See Wang (王晓雁) 2010.

[34] The People's Bank of China (中国人民银行).

[35] China Insurance Regulatory Commission (中国保险监督管理委员会); China Securities Regulatory Commission (中国证券监督管理委员会); China Banking Regulatory Commission (中国银行业监督管理委员会).

[36] See Liao (廖凡) 2012, pp. 103–104.

consumers should enjoy the protection provided by the law as a basic point. The financial consumers are believed to have suffered great losses because of the traders' unfair standard terms and fraudulent statements, so the legislator believes that the special protection is necessary. Furthermore, although the financial consumers are sometimes also the investors, as long as the ultimate target is to satisfy the requirements of daily and family use, it is acknowledged that these investors should be protected by the Consumer Protection Law.[37] Despite that Article 2 itself does not regulate it with clear words, Article 28 of the Consumer Protection Law 2013 clarifies the duties of the business operators who provide stock, insurance and banking services, which means the identity of consumer in these fields has been confirmed.[38] In practice, people's courts also rule that provisions regulated by the Consumer Protection Law are applicable to securities trading services contracts.[39] However, Article 28 only regulates the basic information requirements. Rules on further detailed protection are still provided by special laws.

3.2.2 Abuse of the Status of Consumer: The Case of 'Hai Wang'

Another issue regards the question whether a person should be deprived of the identity of consumer in some specific contexts. Compared with the issues of legal persons, patients, students and financial investors, the private actors in this case are not different from normal consumers in terms of the conduct of consumption or the goods they purchase. However, it is still in dispute whether the special protection should be applicable, because in these cases the consumers are buying fake or defective goods on purpose in order to seek profit. The specific method is to claim increased compensation pursuant to Article 49 of the Consumer Protection Law 1993, which is twice the contract price, and Article 55 of the Consumer Protection Law 2013, which is four times the contract price. The compensation other than the compensation for the original contract price is indeed a type of punitive damage. Thus, it is worth discussing whether there is abuse of the status of consumer.

---

[37] See Jia (贾东明) 2013, pp. 9–10.

[38] It reads: 'Business operators providing commodities or services on the Internet, on television, over telephone, or by mail order, among others, and business operators providing securities, insurance, banking, and other financial services shall provide consumers with information on their business addresses and contact methods, the quality, quantity, and prices or fees of commodities or services, the duration and manner of performance, safety precautions and risk warnings, after-sales services, and civil liability'.

[39] See, for example, Shaoqing Li v Guosen Securities Co Ltd. Shenzhen Middle Shennan Road Securities Sales Department, Guosen Securities Co Ltd.(李少清与国信证券股份有限公司深圳深南中路证券营业部、国信证券股份有限公司证券欺诈责任纠纷), Civil Judgment (2016) Yue-03-Min-Zhong No. 4548 of the Shenzhen Intermediate People's Court (深圳市中级人民法院(2016)粤03民终4548号民事判决书).

In this context, a celebrity should be introduced first. His name is Hai Wang. He started a series of legal actions from 1995, which share a common title: *Wang Hai Da Jia* ('王海打假', which literally means 'Hai Wang cracks down on counterfeits'). These actions are announced as fighting against traders' selling fake by mass-purchasing fake products and afterwards claiming for a high amount of punitive damages on the grounds of the relevant article in the Consumer Protection Law. However, although Hai Wang and his imitators affirm that their actions are for public welfare, not all courts support their claims. A negative opinion can be observed from the following case.

Hai Wang v Yong'an Company[40]

Rule: The buyer who purchases goods without the intention of daily use while being aware of the defect of the goods cannot be treated as a consumer.

Facts and Claims: On 15 September 1996, Hai Wang (hereinafter 'the plaintiff') bought two SONY cordless telephones from Yong'an Company (hereinafter 'the defendant'). The price of each was 3173 RMB so he paid 6346 RMB in total. On 7 October, he complained to the defendant that this type of SONY cordless telephone failed to meet the requirements of national standards of frequency, which is regulated by the State Radio Regulatory Commission ('国家无线电管理委员会'). As a result, there was no network access license granted to the goods, which means these goods were actually banned from sale and use in the light of the law. Thus, the plaintiff alleged that the defendant's act of selling had been a fraudulent act, so he claimed for twice the value of the goods as compensation on the grounds of Article 49 of the Chinese Consumer Protection Law 1993. The defendant argued that the plaintiff had not purchased for the purpose of daily consumption. Therefore, the Consumer Protection Law should not be applied. According to the investigation by the court, the plaintiff had bought 23 cordless telephones of the same type involved in this case in different markets and sued simultaneously in the other courts of competence for the same claim and reason.

Judgment: Selling forbidden products is a conduct which violates the law. However, the fact that the plaintiff bought 23 cordless telephones and claimed punitive damage separately from different sellers reveals that the plaintiff was aware that the subject matter was not permitted to access the network. The plaintiff bought so much modern communication equipment in one month, so the conduct of purchase cannot be regarded as 'daily consumption'. Thus, the Consumer Protection Law 1993 and its Article 49 do not apply to this case. The telephones should be handed over to the relevant administrative department for telecommunications. The contractual relation between the plaintiff and the defendant is invalid and the defendant has to compensate the plaintiff with the amount which is equal to the price of cordless telephones.

In several similar cases, the plaintiffs, Hai Wang and his imitators, who bought fake items on purpose, have won a part of them and also some of them have not been supported by the court. In *Zhongkai Hu v Tianhua Mansion*,[41] the court granted the plaintiff the status of consumer, even though the plaintiff has bought 100 wallets and

[40] Hai Wang v Yong'an Company (王海诉天津市龙门大厦永安公司买卖纠纷案), Civil Judgment (1997) Bei-Min-Chu-Zi No. 2 of the People's Court of Hebei District of Tianjin City (天津市河北区人民法院(1997)北民初字第2号民事判决书).

[41] Zhongkai Hu v Tianhua Mansion (胡仲凯诉新昌县天华商厦买卖金利来票夹索赔案), Civil Judgment (1998) Shao-Zhong-Fa-Jing-Zhong-Zi No. 330 of the Shaoxing Intermediate People's Court in Zhejiang Province (浙江省绍兴市中级人民法院(1998)绍中法经终字第330号民事判决书).

obviously most of them would not be used and the purchase was not a 'daily consumption'.

In academia, the debate is rather heated. Two leading scholars in private law hold opposite viewpoints. Huixing Liang suggests that the person who purchases with the awareness of fake and intends to seek punitive damages should not be identified as a consumer, because further interpretation is only necessary when literal interpretation has multiple possibilities. However, Article 2 of the Consumer Protection Law 1993 has already clarified that the purchase should be within the scope of 'daily consumption'. Furthermore, it is not clear whether buying fake on purpose will benefit the society, but reporting to a competent authority is apparently more reasonable and helpful. When deciding what is 'daily consumption', Huixing Liang argues that reasonableness and common sense should be taken into account as true intention is usually too difficult to identify. Therefore, it is reasonable to buy 1 or 2 telephones for 'daily consumption', but buying more than 20 telephones at once is obviously not.[42] In contrast, Liming Wang considers that the concept of consumer is an opposite concept to 'business operator'. Even if the purchase is based on the awareness of defectiveness or fake, the designation of consumer should never be refused so long as the purchase is not for further selling or providing service. In addition, the resource and ability of competent authorities is restricted. The fewer the people who claim their rights and interests, the more sellers who sell defective products could benefit.[43] Apart from their arguments, Yunliang Chen applies a mathematical model to argue that the concept of consumer is a vague one, so whether Hai Wang is a consumer will depend on his specific consumption, such as indeed how many telephones did he buy.[44] Although the Consumer Protection Law brings the controversy, some local regulations have provided a more specific solution when they implement the law. For example, Zhejiang Province has clarified that 'business operators should not be exempt from their liability for providing defective products on the basis of the quantity of the consumer's purchase.[45]

Regarding buying fake on purpose, the Understanding of authority states frankly that a thorough investigation was done prior to the amendment, but it is so controversial that it is impossible for the law to provide a clear answer. Thus, the solution is, still, to leave it blank at this point and come back in the future when the time is ripe.[46]

However, the Supreme People's Court clarified its opinion on this issue in the Guiding Case No. 23, which was published in 2014 with the other three cases of the sixth group of guiding cases.[47]

---

[42] See Liang (梁慧星) 2001.

[43] See Wang (王利明) 2002, pp. 8–9.

[44] See Chen (陈云良) 2006, pp. 83–88.

[45] Relevant introduction and commentary can be found in Fujian Fang's article. See Fang (方福建) 2002, p. 138.

[46] See Jia (贾东明) 2013, p. 12.

[47] See Notice of the Supreme People's Court on Issuing the Sixth Group of Guiding Cases (《最高人民法院关于发布第六批指导性案例的通知》), Instrument No. 18 [2014] of the Supreme People's Court (法[2014]18号)

Guiding Case No. 23: Yinshan Sun v Jiangning Store of Nanjing Auchan Supermarket Co Ltd[48]

Rule: Regardless of whether the plaintiff knew that the food did not meet the requirements of the standard of safety at the time of purchase, the plaintiff should be deemed as a consumer, and his claim that the seller or producer should compensate him in the amount of ten times the money paid under the Food Safety Law 2009[49] *or compensate the consumer according to other statutory compensation standards should be supported by the people's court.*

Facts and Claims: On 1 May 2012, Yinshan Sun (hereinafter 'the plaintiff') bought 15 packs of the 'jade-rabbit' brand sausage from Jiangning Store of Nanjing Auchan Supermarket Co Ltd (hereinafter 'the defendant'). Among all these goods, the expiration period of 14 packs of sausage, whose value is 558.6 RMB, had already elapsed. After paying the bill at the cashier desk, the plaintiff directly went to the service desk to seek compensation. Since no common view had been reached, the plaintiff brought a lawsuit to the court and claimed the punitive damages which are 10 times the value of 14 packs of the sausage, 5586 RMB.

Judgment: With regard to the issue of whether the plaintiff is a consumer, it should be referred to Article 2 of the Consumer Protection Law. To be specific, 'consumer' is a concept opposite to producer and seller. Only if a private actor is purchasing and using the commodities, or accepting services, for the purposes of individual or family demands, but not the purposes of producing, business or professional demands, he should be identified as a 'consumer'. The contract he signed with a business operator shall fall into the applicable scope of the Consumer Protection Law. In this case, the plaintiff and the defendant have no disputes on the fact that the plaintiff has purchased sausage from the defendant, and the plaintiff did not invest the sausage he bought into further selling or other business activities. The defendant did not provide any evidence to prove the plaintiff's purchase was for further producing and selling activities as well. It is enforcing his legal right that the plaintiff claimed the compensation because he bought the food of which the period of quality guarantee had expired. Therefore, the argument held by the defendant that the plaintiff is not a consumer because he bought the defective food on the basis of his awareness cannot be supported.

With regard to the issue on bearing liability, the compensation is regulated by Article 96 of the Food Safety Law 2009. (…) In this case, the benefit that the plaintiff claimed is the benefit protected by law. The law itself does not impose any limitation with regard to the motivation of the consumer's purchase. (…)

From the viewpoints revealed from this guiding case, it is apparent that the opinion suggested by Liming Wang, as mentioned above, was favoured by the Supreme People's Court. It was explained that the interpretation of 'daily consumption' can be simply based on an opposite interpretation of the concepts of 'producing' and 'selling', which are imposed to define a 'business operator'. In a word, as long as a private actor does not purchase for these business or professional purposes, he is a consumer. Furthermore, as long as there is no restriction on the motivation of the purchase, the specific provisions on increased compensation for infringing consumer's rights and interest can be invoked.

---

[48] Yinshan Sun v Jiangning Store of Nanjing Auchan Supermarket Co Ltd. (孙银山诉南京欧尚超市有限公司江宁店买卖合同纠纷案), Civil Judgment (2012) Jiangning-Kai-Min-Chu-Zi No. 646 of the People's Court of Jiangning District of Nanjing City in Jiangsu Province (江苏省南京市江宁区人民法院(2012)江宁开民初字第646号民事判决书).

[49] Food Safety Law of the People's Republic of China (《中华人民共和国食品安全法》).

Nevertheless, these rules have not been incorporated into the law yet, which should not be forgotten. Even the Supreme People's Court tends to change the standpoint it adopted in Guiding Case No. 23: it stated in an official reply that the negative effects brought by 'Hai Wang phenomenon' have emerged recently. Buying fake products on purpose becomes a commercial act. The buyers' motives are not purifying the market but seeking for profits and racketeering. These acts severely violate the principle of good faith and waste judicial resources. We do not support this approach which is like quenching a thirst with poison.[50] Besides, Shiyuan Han suggests that the 'Hai Wang phenomenon' is not only relevant to whether the status of consumer should be granted. It is also related to whether the requirements of 'fraudulent act' can be met.[51]

3.3 EU Law

3.3.1 Definitions of Consumer and Trader

3.3.1.1 Legislative Expression in the Directives

Most EU directives provide the definitions of 'consumer' and 'trader' at the beginning of the directive. Considering the specific topics which are discussed in the next chapters, the directives regarding unfair terms and withdrawal rights are introduced as examples.

To be specific, Article 2 of the Unfair Contract Terms Directive[52] recognises 'consumer' as 'any natural person who, in contracts covered by this Directive, is acting outside his trade, business or profession', while 'trader'[53] refers to any natural or legal person who is acting for purposes relating to his trade, business or profession, whether publicly owned or privately owned. In the Distance Selling Directive,[54] the definition of consumer remains exactly the same as the one provided in the Unfair Contract Terms Directive. The definition of trader[55] is shortened to any natural or legal person who is acting in his commercial or professionally capacity, where the

[50] See Reply of the General Office of the Supreme People's Court to Suggestion No. 5990 of the Fifth Session of the Twelfth National People's Congress (最高人民法院办公厅对十二届全国人大五次会议第5990号建议的答复意见), Letter No. 181 [2017] of the General Office of the Supreme People's Court (法办函[2017]181号).

[51] See Han (韩世远) 2015, pp. 87–88.

[52] Council Directive 93/13/EEC of 5 April 1993 on unfair terms in consumer contracts [1993] OJ L95/29.

[53] In this directive the terminology of 'seller or supplier' is still imposed. See Article 2(c) of the Unfair Contract Terms Directive.

[54] Directive 97/7/EC of the European Parliament and of the Council of 20 May 1997 on the protection of consumers in respect of distance contracts [1997] OJ L144/19.

[55] 'Supplier' is the terminology employed by this directive. See Article 2(3) of the Distance Selling Directive.

core meaning has not been changed. In the Consumer Credit Directive[56] and the Timeshare Directive,[57] the wording used to define consumer is kept consistent with the one used in the former directives, and the definition of 'trader' provided by the Timeshare Directive not only mentions 'a natural or legal person who is acting for purposes relating to that person's trade, business, craft or profession' but also adds 'anyone acting in the name of or on behalf of a trader'.[58] In the Consumer Rights Directive,[59] the definition of consumer is still the same as the one provided approximately 20 years ago.[60] With regard to 'trader', the legislator combines all the elements mentioned by the former directives and puts them into one definition: '"trader" means any natural person or any legal person, irrespective of whether privately or publicly owned, who is acting, including through any other person acting in his name or on his behalf, for purposes relating to his trade, business, craft or profession in relation to contracts covered by this Directive'.[61]

Although the definition provided by the directives is consistent, there are still some issues worth discussing.

3.3.1.2 Several Specific Issues

3.3.1.2.1 Mixed Situations

The first issue is whether a private actor can be granted the identity of consumer when he is acting partly for purposes related to his trade and partly outside his trade. The discussion can start with a famous case decided by the CJEU in 2005.

Johann Gruber v Bay Wa AG[62]

Rule: The identity of consumer under the Brussels Convention[63] *cannot be granted when the contract partly concerns the buyer's trade, unless the trade or professional purpose is so limited as to be negligible in the overall context of the supply.*

56 Directive 2008/48/EC of the European Parliament and of the Council of 23 April 2008 on credit agreements for consumers and repealing Council Directive 87/102/EEC [2008] OJ L133/66.

57 Directive 2008/122/EC of the European Parliament and of the Council of 14 January 2009 on the protection of consumers in respect of certain aspects of timeshare, long-term holiday product, resale and exchange contracts [2009] OJ L33/10.

58 Article 2(1)(e) of the Timeshare Directive.

59 Directive 2011/83/EU of the European Parliament and of the Council of 25 October 2011 on consumer rights, amending Council Directive 93/13/EEC and Directive 1999/44/EC of the European Parliament and of the Council and repealing Council Directive 85/577/EEC and Directive 97/7/EC of the European Parliament and of the Council [2011] OJ L304/64.

60 Article 2(1) provides that consumer 'means any natural person who, in contracts covered by this Directive, is acting for purposes which are outside his trade, business, craft or profession'.

61 Article 2(2) of the Consumer Rights Directive.

62 Case C-464/01 [2005] ECR I-00439.

63 Convention on jurisdiction and the enforcement of judgements in civil and commercial matters, Convention adopted on 27 September 1968 [1972] OJ L 299.

Facts: Mr Gruber is a farmer who owned a farm building and he used about a dozen rooms as a dwelling for himself and his family. Wishing to replace the roof tiles of his farm building, he contacted an employee of Bay Wa, a German firm publishing brochures which were also distributed in Austria, without mentioning he was a farmer on the phone. The employee made him an offer by telephone but Mr Gruber wished to inspect the tiles on site. On his visit to the premises of Bay Wa, he stated that he had a farm and wished to tile the roof of the farm building. He stated he also owned ancillary buildings that were used principally for the farm, but did not clarify whether the building to be tiled was used mainly for business or for private purposes. After the conclusion of the contract, Gruber considered that the tiles delivered by Bay Wa to tile the roof varied significantly in colour despite the warranty that the colour would be uniform, which also led to the result that the roof would have to be retiled. Therefore, Gruber decided to bring proceedings on the basis of the warranty together with a claim for damages, seeking reimbursement of the cost and of the expense of removing them and retiling the roof and a declaration of liability for any future expenses. However, Bay Wa contested the competence of the court, which is Landesgericht Steyr (Austria), under Article 13 of the Brussels Convention[64] *on jurisdiction over consumer contracts. Subsequent to the fact that the Landesgericht Steyr and the Oberlandesgericht (Higher Regional Court) Linz (Austria) held different views on this issue, Mr Gruber then brought an appeal to the Oberster Gerichtshof (Supreme Court). The latter referred several questions to the CJEU. It wondered whether the rules of jurisdiction laid down by the Brussels Convention must be interpreted as meaning that a contract which relates to activities which are partly business and partly private must be regarded as having been concluded by a consumer for the purposes of the first paragraph of Article 13 of the Convention.*

Judgment: (…) In that regard, it is already clearly apparent from the purpose of Articles 13 to 15 of the Brussels Convention, namely to properly protect the person who is presumed to be in a weaker position than the other party to the contract, that the benefit of those provisions cannot, as a matter of principle, be relied on by a person who concludes a contract for a purpose which is partly concerned with his trade or profession and is therefore only partly outside it. It would be otherwise only if the link between the contract and the trade or profession of the person concerned was so slight as to be marginal and, therefore, had only a negligible role in the context of the supply in respect of which the contract was concluded, considered in its entirety.

From the wording of the judgement, it is clear that the CJEU at that time held the opinion that, in the case of a mixed situation, the person who concludes a contract for purposes which are partly within and partly outside his trade or profession should not be granted the identity of consumer. This is because the party is deemed

[64]Article 13 reads: 'In proceedings concerning a contract concluded by a person for a purpose which can be regarded as being outside his trade or profession, hereinafter called 'the consumer', jurisdiction shall be determined by this Section, without prejudice to the provisions of Articles 4 and 5(5), if it is: (1) a contract for the sale of goods on instalment credit terms; or (2) a contract for a loan repayable by instalments, or for any other form of credit, made to finance the sale of goods; or (3) any other contract for the supply of goods or a contract for the supply of services, an (a) in the State of the consumer's domicile the conclusion of the contract was preceded by a specific invitation addressed to him or by advertising; and (b) the consumer took in that State the steps necessary for the conclusion of the contract'. As Brussels Convention has been replaced by the Brussels I Regulation, now the relevant contents are regulated by Article 15 of the Brussels I Regulation.

to be on an equal footing with the other party if the contract is entered into for his trade or professional purposes.[65]

In the Green Paper on the Review of the Consumer Acquis, it is asked whether 'primarily' should be added to the notion of consumer and professional, which means the consumer can invoke the special rules when he is acting for purposes falling primarily, but not totally, outside his trade, business and profession.[66] Besides, the viewpoint provided by the *Gruber* case was followed by the Consumer Rights Directive as well. It is clarified by the Recital 17 that 'in the case of dual purpose contracts, where the contract is concluded for purposes partly within and partly outside the person's trade and the trade purpose is so limited as not to be predominant in the overall context of the contract, that person should also be considered as a consumer'. However, it should be noticed that the idea has started changing subtly from the Green Paper on the Review of the Consumer Acquis that the purpose of trade does not have to be 'negligible' in order to make consumer protection rules applicable. On the contrary, it is enough to recognise a consumer contract when the purpose outside trade is 'primary' or 'predominant'.

3.3.1.2.2 Intermediary

Another issue to be addressed is about the case in which an intermediary, who is usually a professional actor, is involved in the transaction. This issue is worth discussing, because sometimes although the parties are both consumers, the seller who hires an intermediary may benefit from his expertise. Under this circumstance, is it possible for the buyer to invoke the rules on consumer protection?

In most cases, the answer is 'no', because in most directives, the application of consumer protection rules requires that the target contract has to be concluded between a consumer and a trader, but not two consumers. However, this issue is still discussed in the Green Paper on the Review of the Consumer Acquis, because it is controversial. On the one hand, it would be rather difficult to decide when consumer protection rules should be applicable due to the strong influence of the intermediary, while on the other hand the buyer without the help of intermediary is truly sometimes in a weaker position. Nevertheless, if a contracting party without hiring an intermediary can invoke consumer protection rules, it may not be fair to his counterparty, because he might not realise that hiring an intermediary might put him in a position which makes him equivalent to a trader. Besides, 'there may be a risk of unforeseen and negative knock-on effects on markets on which private persons trade with private persons'.[67] It should be noted as well that the notion of intermediary

[65] See paragraph 40 of the judgement.

[66] Green Paper on the Review of the Consumer Acquis (presented by the European Commission), COM(2006) 744 final.

[67] COM(2006) 744 final, p. 16.

would not contain trading platforms for sellers and consumers, e.g. on the Internet, where the platform did not participate in the conclusion of the contract.[68]

However, if a trader acting as intermediary on behalf of a private individual fails to duly inform the consumer of the fact that the owner of the goods sold is a private individual, it shall be seen as a 'seller'. This is clarified by the CJEU in *Sabrina Wathelet v Garage Bietheres & Fils SPRL*.[69]

3.3.2 Legal Persons: A Focus on SMEs

In the EU directives, only a natural person is recognised as a consumer. Legal persons cannot enjoy the specific rules aiming at consumer protection. This can be easily observed from a literal interpretation. In addition, the possibility that a legal person may also invoke the rule of consumer protection is denied by the case law of the CJEU. This rule was confirmed in the famous *Di Pinto* case, in which it is provided that 'a normally well-informed trader simply could not be considered to be in a similar position to a consumer since he may be aware of his legal position and his interests'.[70] Subsequently, in *Cape Snc v Idealservice Srl*, it is further clarified in the judgement that 'it is thus clear from the wording of Article 2 of the directive (the Unfair Contract Terms Directive) that a person other than a natural person who concludes a contract with a seller or supplier cannot be regarded as a consumer within the meaning of that provision'.[71]

Nevertheless, although the legislation and the CJEU have already made it rather clear, there is still a discussion from a normative perspective. Some scholars suggest that in some circumstances small and medium enterprises (SMEs)[72] should be protected as consumers at the EU level. The reason is that 'SMEs often lack specific expertise, experience, information and bargaining power, in a way very similar to consumers, especially when they act outside their field of usual business'.[73] Indeed, in the EU directives aiming at some specific areas, it has already been pointed out that SMEs sometimes lack professional knowledge and information. With respect to the inequality of bargaining power, there is no difference between a SME and a consumer. The best example can be observed in the new Package Travel Directive

[68] Nevertheless, sometimes this issue is also complex because the consumer who purchase online does not know with whom he is dealing. See Micklitz et al. 2010, p. 38.

[69] Case C-149/15 [2016] ECLI:EU:C:2016:840.

[70] Case C-361/89 [1991] ECR I-01206. Quoted in Loos and Samoy 2014, p. 2.

[71] Case C-541/99 [2001] ECR I-09049, para. 16.

[72] The definition of 'SME' can be found in the Annex to Commission Recommendation 2003/361/EC. Its Article 2 provides: 'The category of micro-, small- and medium-sized enterprises (SMEs) is made up of enterprises which employ fewer than 250 persons and which have an annual turnover not exceeding EUR 50 million and/or an annual balance sheet total not exceeding EUR 43 million.

[73] Micklitz et al. 2010, p. 34.

2015.[74] It is suggested that a similar level of protection is required to apply to the travellers who are the representatives of small businesses or professionals, since they book trips related to their business or profession through the same booking channels as consumers.[75] Thus, another terminology 'traveller' is employed in order to distinguish from the EU definition of 'consumer' in the directive,[76] so the applicable scope is exactly expanded to non-natural persons.

Compared with the strict approach adopted by the directives and the CJEU's case law, some national laws and proposed optional instruments go a step further on this issue. In this area, France is a good example, since in French law small professionals are also protected against unfair contract terms.[77] Speaking of optional instruments, the now withdrawn CESL also extended the scope of protection to SMEs when dealing with unfair terms.[78]

3.4 Concluding Remarks

3.4.1 Comparison Between China and the EU

Based on the above description and analysis, several remarks can be made.

Firstly, with regard to the legislative expression of the definition of 'consumer', it is not difficult to find that the legislative technique employed by EU is a more logical one because the EU legislator imposes another phrase referring to a group of people, 'natural person', to define the word 'consumer'. In contrast, the Chinese legislators have not pointed out explicitly what kind of private actors could be granted the status of consumer. If we seek the answer from Article 2 of the Consumer Protection Law 2013 literally, the answer to 'who is a consumer' would be circular as 'a consumer is a consumer'.

The next question we have to envisage is whether legal persons can be regarded as consumers. In this regard, if 'legal certainty' is used as a criterion to evaluate these two approaches, the EU approach definitely prevails because it precisely states that the consumer can only be a natural person. However, on the other hand, Chinese law is more flexible because it leaves enough room for courts and local legislators to include legal persons into the scope of protection, while in the EU context it is only possible to modify the specific legislation. This issue can also be discussed from a normative perspective, which is 'whether the small and medium legal persons

[74] Directive (EU) 2015/2302 of the European Parliament and of the Council of 25 November 2015 on Package Travel and Linked Travel Arrangements, amending Regulation (EC) No 2006/2004 and Directive 2011/83/EU of the European Parliament and of the Council and Repealing Council Directive 90/314/EEC [2015] OJ L326/1

[75] See Preamble no. 7 of the Package Travel Directive 2015.

[76] See Article 3(6) of the Package Travel Directive 2015.

[77] See Micklitz et al. 2010, pp. 32–34.

[78] See Article 7.2 of the CESL.

should be regarded as consumer in some circumstances'. If we consider that the disparity of information and negotiating power is the reason for introducing special protection, there is no reason to deny that the SMEs should enjoy the same protection. However, on the basis of most EU directives, there is not much room for including legal persons into the scope of consumer protection. In contrast, in Chinese law it is possible to interpret Article 2 of the Consumer Protection Law 2013, but it may not be the optimal solution. Compared with EU legislation, there is no restriction on legislative competence so separate legislation could be introduced when the legislator thinks it is indeed necessary to grant legal persons specific protection in a very specified area.

Thirdly, the method of imposing limitations to define 'consumer' is also different. The EU directive applies a negative approach which requires that the consumption should not be related to the actor's trade, business or profession, whereas the Chinese Consumer Protection Law 2013 employs a positive way that the acting has to be relevant to 'daily consumption'. Indeed, most specific issues we discuss in this chapter are relevant to this limitation. We can observe that sometimes a negative approach is more practicable. If a positive approach is adopted, there will be more interpretative work to do. For example, if we use the limitation imposed by the EU legislator to deal with the Chinese issues, it is not difficult to find that a patient or a student is a consumer because the contracts concluded with hospitals or schools are undoubtedly for purposes outside their trade, business or profession. However, in some other circumstances, the positive way may provide a clearer answer. For example, to the mixed situations, such as the illustration that an author bought a laptop for the purpose of writing a new novel but watching online shows and playing computer games as well, the EU approach adds a new criterion that the purpose for trade has to be negligible or the purpose outside the trade has to be predominant. In the Chinese context, this issue can be easily resolved, because the positive approach only requires the purpose of 'daily consumption', which means the special protection is always applicable where the subject matter can be possibly applied for daily use unless it is obviously a productive consumption, such as a machine tool, or the subject matter will be used only for the purpose of seeking profits.

Fourthly, with regard to the 'Hai Wang' phenomenon, actually his purchase can be absolutely regarded as a consumer's purchase in the context of EU directives because it is outside his trade, business and profession, unless he builds up a company and makes profit via purchasing defective goods.[79] But in China, the question whether he is a consumer is remarkably controversial. However, in Guiding Case No. 23, the Supreme People's Court holds that, as long as the motivation for purchasing is not required by the law, the consumer can claim the special consumer protection rules regardless of whether he is aware of the defectiveness. From this

[79] As Hai Wang set up a company to crack down on the fakes these years, his previous identity of consumer will be questionable. See Lingjun Kong (孔令君), 'Hai Wang's These Years as a Professional in Cracking down on Counterfeits' (《职业打假人王海的这些年》), Jiefang Daily, 21 March 2012, available at: <http://focus.news.163.com/12/0321/01/7T361DLT00011SM9.html>, last visited: 2013/10/25.

viewpoint, we can observe that, from the Supreme People's Court's perspective, the reason for introducing consumer protection rules is not limited to the weakness of the consumer. Even though the consumer is not weak at all, fraud or other illegal behaviour of the trader should still be punished. This is the case at least in the areas of food and drug.

Fifthly, with regard to the identity of 'trader', the definition in Chinese law is also rather vague, as it only contains the message of providing commodities and services, while the EU definition mentions four keywords which are relevant to the requirement of 'purpose': trade, business, craft and profession. Based on the difference in definition, it is clear that the Chinese problem can be simply solved in the European context: hospitals and schools are definitely traders because they provide their services for the purpose relating to their profession. However, in China this is sometimes not the case because the courts and scholars suggest that there is a lack of seeking-for-profits purpose, which is also required by the identity of trader. The circumstance where an intermediary is involved is also noteworthy. In the EU context, it is rather clear that a contract concluded on an e-platform does not inevitably grant the consumer special protection, unless the e-platform itself is involved in the conclusion of the contract. Indeed, whether the counterparty is a trader is the core of the topic. This viewpoint should be also applicable to the Chinese context.[80]

Finally, it should be noticed that there are some specific areas where Chinese law and EU law may hold different ideas simply because of policy reasons. For example, in Chinese law a farmer can invoke the rules in the Consumer Protection Law 2013 when purchasing agricultural products, although he is not a natural consumer. In contrast, in EU law, a farmer cannot enjoy the special protection.

3.4.2 *Explanatory Analysis*

From the foregoing comparative review, it is not difficult to find that the biggest difference in the context of the concept of consumer contract between China and the EU is the level of clarity. The Chinese definitions, especially 'consumer' and 'trader', are much vaguer, while the EU definitions are more concrete.

This can be explained by the hypothesis (1) raised in Chap. 1: 'With a more regulated market, China has a lower level of demand for consumer law rules and the level of requirement for the clarity and concreteness of the rules is also lower. On the contrary, the demand for consumer law rules and their clarity and concreteness in the EU, which has a more competitive market, should be much higher'.

To be specific, a jurisdiction with a competitive market usually has a higher demand for a concrete and unequivocal consumer law. This is not difficult to understand: as mentioned, a competitive market is always linked with sufficient contract freedom. Considering that the consumer law contains a great number of

[80]Thus, the opinion that 'withdrawal rights shall be applicable to all transactions on e-platforms' may not be correct. See Cheng (成慧) 2014.

mandatory rules, the clearer the law is, the more freedom can be assured.[81] Indeed, most EU directives provide a list of definitions at the beginning of the main text and adopt a rather legible approach to demonstrate the connotations of these definitions. This approach fits in with the competitive market well, because the higher level of concreteness helps with creating the legal certainty, which is conducive to reducing the traders' information cost when they want to enter the market.

Inversely, in a regulated market jurisdiction, the legal rules do not have to be relatively clear and concrete because vagueness can be used for further interpretation and administrative reaction.[82] This is exactly the case in the context of definitions as well: China has a more regulated market, and its legal definitions are much simpler and vaguer. This leaves courts and administrative authorities greater room in practice to acquire their expected consequences. For example, in the context of hospitals and schools, Chinese legislators have not yet decided whether to grant to students and patients the status of consumer. It should be taken into account that the background context of these contracts in China is considerably complicated because many hospitals and schools are seen as a part of the social welfare system and they do not act for purposes of seeking profits so they are radically different from normal traders. Some people suggest it may not be appropriate to apply consumer protection rules to these specific circumstances at this stage. Therefore, even if the legislator had the opportunity to make the definitions more precise during the process of enacting amendment, they refused to do so, because the controversy had not been solved. In this sense, the Chinese approach could be vaguer but more suitable to the domestic context.

With regard to the dissimilar treatment of farmers, it shows the differences of social background and policy consideration. In China, the farmers are recognised as impecunious and weak. Consumer law is seen as an instrument which is employed to protect the weak party in society. In order to maintain the social order, which is a part of the motivations of enacting consumer protection rules, the government believes that it is necessary to protect the farmers as if they are consumers. Nevertheless, this is not the case in the EU, so the special treatment does not exist in the EU context.

References

(Chen (陈云良) 2006) 陈云良[Yunliang Chen]:"消费者概念之模糊性分析——模糊法学的一个应用"[The Fuzziness of the Concept of Consumer: an Application of Vague Legal Doctrine], 《法学》2006年第10期[Law Science, 2006(10)],第83—88页[p. 83–88]。

(Cheng (成慧) 2014) 成慧[Hui Cheng]:"7天无理由退货怎么退"[How to Return the Goods through the Right of Withdrawal], 《人民日报》2014年2月21日第4版[People's Daily, 2014/2/21, Page 4]。

[81] See Chap. 1, Sect. 3.3.1.

[82] See Chap. 1, Sect. 3.4.1.

(Fang (方福建) 2002) 方福建[Fujian Fang]:“论‘消费者’概念的法律界定”[On the Legal Definition of Consumer],《当代法学》2002年第2期[Contemporary Law Review, 2002(2)], 第136—138页[p. 136–138]。

(Gao & He (高虹、何忠正) 1998) 高虹、何忠正[Hong Gao, Zhongzheng He]:“《消费者权益保护法》适用于处理医疗纠纷吗”[Is Consumer Protection Law Applicable to Medical Disputes?],《中国卫生事业管理》1998年第12期[Chinese Health Service Management, 1998(12)],第645—649页[p. 645–649]。

(Han (韩世远) 2011) 韩世远[Shiyuan Han]:《合同法总论》[The Law of Contract],法律出版社2011年第3版[Law Press, 2011, 3rd Edition]。

(Han (韩世远) 2015) 韩世远[Shiyuan Han]:“消费者合同三题:知假买假、惩罚性赔偿与合同终了”[Three Problematic Issues in Consumer Contracts: Buying Fake on Purpose, Punitive Damage and the End of Contract],《法律适用》2015年第10期[Journal of Law Application, 2015(10)],第87—92页[p. 87–92]。

(He (何春雷) 2009) 何春雷[Chunlei He]:“患者是不是消费者再引关注”[‘Whether Patients are Consumers’ Attracts Attention Again],《中国消费者报》2009年4月17日第A2版[China Consumer News, 2009/4/17, Page A2]。

(Howell & Wilson 2016) Nicola Howell & Therese Wilson, ‘The Limits of Competition: Reasserting a Role for Consumer Protection and Fair Trading Regulation in Competitive Markets’, in Deborah Parry, Annette Nordhausen, Geraint Howells & Christian Twigg-Flesner (eds.), *The Yearbook of Consumer Law 2009*, New York: Routledge, 2016, p. 147–174.

(Jia (贾东明) 2013) 贾东明主编[Dongming Jia (ed.)]:《中华人民共和国消费者权益保护法解读》[Understanding on the Law of the People’s Republic of China on the Protection of Consumer Rights and Interests],中国法制出版社2013年版[China Legal Publishing House, 2013]。

(Jiang (强美英) 2010) 强美英[Meiying Jiang]:“关于医疗服务选择适用《消费者权益保护法》的思考”[Thoughts on Applying the Consumer Protection Law to Medical Services],《法律适用》2010年第5期[Journal of Law Application, 2010(5)],第28—32页[p. 28–32]。

(Liang (梁慧星) 2001) 梁慧星[Huixing Liang]:“消费者权益保护法第49条的解释与适用”[On Interpretation and Application of Article 49 of the Consumer Protection Law],《人民法院报》2001年3月29日第3版[People’s Court Daily, 2001/03/29, Page 3]

(Liao (廖凡) 2012) 廖凡[Fan Liao]:“金融消费者的概念和范围: 一个比较法的视角”[Definition and Scope of the Concept of ‘Financial Consumer’: A Comparative Perspective],《环球法律评论》2012年第4期[Global Law Review, 2012(4)],第95—104页[pp. 95–104]。

(Loos & Samoy 2014) Marco B.M. Loos & Ilse Samoy, ‘The Position of Small and Medium Sized Enterprises in European Contract Law: An Introduction’, in Marco B.M. Loos & Ilse Samoy (eds.), *The Position of Small and Medium Sized Enterprises in European Contract Law*, Cambridge: Intersentia, 2014, p. 1–9.

(Micklitz, Stuyck & Terryn 2010) Hans-W. Micklitz, Jules Stuyck, Evelyne Terryn (eds.), *Cases, Materials and Text on Consumer Law*, Portland: Hart Publishing, 2010.

(Qian (钱玉文) 2006) 钱玉文[Yuwen Qian]:“消费者概念的法律再界定”[The Re-identification of the Concept of Consumer],《法学杂志》2006年第1期[Law Science Magazine, 2006(1)], 第136—138页[p. 136–138]。

(Wang (王利明) 2002) 王利明[Liming Wang]:“消费者的概念及消费者权益保护法的调整范围”[The Concept of Consumer and the Applicable Scope of the Consumer Protection Law],《政治与法律》2002年第2期[Political Science and Law, 2002(2)],第3—12页[p. 3–12]。

(Wang (王伟玲) 2002) 王伟玲[Weiling Wang]:“金融消费者权益及其保护初探”[On Protection of Rights and Interests of Financial Consumers],《重庆社会科学》2002年第5期[Chongqing Social Sciences, 2002(5)],第34—36页[pp. 34–36]。

(Wang (王晓雁) 2010) 王晓雁[Xiaoyan Wang]:“5到10年内‘金融消费者’有望成为法律概念”[‘Financial Consumer’ is Expected to Become a Legal Concept in 5 to 10 Years],《法制日报》2010年3月15日第6版[Legal Daily, 2010/3/15, Page 6]。

(Yang (杨立新) 2013) 杨立新[Lixin Yang]:“消法关于消费者概念的规定应当修改”[The Provision on the Concept of Consumer of the Consumer Protection Law Should be Amended], 《中国审判》2013年第6期[China Trial, 2013(6)],第24—25页[p. 24–25]。

(Yu 2017) Xiaowei Yu, *Preventing Medical Malpractice and Compensating Victimised Parents in China: A Law and Economics Perspective*, Cambridge: Intersentia, 2017.

(Zeng (曾锦) 2013) 曾锦[Jin Zeng]:“金融消费者的概念界定”[On the Definition of Financial Consumer],《经济界》2013年第4期[Economic Affairs, 2013(4)],第32—36页[p. 32–36]。

Chapter 4
Unfair Terms

4.1 Introduction

The law has to evolve and reflect economic and societal developments in order to adapt to the new circumstances it needs to regulate.[1] Nowadays, contract terms are scarcely negotiated in a real sense. This development challenges the traditional approach of contract law and raises the question: how should contract law adapt to this new reality? Put differently, with the widespread use of pre-formulated or standard contracts, it is necessary to reconsider the traditional understanding of contract law in line with the principles of 'party autonomy' and 'freedom of contract'. These principles have to reflect this new trend and to some extent change in several fundamental ways.[2] For example, the traditional understanding of the principle of party autonomy suggests that the parties can decide the substantive content of their contract and the law should not interfere. However, nowadays the substantive fairness of such contract is addressed in most jurisdictions, primarily to protect the weaker party.[3] In this context, the law needs to first establish legitimacy to interfere with contracts so as to achieve these policy objectives, and then develop legal mechanisms to control these terms.

Regarding the reasons for monitoring pre-formulated contract terms, there are at least two kinds of mainstream theory. The first theory is about transaction costs and informational asymmetries. It is believed that a party using pre-formulated terms is

---

[1] Reversely, as pointed out by Lei Chen, well-functioning legal institutions are conducive to economic development. See Chen 2010, p. 984.

[2] It is believed that the phenomenon of standard form conditions provoked discussion as early as the beginning of the twentieth century. The French lawyer Raymond Saleilles (1901) proposed that the phenomenon that he called contrat d'adhésion should be distinguished from proper contract law. Quoted in Wilhelmsson 2011, p. 574.

[3] Yan Zhu suggests that autonomy of will, weaker party protection, responsibility for unlawful acts and reliance are all values underlying private law, and weaker party protection requires contract law to provide special rules on standard terms. See Zhu (朱岩) 2010, p. 155.

J. Ge, *A Comparative Analysis of Policing Consumer Contracts in China and the EU*, https://doi.org/10.1007/978-981-13-2989-0_4

usually better informed about the content of the terms than the other party and the cost for the other party of acquainting himself with the conditions is much more expensive than for the user. Thus, the informational asymmetries and the uneven distribution of transaction costs have to be balanced by reviewing the pre-formulated terms. Another theory is recognised as the 'abuse theory'. On the grounds of this theory, the control of pre-formulated terms aims to protect a specified class of persons due to the imbalance in bargaining power and knowledge.[4]

Regarding the legal mechanisms for controlling standard terms, in China, the principle of fairness plays an essential role. This principle is emphasised as one of the basic principles of the Contract Law 1999,[5] together with the principles of equity of the parties' legal status, freedom of contract, good faith, public order and social ethics, and sanctity of contract.[6] It guides the interpretation and supplementation of the Contract Law 1999 as well as the interpretation, policing and supplementation of contracts.[7] The principle itself and the related contract law rules which implement this principle point to the fact that the value of substantive fairness is still the core element of a Chinese socialistic market economy. Although the state does not interfere in the transactions between private actors as much as it did during the age of the planned economy, contractual freedom is still restricted by the idea of fairness. The regulation of unfair terms in consumer contracts is a good example, especially where the contract is concluded on the basis of standard terms.

In European law, the methods applied to control standard terms can be divided into two categories. The first category focuses on whether real consensus exists when the contract is concluded. Put differently, it is a consent-oriented paradigm including mechanisms, such as the obligation to draw attention to the terms, to safeguard genuine consent to the terms. The second category focuses on the substantive content of standard terms and 'the (un)fairness, (un)balanced character or (un)suitability of a term in the conditions, or of the conditions as a whole'.[8] The first category is also referred to as 'formal control', while the latter is recognised as 'substantive control'.[9]

Under the EU multi-level governance system, national jurisdictions have legislative rules and judicial practice with regard to policing contracts to control unfair terms, which have developed over decades. To establish the internal market, the Unfair Contract Terms Directive[10] provides the benchmark for all EU Member States to achieve a minimum level of protection in the area of unfair terms.

---

[4] See Micklitz et al. 2010, p. 280. In addition, new insights can be found in Cseres 2008; Faure and Luth 2011.

[5] Contract Law of the People's Republic of China (《中华人民共和国合同法》).

[6] See Articles 3–8 of the Contract Law 1999.

[7] See Han (韩世远) 2011, p. 35.

[8] Wilhelmsson 2011, pp. 573–574.

[9] See Nebbia 2010, pp. 220–226.

[10] Council Directive 93/13/EEC of 5 April 1993 on unfair terms in consumer contracts [1993] OJ L95/29.

In this chapter, the legislative rules and judicial practice with regard to unfair terms in consumer contracts in China and the EU are introduced. For EU law, the focus is on the Unfair Contract Terms Directive. Firstly, this chapter discusses the legislative framework and introduces the most important legal sources (Sect. 4.2). After that, several topics including applicable scope (Sect. 4.3), formal control (Sect. 4.4), substantive control (Sect. 4.5) and public mechanisms for controlling unfair terms (Sect. 4.6) are addressed. In each section, the description and analysis of Chinese and EU legislation and practice are addressed separately and followed by a comparison. Finally, some concluding remarks are provided (Sect. 4.7.1) and used to verify the hypotheses proposed in Chap. 1 (Sect. 4.7.2).

4.2 Legislative Framework and Technique

4.2.1 Chinese Law

In Chinese law, a variety of provisions address unfair standard terms. Article 5 of the Contract Law 1999[11] and Article 6 of the General Provisions of the Civil Law 2017[12] concerns the principle of fairness. Unfair terms in contracts are forbidden pursuant to this principle. It is not common to apply this article as the sole basis of a claim.[13] Rather, more specific articles in the Contract Law 1999 implement this principle and provide specific rules to realise the objective of this principle. Furthermore, the principle of equal value which is regulated by Article 4 of the General Principles of the Civil Law 1987[14] is implied in the principle of fairness.

In order to implement the principle of fairness mentioned above, Articles 53 and 54 of the Contract Law 1999, which deal with 'exemption clauses' and 'obviously unfair terms', lay down the general provisions which apply to all contracts, regardless of whether standard terms are used. In contrast, Articles 39, 40 and 41 are applicable only when standard terms are used. What should be noticed is that the Chinese legislator did not adopt a separate contract law for consumer contracts. The rules laid down in the Contract Law 1999 therefore apply to B2C contracts as well as B2B contracts.[15]

[11] Article 5 states: 'The parties shall abide by the principle of fairness in defining the rights and obligations of each party.'

[12] General Provisions of the Civil Law of the People's Republic of China (《中华人民共和国民法总则》).

[13] This means actors cannot find a basis of claim derived from this article itself. This could be observed not only through a practical perspective, but also the nature of these articles which manifests that there is no content concerning legal consequences if somebody violates the principle. If no specific rule could be found in later articles, the principles would become the articles with purely declarative function and it would turn law into 'a tiger without teeth'.

[14] General Principles of the Civil Law of the People's Republic of China (《中华人民共和国民法通则》).

[15] Some scholars who participated in the legislative process mention that the articles regulating

Apart from the Contract Law 1999, Article 26 of the Consumer Protection Law 2013[16] regulates unfair terms in consumer contracts. In this sense, the Consumer Protection Law 2013 is also an important source in addition to the Contract Law. In practice, these two statutes could be applied in combination in B2C cases, although the Consumer Protection Law 2013 is superior to the Contract Law 1999 if they regulate one and the same problem due to it being the special law (*Lex specialis derogat legi generali*).[17]

We can also find specific provisions dealing with unfair terms in some statutes dealing with specific types of consumer contracts, such as the Insurance Law 2015.[18] For example, Article 17 of the Insurance Law 2015 provides rules for insurance contracts that are entered into by using standard terms and Article 19 further regulates two specific types of invalid standard terms.

4.2.2 *EU Law*

4.2.2.1 Introduction

At the EU level, the Unfair Contract Terms Directive (93/13/EEC) harmonises the national rules on unfair terms in order to realise the function and objective provided by the TFEU. The Unfair Contract Terms Directive, unlike the national legislation dealing with unfair terms to protect the weaker party in the transaction, not only has the objective to protect consumers, it also aims to reinforce the internal market. Because of the EU's limited legislative competence, this directive has some constraints in the scope of application. It is only applied to non-individually negotiated terms in consumer contracts. In line with the common practice in the Member States, the Unfair Contract Terms Directive contains rules concerning both 'formal control' and 'substantive control'. This is further elaborated in the coming sections.

At the national level, German law provides most rules on standard terms in its Civil Code (*Bürgerliches Gesetzbuch*, hereinafter 'BGB'). English law used to rely on common law cases to control these terms and now put more emphasis on statutory law. In this section, an introduction to the structure and contents of the Unfair Contract Terms Directive is provided (Sect. 4.2.2.2). Then the relevant legislation and case law in German law and English law are briefly introduced (Sects. 4.2.2.3 and 4.2.2.4).

standard terms in the Contract Law are primarily designed to deal with unfair terms in B2C contracts. See Liang (梁慧星) 2000, pp. 25–26. See also Cui (崔建远) 2014, p. 48.

[16] Law of the People's Republic of China on the Protection of Consumer Rights and Interests (2013 Amendment) (《中华人民共和国消费者权益保护法(2013修正)》).

[17] See Han (韩世远) 2011, p. 734. See also Liang (梁慧星) 2002, pp. 211–212.

[18] Insurance Law of the People's Republic of China (2015 Amendment) (《中华人民共和国保险法(2015修正)》).

4.2.2.2 The Unfair Contract Terms Directive

Regarding the significance of the Unfair Contract Terms Directive under the topic of regulating unfair contract terms, it is said that the directive 'has established a contractual fairness principle for the whole European Union, at least in the field of consumer law.'[19] The Unfair Contract Terms Directive provides the EU with a common approach to the concept of 'fairness' to be implemented by all the Member States to achieve a common level of consumer protection.[20] Like other EU directives, the Unfair Contract Terms Directive only focuses on the result to be achieved. The actual method of implementation is left to be decided by the Member States when they transpose the Unfair Contract Terms Directive. During this process, some jurisdictions, such as the UK, were compelled to significantly adapt their national law to accommodate the directive. In 2011, the Unfair Contract Terms Directive was amended by the Consumer Rights Directive,[21] requiring further adaptation of national laws.[22]

The Unfair Contract Terms Directive comprises three parts: Recitals, Articles and an Annex. Based on the fact that most directives have the first two parts, the Annex provided by the Unfair Contract Terms Directive is of peculiarity in the sense of legislative technique.

The Unfair Contract Terms Directive has a part with 23 recitals to set out the statement of reasons for the directive. Besides the legislative reasons where the objectives and the most important concerns have been emphasised, some of the recitals providing specific reasons can be helpful to clarify and interpret the articles that follow.[23]

---

[19] Wilhelmsson 2011, p. 582.

[20] Nevertheless, there is also research pointing out that the Unfair Contract Terms Directive has an unfitting form for the goal it is supposed to reach – harmonising the law of unfair standard terms, and it should be ascribed to minimum harmonisation, no reference to self-regulation, the use of general clauses, the absence of a black list as well as a very heavy load of case law from the CJEU. The interpretation and application of key provisions depend to a great extent on national law. See Goanta 2016, p. 281.

[21] Directive 2011/83/EU of the European Parliament and of the Council of 25 October 2011 on consumer rights, amending Council Directive 93/13/EEC and Directive 1999/44/EC of the European Parliament and of the Council and repealing Council Directive 85/577/EEC and Directive 97/7/EC of the European Parliament and of the Council [2011] OJ L304/64.

[22] Article 32 of the Consumer Rights Directive reads: 'In Directive 93/13/EEC, the following Article is inserted: 'Article 8a/1. Where a Member State adopts provisions in accordance with Article 8, it shall inform the Commission thereof, as well as of any subsequent changes, in particular where those provisions: /–extend the unfairness assessment to individually negotiated contractual terms or to the adequacy of the price or remuneration; or, /–contain lists of contractual terms which shall be considered as unfair, /2. The Commission shall ensure that the information referred to in paragraph 1 is easily accessible to consumers and traders, inter alia, on a dedicated website. /3. The Commission shall forward the information referred to in paragraph 1 to the other Member States and the European Parliament. The Commission shall consult stake holders on that information.'

[23] One example is Recital 16 in terms of good faith. It is elaborated in Sect. 4.5 of this chapter. Another example is Recital 20 which offers the legality of Article 5 of clarity and contra proferen-

In the provisions, the main text of the directive provides the core elements of a fairness test at the EU level. Article 1 and Article 2 lay down the purpose of the directive and the relevant definitions. Article 3 elucidates the applicable scope and the specific criteria of the fairness test with two crucial elements: 'good faith' and 'significant imbalance'. Article 4 provides the conditions and terms subject to the fairness test. Article 5 lays down a requirement of clarity and a rule of interpretation *contra proferentem* (interpretation against the party who uses the standard terms). The consequences of unfair terms are stated in Article 6. Article 7 mentions that measures should be adopted to ensure the protection of the consumer's interest. Finally, Articles 8 to 11 regulate the issues related to harmonisation.

Besides the main text, an Annex is provided with an indicative and non-exhaustive list of unfair terms. In *Commission of the European Communities v Kingdom of Sweden*, the CJEU confirmed that the list in the Annex to the directive is an indicative one, which means 'a term appearing in the list need not necessarily be considered unfair and, conversely, a term that does not appear in the list may none the less be regarded as unfair'.[24] Thus, the list in the Annex is supposed to be a 'grey list'. It distinguishes itself from a 'black list', which means a term contained in the list is invalid in all circumstances without the possibility of evaluation.[25] Therefore, if a term corresponds to one of the model clauses in the Annex, it is still not automatically presumed to be unfair without any specific explanation. In practice, judges can assess the fairness of a term by reference to the Annex in conjunction with the abstract criteria in Article 3. What should be noted is that in the proposal of the Consumer Rights Directive a new division of black list and grey list was provided. But ultimately it was not adopted in the final version.[26]

4.2.2.3 German Law

In Germany, the issues with respect to standard terms had not been taken into consideration when the BGB was introduced. However, at the end of nineteenth century, the industrialisation of the production process led to an increased standardisation of contract terms in Germany.[27] Judges discovered that they have to deal with a new kind of contractual term which was not concluded on the grounds of the parties' voluntarily negotiation. Before the introduction of subsequent legislation, judges

tem. Recital 20 reads: 'Whereas contracts should be drafted in plain, intelligible language, the consumer should actually be given an opportunity to examine all the terms and, if in doubt, the interpretation most favourable to the consumer should prevail.'

[24] Case C-478/99 [2002] ECR I-4147, para. 20.

[25] See Smits 2014, p. 153. See also Markesinis et al. 2006, p. 167. Some scholars consider that the list in the Annex is neither a black list nor a grey list. They suggest that it is possible to distinguish so-called 'black lists' of absolutely unlawful clauses, 'grey lists' of clauses that are presumed to be unfair, from 'indicative lists' of clauses that may be unfair. See Micklitz et al. 2010, p. 291.

[26] See Annex II and III of the Proposal for a Directive of the European Parliament and of the Council on Consumer Rights, COM (2008) 614 final.

[27] See Markesinis et al. 2006, p. 164.

initially used the rules on immorality (§ 138 BGB), good faith (§ 242 BGB) and situations where the equitable discretion of courts could be exercised if one party was empowered to specify the performance unilaterally (§ 315 BGB) to dispose of unfair standard terms. Though all these articles provided the legitimacy for the courts to intervene in contractual relationships, it is mentioned that good faith was the most flexible and reliable basis.[28]

In 1976, Germany introduced the Act on General Conditions (or Standard Terms Act, *Gesetz zur Regelung des Rechts der Allgemeinen Geschäftsbedingungen*, hereinafter 'AGBG'). It provided rules on incorporation, surprising clauses and the rule of *contra proferentem*, as well as substantive rules which comprised a black list and a grey list. The AGBG served as a model for subsequent EC legislation (the Unfair Contract Terms Directive).[29] In 1996, the German legislator implemented and transposed the Unfair Contract Terms Directive into the AGBG. In Germany, the directive did not require too many amendments to the AGBG, because the directive itself was inspired, to some extent, by the AGBG. The sole changes include a re-definition of 'consumer contract', a re-formulation of the applicable scope and a requirement of transparency.[30] Later, in the German reform of the law of obligations (*Schuldrechtsreform)*, the core provisions in the AGBG were incorporated in the German Civil Code, in a separate chapter from § 305 to § 310. The regulations in terms of procedural rights and protection of consumers' rights and interests have been incorporated in the German Act on Injunctions for the Protection of Consumers' Interests (*Gesetz über Unterlassungsklagen bei Verbraucherrechts- und anderen Verstößen*, hereinafter 'UKlaG').

4.2.2.4 English Law

Regarding how English law deals with unfair contract terms, two stages can be observed: English law used to rely on common law cases to identify and control unfair terms, especially exemption clauses, and nowadays more emphasis is on the statutory law.

In English common law, the courts' attitude to the use of exemption clauses and the methods to control these clauses can be found in many important judgments. For example, in the Court of Appeal decision in *George Mitchell (Chesterhall) Ltd v Finney Lock Seeds Ltd*, Lord Denning said the following about the use of exemption clauses reflecting the courts' attitude: '(exemption clauses) were printed in small

---

[28] See Markesinis et al. 2006, p. 164.

[29] See Micklitz et al. 2010, p. 281.

[30] 'The main changes include a presumption that standard terms were to be regarded as having been presented by the trader unless they were introduced into the contract by the consumer (§24a Standard Terms Act). For B2C contracts the AGBG also applied even if the terms have been used only once, whereas the AGBG in general only applied to terms that are used several times. The requirement of transparency was only expressly included in 2000, with the reform of the law of obligations.' Micklitz et al. 2010, p. 287.

print on the back of tickets and order forms and invoices. (…) No one ever did object. He never read them or knew what was in them. (…) No freedom for the little man who took the ticket or order form or invoice. The big concern said, "Take it or leave it". The little man had no option but to take it. The big concern could and did exempt itself from liability in its own interest without regard to the little man. …It was a bleak winter for our law of contract. (…) Faced with this abuse of power – by the strong against the weak – by the use of the small print of the conditions – the judges did what they could to put a curb on it.'[31] In terms of the specific methods to control these terms, for example, Lord Denning defined the famous 'red hand rule' in *Spurling Ltd v Bradshaw*,[32] which is further introduced in Sect. 4.4.3.3.1 of this chapter.

At the statutory level, the Unfair Contract Terms Act was introduced in 1977 (hereinafter 'UCTA 1977'). On the grounds of this legislation, whether the exemption clauses are enforceable or not depends on an assessment of reasonableness. Although the applicable scope of the UCTA 1977 is not limited to consumer contracts, there is still 'a clear policy distinction in the decisions between the operation of clauses in the commercial and consumer contexts'.[33] In order to implement the Unfair Contract Terms Directive on the national level, a new statutory instrument was adopted: the Unfair Terms in Consumer Contracts Regulations 1994, later replaced by the 1999 Regulations (hereinafter 'UTCCR 1999'). The text of the Regulations is rather close to the text of the directive. However, the Unfair Contract Terms Act 1977 was not repealed, hence in the UK both instruments operated alongside each other until the Consumer Rights Act 2015 (hereinafter 'CRA 2015'). The CRA 2015 integrates and develops the law regarding consumer protection and consumer rights, and consolidates consumer contract law into one single act. In the area of unfair terms, it replaces the UCTA and the UTCCR in the area of B2C contracts. It provides, for example, a rule requiring that the key terms need to be 'prominent and transparent',[34] and there is a new grey list mentioning several new categories of terms that are likely to be considered unfair.[35] However, the CRA 2015 only applies to contracts entered into after 1 October 2015. If a consumer entered into a contract before that date, the contract will still be governed by the UTCCR 1999. Besides, the UCTA 1977 continues to remain in force for B2B contracts. Thus, in order to obtain a more comprehensive understanding of the English rules on unfair terms, the UCTA 1977 and the UTCCR 1999 are still introduced in this chapter.

---

[31] George Mitchell (Chesterhall) Ltd. v Finney Lock Seeds Ltd. [1983] 2 A.C. 803. Quoted in Markesinis et al. 2006, pp. 166–167.

[32] Spurling Ltd. v Bradshaw [1956] 1 W.L.R. 461.

[33] Poole 2012, p. 229.

[34] See Sect. 4.4.3.3 of this chapter.

[35] See Sect. 4.5.3.3 of this chapter.

4.3 Applicable Scope

4.3.1 Introduction

The rules concerning unfair terms are not applied to all contracts. Legislators usually take two aspects into account to set the scope of application: the nature of the contracting party and the nature of the term. The former aspect addresses whether there is a weaker party in need of special protection, and the latter aspect focuses on whether the term is drafted on the basis of individual negotiation. Some scholars discuss the issues relevant to the former aspect under the topic of 'subjective scope of application', and the latter under the topic of 'objective scope of application'.[36] This study also uses these concepts to discuss the relevant issues.

For the subjective scope of application, the following question needs to be answered: who is protected under the rules on unfair terms in Chinese, EU, German and English law. Although it is very common to establish a mechanism with special rules preventing unfair terms from being used in consumer contracts, not all of these provisions are only applicable to the specific situation of consumer contracts. Depending on the jurisdiction, a consumer may claim that a contractual term is unfair on the grounds of both a provision which is applicable to all types of contract and a provision which is only applicable to consumer contracts. Taking the different legal strategies and approaches adopted for different types of contracts into account, the distinction between general rules and rules aimed only at consumer contracts is instrumental to understanding the substance of the rules better.

For the objective scope of application, two questions need to be answered. The first is 'what type of contract terms by their nature are subject to control' and the second is 'within these terms, are there any exceptions'. The first question has been raised because not all terms should be examined. Even if it is believed that the consumer should be provided with increased protection, economic efficiency would be weakened and sacrificed if the validity of every consumer contract term could be challenged. The law needs to identify the kind of contract terms that can be challenged. This is necessary because some contract terms are prepared in advance whereas others are the result of negotiation. With respect to the former type, some terms are prepared for repeatable use and others are made for one-off use. Also, contracting parties sometimes could adapt the substantive contents of standard terms through subsequent negotiation and sometimes they have no choice but to take it or leave it. Thus, it is necessary to find out, within all these types of contract terms and situations, which are subject to control. The second question is about the specific content of contracts. In this regard, the focus is on the details of terms. It is not always the case that all contract terms which fall into the previously mentioned group are subject to the fairness test. Therefore, even if terms are by their nature examinable, there are still some exceptions.

---

[36] See Nebbia 2007, pp. 69–134.

In this section, the relevant rules in the Chinese statutes, the Unfair Contract Terms Directive, the BGB and English legislation are introduced (Sects. 4.3.2 and 4.3.3) and subsequently compared (Sect. 4.3.4).

4.3.2 Chinese Law

4.3.2.1 Subjective Scope of Application

In China, the most important sources in the context of consumer contracts are the Contract Law 1999 and the Consumer Protection Law 2013. As previously mentioned, in the Contract Law 1999, Article 53 deals with exemption clauses and Article 54 states that obviously unfair contracts are voidable. In addition, there are also three articles (Articles 39–41) dealing with standard terms in particular. In the Consumer Protection Law 2013, Article 26 lays down the duty to draw attention to terms and the fairness control when standard terms are used.

There is no limitation in the scope of application of the articles in the Contract Law 1999. They are applicable to all types of contract, irrespective of whether it is a B2B contract, a B2C contract, or a contract between two individuals. For example, the content of a contract cannot violate the mandatory provisions of laws and administrative regulations,[37] and under Article 54, any obviously unfair term is voidable,[38] no matter whether the contract is concluded by a trader and a consumer or two businesses. This means that not only could a consumer claim a contract term is obviously unfair and voidable in accordance with Article 54, but a business actor could as well. It is the same case in the application of Article 53 and Articles 39, 40 and 41 concerning standard terms.[39]

In contrast, Article 26 of the Consumer Protection Law 2013 is only applicable to consumer contracts. It can be easily observed from the formulation of the article that the two parties concerned are a business operator and a consumer. The legislator has specifically regulated the issue of standard terms, due to the imbalance of information between the business operator and the consumer who was already in an unfavourable position during the negotiation and which has become more severe due to the increased use of long and obscure standard terms.[40]

---

[37] See Article 52, item (5) of the Contract Law 1999.

[38] See Article 54, item (2) of the Contract Law 1999.

[39] For the type of individual contracts, it would be questioned whether a non-business individual is regulated by Articles 39–41. It should be noticed that the word used in the Contract Law is the ‘supplier’ of the standard terms. This means the fairness test only focuses on the use of standard terms itself regardless of whether the supplier made the term himself or whether he is a business operator. Therefore, even if the contracting party is an individual dealing without his trade, business or profession, he is still requested to fulfil the obligations required by the law where standard terms are used in concluding a contract.

[40] See Jia (贾东明) 2013, p. 112.

In addition to the Contract Law 1999 and the Consumer Protection Law 2013, there are also some special statutes dealing with unfair terms in special areas, such as the Insurance Law 2015.[41] In these statutes, the subjective scope of application depends on the legal relationship concerned. For example, the insured can claim that a term exempting the insurer from a statutory obligation is void pursuant to Article 19 of the Insurance Law 2015.

4.3.2.2 Objective Scope of Application

As aforementioned, the Chinese Contract Law 1999 provides the basic requirements for all contracts. Therefore, in principle, all contract terms are subject to the provisions, no matter how they are drafted or concluded. However, there are still provisions that are only applicable to certain types of contract terms. Specifically, the scope of Article 53 is restricted to two types of exemption clauses, and the scope of Articles 39–41 is restricted to 'standard terms'. In the new Chinese Consumer Protection Law 2013, the phrase 'standard terms' has also been adopted to substitute the previous phrase 'standard contracts' (Article 26) in regulating unfair terms. Furthermore, some specific provisions on 'standard clauses' have been laid down in the specific statutes, such as Article 19 of the Insurance Law 2015.[42]

On the basis of this description, it is not difficult to observe that Chinese legislation focuses on the 'standard terms'. Pursuant to the second paragraph of Article 39 of the Contract Law 1999, 'standard terms' are terms which are prepared in advance for general and repeatable use by one party and which are not negotiated with the other party in concluding a contract. In the previous legislation, the Chinese Consumer Protection Law 1993,[43] the legislator employed the phrase '*geshi hetong*' ('格式合同', which literally means 'standard contracts') in Article 24, but not '*geshi tiaokuan*' ('格式条款', which literally means 'standard terms'). Haopeng Su suggests that the phrase 'standard contracts' is not precise enough, because a contract could be constituted by only standard terms, whereas it is also possible that the terms in a contract are composed of both standard terms and non-standard terms.[44] If the phrase of 'standard contracts' is adopted, the previously mentioned second type of contract which contains both standard terms and non-standard terms may escape control. However, the standard terms part should be subjected to the fairness test. Therefore, the Contract Law 1999 uses the phrase 'standard terms' instead.

---

[41] See Articles 17 and 19 of the Insurance Law 2015.

[42] Article 19 of The Insurance Law 2015 provides: 'The following clauses in an insurance contract using the standard clauses of the insurer shall be null and void: (1) A clause exempting the insurer from any legal obligation or aggravating the liability of the insurance applicant or insurant; and (2) A clause excluding any legal right of the insurance applicant, insurant or beneficiary.'

[43] Law of the People's Republic of China on the Protection of Consumer Rights and Interests (《中华人民共和国消费者权益保护法》).

[44] See Su (苏号朋) 2004, p. 187.

This means, regardless of the type of the contract, as long as there are standard terms in the contracts, Articles 39–41 are applicable.

In the new Chinese Consumer Protection Law 2013, the phrase ‘standard contracts’ has been changed as well to maintain the consistency with the Contract Law 1999. On the grounds of the understanding given by the Research Office of the Legislative Affairs Commission of the Standing Committee of the National People’s Congress, ‘standard terms’ are terms which have been prepared in advance for the purpose of repeatable use without individual negotiation during the process of concluding the contract.[45] This definition is consistent with the one provided by the Contract Law 1999.

To determine whether a term is a standard term or not, Chinese scholars offer some further discussion other than the criteria given by law. Haopeng Su considers that ‘for the purpose of repeatable use’ solely refers to the intention of the provider of the standard terms. This means even if the term is applied for the first time the consumer can still claim that it is a standard term only if the other requirements, such as there is no individual negotiation during the conclusion of the contract, have been met.[46] Liming Wang argues that it is too rigorous for the other party to prove the fact that the terms were reused.[47]

Nevertheless, it is suggested that standard terms do not have to be examined on every occasion. Although the Contract Law 1999 and Consumer Protection Law 2013 have not provided explicit rules on this, scholars still enumerate several conditions under which it is not necessary to test standard terms. According to Haopeng Su, if the provider of standard terms just directly incorporates the law and administrative regulation, the relevant terms will escape examination. In addition, the same is true where an administrative organ has already examined the standard terms.[48] In contrast, it is said that the terms should be examined, even though they incorporate administrative regulations, if they only reflect the interest of the government.[49]

Apart from standard terms, pursuant to Article 26(2) of the Consumer Protection Law 2013, notices, announcements and entrance hall bulletins need to be examined as well. In some special areas such as food and recreation services, another concept describing unfair standard terms, ‘*Bawang Tiaokuan*’ (‘霸王条款’, which literally means ‘hegemon clauses’), is adopted. This is not a legal concept but it is widely used in news, reports and documents published by the government. In practice, the best examples of this kind of clause are notices stating ‘customers are not allowed to BYO (bring your own)’ and ‘invoices will not be provided if customers bring their own food and drinks’ posted in halls of restaurants. As hegemon clauses are also standard terms, the test of fairness provided for standard terms can be also applied in this context.

[45] See Jia (贾东明) 2013, p. 112.
[46] See Su (苏号朋) 2004, pp. 151–152.
[47] See Wang (王利明) 2002a, p. 380.
[48] See Su (苏号朋) 2004, pp. 301–302.
[49] See Hu (胡康生) 2013, p. 79.

4.3.3 *EU Law*

4.3.3.1 The Unfair Contract Terms Directive

4.3.3.1.1 Subjective Scope of Application

On the EU level, due to the restriction of the EU legislative competence in this area, the Unfair Contract Terms Directive (93/13/EEC) focuses on consumer contracts. Pursuant to Article 1 of the directive, its purpose is 'to approximate the laws, regulations and administrative provisions of the Member States relating to unfair terms in contracts concluded between a seller or supplier and a consumer'. Apparently, the applicable scope here only includes consumer contracts.

Article 2 of the Unfair Contract Terms Directive follows the general approach adopted in most EU legislation in this field and provides that 'consumer' refers to any natural person who is acting outside his trade, business or profession. Although this chapter does not discuss the definition of consumer in depth,[50] it is still noteworthy that the directive has provided a definition of the concept itself.

In its case law, the CJEU sometimes clarifies that the directive applies to some specific types of contract. For example, in *Dirk Frederik Asbeek Brusse, Katarina de Man Garabito v Jahani BV*, it was pointed out that a residential tenancy agreement concluded between a professional landlord and a consumer should be covered by the directive.[51] In the same case, the CJEU also clarified that, even if a Member State did not use a general term to identify the consumer but only mentioned the 'seller' (e.g., '*verkoper*', the Dutch version of Article 1(1) of the directive), it should never prevent the directive from applying to no sale contracts.[52]

4.3.3.1.2 Objective Scope of Application

In accordance with the Unfair Contract Terms Directive, the objective scope of application is determined by three elements.

Firstly, the provisions of directive are only applicable to non-individually negotiated terms.[53] What is considerably noteworthy is that the phrase 'non-individually negotiated terms' is broader than 'standard terms' because non-individually negotiated terms which have been drafted in advance for a one-off transaction are included

---

[50] See Chap. 3, Sect. 3.3 of this study.

[51] See Case C-488/11 [2013] ECLI:EU:C:2013:341.

[52] See Case C-488/11 [2013] ECLI:EU:C:2013:341, paras. 23–34.

[53] During the preparation of this directive, the applicable scope was not limited to the non-individually negotiated terms but cover all contracts regardless of whether they are concluded by standard forms or individual negotiation. See Proposal for a Council Directive on unfair terms in consumer contracts, COM(90) 322 final, Article 2. However, it was criticised that the fairness control of individually negotiated contracts was in conflict with private autonomy and the functioning of the market economy. See Brandner and Ulmer 1991, pp. 652–653.

within the scope of the former but not the latter (Article 3(1)).[54] Article 3(2) states that the determination of whether the term is not individually negotiated will depend on whether the consumer is able to influence the substance of the term. Meanwhile, this directive is still applicable to a pre-formulated standard contract from a general view even though certain aspects of a term or one specific term have been individually negotiated. On these grounds, the phrase 'standard term' will still determine the objective scope of application. Besides, not only written pre-formulated contracts but also oral pre-formulated contracts fall within the scope of application.[55] What should be noticed is that, in line with Article 3(2), where any seller or supplier claims that a standard term has been individually negotiated, the burden of proof in this respect will be imposed on him.[56]

Secondly, the fairness test of this directive is not applicable to terms describing the main subject matter of the contract or the quality/price ratio of the goods or services supplied. But in assessing the fairness of terms, the two elements mentioned are still taken into account. Recital 19 of the directive provides a good example in relation to insurance. It states that 'the terms which clearly define or circumscribe the insured risk and the insurer's liability shall not be subject to such assessment since these restrictions are taken into account in calculating the premium paid by the consumer.'[57] As a result, Article 4 has confirmed the viewpoint in Recital 19 and emphasised that 'assessment of the unfair nature of the terms shall relate neither to the definition of the main subject matter of the contract nor to the adequacy of the price and remuneration, on the one hand, as against the services or goods supplied in exchange, or on the other, in so far as these terms are in plain intelligible language'.[58] This principle indicates that the Unfair Contract Terms

[54] It is noteworthy that the regulating mode adopted by the EU was not the same as its Member States when it was introduced. There were at least three modes to regulate the unfair terms from a comparative perspective: the first one is a 'standard terms mode'. The law focuses on the approach to concluding contracts because of the disparity in the transactional parties. This means the terms of contracts will be judged through the fairness test as long as they adopt the formation of standard terms, irrespective of the distinction between B2B and B2C contracts. This mode has been adopted by German law (German mode). The second one is a 'consumer contracts mode', where the law put more emphasis on the actors which came into the contractual relationship, in the light of the consumers' unfavourable position in bargaining power, information and knowledge. French consumer law is the representative of this method whose rationale is more about weaker party protection (French mode). The third mode is a combination of these two modes above. The English Unfair Contract Terms Act adopts this mode.

[55] This is on the basis of the Recital 11 of the Unfair Contract Terms Directive: 'Whereas the consumer must receive equal protection under contracts concluded by word of mouth and written contracts regardless, in the latter case, of whether the terms of the contract are contained in one or more documents.'

[56] See the last paragraph of Article 3(2).

[57] See Recital 19 of the Unfair Contract Terms Directive.

[58] See Article 4(2) of the Unfair Contract Terms Directive. Article 4(1) reads: 'Without prejudice to Article 7, the unfairness of a contractual term shall be assessed, taking into account the nature of the goods or services for which the contract was concluded and by referring, at the time of conclusion of the contract, to all the circumstances attending the conclusion of the contract and to all the other terms of the contract or of another contract on which it is dependent.'

Directive does not aim to regulate the core of the contractual relationship otherwise the parties' contractual freedom would be infringed.[59] In other words, the price/quality ratio itself is exempted from the fairness assessment although it may be taken into account in assessing the fairness of the other terms.

Thirdly, on the grounds of Article 1(2), 'The contractual terms which reflect mandatory statutory or regulatory provisions and the provisions or principles of international conventions to which the Member States or the Community are party, particularly in the transport area, shall not be subject to the provisions of this Directive.' Nebbia explains that 'the rationale for this provision is that statutory or regulatory provisions usually establish solutions which the legislator has considered to be the most equitable ones.'[60]

4.3.3.2 German Law

4.3.3.2.1 Subjective Scope of Application

Within the context of the German Civil Code, from § 305 to § 310 BGB, most provisions are applicable to all contracts. Only § 310(3) BGB provides some special rules for B2C contracts. This is further discussed in the following section.

4.3.3.2.2 Objective Scope of Application

The German Civil Code focuses on 'standard terms'. § 305(1) BGB states that standard terms are all contractual terms pre-formulated for more than two contracts which one party to the contract (the user) presents to the other party upon entering into the contract. It is clarified that contract terms are not standard business terms if they have been negotiated in detail between the parties. This means the standard terms have to be non-individually negotiated. In the context of consumer contracts, § 310(3) extends the applicable scope from terms intended for repeatable use to terms intended for one-off trade. However, this is only applicable when the consumer, by reason of pre-formulation, had no influence on their contents. Besides, if terms of a third party are used, such terms are imputed to the user as well on the grounds that 'all standard terms are attributed to the dealer if the consumer did not put them forward'.[61]

§ 305(a) BGB regulates some special cases related to public service, where standard terms can be incorporated if the other party agrees to their application even without compliance with requirements mentioned in § 305(2), such as the

---

[59] This principle is derived from German law and it was introduced at the end of the preparatory stage. See Nebbia 2010, p. 219.

[60] Nebbia 2010, p. 220.

[61] Markesinis et al. 2006, p. 172.

requirement on referring to the other party to the standard terms explicitly.[62] § 310(3) BGB regulates that the standard terms are deemed to be provided by the user, unless they were introduced into the contract by the consumer. On the basis of this, it is envisaged that the consumer could also be the provider of the standard terms, but in that case the fairness control provided by § 307 BGB is not applicable.

To sum up, the objective scope of application in German law is rather complicated and detailed.

4.3.3.3 English Law

4.3.3.3.1 Subjective Scope of Application

Under English Law, the starting point is the UCTA 1977 which focuses on exemption and limitation clauses. Since the adoption of the CRA 2015, the protective scope of the UCTA 1977 is now limited to B2B contracts.

The UTCCR 1999, which implemented the Unfair Contract Terms Directive, applies to contracts concluded between a consumer and a seller or supplier who is acting for purposes relating to his trade, business or profession, which is exactly the same as the directive. It has now been replaced by the CRA 2015.

Part 2 of the CRA 2015 provides the rules protecting consumers against unfair terms. As the title of the act reveals, its Section 61 clearly states that 'This Part applies to a contract between a trader and a consumer'. The definition of 'trader' and 'consumer' remain mostly the same as the UTCCR. Nevertheless, it should be noted that the concept of 'consumer' has changed slightly. It is explicitly mentioned that, not only individuals acting for purposes 'wholly' outside their trade, etc., but also an individual acting for purposes that are 'mainly' outside that individual's trade, business, craft or profession shall be deemed a 'consumer'.[63]

---

[62] § 305(a) BGB provides: 'Even without compliance with the requirements cited in § 305(2) nos. 1 and 2, if the other party to the contract agrees to their applying the following are incorporated, /1. the tariffs and regulations of the railways issued with the approval of the competent transport authority or on the basis of international conventions, and the terms of transport approved under the Passenger Transport Act, of trams, trolley buses and motor vehicles in regular public transport services, /2. the standard business terms published in the gazette of the Federal Network Agency for Electricity, Gas, Telecommunications, Post and Railway and kept available on the business premises of the user, /a) into transport contracts entered into off business premises by the posting of items in postboxes, /b)into contracts on telecommunications, information services and other services that are provided direct by the use of distance communication and at one time and without interruption during the supply of a telecommunications service, if it is disproportionately difficult to make the standard business terms available to the other party before the contract is entered into.'

[63] See Section 2(3) CRA 2015.

4.3.3.3.2 Objective Scope of Application

In the context of the UCTA 1977, the courts are not entitled to simply strike out any unreasonable or unfair term in B2B contracts. The regulatory target is the exemption clause, including both clauses excluding and limiting liabilities. Section 13 provides that exemption clauses refer to the terms which make the liability or its enforcement subject to restrictive or onerous conditions; exclude or restrict any right or remedy in respect of liability, or subject a person to any prejudice in consequence of his pursuing any such right or remedy; exclude or restrict rules of evidence or procedure. Section 3 deals on the other's written standard terms of business. Sections 2 and 5 to 7 also prevent excluding or restricting liability by reference to terms and notices which exclude or restrict the relevant obligation or duty. With regard to the clauses which are not targeted, Section 13(2) provides that arbitration clauses are not to be treated as excluding or limiting liability.[64]

In practice, the Court of Appeal held that a contract term which includes a prohibition on a payment or credit being set off against the price claimed is *prima facie* unreasonable. This means this type of term falls within the ambit of the UCTA 1977.[65] The contract clause which 'purports to modify the expected contractual obligation or duty' also falls under the scope of the UCTA 1977.[66]

In terms of the scope of the UTCCR 1999, Regulation 5 refers to non-individually negotiated terms,[67] which follows the approach adopted by the Unfair Contract Terms Directive. As regards the description of 'non-individually negotiated terms', Regulation 5(2) reads: 'A term shall always be regarded as not having been individually negotiated where it has been drafted in advance and the consumer has therefore not been able to influence the substance of the term.' In addition, Regulation 6(2) UTCCR provides that the assessment of fairness shall not relate to the adequacy of the price or remuneration, as against the goods or services supplied in exchange. It also complies with the directive.[68] However, Regulation 6(2) shall be interpreted in a restrictive way. The case *Bairstow Eves London Central Ltd v Smith*[69] is a good example to show how the evaluation works in practice. The term which provided for a commission rate of 3% was a default provision which only came into play if the client failed to pay the 1.5% commission within 10 days. This led to the consequence that the term that made provision for a commission rate of 3% fell under the scope of the UTCCR and was not a clause which regulated the price to be paid for the estate agents' services.

---

[64] To be specific, see Poole 2012, pp. 242–243

[65] See Stewart Gill Ltd. v Horatio Myer and Co Ltd. [1992] Q.B. 600.

[66] See Poole 2012, p. 242. Smith v Eric S Bush [1990] 1 A.C. 831.

[67] Regulation 5(1) states: 'A contractual term which has not been individually negotiated shall be regarded as unfair if, contrary to the requirement of good faith, it causes a significant imbalance in the parties' rights and obligations arising under the contract, to the detriment of the consumer.'

[68] For further discussion, see Twigg-Flesner 2007, pp. 9–10.

[69] Bairstow Eves London Central Ltd. v Smith [2004] EWHC 263 (QB).

In the new CRA 2015, the rules on unfair terms apply to all consumer contracts. It therefore does not matter whether 'standard terms' or 'non-individually negotiated terms' are regulated. With respect to the applicable scope, it does not distinguish between negotiated and non-negotiated contracts.[70] This is different from the UTCCR and extends the applicable scope which is set by the EU directive. As it has been suggested in academic works,[71] Section 61(4) CRA 2015 extends the assessment of fairness to the notice if it relates to rights or obligations as between a trader and a consumer, or purports to exclude or restrict a trader's liability to a consumer.[72] Furthermore, the aforementioned notice does not have to be in writing, but includes an announcement or any other communication or purported communication as long as it is reasonable to assume it is intended to be seen or heard by a consumer.[73] Still, the core terms that 'specify the main subject matter of the contract' or regarding the 'appropriateness of the price payable under the contract by comparison with the goods, digital content or services supplied under it' may not be assessed for fairness, as long as they are transparent and prominent.[74] And the terms and notices which reflect the mandatory statutory or regulatory provisions or the provisions or principles of an international convention to which the UK or the EU is a party need not necessarily be assessed as well.[75]

4.3.4 Comparative Review

With respect to the question of the subjective scope of application, the rules in Chinese Contract Law 1999 (Articles 39–41, 53, 54) are applicable to all contracts irrespective of a distinction between a consumer contract and a non-consumer contract. Meanwhile the Consumer Protection Law 2013 (Article 26) provides a special rule in the area of consumer contracts, although the contents are not very different from the version regulated by the Contract Law 1999.

In the EU, the Unfair Contract Terms Directive (Article 1) is only applicable to a contractual relationship where one party is a consumer and the counterparty is a professional seller or supplier. At the national level, both German law (§§ 305–310 BGB) and English Law (UCTA 1977) have general provisions which are applicable to all circumstances, and special provisions (§ 310(3) BGB and CRA 2015) that are applicable specifically where a person is a consumer or 'dealing as a consumer'.

---

[70] See Section 61.

[71] For example, Twigg-Flesner mentions that 'where no written contract is used, but reference to the terms of a contract is made by notice, these terms will be incorporated into the contract if the notice given to the contracting party was reasonable.' Twigg-Flesner 2007, p. 2.

[72] See Section 61(4) CRA 2015.

[73] See Sections 61(8) and 61(6) CRA 2015.

[74] See Section 64(1) and (2) CRA 2015.

[75] See Section 73(1) CRA 2015.

In comparison, it is not difficult to find that both Chinese and European legislators tend to design a 'double-decker structure' to regulate unfair terms. Except that at the EU level the legislators have no competence to touch the general contract law rules, both German law and English law have their basic rules for all contracts and special rules for consumer contracts. It can be observed that the threshold is higher under the general rules, whereas the special rules provide a lower threshold in the case of consumer transaction. This design implies the value of the protection of the weaker party.

With respect to the objective scope of application, it can be observed that the Unfair Contract Terms Directive is only applicable to 'non-individually negotiated terms' as the minimum requirement of consumer protection (Article 3(1)). This means in European law, as long as it is not individually negotiated by the contracting parties, a contract term is subject to examination under the rules provided by the directive on unfair terms implemented in national legislation. As noted earlier, 'individual negotiation' does not demand that parties together and have a real talk. The assessment will depend on whether the consumer is able to influence the substance of the term (Article 3(2)). In national jurisdictions, the UCTA 1977 of English law provides the rules on exemption clauses in B2B contracts and the UTCCR 1999 followed the directive to regulate non-individually negotiated terms. The new CRA 2015, however, has extended the applicable scope of the terms that need to be assessed for fairness to a broader sense including all consumer contracts. German law employs the phrase 'standard terms' but the focus is on 'non-individually negotiated' terms.

In China, all consumer contract terms have to be examined under the general articles with respect to fairness of the Contract Law 1999 (Article 54), but only standard terms can be examined by a special test regulated by Articles 39–41 of the Contract Law 1999 and Article 26 of the new Consumer Protection Law.[76] Pursuant to the new Consumer Protection Law 2013, besides the standard terms, it is also forbidden to include unfair contents in notices, announcements and entrance hall bulletins. Within the context of Chinese Contract Law 1999, standard terms refer to contract terms which were prepared in advance for the purpose of repeatable use and which were not negotiated with the other party (Article 39(2)).

Comparing the two strategies mentioned above, it is apparent that the legislators, both in EU and China, focus on non-individually negotiated terms. This criterion is the core of the EU directive as well as the main standard to determine whether a term is a standard term in Chinese law. However, the perspectives of these two approaches are still considerably different.

In the EU directive, the lack of individual negotiation is the sole requirement for the term to be assessed, while in China there is a superordinate concept called 'standard terms'. Within the Chinese context, it is insufficient for a term to be examined

[76] What is noteworthy is that the first paragraph of Article 26 of the Consumer Protection Law provides that business operators shall remind consumers to pay attention to any terms and conditions which are vital to the interests of consumers. This rule of formal control does not involve any limitation in respect to core or price/ratio terms. For further details, see Sect. 4.5 of this chapter.

if it is only not individually negotiated. There is another requirement that it should be prepared in advance for the purpose of repeatable use – it is only one requirement but not two because it is obvious that 'prepared in advance' is the precondition of 'for repeatable use'. As a result of this, if a term was made for a one-off trade but it was not individually negotiated, it is appropriate to assess it under the EU rules but it is not sufficient to examine it within the context of Chinese consumer law. Chinese scholars often criticise that the requirement of repeatable use is not necessary. Within the context of German law, the BGB explicitly states that the provisions are able to apply to one-off trades, and the English CRA 2015 applies to all consumer contracts.

Regarding the specific assessment of 'non-individually negotiated' terms, the EU directive clarifies that a 'non-individually negotiated' term refers to the situation where the consumer could not influence the substance of the term. The underlying Chinese legislative intention of the requirement of being prepared in advance is considerably similar since it focuses on whether the consumer could participate in the process of contract formation. It is rather likely that the parties' autonomy would be affected because only one party's will could be included. Compared with the approach adopted by the EU directive, the formulation provided by the Chinese Contract Law 1999 is more tortuous in pursuing the legislative aim. The Chinese criteria would have been more facilitative in practice if 'made in advance for the purpose of repeatable use' were the sole requirement for a standard term: it would be much easier to decide whether a term is made in advance for the purpose of repeatable use than to find out whether the consumer has influenced the substance of the term. As a matter of fact, it is still necessary for the Chinese judges to determine whether a term is individually negotiated.

Besides, the Chinese Consumer Protection Law 2013 also provides that the other three types of texts – notices, announcements and entrance hall bulletins – should be examined under the fairness test even if they are not always included in written contracts. Since the substance of these texts are also binding and imposes material rights and obligations on consumers, this enumeration is important since it points out the types of documents that are similar to standard terms. This specific elaboration can also be observed in English law.

To sum up, in terms of the protective scope in light of the nature of the terms, the scope regulated by the EU directive is broader than regulated by Chinese law because the non-individually negotiated terms being prepared for a one-off trade are also included, and English law is even broader since it applies also to individually negotiated terms. Chinese law provides an enumeration which clarifies that the texts supplied by business operators which are similar to standard terms in nature should also be placed under the unfairness test. And the specific criterion to determine whether a term is 'non-individually negotiated' is particular in EU Law.

Concerning the question about exceptions, the rule mentioned in the Unfair Contract Terms Directive that the fairness control is not applicable to terms concerning the description of the main subject matter of the contract or the quality/price ratio of the goods or services supplied is an obvious feature (Article 4(2)).

In the Chinese context, there is no such provision in either the Contract Law 1999, the Consumer Protection Law 2013, the Insurance Law 2015 or other legislation. This means that it is possible for a consumer to claim that a contract is voidable just because the price is too high on the grounds of Article 54 of the Contract Law 1999, although, as will be seen in Section 5, this kind of case is rarely seen in practice. In addition, pursuant to Article 40 and its interpretation, a contract term will be deemed to be void if it exempts the supplier from its liabilities, increases the liabilities of the other party, or deprives the material rights of the other party. Article 26(2) of the new Consumer Protection Law 2013 also follows the wording of the Contract Law 1999. Therefore, a standard contract term is very likely to be examined even if it is a 'core term', because in Article 40 it is provided that whether a standard term is fair or not sometimes depends on an examination of main obligations and rights.

As a result, although there is a concern in Europe that freedom of contract would be infringed upon if the legislation intervened too much, it seems the Chinese legislator still considers control of substantive fairness as a high priority.

Apart from this, both in the Unfair Contract Terms Directive, the BGB and the CRA 2015 we can find an exception with regard to terms which were directly incorporated from mandatory statute, regulation, convention etc. Although there are Chinese scholars who argue that Chinese law should also put such an exception in Chinese legislation, similar provisions cannot be found in the statutes, even if in the latest Consumer Protection Law 2013 (Table 4.1).

4.4 Formal Control

4.4.1 Introduction

The methods applied to control standard terms can be divided into two categories: formal control which focuses on whether a real consent exists and how to establish the actual meaning of the term, and substantive control which focuses on the substantive distribution of rights and obligations. This section addresses the issues relevant to formal control. It includes the rules which 'do not involve a direct assessment of the substance of contractual terms, but rather compliance with certain general, formal, requirements for their validity and enforceability'.[77]

Generally speaking, the binding force of the contractual terms is based on the consent of the parties, but in the case of standard terms or non-individually negotiated terms, the situation is rather different, since the consent of the consumer here is rather weak due to the lack of negotiation. This is known as the 'incorporation problem'.[78] In addition, the text of the contract will require interpretation. When the

---

[77] Nebbia 2007, p. 45.

[78] To a Chinese leading scholar of civil law, Jianyuan Cui, this is 'due to the reason that some standard terms are not printed along with the other parts of the contract, some are elevated in the business premises and some are too complex for the consumers to understand.' Cui (崔建远) 2008, pp. 142–143.

Table 4.1 Applicable scope

	General rules	Consumer contracts	Types of terms and their definition	Exceptions
Chinese Contract Law	Articles 39, 40, 41		Standard terms (Articles 39–41)	
	Articles 53, 54		Definition:	
			(1) Being prepared in advance for the purpose of repeatable use;	
			(2) Non-individually negotiated (Article 39(2))	
Chinese Consumer Protection Law		Article 26	Standard terms (Article 26)	
			Notices, announcements, entrance hall bulletins (Article 26)	
EU Unfair Contract Terms Directive		The whole directive	Non-individually negotiated terms (Article 3(1))	Core terms (Article 4(2))
			Definition:	Article 1(2)
			Consumer is unable to influence the substance of the term (Article 3(2))	
German Law	§§ 305–310	§ 310(3)	Standard terms (§ 305(1))	§ 305a (incorporation)
			Definition:	§ 310(3) (fairness test)
			(1) Non-individually negotiated (§ 305(1))	
			(2) Also applied to the pre-formulated terms for one-off trade to the extent that the consumer has no influence on that term (§ 310(3))	
English Law	UCTA 1977 (now only applies to B2B)	UTCCR 1999 (now CRA 2015)	All consumer contracts (Section 61 CRA 2015)	Core terms (Section 64 CRA 2015)
			Exemption clauses (UCTA 1977, now only applies to B2B)	
			Notices (Section 61(4) CRA 2015)	

parties, or the judge, have to interpret the actual meaning, they start from the text and generally apply a textual approach to interpretation. In many jurisdictions, it is suggested that interpreters are allowed to apply other interpretative approaches only if there are more than two ways to interpret the text.[79] However, with standard terms, the language used may be vague or biased, which leads to an 'interpretation problem'.

[79] This is further discussed in the following sections.

Thus, this section tries to answer two questions. Firstly, 'is a consumer bound if he is not acquainted with a contract term which has been included in the contract'. 'Not being acquainted with the terms' refers to a lack of awareness of the consumer because, for instance, the supplier of the contract did not provide an opportunity for the consumer to take notice of or examine the contract terms. The second one is 'how to decide which interpretation prevails when dispute occurs'. This question concerns the situation that the text of the contract is so vague that the parties have different understandings of it and the sole and actual meaning must be established.

In this section, the relevant legislative provisions and judicial decisions in China are introduced firstly (Sect. 4.4.2). The duty to draw attention (Sect. 4.4.2.1) and the method to interpret the contract (Sect. 4.4.2.2) are addressed separately. Then the approach under EU law is presented (Sect. 4.4.3). The Unfair Contract Terms Directive (Sect. 4.4.3.1), the German Civil Code and related legislation (Sect. 4.4.3.2), and English law, especially the CRA 2015, (Sect. 4.4.3.3) are considered. Afterwards a comparative review is given (Sect. 4.4.4).

4.4.2 Chinese Law

4.4.2.1 Incorporation Problem

To answer the question 'what would happen when a consumer is not acquainted with a contractual term', in the context of the Chinese Contract Law 1999, Article 39 which regulates the duty of drawing attention should be noticed first.

Among the three articles concerning standard terms, Article 39 provides the general principle of fair dealing and it also mentions the duty of offering notice and information. The first paragraph of Article 39 reads: 'Where standard terms are adopted in concluding a contract, the party supplying the standard terms shall define the rights and obligations between the parties abiding by the principle of fairness, and shall inform the other party to note the exclusion or restriction of its liabilities in a reasonable way, and shall explain the standard terms upon request by the other party.'

In determining whether the duty of drawing attention has been fulfilled 'in a reasonable way', the Interpretation II of the Supreme People's Court of Several Issues concerning the Application of the Contract Law of the People's Republic of China ('Interpretation No. 5 [2009] of the Supreme People's Court')[80] provides: 'Where, at the time of concluding a contract, the party providing the standard terms adopted special characters, symbols, fonts and other signs sufficient to arouse the other party's attention to the content of the standard terms regarding liability exemptions or restrictions in favour of the party providing the standard terms, and

[80] Interpretation II of the Supreme People's Court of Several Issues concerning the Application of the Contract Law of the People's Republic of China (《最高人民法院关于适用〈中华人民共和国合同法〉若干问题的解释(二)》) (Interpretation No. 5 [2009] of the Supreme People's Court (法释[2009]5号)).

made an explanation of the standard terms according to the requirements of the other party, the people's court shall determine that the requirement of "a reasonable way" in Article 39 of the Contract Law has been satisfied.'[81] Scholars also provide some specific criteria. For example, Shiyuan Han demonstrates that some elements such as 'the appearance of the document',[82] 'the approach to remind',[83] 'the level of clarity',[84] 'the time of giving reminder'[85] and 'the degree of drawing attention'[86] should be considered.[87]

With regard to the assessment in practice, in some judgments with regard to carriage contracts, judges assert that the words of 'special reminder' printed on the waybill and the fact that the consignor has filled in the waybill herself,[88] or words in red printed in a prominent place,[89] result in the fulfilment of the duty of drawing attention. However, some cases reveal that a result-oriented approach has been adopted whereby the courts are more concerned with whether the corresponding party has been made aware of the specific standard terms than whether the supplier has fulfilled the duty of drawing attention. The courts hold that the standard term is legally binding on the parties because the party should have known about it regardless of whether the party who provides the standard terms has drawn his attention to them. Furthermore, the supplier of standard terms also has to prove that the duty has been fulfilled and the fact that the corresponding party as an ordinary person can understand his reminder and the designated terms.[90]

---

[81] Article 6(1).

[82] See Han (韩世远) 2011, p. 742. 'The appearance of the document' refers to the appearance of the contract that should leave an impression to the other party that it is a legal document which would influence his rights and interests.

[83] See Han (韩世远) 2011, p. 742. 'The approach to remind' mentions the different approaches to ask the other party to notice. Reminding individually and proclaiming in public are the two approaches of mainstream. However, the former should be the principle and the latter should be the exception. That means only if reminding individually is too difficult in practice the supplier could use the approach of proclaiming in public.

[84] See Han (韩世远) 2011, p. 742. 'The level of clarity' requires that the words utilised to inform the other party to notice must be plain and intelligible.

[85] See Han (韩世远) 2011, p. 742. 'The time of giving the reminder' implies that if the reminder is delayed the reminder will be worthless.

[86] See Han (韩世远) 2011, p. 742. 'The level of drawing attention' provides the relativity between the approach to draw attention and the level of surprise of the standard term. Put differently, the more surprising the term is, the higher the level of approach is required to be.

[87] See also, Su (苏号朋) 2004, pp. 156–162.

[88] See Meiya Lu v Shaoxing Lutong Express Service Ltd. Co (鲁梅雅与绍兴路通快递服务有限公司邮寄服务合同纠纷上诉案), Civil Judgment (2010) Zhe-Shao-Min-Zhong-Zi No. 833 of the Shaoxing Intermediate People's Court in Zhejiang Province (浙江省绍兴市中级人民法院(2010)浙绍民终字第833号民事判决书).

[89] See Nanjing Zhiheng Technology Ltd. Co v Shanghai Qisu Express Ltd. Co (南京智恒科技有限公司诉上海奇速快递有限公司货物运输合同案), Civil Judgment (2006) Chang-Min-Er-Shang-Chu-Zi No. 811 of the People's Court of Changning District of Shanghai City (上海市长宁区人民法院(2006)长民二(商)初字第811号民事判决书).

[90] See Piyan Zhang v China Life Insurance Ltd. Co Linli Branch (张丕岩与中国人寿保险股份有限公司临澧支公司意外伤害保险合同纠纷), Civil Judgment (2013) Lin-Min-Er-Chu-Zi No. 101 of the People's Court of Linli County in Hunan Province (湖南省临澧县人民法院(2013)临

In addition, in spite of not being clarified in legislation, the rule of 'signature deems commitment' finds support in scholarly writing and judicial practice.[91] That means the signature of the corresponding party will definitely show that the duty of drawing attention has already been performed sufficiently by the supplier of the standard terms.

With regard to a standard term to which the supplier did not draw attention, there are two opinions. The first one is supported by scholars: this term shall not be incorporated.[92] In some judgments it is also described as 'not effectively binding'.[93] These expressions all point to the failure of consent which leads to the conclusion that the term should not be a part of the contract. In sharp contrast, however, the judicial interpretation adopts a different and 'ingenious'[94] approach that this term shall be voidable, which states 'where the party providing the standard terms violates the provision of paragraph 1 of Article 39 of the Contract Law 1999 regarding the obligation to draw attention and give an explanation, and causes the other party's failure to notice the terms regarding liability exemptions and restrictions in favour of the party providing the standard terms, the people's court shall support the other party's application for invalidating the standard terms'.[95] Put differently, the Interpretation No. 5 [2009] of the Supreme People's Court does not follow the academic opinion. It chooses a compromising approach between the approach that 'the terms are not incorporated'[96] and another approach that 'the terms are null and void',[97] because the Supreme People's Court considers that it is too complicated and difficult for ordinary consumers to understand the consequence that 'the terms are not incorporated'. Meanwhile, it is also considered to be too strict if the terms are held to be null and void.[98] In practice, following the rule ascertained by the judicial interpretation, most people's courts hold that if the standard terms have not been drawn to the consumer's attention, the consumer will be entitled to invalidate the terms.[99]

民二初字第101号民事判决书). The legal basis of the distribution of burden of proof is Article 6(2) of the Interpretation No. 5 [2009] of the Supreme People's Court.

[91] See, for example, Wang (王利明) 2002b, p. 395.

[92] See, for example, Han (韩世远) 1994, p. 484 ff; Wang (王利明) 2002b, p. 393 ff.

[93] See, for example, Tianan Insurance Ltd. Co Rugao Branch v Yuanxing Sun (天安保险股份有限公司如皋支公司与孙元兴等保险合同纠纷上诉案), Civil Judgment (2010) Tong-Zhong-Min-Zhong-Zi No. 1352 of the Nantong Intermediate People's Court in Jiangsu Province (江苏省南通市中级人民法院(2010)通中民终字第1352号民事判决书).

[94] See Han (韩世远) 2011, p. 741.

[95] Article 9 of the Interpretation No. 5 [2009] of the Supreme People's Court.

[96] See, for example, Wang (王利明) 2002b, p. 394.

[97] See, for example, Yin (尹华广) 2005, p. 49.

[98] See Research Office of the Supreme People's Court (最高人民法院研究室) 2009, p. 87.

[99] See, for example, China Dadi Property Insurance Ltd. Co Chongqing Branch v Chongqing Jiafeng Industry Ltd. Co (中国大地财产保险股份有限公司重庆分公司与重庆嘉峰实业(集团)有限公司财产损害赔偿纠纷上诉案), Civil Judgment (2011) Yu-Wu-Zhong-Fa-Min-Zhong-Zi No. 367 of the Chongqing No. 5 Intermediate People's Court (重庆市第五中级人民法院(2011)渝五中法民终字第367号民事判决书).

Indeed, this approach causes a chain reaction because the judicial interpretation applies the word '*Chexiao*' ('撤销', which literally means 'withdraw' or 'avoid'), which is mostly regulated by Article 54 of the Contract Law 1999 for the circumstances where the contract was concluded as a result of significant misconception or the contract is obviously unfair at the time of conclusion. The common rationale here is probably that there is a failure of consent in all these different situations. In any event, this means the existence and the legal consequences of this right are provided by the articles regulating the right to avoid the contract. Furthermore, if the consumer does not claim that the duty of drawing attention has not been fulfilled or the right is extinguished due to the reasons specified by Article 55, the consumer will be legally bound by the standard term. Compared with the approach of 'not incorporated', it is clear that the protective level of the Interpretation's approach is lower. Nevertheless, even if the unfair term has been incorporated, the methods offered by the fairness test (substantive control) could still prevent it from being binding.

In terms of the range of the contractual terms that the supplier should draw attention to, scholars and judges criticise the limitation set by Article 39 which mentions the duty of providing notice and information, and is only applied to the terms that exclude or limit the party's liabilities, which is unnecessary. The consequence of non-performance of this information duty, is that the terms may be set aside, and this should be applied by analogy to other types of standard terms.[100]

Besides Article 39 of the Contract Law 1999, the first paragraph of Article 26 of the Consumer Protection Law 2013 also provides that business operators that use standard terms and conditions in business activities shall, in a conspicuous manner, should remind consumers to pay attention to the quality, quantity, and prices or fees of commodities or services, duration and manner of performance, safety precautions and risk warnings, after-sales service, civil liability, and other terms and conditions vital to the interests of consumers, and provide explanations as required by consumers. That means, in the context of consumer contracts, that if the supplier of standard terms is the business operator, he has to remind the consumer to pay attention to not only the terms about the exclusion and restriction of its liability but also the terms which are vital to the interests of consumers, which is in line with the opinion suggested by scholars and judges.

What should be noticed is that the Consumer Protection Law 2013 does not provide the legal consequence for the failure of the performance of the legal duty to draw attention. The approach which was adopted by the Interpretation No. 5 [2009] of the Supreme People's Court is not restated in this statute. In the book <Understanding on Law of the People's Republic of China on the Protection of Consumer Rights and Interests>, it is stated that the terms will not become a part of the contract if the business operator does not perform the duty to remind the consumer to pay attention.[101] It seems that in the context of consumer contracts, the rule

[100] See Tan & Hu (谭振亚、胡建) 2012, pp. 140–142.

[101] See Jia (贾东明) 2013, p. 117.

set by the Interpretation No. 5 [2009] of the Supreme People's Court that the term is voidable has been amended. The previous opinion supported by scholars prevails in the new Consumer Protection Law. However, the Understanding of authority further states that there is still an exception that could restore the terms if the consumer claims the term should be applied. Thus, it is clarified that the legal consequence is still that 'the target term is voidable in nature'.[102]

From a traditional contract law perspective, this argument is rather farfetched because a voidable term should be deemed as an effective one if the right to avoid has not been exercised. This means contracting parties can rely on this voidable term to claim for the performance in the absence of an action to avoid it. But if a term is 'not incorporated', a party could not claim its performance. Therefore, the nature of 'not incorporated' contradicts the nature of 'voidable'. Considering that the official text of the Consumer Protection Law 2013 does not provide a clear answer it is difficult to allege that the approach provided by the Interpretation No. 5 [2009] of the Supreme People's Court has already been revised. This means that in accordance with the interpretation terms that have not been drawn to the consumer's attention are 'voidable'.

4.4.2.2 Interpretation Problem

The first paragraph of Article 125 of the Contract Law 1999 provides the general rule for contract interpretation which states the interpretation must consider the words and sentences used in the contract, the relevant provisions in the contract, the purpose of the contract, the relevant transaction practices and the principle of good faith. In addition, within the context of standard terms, Article 41 provides: 'If a dispute over the understanding of the standard terms occurs, it shall be interpreted according to general understanding. Where there are two or more kinds of interpretation, an interpretation unfavourable to the party supplying the standard terms shall be preferred. Where the standard terms are inconsistent with non-standard terms, the latter shall be adopted.'

'General understanding' refers to the understanding of the ordinary people in society.[103] It adopts a reasonable third-party standard when determining the meaning of a standard term. This is not similar to the starting point adopted in the context of individually negotiated terms where a subjective approach has been accepted to explore the 'true meaning' or actual intention of the parties.[104] The emphasis has

---

102 See Jia (贾东明) 2013, p. 117.

103 See Liang (梁慧星) 2002, p. 264.

104 Article 125(1) provides: 'If any disputes arise between the parties over the understanding of any clause of the contract, the true meaning thereof shall be determined according to the words and sentences used in the contract, the relevant provisions in the contract, the purpose of the contract, the transaction practices and the principle of good faith.' The word 'actual' (真实) which is always used to emphasise something that is real or exists in fact directs to the parties' intention in reality but whether it is actual or not has not been taken into account when the intention is determined by objective approach

been put on the objective approach because standard terms are made in advance for the purpose of repeatable use and they will be applied to transactions with unspecified people. Therefore, due to their widespread application, attributing a separate meaning in each single but identical standard contract is abandoned.[105]

In a case involving a telecom contract, the consumer and the provider of telecom service had a different understanding of the contractual term 'telephone bill enquiry'. The consumer claimed that a printed telephone bill list is within the scope of 'telephone bill enquiry' and the provider claimed the opposite opinion. The judge held that a printed bill list is certainly one of the ways to request a telephone bill. Therefore, the consumer's understanding prevailed on the grounds of 'general understanding'.[106] This rule could also be applied to the situation where there are two different meanings attached to one single word and one is its general meaning whilst the other is its professional meaning which is not known by the ordinary consumer. According to Article 41 of the Contract Law 1999, the former will prevail. Besides, when the supplier of standard terms attaches some unusual meanings to the term by another 'interpretative term', such as giving a new definition to legal terminology that has already been defined by law, the other party is entitled to claim the invalidity of this interpretative term in light of Article 41. For instance, it is not allowed for the supplier of standard terms to define the meaning of 'lineal relative' or 'family member' by contractual terms since they are already defined by law.[107]

The second sentence of Article 41 of the Contract Law 1999 is the rule of interpretation *contra proferentem*. What is noteworthy is that the pre-condition of applying this article is that 'there are more than two ways to interpret the words' and these two ways should both fall into the probable scope of the literal meaning of the terms. According to a judgment published by the Supreme People's Court, 'When searching for the actual intention of declaration between two parties, the approach of most priority is assessing the literal meaning. Only where it is impossible to confirm the actual intention by literal approach, could the other approaches be applied to determine the meaning of contractual terms and fill in the gap of the contract.'[108] In judicial practice, it is very common for the judge to support an interpretation

[105] See Su (苏号朋) 2004, p. 223.

[106] See Hongjian Lin v China Mobile Fujian Ltd. Co Changle Branch (林宏剑诉中国移动通信集团福建有限公司长乐分公司电信服务合同纠纷案), Civil Judgment (2009) Rong-Min-Zhong-Zi No. 147 of the Fuzhou Intermediate People's Court (福州市中级人民法院(2009)榕民终字第147号民事判决书).

[107] See Shuling Yang v China Pingan Property Insurance Ltd. Co Tianjin Baodi Branch (杨树岭诉中国平安财产保险股份有限公司天津市宝坻支公司保险合同纠纷案), Gazette of the Supreme People's Court of the People's Republic of China, 2007(11) (《中华人民共和国最高人民法院公报》2007年第11期).

[108] See Zibo Wanjie Hospital v China Bank Ltd. Co Zibo Boshan Branch etc. (淄博万杰医院与中国银行股份有限公司淄博博山支行、淄博博易纤维有限公司、万杰集团有限责任公司借款担保合同纠纷管辖权异议案), Gazette of the Supreme People's Court of the People's Republic of China, 2007(12) (《中华人民共和国最高人民法院公报》2007年第12期).

unfavourable to the party supplying the standard terms, if the literal meaning of the term could lead to several possibilities.[109]

4.4.3 EU Law

4.4.3.1 The Unfair Contract Terms Directive

4.4.3.1.1 Incorporation Problem

The Unfair Contract Terms Directive (93/13/EEC) adopts a 'consent-oriented' approach concentrating on whether a consensus really exists. Some scholars term this as the 'incorporation problem' which refers to 'a minimum requirement for the conditions to become binding on a party that this party has had at least an opportunity to acquaint itself with the conditions when the contract was made.'[110] Pursuant to scholars, it refers to a 'formal requirement of transparency'[111] or a 'transparency principle'[112] lying in Article 5.

The first sentence of Article 5 provides: 'In the case of contracts where some or all certain terms offered to the consumer are in writing, these terms must always be drafted in plain, intelligible language.' The purpose of this provision is to provide the consumer with an actual opportunity to examine all the terms.[113]

This is further elaborated in the Annex, under example (i), which provides that a term that has the object or effect of 'irrevocably binding the consumer to terms with which he had no real opportunity of becoming acquainted before the conclusion of the contract' is an unfair term in accordance with Article 3. If the consumer has no opportunity to become acquainted with the term because the language is not plain and intelligible, this term will not bind the consumer.

Article 5 simply includes a duty to use plain and intelligible language so that consumer can understand the rights and obligations under the contract. However, there is no provision in the Unfair Contract Terms Directive requiring the user to draw attention to the terms. The issue of incorporation of the standard terms is thus not dealt with in the Unfair Contract Terms Directive.[114]

---

[109] For example, a case in terms of the dispute concerning the different understanding on starting date of an airline membership card could be noticed. See Jianhua Liu v Hainan Airline Ltd. Co (刘建华与海南航空股份有限公司消费服务合同纠纷上诉案), Civil Judgment (2013) Hai-Zhong-Fa-Min-Er-Zhong-Zi No. 300 of the Haikou Intermediate People's Court in Hainan Province (海南省海口市中级人民法院(2013)海中法民二终字第300号民事判决书).

[110] Wilhelmsson 2011, p. 578.

[111] Nebbia 2007, p. 135.

[112] Nebbia 2010, p. 225.

[113] See Recital 20 of the Unfair Contract Terms Directive.

[114] Some scholars consider that incorporation of standard terms in the contract is not dealt with the Unfair Contract Terms Directive for fear that this would interfere too much with national laws on the formation of contracts. The issue of incorporation is therefore a matter for the applicable national law. See Micklitz et al. 2010, p. 282.

Consequently, it is suggested that this formal requirement of transparency in the Unfair Contract Terms Directive does not completely accomplish its mission. Nebbia suggests that it is not clear whether 'transparency' is limited to some sort of negative control which allows at most the elimination of unclear and incomprehensible contract terms, or whether it might be understood as providing for positive information duties.[115] She also criticises the directive for failing to regulate the language in which clauses should be presented to the consumer, which is important in a cross-border setting, and not clearly stating the sanctions for infringement of the transparency requirement. Furthermore, it is not clear what standard of transparency is required under the directive, which refers to 'what model of "consumer" transparency would be assessed'.[116]

4.4.3.1.2 Interpretation Problem

It should be first noticed that no general interpretation rule can be found in the EU directives. The Unfair Contract Terms Directive also does not contain such rule. It only addresses a specific interpretation problem in relation to standard terms.

In comparison with the incorporation problem, the rule provided by the directive regarding interpretation is clearer and more specific. The second sentence of Article 5 incorporates the rule of interpretation *contra proferentem*, a rule which has roots in Roman law, and has been codified in many EU jurisdictions and model laws nowadays,[117] in European contract law. It provides: 'Where there is doubt about the meaning of a term, the interpretation most favourable to the consumer shall prevail.' This rule 'is derived from the argument that it is in the hands of the user of standard terms to phrase them in plain and unambiguous language' and therefore he should bear responsibility or the risk for using ambiguous language.[118] In the Unfair Contract Terms Directive, the rule of *contra proferentem* is seen as one of the consequences where the term is not drafted in plain and intelligible language, because the language requirement and this interpretation rule are regulated in the same article. It is stated in the Recital that the language requirement is regulated for consumers to have an opportunity to examine all the terms.[119] In the case of an ambiguity, where the trader fails to comply with the requirement of using plain and intelligible language, the EU legislator considers that the consumer would lose the opportunity to examine the term. Therefore, the contract must be interpreted against the person who drafted it, in order to protect the consumer from being bound by the terms with which he is not familiar.

---

[115] See Nebbia 2007, p. 137.

[116] For the elaboration, see Nebbia 2007, p. 137.

[117] Beale et al. 2010, pp. 702–710.

[118] See Markesinis et al. 2006, p. 174.

[119] See Rectial 20 of the Unfair Contract Terms Directive.

4.4.3.2 German Law

4.4.3.2.1 Incorporation Problem

Since the Unfair Contract Terms Directive does not deal with incorporation, it is necessary to consider the national rules on incorporation. In Germany, an agreement to apply the standard terms is necessary. Pursuant to § 305(2) BGB, standard terms become a part of a contract if the user refers the other party to them explicitly or, where explicit reference to the nature of the conclusion of the contract is only possible with considerable difficulties, by posting a clearly visible notice at the place of the conclusion of the contract. Standard terms are also incorporated if the user provides the other party with the opportunity of taking notice of their contents. This must take place in an acceptable manner, also appropriately taking into account a physical handicap of the other party discernible by the user. Besides, an agreement with the standard terms' application is indispensable to the incorporation.

§ 305c(1) BGB deals with so-called 'surprising' terms. It provides that standard terms will not be incorporated where they are so unusual that the other party need not expect to encounter them, in particular with regard to the outward appearance of the contract.[120] The rationale behind this provision is that it is reasonable for the counterparty to expect the standard terms to regulate ordinary rights and obligations, but it would be unfair to place the burden on that party – especially in light of the relatively easy incorporation of standard terms – to check the terms for unusual terms as well as to object to their incorporation. Thus, a term is considered as 'surprising' if, for example, it contains terms that are alien to the type of contract at issue; if it modifies abnormally the subject matter of the contract; if it is too far from the directing image of the contract; if it betrays the legitimate expectation of the customer.[121] Although it is not explicitly provided by the BGB, scholars point out the 'surprising terms' rule implies a higher requirement for duty to draw attention: if the counterparty has become aware of the term before or during the conclusion of the contract, it is not surprising anymore.[122] This makes this rule similar to the 'red ink' rule in English law,[123] which is discussed in the next section. However, although this rule concerns the incorporation issue, the assessment of a surprising term is to some extent very similar to the substantive fairness test to be discussed in Sect. 4.6 of this chapter. It is difficult to draw a clear line between them, because the surprising effect of a term depends on the degree to which it deviates from the default rules of the Code, and this is more relevant to the test in terms of substantive fairness.[124]

---

120 See Markesinis et al. 2006, p. 173.

121 See Nebbia 2007, p. 49.

122 See Nebbia 2007, p. 49.

123 See Micklitz et al. 2010, p. 286. Some scholars suggest the English rule does not go so far as the German treatment of unexpected or unusual terms: 'instead, these are treated as subject to the general rules on notice.' See Markesinis et al. 2006, p. 173.

124 See Markesinis et al. 2006, p. 173.

Where these duties have not been fulfilled, the terms are 'not incorporated in the contract' on the basis of §§ 305(2), 305c(1) BGB. § 306(1) BGB provides that if standard terms in whole or in part have not become part of the contract, the remainder of the contract remains in effect. The second paragraph provides that the content of the contract will then be determined by the relevant statutory provisions.'

4.4.3.2.2 Interpretation Problem

The general rules for contract interpretation are regulated in § 133 and § 157 BGB. § 133 provides that when interpreting a declaration of intention, the actual intention should be sought without regard to the declaration's literal meaning. However, the application of this article is limited in practice, because in most cases that have to be dealt with by the court the parties do not share a common meaning.[125] Thus, § 157 adds an objective approach by providing that the contracts should be interpreted according to good faith giving consideration to common practice.

In the field of standard terms, § 157 BGB plays an even more important role, because only one party drafted the contract. It is difficult to find out the 'actual intention'. Besides, the general rules for contract interpretation sometimes are altered by special rules, e.g. the rule of interpretation *contra proferentem*. In German law, this rule already existed prior to the implementation of the Unfair Contract Terms Directive. It was regulated in the AGBG 1976.[126] Now this rule is laid down in § 305c BGB, which provides that any doubts in the interpretation of standard terms should be resolved against the user. It should be highlighted that the German courts require the presence of genuine ambiguity as to the true meaning of a term for the application of this rule. It is not sufficient that the meaning is disputed between the parties.[127] In this sense, the German rule of interpretation *contra proferentem* is indeed relevant to the requirement that the user of standard terms should phrase them in plain and intelligible language.

4.4.3.3 English Law

4.4.3.3.1 Incorporation Problem

In English law, the person who signs the contract will be legally bound by it regardless of whether he has actually read or not.[128] This means that by signing the contract, a person is deemed to have read and agreed to the terms of the contract.

English courts have developed a series of rules related to drawing the other party's attention to the term. In general, the more unusual and unexpected the terms are,

[125] See Kornet 2006, p. 97.

[126] See Sect. 4.2.2.3 of this chapter.

[127] See BGH NJW 2002, 3232, quoted in Markesinis et al. 2006, p. 174.

[128] L'Estrange v F Graucob Limited [1934] 2 K.B. 394.

the higher the degree of notice that is required.[129] This is the famous 'red hand' rule. In *Spurling Ltd. v Bradshaw*, Lord Denning clarified that 'the more unreasonable a clause is, the greater the notice which must be given of it…some clauses I have seen would need to be printed in red ink on the face of the document with a red hand pointing to it before the notice could be held to be sufficient.'[130] Such notice should be given before, or at least at the moment of the conclusion of the contract. The following case illustrates this issue.

Olley v Marlborough Court Ltd[131]

Rule: A hotel could not rely on a notice displayed in its bedroom to exempt it from liability for negligence. Guests would not see the notice until they had been accepted as guests, meaning that it could not form part of the contract between hotel and guest.

Facts and Claims: The appellant hotel owner appealed against a decision that it had negligently allowed the theft of the possessions of the respondent guest from its hotel. Marlborough ran a residential hotel where Olley had stayed for several months. In Olley's bedroom there was a notice stating that Marlborough would not be liable for articles lost or stolen unless handed to Marlborough for safe custody. Olley went out of the hotel, leaving her room key on a key rack in reception. While Marlborough's staff were not watching, a man took the key and stole items from Olley's room. The judge found that Marlborough had been negligent, that the negligence had caused Olley's loss, that the hotel was a private hotel rather than a common inn, and that although Olley had seen the notice, its terms were ambiguous and had not absolved Marlborough from liability. Marlborough argued that (1) on the facts, it had not been negligent; (2) the notice formed part of the contract between it and operated to exempt it from liability for negligence; (3) its liability was limited to that of a residential hotel.

Judgment: (DENNING L.J.) The first question is whether that notice formed part of the contract. Now people who rely on a contract to exempt themselves from their common law liability must prove that contract strictly. Not only must the terms of the contract be clearly proved, but also the intention to create legal relations – the intention to be legally bound – must also be clearly proved. The best way of proving it is by a written document signed by the party to be bound. Another way is by handing him before or at the time of the contract a written notice specifying its terms and making it clear to him that the contract is on those terms. A prominent public notice which is plain for him to see when he makes the contract or an express oral stipulation would, no doubt, have the same effect. But nothing short of one of these three ways will suffice. (…) So, also, in my opinion, notices put up in bedrooms do not of themselves make a contract. As a rule, the guest does not see them until after he has been accepted as a guest. The hotel company no doubt hope that the guest will be held bound by them, but the hope is vain unless they clearly show that he agreed to be bound by them, which is rarely the case.

To implement the Unfair Contract Terms Directive, Regulation 7(1) UTCCR 1999 provides that a seller or supplier will ensure that any written term of a contract is expressed in plain, intelligible language. Nevertheless, just like the directive, it is pointed out that 'there is no specific sanction envisaged under the UTCCR for circumstances where a term does not comply with the requirement of transparency'.

---

[129] Peel and Treitel 2007, pp. 241–243. In terms of case law, see Parker v The South Eastern Railway Company (1877) 2 C.P.D. 416.

[130] Spurling Ltd. v Bradshaw [1956] 1 W.L.R. 461.

[131] Olley v Marlborough Court Ltd. [1949] 1 K.B. 532.

Only the application of the interpretation rule *contra proferentem* can be seen as one of the consequences. Under the new CRA 2015, a consumer contract or a consumer notice needs to be 'transparent'. This requirement will be met if the notice is expressed in plain and intelligible language, and it is legible.[132] In terms of the legal consequences, it is stated in Schedule 3 that a regulator may apply for an injunction or interdict (in Scotland) against the person who uses, or proposes or recommends the use of, a non-transparent term/notice.[133] Furthermore, it is likely that the court will take whether a term is transparent into account when deciding whether or not a term is unfair.[134]

4.4.3.3.2 Interpretation Problem

The general approach to contract interpretation in English law is an objective one. The English courts do not aim to discover the subjective intention of the contracting parties, but to promote certainty and expediency in litigation.[135] Interpretation is deemed as 'the ascertainment of the meaning which the document would convey to a reasonable person having all the background knowledge which would reasonably have been available to the parties in the situation in which they were at the time of the contract.'[136] For specific rules of interpretation, it is noteworthy that *contra proferentem* is a general rule. English law already recognised this rule in case law prior to the implementation of the Unfair Contract Terms Directive.[137]

With the implementation of the directive in the UTCCR, this rule was laid down in statute and applied to consumer contracts. Regulation 7(2) UTCCR reads: 'If there is doubt about the meaning of a written term, the interpretation which is most favourable to the consumer shall prevail.'[138] The new CRA 2015 now deals with *contra proferentem* in Section 69(1) which provides: 'If a term or a notice could have different meanings, the meaning that is most favourable to the consumer shall prevail.'[139] Scholars suggest that according to this rule 'any ambiguity in a term must be resolved against the party who is relying upon it.'[140]

---

[132] See Section 68(1) CRA 2015.

[133] See paragraph 3(1), (5) of Schedule 3 CRA 2015.

[134] See McKendrick 2016, p. 471.

[135] See Kornet 2006, p. 179.

[136] Scheme Ltd. v West Bromwich Building Society [1998] 1 W.L.R. 896.

[137] See Houghton v Trafalgar Insurance Co Ltd. [1954] 1 Q.B. 247; Alisa Craig Fishing Co Ltd. v Malvern Fishing Co [1983] 1 All ER 92. See also Beale 1999, p. 667.

[138] Regulation 7(2) UTCCR 1999.

[139] See Section 69(1) CRA 2015.

[140] McKendrick 2016, p. 472.

4.4.4 Comparative Review

To answer the question 'what can a consumer claim if he is not acquainted with a contractual term which has already been written in the text of contract', attention can first be directed at whether the seller or supplier has a duty to draw attention to or give notice of the terms it uses.

Provisions or rules regulating this issue can be found in Chinese, German and English law. In China, the first paragraph of Article 39 of the Contract Law 1999 and its relevant provisions in the judicial interpretation, as well as Article 26 of the Consumer Protection Law 2013, can be identified. Article 39 of the Contract Law 1999 provides that the supplier of standard terms should draw the other party's attention to the terms which exclude or limit its liability and the supplier should explain such terms upon the other party's request. The first sentence is always regarded as a duty to draw attention. The corresponding part in the BGB is § 305(2) and § 305c(1), which require the user to refer the other party to the standard terms explicitly. In English law, the court has given the criteria to evaluate whether the notice is sufficient and the rule that one is bound by his signature. The general rules on notice provide that the level of notice will increase where the term in question is more unusual or unexpected. The effect of this rule is similar to the rule 'surprising terms' in German law. The EU directive does not contain an explicit duty to draw attention to the standard terms, although example (i) of the Annex provides that the consumer should be given a real opportunity to become acquainted with the term before the conclusion, otherwise the term will not bind the consumer.

Among these three jurisdictions, German law provides the most detailed rules in its legislation. This is also the reason why some Chinese scholars suggest that Chinese law should, following § 305c(1) BGB, adopt the rule of 'surprising terms' to mitigate the strictness of the rule of 'signature deems commitment'. Besides, to assess whether the duty to draw attention to the terms has been sufficiently fulfilled, scholars propose for a more detailed approach. For example, if the consumer is mentally or physically handicapped, or blind, this should be taken into account. In these circumstances, if the consumer has tried his best but he is still not aware of the content of exemption terms, these terms shall not be incorporated.[141] This is in line with § 305(2) BGB.

Apart from the similarities, there is an obvious distinction in terms of the legal consequence when the duty has not been fulfilled. Chinese judges adopt an extraordinary approach: the Interpretation No. 5 [2009] of the Supreme People's Court provides that the consequence of the non-performance of this calling-attention or information duty is that the term is voidable. In sharp contrast, the consequence in German law and English law is that the term should not be incorporated because of the lack of consent. This distinction will also lead to the difference in terms of the nature between a voidable term and a non-incorporated term. The former will be deemed as a valid one until the party avoids it and it will also be restricted

[141] See Cui (崔建远) 2008, p. 145.

by the rule of extinguishment of the right to avoid. In the context of Chinese law, Article 55 of the Contract Law 1999 will be applied. If the consumer, having the right to invalidate the contract, fails to exercise the right within one year from the day on which he knows or ought to have known the causes of avoidability, or explicitly expresses or act in a way to waive the right, the right to avoid the contract shall extinguish and the consumer will remain bound by the term. Another difference is that Article 26 of the Consumer Protection Law 2013 requires the business operator to inform the consumer to notice every term which is related to their vital interests, not only the standard terms. In contrast, according to German and English law, the user of standard terms is required to make the counterparty acquainted with the terms, otherwise the terms are not incorporated. This duty can be simply fulfilled by making reference to the terms. However, even if a standard term is incorporated, it has to undergo the fairness test.

Turning to the requirements of language, the Unfair Contract Terms Directive requires that the terms should be expressed in plain and intelligible language (Article 5) under the idea that the consumer should be given an opportunity to examine all the terms. The directive thus focuses on whether there is actual consent. After all, if the consumer has no opportunity to become acquainted with the contractual terms, the terms are not incorporated because of a lack of consent. Both German and English law implemented this in national legislation. This is recognised as a requirement of transparency, but in China no similar rule can be found.

Apart from the rule of interpretation *contra proferentem*, the Unfair Contract Terms Directive has not provided other legal consequences for when the duty to draft in plain and intelligible language has not been performed. This problem was left to the Member States. However, in German law and English law, it is still difficult to find rules regulating this specific issue. Only the new CRA 2015 now provides that an injunction can be sought. On the national level, sometimes it can be observed that the requirement of transparency is regulated to supplement the fairness test, which is discussed in the next section.

If the standard term was not drafted in plain and intelligible language, the problem of interpretation arises. It is noteworthy that there is no general rule on contract interpretation in the EU directives. Thus, the standard terms need to be interpreted in accordance with national rules first. In this regard, Chinese law, German law and English law all adopt an objective approach to ascertain the meaning of the term, since only one party drafted the contract. Although no general rule can be found, the Unfair Contract Terms Directive provides the rule of interpretation *contra proferentem* and this rule can also be found in Chinese law, German law and English law. According to this rule, in case of doubt about the meaning of a standard term, the interpretation which is most favourable to the consumer should prevail (Article 41 of the Contract Law 1999, Article 5 of the Unfair Contract Terms Directive, § 305c(2) BGB and Section 69(1) CRA 2015) (Table 4.2).

Table 4.2 Formal control

	Duty to draw attention	Legal consequences	Plain language and the rule of *contra proferentem*	Legal consequences
Chinese Contract Law	Article 39(1) (shall inform the other party to notice the… terms upon the request of the other party)	Article 9 of the Interpretation No. 5 [2009] of the Supreme People's court (the right of avoidance)	Article 41 (if a dispute occurs, the understanding of standard terms shall be interpreted in accordance with common understanding)	Article 41 (the interpretation unfavourable to the party supplying the standard terms shall prevail)
Chinese Consumer Protection Law	Article 26 (shall draw the consumer's attention to notice the quantity, quality…)			
EU Unfair Contract Terms Directive			Article 5 (plain, intelligible language)	Recital 20
			Recital 20 (the consumer should actually be given an opportunity to examine all the terms)	Article 5 (the interpretation most favourable to the consumer shall prevail)
German Law	§ 305(2) BGB	§ 305(2) BGB	§ 305c(2) BGB	§ 305c(2) BGB (the interpretation unfavourable to the party supplying the standard terms shall prevail)
	§ 305a BGB	§ 305c(1) BGB		
	§ 305c(1) BGB (surprising terms)	§ 306 BGB (not incorporated)		
English Law	Case Law (notice of contract terms)	Case Law (not incorporated)	Section 68(2) CRA 2015 (plain, intelligible language)	Section 69(1) CRA 2015 (the meaning that is most favourable to the consumer is to prevail)

4.5 Substantive Control

4.5.1 Introduction

In the context of the control of unfair terms, the substantive fairness test is the central topic. Rather than focusing on whether the parties consented to the terms, as discussed in the previous section, the substantive control primarily focuses on the content or the substance of the term.

This section answers the question: 'Under what circumstances can a consumer claim a contractual term is "unfair" and escape from being bound by it?' In addressing this question, the focus is on the approaches used by the courts. In the context of consumer protection, the relevant rules are not only regulated by the general principles of contract law, but also in some specific provisions regulating standard or non-individually negotiated terms. In dealing with fairness issues, legislators are concerned about the substantive balance of the rights and obligations, because the supplier of the terms could insert terms that favour him into the contract while the consumer is unable to influence the substance of the contract through negotiation. In China and the EU, the legislators have provided both procedural and substantive ways to prevent consumers from being bound by unfair terms.

In many jurisdictions, legislators concentrate on a special type of contract term – exemption clauses – because their contents are generally linked with the higher possibility of unfairness. An exemption clause is a clause which seeks to exclude a party's liability for not fulfilling his duty. What should be noticed is that limitation clauses which limit the liability to a specified amount are also included when discussing exemption clauses, since a limitation clause can be seen as partly exempting a party from his liability.

In China, Article 5 of the Contract Law 1999 lays down a general principle of fairness. This principle is worked out further in Articles 53 and 54. Article 53 of the Contract Law 1999 prohibits two specific types of exemption clauses and Article 54 provides that contract terms should not be 'obviously unfair'. Whereas Articles 53 and 54 apply to all contracts, Articles 39 and 40 of the Contract Law 1999 police the fairness of standard terms. Apart from these articles, Article 26 of the Consumer Protection Law 2013 is also relevant.

In the EU, Article 3(1) of the Unfair Contract Terms Directive (93/13/EEC) offers two criteria for the assessment of fairness of non-individually negotiated terms. German law and English law have implemented the rules on the national level. In addition, mature rules with respect to exemption clauses and the substantive fairness test can be found in national law.

In the following analysis, the rules regarding the substantive control in Chinese law (Sect. 4.5.2), the EU directive (Sect. 4.5.3.1), German law (Sect. 4.5.3.2) and English law (Sect. 4.5.3.3) are addressed respectively, and a comparison of the interpretation of the requirements and the legal consequences of the rules is given. In addition, some comments on several controversial topics are offered and at the end of this section a comparative review is given (Sect. 4.5.4). To address the relevant issues, the contract terms are divided into two types: exemption clauses and other contract terms. They are dealt with separately.

4.5.2 *Chinese Law*

4.5.2.1 Introduction

In terms of the substantive control in Chinese law, Articles 39, 40, 53 and 54 of the Contract Law 1999 and Article 26 of the Consumer Protection Law 2013 are the most important provisions.

When the issues regarding exemption clauses are addressed, Article 53 of the Contract Law 1999 should be considered first. It should be noted that the application of Article 53 is not redirected to standard terms. It applies to all contracts. It is a 'general provision', in the sense that it is a provision that governs the fairness test in general, regardless of the division between standard terms and individually negotiated terms. Article 53 of the Contract Law employs the phase '*mianze tiaokuan*' ('免责条款', which literally means 'exemption clauses') in Chinese. It refers to the clauses which allow one party to exclude the liability for breach or to limit such liability. Sometimes it is also translated as 'immunity clauses'[142] or 'clauses on liability exemption'.[143] On the grounds of this article, a clause will be null and void if it exempts liability for personal injury to the other party or property damage to the other party as a result of an intentional act or gross negligence. In addition to this general provision, there are also rules regulating exemption clauses in specific areas, also regardless of the distinction between standard terms and individually negotiated terms. Article 126 of the Maritime Law 1992[144] is the representative.[145] In the specific context of standard terms, Article 40 of the Contract Law 1999 and Article 26 of the Consumer Protection Law 2013 contain the rule that a contract term exempts the supplier's liability is null and void.

Like Article 53 of the Contract Law 1999, Article 54 is also a general provision that can be applied to all contracts. However, compared with Article 53, it is more complicated. This is particularly the case when interpreting the phrase '*xian shi gongping*' ('显失公平', which literally means 'obvious unfairness'). Pursuant to

[142] This version is translated by the Supreme People's Court of the People's Republic of China, available at: <http://en.chinacourt.org/public/detail.php?id=97>, last visited: 2016/9/9.

[143] This version is translated by China.org.cn, available at: <http://www.china.org.cn/china/LegislationForm2001-2010/2011-02/12/content_21908031.htm>, last visited: 2016/9/9.

[144] Maritime Law of the People's Republic of China (《中华人民共和国海商法》).

[145] Article 126 of the Maritime Law 1992 reads: 'Any of the following clauses contained in a contract of carriage of passengers by sea shall be null and void: (1) Any clause that exonerates the statutory responsibility of the carrier in respect of the passenger; (2) Any clause that reduces the limitation of liability of the carrier as contained in this Chapter; (3) Any clause that contains provisions contrary to those of this chapter concerning burden of proof; and (4) Any clause that restricts the right of claim of the passenger.'

Article 54 of the Contract Law 1999, a party is entitled to request the people's court or an arbitration institution to modify or avoid the contract, if it is concluded as a result of serious misunderstanding, or if it is 'obviously unfair'. Although this phrase follows the wording of Article 59 of the General Principles of the Civil Law 1987 and it has been elaborated on by Article 72 of Instrument No. 6 [1988] of the Supreme People's Court,[146] it is still disputed whether a subjective element is necessary. The borderline between 'obvious fairness' and 'exploitation of the other party's unfavourable position' is also a controversial point.[147]

When dealing with standard terms, Article 39 of the Contract Law 1999 provides the general principle of fairness, which emphasises the principle mentioned by Article 5 of the Contract Law 1999. The first sentence of the first paragraph of Article 39 reads: 'Where standard terms are adopted in concluding a contract, the party which supplies the standard terms shall define the rights and obligations between the parties abiding by the principle of fairness.' Article 40 of the Contract Law 1999 deals further with the specific types of standard terms that are deemed as 'null and void'. It provides: 'When standard terms are under the circumstances stipulated in Article 52 and Article 53 of this Law, or the party which supplies the standard terms exempts itself from its liabilities, weights the liabilities of the other party, or excludes the major rights of the other party, the terms shall be null and void.'

In addition, Article 26 of the Consumer Protection Law 2013 restates the position under Article 40 of the Contract Law 1999 for consumer contracts: 'Business operators shall not, by standard terms and conditions, notices, declarations, on-site posters, and other means, impose unfair or unreasonable rules on consumers to exclude or restrict consumer rights, reduce or waive the responsibilities of business operators, or aggravate the responsibilities of consumers, among others, and shall not force consumers into any transactions by standard terms and conditions and technical means.' What is noteworthy is that the wording used is not the same as the wording of Article 40.

In this section, relevant problems in relation to consumer contracts are discussed on the basis of the interpretation of the aforementioned articles. The requirements and consequences of an unenforceable exemption clause, an obviously unfair contractual term and an unfair standard term are elaborated respectively (Sects. 4.5.2.2 and 4.5.2.3). Several disputed questions are addressed. Some judgments are introduced to illustrate how Chinese judges consider the concept of 'fairness' and how they apply these provisions.

---

[146] Opinions of the Supreme People's Court on Several Issues concerning the Implementation of the General Principles of the Civil Law of the People's Republic of China (For Trial Implementation) (《最高人民法院关于贯彻执行〈中华人民共和国民法通则〉若干问题的意见(试行)》), Instrument No. 6 [1988] of the Supreme People's Court (法(办)发[1988]6号).

[147] It should be noticed that the General Provisions of the Civil Law 2017 has already merged two provisions ('obvious fairness' and 'exploitation of the other party's unfavourable position') into one (Article 151 provides: Where a juridical act is evidently unfair when it is formed as a result of one party taking advantage of the other party's distress or lack of judgment, among others, the aggrieved party shall have the right to request a people's court or an arbitral institution to revoke the act.) for judicial acts. Thus, it is very likely that the Book of Contract Law of Chinese Civil Code will adopt the same standpoint in the future.

4.5.2.2 Exemption Clauses

4.5.2.2.1 Exemption Clauses in General

4.5.2.2.1.1 Article 53: Two Enumerated Categories

Article 53 of the Contract Law 1999 prohibits two specific types of exemption clauses on the grounds of the principle of fairness and good faith.[148] The first category refers to exemption clauses that exempt the party from liability for personal injury and the second category refers to exemption clauses that exempt the party from liability for property damage as a result of an intentional act or gross negligence.[149]

With regard to the first category, exemption clauses that exempt liability for personal injury have been prohibited since an official reply[150] introduced by the Supreme People's Court in 1988. Some employers had provided in the labour contracts that they would not be responsible for work-related injuries. In the official reply, the Supreme People's Court pointed out that these clauses are null and void because they violate the Constitution and legislation in the field of labour protection. They are also against the social morality.[151] This viewpoint was widely complimented by scholars and finally adopted in the Contract Law 1999,[152] in Article 53.

---

[148] Good faith as the supreme clause in civil law is emphasised in Article 6 of the Contract Law. It states: 'The parties must act in accordance with the principle of good faith, no matter in exercising rights or in performing obligations.' For an analysis from an etymologic perspective and on how Chinese judges apply this principle, see Novaretti 2010.

[149] Article 53 of the Contract Law 1999 reads: 'The following exemption clauses in a contract shall be null and void: (1) those that cause personal injury to the other party; (2) those that cause prop erty damage to the other party as a result of intention or gross fault.'

[150] 'Official reply'(translated from the Chinese phrase '批复') refers to a sort of official written documents that superior provide inferior with certain answer or indication to some specific queries. The Supreme People's Court's power to introduce official replies derives from Articles 16 and 32 of the Organic Law of the People's Courts of the People's Republic of China (2006 Amendment) (《中华人民共和国人民法院组织法(2006修正)》): Article 16 clarifies that the judicial work of lower courts shall be supervised by superior courts and Article 32 authorises the Supreme People's Court the power to introduce judicial interpretation dealing with how to apply statutes and regulations during the process of judicial work. As a result of this, introducing official reply, as well as another channel called 'Telephone reply' (translated from the Mandarin phrase '电话答复'), has become an essential method to indicate lower courts how to interpret law on the basis of a specific case and it is in accord with the superior situation of the Supreme People's Court. Even to this day, it is still a channel of introducing judicial interpretation of great importance, although it has been criticised by scholars for a long time that it may arrogate the legislative power of the National People's Congress and deprive the party of the right of appeal. See Suli (苏力) 2003, pp. 27–28. See also, Wang (汪世荣) 2000, pp. 16–28.

[151] See The Official Rely of the Supreme People's Court Concerning Issues Employment Contract Shall Strictly Implement the Labour Protection Laws and Regulations (《最高人民法院〈关于雇工合同应当严格执行劳动保护法规问题的批复〉》), Interpretation No. 1 [1988] of the Supreme People's Court ([1988]民他字第1号).

[152] See Liang (梁慧星) 1993, pp. 280–283. See also Han (韩世远) 2011, p. 744.

Some scholars suggest, however, this kind of exemption clause should not be policed as 'null and void'. For example, Liming Wang notes that some branches involve relatively high risk, such as operation on patients and driving training. If it were not permitted to include exemption clauses to exempt liability for personal injury, the regular activities and further development of these branches would be restricted and impeded. Ultimately, the rights and interests of the consumer would be harmed.[153] Thus, in line with provisions on tort liability such as Article 55 of Tort Liability Law 2009,[154] it is reasonable to say some special rules should be applied in this area.

The second category relates to exemption clauses concerning property damages as a result of an intentional act or gross negligence. According to Shiyuan Han, the legislative reason for Article 222 of the Taiwan Civil Code can contribute to the understanding of this article: although a contracting party may exempt liability for common negligence, the legislators see no reason to allow exemption from liability for an intentional act or gross negligence.[155]

4.5.2.2.1.2 Article 53 in Practice

In practice, the first category is rare. Most cases of the people's courts citing Article 53 of the Contract Law 1999 are concerned with the second category and this sort of exemption clause is often seen in the contracts of carriage. The following case provides a good example.

Guo v Shanghai Xinbang Logistic Ltd Co[156]

Rule: If gross negligence in a logistic company's conduct could be inferred from the specific circumstances of the case, the clauses that limit the scope of liability shall be null and void. The logistic company is responsible for the loss of the consignor.

Facts and Claims: Mr. Guo (hereinafter 'the plaintiff') signed a contract of carriage with Shanghai Xinbang Logistic Co (hereinafter 'the defendant') in which they agreed that the plaintiff would insure the value of the goods. The insurance costs amounted to

---

[153] See Wang (王利明) 2011b, pp. 432–433.

[154] Article 55 of Tort Law of the People's Republic of China (《中华人民共和国侵权责任法》) provides: 'During the diagnosis and treatments, the medical staff shall explain the illness condition and relevant medical measures to their patients. If any operation, special examination or special treatment is needed, the medical staff shall explain the medical risks, alternate medical treatment plans and other information to the patient in a timely manner, and obtain a written consent of the patient; or, when it is not proper to explain the information to the patient, explain the information to the close relative of the patient, and obtain a written consent of the close relative. /Where any medical staff member fails to fulfil the duties in the preceding paragraph and causes any harm to a patient, the medical institution shall assume the compensatory liability.'

[155] See Han (韩世远) 2011, pp. 744–745. Article 222 of Taiwan Civil Code provides: 'Responsibility for intentional or gross negligent acts shall not be released in advance.' This translation can be found at: <faculty.pccu.edu.tw/~borshan/ROC%20Obligations.doc>, last visited: 2017/1/25.

[156] Guo v Shanghai Xinbang Logistic Ltd. Co (过某某与上海新邦物流有限公司运输合同纠纷上诉案), Civil Judgment (2011) Hu-Er-Zhong-Min-Si-Shang-Zhong-Zi No. 320 of the Shanghai No. 2 Intermediate People's Court (上海市第二中级人民法院(2011)沪二中民四(商)终字第320号民事判决书).

0.3% of the price of the goods. The contract contained an exemption clause mentioned whereby the defendant limited the compensation to be paid to between double and quadruple the freight of the lost goods, provided the loss was not caused by force majeure, if the plaintiff did not ensure the value of the goods or pay the costs. Afterwards, 5 of the 16 goods were lost during the transportation. The defendant stated that they would only be responsible for compensation that ranged between double and quadruple the value of the lost goods' freight because the consignor did not claim insurance for the value. The plaintiff claimed gross negligence that the defendant did not know about the specific reason for the loss of the goods. On the grounds of the Contract Law, the exemption clause was null and void. The defendant should pay compensation according to the true value of the goods.

Judgment: The court held that he defendant, as the carrier bears the burden of proof to show why the goods were lost and whether there was gross negligence because it knew the particular case of the transportation well. In this case, the defendant failed to provide relevant evidence about the reasons for the loss of the goods. It even did not report to the security authorities immediately after the goods were lost. Therefore, the court held that the defendant had not performed the duty to take reasonable care, and found gross negligence. Pursuant to Article 53 of the Chinese Contract Law 1999, clauses that exempt liability for loss of property caused by an intentional act or gross negligence are null and void. This includes not only clauses that exempt liability but also clauses that restrict liability. In this case, the clauses included in the carriage contract that restricted the defendant's liability were null and void.

What can be noticed in this judgment is that, according to the people's court, clauses that exempt liability and those that limit liability are both treated as 'exemption clauses' and such. Exemption clauses may not exempt or limit liability for loss caused by gross negligence. In these cases, the party relying on the exemption clauses generally bears the burden to prove there was no gross negligence.[157]

4.5.2.2.1.3 Some Comments

It can be seen that the approach taken differs depending on the nature of the exemption clauses.

The focus in the first category of exemption clauses is on the expression of the clause. Thus, a clause will be null and void if it reveals an intention to exempt or limit liability for personal injury. In contrast, the validity of clauses in the second category usually cannot be determined on the basis of a literal interpretation alone. The court must determine whether there was gross negligence after the conclusion of contract. A clause that exempts or limits liability for property damage is consequently valid, unless it exempts or limits liability for damage caused by an intentional act or gross negligence and an intentional act or gross negligence can be factually established.

---

[157] For example, if the vehicle which transported the subject matter ignited itself and this caused the loss of the subject matter, the logistic company needs to prove that there was no gross negligence. See Shanghai Yuantong Express Ltd. Co v Shanghai Dinghang Electric Engineering Ltd. Co (上海圆通速递有限公司与上海鼎航电气工程有限公司运输合同纠纷上诉案), Civil Judgment (2010) Hu-Er-Zhong-Min-Si-Shang-Zhong-Zi No. 815 of the Shanghai No. 2 Intermediate People's Court (上海市第二中级人民法院(2010)沪二中民四(商)终字第815号民事判决书).

4.5.2.2.2 Exemption Clauses in Standard Terms

Article 40 of the Contract Law 1999 and Article 26 of the Consumer Protection Law 2013 provide rules where standard exemption clauses are used. Article 40 deals with clauses that exempt the supplier of standard terms from liability, whereas Article 26 provides that business operators must not take advantage of standard terms to reduce or waive their responsibilities.

The people's courts regard clauses that reduce or limit the supplier's liability as exemption clauses under Article 40 of the Contract Law 1999. The same conclusion can be reached under Article 26 of the Consumer Protection Law 2013. Pursuant to these provisions, standard terms that exempt a party's liability for infringing the consumers' rights and interests are invalid.[158]

The broad formulation of Article 40 ('exempt itself from liabilities') is widely criticised by scholars.[159] To be specific, extending a literal meaning to the provision could undermine the legislative objective. Jianyuan Cui argues, for instance, that if an exemption clause is necessary for an enterprise's reasonable operation, or it merely exempts the party from liability for ordinary negligence or for trivial breach of contract, and the supplier has performed its duty to draw attention, the exemption clause should not be null and void.[160] Furthermore, Article 53 provides that only the two types of exemption clause enumerated are null and void. Even though it could be argued that a higher standard should be applied in the context of non-individually negotiated situation, it is still inappropriate to prohibit all exemption clauses, since this would completely deviate from the daily and commercial practice.

On the basis of these arguments, it can be concluded that there is a legal gap in Article 40 of the Contract Law 1999, since the boundaries of the fairness test are uncertain. Therefore, it is necessary to restrict the scope of application by means of '*mudi xing xiansuo*' ('目的性限缩', which literally means 'narrow the applicable scope in terms of the legislative objectives', or teleological or purposive interpretation).[161] Some scholars suggest that the phrase 'exempt itself from liabilities' should be restricted and interpreted as 'exempt the supplier from major obligations'.

The same problem arises in Article 26 of the Consumer Protection Law 2013, but can be resolved in a different way. The application of Article 26 is restricted by a systematic interpretation with Article 23 of the Consumer Protection Law 2013.

---

[158] See Article 40 of the Contract Law 1999 and the third paragraph of Article 26 of the Consumer Protection Law 2013.

[159] See Rougier-Brierre 2007, pp. 168–169.

[160] See Cui (崔建远) 2008, p. 291. This is also supported by Huixing Liang and Shiyuan Han. See Han (韩世远) 2011, p. 744.

[161] Teleological interpretation has been emphasised since the 1990s by civil lawyers for the interpretation of statutes and to fill the gaps. For Huixing Liang, teleological interpretation is a method to fill a cryptic legal gap. A cryptic legal gap exists where the legislator should have established boundaries according to the legislative intention but it did not, as a result of this the formulation of the article is too broad. Therefore, judges and scholars should use teleological interpretation to make the article meet the objectives of the legislation. See Liang (梁慧星) 1995, p. 274.

Article 23 provides that where a consumer knew of a defect in a commodity or service when the contract was concluded, the business operator is not required to guarantee the quality, performance, or use of the commodity or service. Consequently, where Article 23 would apply, an exemption clause should be valid.[162]

4.5.2.3 Unfair Contract Terms

4.5.2.3.1 Obviously Unfair Terms

Article 54(1) of the Contract Law 1999 provides that a party shall have the right to request the people's court or an arbitration institution to modify or avoid contracts that are obviously unfair at the time when concluding the contract. It is a general provision that is applicable to all contracts. The question of what is an 'obviously unfair' contract remains controversial. Some scholars consider that there is only an objective element required to constitute 'obvious unfairness' (single-element approach')[163] while other scholars argue that there are two required elements: an objective one and a subjective one ('dual-element approach').

4.5.2.3.1.1 Single-Element or Dual-Element?

A literal interpretation of Article 54(1) of the Contract Law 1999 leads to a 'single-element approach', because no subjective element can be found in the wording of the provision. It is simply a 'result-oriented' provision.[164] Besides, 'obvious unfairness' in the sense of an obvious imbalance in the rights and obligations of the parties often emerges as the result of fraud, coercion or exploitation of the other party's unfavourable position, which are the other types of voidable contract regulated by Article 54(2). Therefore, Article 54(1) seems to be a fallback provision to cover other situations other than fraud, coercion and exploitation of the other party's unfavourable position, where the allocation of the parties' rights and obligations is unbalanced.[165]

The 'dual-element approach' requires not only the disparity between rights and obligations but also a subjective element of bad faith, in the sense that one party

---

[162] The first two paragraph of Article 23 of the Consumer Protection Law 2013 state: 'Business operators shall guarantee the quality, performances, use, and useful life of their provided commodities or services in the normal use of the commodities or receipt of services, except that consumers have known the existence of defects before purchasing the commodities or receiving the services and the existence of defects does not violate the mandatory provisions of law. /Business operators which indicate the quality of commodities or service by advertising, product instructions, real samples, or other means shall guarantee that the actual quality of their provided commodities or services is consistent with the quality indicated.'

[163] See Liang (梁慧星) 2007, p. 209.

[164] See Cui (崔建远) 2007, p. 109.

[165] See Yin (尹田) 1995, p. 104 ff.

takes advantage of the counterparty's imprudence, exigency or lack of experience.[166] This approach is based on Article 72 of Instrument No. 6 [1988] of the Supreme People's Court, which provides: 'In case any party makes use of his own advantages or takes advantage of the other party's lack of experiences to have the rights and obligations of the two parties obviously violate the principle of fairness and making compensation for equal value, it shall be determined as obviously unfair.'

The 'dual-element approach' is also supported from a legislative perspective. In the book <Paraphrase on Contract Law of the People's Republic of China>, edited by the Research Office of the Legislative Affairs Commission of the Standing Committee of the National People's Congress,[167] it explains that it will violate the principle of equal value if one contracting party suffers a serious economic loss from undertaking too many obligations and only a few rights are entitled to him, while the counterparty acquires excessive profits at a low expense. In addition, the circumstances of the conclusion of the contract are also relevant. The party which suffers the loss must have had some immediate needs, or been in an unfavourable position that he had to look to others for help, or he simply lacked experience, while the counterparty took advantage of this predicament by concluding the contract in order to pursue extra profit.[168] These combined factors will constitute a subjective requirement of 'obvious unfairness'.

It should be noticed that 'exploitation of the other party's unfavourable position' is another type which causes the avoidability of a contract.[169] It is regulated in Article 54(2) of the Contract Law 1999 and parallel to the type of 'obvious unfairness'. If a 'dual-element approach' for obvious unfairness is adopted, an overlap emerges. Nevertheless, they are still different types, because sometimes 'exploitation of the other party's unfavourable position' is not relevant to a serious economic loss, which is required for an obviously unfair term. Put differently, sometimes it is difficult to affirm that a contract is economically unfair, but it still constitutes 'exploitation' if one party goes against the counterparty's true intention. For example, a contract to sell one's favourite object against one's will that is concluded by taking advantage of one's distress will be treated as a contract of 'exploitation', even though the contract is not 'unfair' from an economic perspective. In contrast, 'obvious unfairness' concentrates on the economic imbalance of the profits, and in a dual element approach the subjective element not only focuses on the 'exploitation' but also the imbalanced position of the parties and the inexperience of the injured party.[170] To sum up, there is value to regulate two different types of voidable contract to address different situations.

---

[166] See Wang and Cui (王利明、崔建远) 2000, p. 289.

[167] The original Chinese is '全国人大常委会法制工作委员会研究室'.

[168] See Research Office of the Legislative Affairs Commission of the Standing Committee of the National People's Congress (全国人大法工委研究室编写组) 1999, pp. 84–85.

[169] The phrase used by the Chinese legislator is 'cheng ren zhi wei' ('乘人之危'), which literally means 'exploitation of the other party's unfavourable position'.

[170] See Research Office of the Legislative Affairs Commission of the Standing Committee of the National People's Congress (全国人大法工委研究室编写组) 1999, p. 86.

Thus, the economic inequality is surely the core element of an obviously unfair contract. According to the 'dual-element approach', the subjective part of taking advantage of a dominant position, especially the situations which are not covered by the provision dealing simply with 'exploitation of the other party's unfavourable position', is also necessary.

Although the 'dual-element approach' is approved by judicial interpretation and those in charge of the legislative process of Contract Law 1999, this approach is still questioned by some scholars. Shiyuan Han argues that the 'dual element approach' restricts the scope of application of the rule of 'obvious unfairness' in practice and it will lead to the failure of the objective of this provision.[171] Jianyuan Cui also states that there is no need to limit the application of 'obvious unfairness', since there is already a rule on 'exploitation of the other party's unfavourable position'. It is extremely likely that the boundary between 'obvious unfairness' and 'exploitation' will become blurred.[172] Cui suggests that the article in the judicial interpretation can be interpreted as an enumerative article and this can be read from the expression that 'it shall be determined as obvious unfairness' which implies that there are also other situations of obvious unfairness and the subjective element is not a requirement of 'obvious unfairness'.[173] Han suggests that although the judicial interpretation was introduced after the General Principles of the Civil Law, the Contract Law 1999 did not adopt this viewpoint and it was formulated after the judicial interpretation, which shows the preference of the legislator for a 'single-element approach'.[174]

4.5.2.3.1.2 What Is 'Obvious'?

Article 54 requires the contract to be obviously unfair. This raises the question what is meant with 'obvious'.

According to Mo Zhang, if the gain of a party by unfair means exceeds the limit by the law, the unfairness will be obvious. For example, in an employment contract, if the agreed salary is far below the level in the same or similar sector or industry, such contract with regard to the salary payment would very likely be deemed as obviously unfair.[175] This criterion focuses not only on the limitation of law, but also on the comparison with the level in the same or similar sector or industry, or the market value as well. In this way, 'obvious unfairness' could also be found in the loan contract in which the loan interest is several times higher than the market interest and in the sale contract in which the price is several times higher than the market value.[176]

---

[171] See Han (韩世远) 2011, p. 201.

[172] See Cui (崔建远) 2008, p. 304.

[173] See Cui (崔建远) 2008, p. 305.

[174] See Han (韩世远) 2011, p. 201.

[175] See Zhang 2006, pp. 189–190.

[176] See Research Office of the Legislative Affairs Commission of the Standing Committee of the National People's Congress (全国人大法工委研究室编写组) 1999, p. 84.

4.5.2.3.1.3 Article 54 in Practice

The relevant question is whether in practice the people's courts adopt a 'single-element approach' or a 'dual-element approach'. The following case of the Shanghai No.1 Intermediate People's Court provides a starting point.

Dou etc v Dong[177]

Rule: In order to modify or avoid the contract on the grounds of 'obvious unfairness', a subjective element that the party has taken advantage of the other party's hastiness or inexperience is necessary. In individually negotiated contracts, it can be inferred from the meticulous agreement that one party did not make use of the other party's disadvantaged position.

Facts and Claims: On 12 June 2006, Dou Guang and Dou Zhi (hereinafter 'the plaintiff') signed a lease contract with Dong, Chen and Lin (hereinafter 'the defendant') and agreed that they would lease a building owned by the defendant. The contract clarified that the building is a 635.40 square meter shopping mall. The defendant should hand over the building before 12 June 2006. The rent from 1 September 2006 to 31 August 2016 recorded in the supplementary clauses can be seen as follows.

Year	Price per day per m^2 (RMB)	Total price per month (RMB)
The first year	2.50	48316.81
The second year	2.80	54114.77
The third year	3.30	63778.27
The fourth year	5.00	96633.61
The fifth year	5.00	96633.61
The sixth year	4.63	89482.82
The seventh year	4.63	89482.42
The eighth year	4.73	91415.24
The ninth year	4.73	91415.24
The tenth year	4.73	91415.24

The plaintiff and the defendant also agreed that the rent would be adjusted by reference to the National Urban Consumer Price Index (CPI) in Article 2 of the supplementary clauses. If the CPI increases by 10% or more, the rent will also grow by 10% or the corresponding proportion. If the CPI decreases by 10% or more, the rent will also drop by 10% or the corresponding proportion. The two parties also agreed with the manner of payment, and liability for breach of contract. Later, the plaintiff claimed to the people's court that the contract is an obviously unfair contract: they had not known about the market price of the area where the building is located and afterwards they found that the market price was far below the price on which they agreed. Thus, they claimed that the rent of the fourth and fifth year should be modified to 2.61 RMB per day per square meter.

Judgment: If a contract was concluded as a result of 'obvious unfairness', the party is entitled to request the people's court or an arbitration institution to modify or avoid the contract. A contract concluded as a result of 'obvious unfairness' refers to the contract

[177] Dou etc. v Dong (窦光某等与董某等房屋租赁合同纠纷上诉案), Civil Judgment (2010) Hu-Yi-Zhong-Min-Er-Min-Zhong-Zi No. 3349 of the Shanghai No. 1 Intermediate People's Court (上海市第一中级人民法院(2010)沪一中民二(民)终字第3349号民事判决书).

concluded under the circumstance where one party has some urgent needs or he lacks experience while the entitled rights and obligations are seriously unequal. First of all, in this case, the clauses of the contract are clear, complete and explicit, especially on the agreement on rent year by year. It can be inferred that the contract was concluded on the basis of sufficient negotiation and no evidence can be found to prove that one party has made use of his advantage or the other party's hastiness or inexperience. Secondly, in this case, there is no evidence which manifests that the rent is too high or it leads to gross disparity. Since both of the parties cannot foresee market risk, it was agreed that the rent would be adjusted by reference to the National Urban Consumer Price Index (CPI). This agreement is equal to both of the parties and it does not lead to obvious unfairness. The market price claimed by the plaintiff does not have the function of guidance. Thus, the claims of the plaintiff fail to meet the requirements of 'obvious unfairness' in the Chinese Contract Law.

Pursuant to another judgment from the Supreme People's Court, it can be seen that a subjective element is required. According to the court, the current legislation has not regulated or clarified the specific standard of 'obvious unfairness'. Therefore, if the rights and obligations contained in the contract are complete and there was no duress or lack of experience, 'obvious unfairness' will not be constituted, even if there is an imbalance in the rights and obligations.[178] This viewpoint has been followed by many intermediate people's courts. For example, it is pointed out that a so-called 'obvious unfairness' refers to the case in which one party has concluded an obviously unfair contract under an urgent or inexperienced situation,[179] or that an obviously unfair contract refers to a contract which was concluded as a result of an exigency or lack of experience and its allocation of rights and obligations is seriously unbalanced. There are two elements for an obviously unfair contract. The subjective element is that one party makes use of his advantage and takes advantage of the other's inexperience deliberately; the objective element is that the profit-allocation is not balanced.[180] The adoption of a dual element approach by lower courts is not difficult to explain since the dual-element approach was accepted by the Supreme People's Court. Therefore, lower courts are likely to follow this approach in order not to contradict the superior courts.

However, some courts follow the 'single-element' approach. 'Obvious unfairness' in these cases does not require a subjective element and an unfair result in the sense of an economic imbalance is enough. To establish whether the contract is 'obviously' unfair, the price that is alleged to be too low will be compared to the

[178] Fujian Sanmu Group Inc. v Huangxing Real Estate Development Ltd. Co (福建三木集团股份有限公司与福建省泉州市煌星房地产发展有限公司商品房预售合同纠纷案), Civil Judgment (2004) Min-Yi-Zhong-Zi No. 104 of the Supreme People's Court of the People's Republic of China (中华人民共和国最高人民法院(2004)民一终字第104号民事判决书).

[179] Beijing Yahao Real Estate Broker Ltd. Co v Beijing Badachu Real Estate Development Ltd. Co (北京亚豪房地产经纪有限公司第五分公司与北京八大处房地产开发有限公司委托合同纠纷上诉案), Civil Judgment (2009) Gao-Min-Zhong-Zi No. 514 of the Beijing High People's Court (北京市高级人民法院(2009)高民终字第514号民事判决书).

[180] Nanjing Rixin Fat Chemical Plant Ltd. Co v Jingtai Industry (Group) Ltd. Co (南京日信油脂化工有限公司诉京泰实业(集团)有限公司等购销合同纠纷案), Civil Judgment (2002) Lu-Min-Si-Zhong-Zi No. 3 of the Shandong High People's Court (山东省高级人民法院(2002)鲁民四终字第3号民事判决书).

market value and the number checked and ratified by the Price Bureau, if it is far below the market value, the contract will be voidable for obvious unfairness.[181]

4.5.2.3.1.4 Some Comments

From A Doctrinal Perspective

Whether Article 54 of the Contract Law 1999 adopts a single element or a dual element is a matter of interpretation. As judicial interpretations are legal sources, the viewpoint of the Supreme People's Court cannot simply be ignored. However, the rules of interpretation need to be followed to resolve this issue.

Shiyuan Han and Jianyuan Cui argue that it is not possible to find a subjective element in Article 54 based on a literal interpretation.[182] Furthermore, a historical interpretation also leads to a 'single-element approach'. In the book <The Selection of Materials on Legislation of Contract Law of the People's Republic of China>, it is explained that participants in the drafting process of the Contract Law 1999 suggested that the definition and requirements of 'obvious unfairness' should be clarified that the dual-element approach should be explicitly written down in order to distinguish 'obvious unfairness' from fraud and coercion.[183] What is more significant is that the Third Draft of the Contract Law adopted the 'dual-element approach': its Article 39 provides that one can avoid a contractual clause if it is obviously unfair and concluded by making use of a party's disadvantage or inexperience.[184] Since the dual-element approach was mentioned in a draft, but not officially adopted, it is reasonable to conclude that the dual-element approach was not accepted by the Contract Law 1999.

In light of the basic theories of statutory interpretation, other methods of interpretation should be adopted only if two or more meanings are possible based on a literal interpretation.[185] But indeed, no other interpretation besides the 'single-element approach' can be found through reading the literal expression of Article 54. Moreover, a historical interpretation and a teleological interpretation will also lead to the conclusion that there is only one element required to constitute 'obvious

[181] See Henan Luozhoujie Highway Ltd. Co v Beijing Shizhenger Construction Engineering Ltd. Co (河南省漯周界高速公路有限责任公司与北京市市政二建设工程有限责任公司建设工程合同纠纷上诉案), Civil Judgment (2008) Yu-Fa-Min-Yi-Zhong-Zi No. 19 of the Henan High People's Court (河南省高级人民法院(2008)豫法民一终字第19号民事判决书). See also China Real Estate Development Zhengzhou Ltd. Co v Minhe Chu (中国房地产开发郑州公司诉楚敏和等撤销商品房买卖合同纠纷案), Civil Judgment (2002) Yu-Fa-Min-Yi-Zhong-Zi No. 213 of the Henan High People's Court (河南省高级人民法院(2002)豫法民一终字第213号民事判决书).

[182] See Han (韩世远) 2011, p. 201; Cui (崔建远) 2008, p. 304.

[183] Civil Law Office of the Legislative Affairs Commission of the Standing Committee of the National People's Congress (全国人大法制工作委员会民法室) 1999, p. 86, 151–152.

[184] See Liang (梁慧星) 1999, p. 143.

[185] See Sect. 4.4 of this chapter.

unfairness'. With regard to systematic interpretation, there is no paradox inside the Contract Law 1999 if we adopt single-element approach. Furthermore, the commentary of the Research Office of the Legislative Affairs Commission does not constitute a source of legislative interpretation, it is merely a doctrinal source of higher authority.

To conclude, in the context of the Chinese Contract Law 1999, the 'single-element approach' is more acceptable on the basis of a doctrinal analysis. The dual-element approach of the Instrument No. 6 [1988] of the Supreme People's Court has been already replaced by the single-element approach of the Contract Law 1999.

From A Normative Perspective

However, concluding that the 'single-element approach' is the only answer based on statutory interpretation does not mean that Article 54 of the Contract Law 1999 is good enough. For Shiyuan Han, the internal system of voidable contracts in Chinese Contract Law is rather confusing.[186] In fact, although the 'dual-element approach' cannot be supported, the arguments provided by scholars are worth consideration.

Firstly, the types of voidable contracts regulated by Article 54, such as fraud, coercion, exploitation of the other party's unfavourable position and contracts concluded as a result of a serious misunderstanding, concern defective declarations of intention. That means a contract is voidable only if its contents are not what the contracting party intended. But in a single-element approach to 'obvious unfairness', this rationale cannot be found. Compared with the other types of voidable contract, this result-oriented approach needs further grounds of legitimacy.

Secondly, the result-oriented approach to 'obvious unfairness' shows that Article 54 of the Contract Law 1999 follows the principle of equal value in the General Principles of the Civil Law 1987. However, it entitles the party to avoid the contract so long as the unfair consequence existed when the contract was concluded, regardless of the party's real intention and other specific conditions. This will give the party a right to avoid the contract whenever he no longer wants to be bound or he simply finds a new commercial partner who might give him a lower price, even though he was initially completely willing to accept the 'unfair' contract. This will lead to the violation of the principle of good faith if the principle of equal value/fairness is strictly obeyed. Given the current state of affairs, it is not possible to say which of these two principles prevails over the other.

Thirdly, Article 26 of the Interpretation No. 5 [2009] of the Supreme People's Court has established the rule of 'change of circumstances' (*Rebus sic stantibus*). For the Supreme People's Court, where some material and fundamental changes emerge after the conclusion of contract that were not foreseeable for the parties, and not caused by force majeure or a commercial risk, and specific performance of the contract would be obviously unfair for one party or the purpose of the contract cannot be realised, the people's court should determine upon the party's request whether

[186] See Han (韩世远) 2011, p. 191.

to alter or rescind the contract on the basis of the principle of fairness and the circumstances of the case. This article reveals that even if an unfair situation arrives after the conclusion of the contract which could not be foreseen during the negotiating process, a party cannot simply avoid or alter the contract. It is left to the people's court to decide on the basis of the principle of fairness and the circumstances of the case. In contrast, the contracting party who was fully aware of the unfairness before the conclusion of contract can avoid the contract in the context of Article 54. Therefore, the legislator should set up stricter requirements for the avoidance of the contract in these cases. However, this apparently contradicts the viewpoint of 'single-element approach'.

Finally, the 'single-element approach' will open the gate to legal uncertainty. The parties will find it difficult to foresee the consequences that may arise from their contract and they will not know what is the boundary between normal commercial risk and unfair conduct that is prohibited by law. It is also too difficult for judges to determine whether there is 'obvious unfairness' if there is only a single element because the standard of 'obvious' has not been expounded by law. Put differently, the subjective element would be more feasible in practice and bring more legal certainty.

To conclude, if the legislator is going to revise the Contract Law or introduce a civil code, it should adopt the 'dual-element approach' rather than 'the single-element approach' in the provision on 'obvious unfairness'.[187]

4.5.2.3.2 Unfair Standard Terms

4.5.2.3.2.1 Article 40 of the Contract Law

The legitimacy of policing standard terms is to correct the unbalanced bargaining power and protect the freedom of contract in order to achieve the value of fairness. This value has not only been emphasised as one of China's civil law principles, but also reiterated in Article 39 of the Contract Law 1999, which provides that 'the party supplying the standard terms shall define the rights and obligations between the parties abiding by the principle of fairness'. It shows the value orientation of the legislator and consequently policing standard terms should also follow and be guided by this principle. This article also points out that 'unfairness' refers to the unfair definition of the parties' rights and obligations. However, Article 39 cannot be applied as the basis of a claim itself because it does not contain the specific criteria and legal consequences. It is therefore necessary to refer to Article 40 of the Contract Law 1999. Pursuant to the first half of Article 40, the general rules on void contracts and exemption clauses regulated by Articles 52 and 53 of the Contract Law 1999 are also applied to standard terms. On the grounds of the second half of

[187] As previously mentioned, the General Provisions of the Civil Law 2017 has already adopted a 'dual-element' approach for judicial acts (Article 151). When the Book of Contract Law of Chinese Civil Code is enacted, it is highly possible that the standpoint of 'single-element' will be replaced by 'dual-element'.

Article 40, standard terms shall be invalid if they exempt the party supplying them from liability, increase the liability of the other party, or deprive the material rights of the other party,[188] because such terms violate the principle of fairness laid down in Article 39. In other words, these terms are unfair terms which are 'null and void'.

Nevertheless, even though some limitation has been set for the application of Article 40 of the Contract Law 1999, it is still necessary to categorise the types of terms when policing standard contract terms in line with the legislative objective. A literal interpretation does not clarify what 'material rights' are. To Mo Zhang, the material rights refer to those rights a party normally will have in the kind of contract.[189] But this explanation is not sufficient either, because judges have to determine what are the obligations and rights that the party normally will have.

4.5.2.3.2.2 Article 26 of the Consumer Protection Law

In the context of consumer protection, Article 26 of the Consumer Protection Law 2013 as a special law of Article 40 of the Contract Law 1999 is also relevant.

According to the second paragraph of Article 26, the use of standard terms is prohibited where they impose unfair or unreasonable rules on consumers that exclude or restrict consumer rights, reduce or waive the responsibilities of business operators, or aggravate the responsibilities of consumers. Compared with the previous version,[190] the Consumer Protection Law 2013 provides a provision which is more similar to Article 40 of the Contract Law 1999.

In comparison with Article 40 of the Contract Law, Article 26 clarifies that the contract terms that restrict (not only 'deprive' as in Article 40) consumer rights, or reduce (not only exempt) the responsibilities of business operators should also be policed as invalid. Article 26 also provides a more abstract rule that business operators should not impose other unfair and unreasonable rules on consumers, a similar formulation cannot be found in Article 40.

According to the Understanding of authority, the criteria to assess whether a standard consumer contract term is unfair have been established on the basis of comparative research. The legislator recognised that many jurisdictions provide specific criteria for the fairness test in consumer contracts. For instance, the EU Unfair Contract Terms Directive has identified at least 17 specific types of unfair

---

[188] It has been confirmed by the Supreme People's Court that if there are these terms and the provider also didn't perform the duty mentioned in Article 39, the legal consequence is that these terms are invalid. Article 10 of Interpretation No. 5 [2009] of the Supreme People's Court reads: 'Where the party providing the standard terms violates the provisions of Paragraph 1, Article 39 of the Contract Law, and has one of the circumstances as stipulated in Article 40 of the Contract Law, the people's court shall rule that such standard terms are invalid.'

[189] See Zhang 2006, p. 139.

[190] The first paragraph of Article 24 of the Consumer Protection Law 1993 provides: 'Business operators are prohibited from setting unfair and unreasonable standard terms, or resorting standard terms to mitigate, or exempt themselves from, liabilities for harming the consumers' legitimate rights and interests.'

terms. The legislator considers the similarities which can be identified from different national laws can be used as criteria in applying Article 26.[191]

In line with the general rules on fairness, the consequence of including unfair standard terms in consumer contracts are that the terms should be null and void. Since the criteria provided are considerably abstract, an assessment of fairness has to be done by the court on a case-by-case basis. Questions such as whether the terms are unfair or reasonable, or what are the material rights and obligations, still need to be answered on the basis of the individual circumstances of each case.

4.5.2.3.2.3 Unfair Standard Terms in Practice

The use of standard terms is common in the fields such as transportation, telecom and financial services.[192] This is because these fields are closely related to people's daily life. The traders in these fields have to deal with a large number of consumers. The use of standard terms can immensely decrease the transaction cost, since they do not need to negotiate and draft contracts with every individual consumer. However, the mass use of standard terms brings the phenomenon that some traders incorporate unfair terms in their standard contracts. The following case provides an example.

Jun Gu v the Shanghai Branch of Bank of Communication[193]

Rule: The standard term provided by a bank that requires the depositor to bear any loss caused by the use of a debit card and states that all transactions would be regarded as the depositor's own performance regardless of specific circumstances should be struck down as 'increasing the liability of the other party unfairly'.

Facts and Claims: Jun Gu (hereinafter 'the plaintiff') opened an account with the Shanghai Branch of Bank of Communication (hereinafter 'the defendant') and signed a deposit contract with the defendant. As a result of this, he obtained a debit card. On 9 June 2003, the plaintiff found that the capital on his card had decreased by 10,068 RMB for no reason, and he reported this to the public security organ. The investigation by the public security organ revealed that criminals stole the information and password of his card by setting up a password-stealing device on the access control system of the ATM. After that, the criminals copied the card and withdrew the money with a counterfeit card. However, the defendant refused to pay compensation because a standard term in the deposit contract states 'the bank will not be responsible for any transaction accomplished by password and all these transactions will be regarded as the transac-

[191] See Jia (贾东明) 2013, p. 116.

[192] Guiding Case No. 1 also concerns the fairness of a standard term: A contract term that prevents a purchaser from buying a property by using information provided by an agency but without the involvement of the agency, as it would result in the agency being unable to obtain the agreed commission fee should be held valid, since it did not exempt one party from any liability, increase the other party's liability or exclude any primary right of the other party. See Guiding Case No. 1 (指导案例1号), Shanghai Zhongyuan Property Consultancy Co Ltd. v Dehua Tao (上海中原物业顾问有限公司诉陶德华居间合同纠纷案), Gazette of the Supreme People's Court of the People's Republic of China, 2012(2) (《中华人民共和国最高人民法院公报》2012年第2期).

[193] Jun Gu v the Shanghai Branch of Bank of Communication (顾骏诉上海交行储蓄合同纠纷案), Gazette of the Supreme People's Court of the People's Republic of China, 2005(4) (《中华人民共和国最高人民法院公报》2005年第4期).

tions accomplished by cardholder.' The plaintiff claimed that this standard term had increased the responsibility of the depositor unfairly and had been brought about by the bank unilaterally. According to the plaintiff, this standard term is unfair and therefore null and void. On these grounds, the defendant should pay 10,086 RMB compensation and the interest from 9 June 2003.

Judgment: Setting a password with which the depositor could control the debit card is a method to safeguard the deposit and prevent crime. The facts in this case show that although the depositor has complied with the obligation of confidentiality the criminals were still able to crack, and take advantage of, the password set by the depositor. At the present time, with the rapid technological progress and changing of criminal methods with each passing day, it is contrary to the principle of fairness that banks shift the liability that they should have taken upon themselves onto the depositors. Thus, the standard terms that states 'the bank will not be responsible for any transaction accomplished by password and all these transactions will be regarded as the transactions accomplished by cardholder' increased the liabilities of the consumers unfairly.

This case is a good example that shows a standard term which increases the liabilities of the other party unfairly is null and void. There are also cases dealing with terms that deprive material rights of the other party, such as standard terms eliminate the user's duties required by law. A standard term that requires the employee to buy social insurance himself is also unfair because buying social insurance for employees is a legal duty of an employer according to law. This standard term is consequently unfair on the grounds of Article 40 of the Contract Law 1999.[194]

4.5.2.3.3 Consequences of Unfairness

In contrast to the void nature of exemption clauses and most other unfair terms, the obviously unfair terms are voidable pursuant to Article 54 of the Contract Law 1999. The contract is therefore valid and the parties are required to perform unless and until the contract is avoided. Once a party exercises the right of avoidance, the contract will become null and avoid. The contract will be avoided retroactively (*Void ab initio*), in accordance with Article 56 of the Contract Law 1999, and be treated as if it had never existed. Thus, once the consumer has avoided the contract, the consequences of an obviously unfair term are the same as a void contract term. Article 56 also provides that if part of a contract is policed to be null and void without influencing the validity of the other parts, the other parts of the contract will remain valid.

The right of avoidance expires after one year. If the entitled party declares by words or conduct that it wants to waive the right after it becomes aware of the avoidability, the right to avoid will be extinguished as well.[195]

[194] See Guangqiang Li v Guangzhou Fanyu Guibo Automatic Device Factory (李广强与广州市番禺桂博自动化设备制造厂劳动争议纠纷上诉案), Civil Judgment (2010) Sui-Zhong-Fa-Min-Yi-Zhong-Zi No. 427, 428 of the Guangzhou Intermediate People's Court in Guangdong Province (广东省广州市中级人民法院(2010)穗中法民一终字第427、428号民事判决书).

[195] See Article 55 of the Contract Law. It provides: 'The right to avoid a contract shall extinguish under any of the following circumstances: (1) A party having the right to avoid the contract fails to

Terms in standard contracts that are deemed unfair on the basis of Article 40 of the Contract Law 1999 and Article 26 of the Consumer Protection Law 2013 are null and void. In contrast to the obviously unfair terms in individually negotiated contracts, there is no room for the parties to opt for validity. These terms are 'absolutely void' from the very beginning.

After a term has been avoided or policed to be null and void, Article 58 of the Contract Law 1999 lays down a duty to return property.[196] The aim of the legislator is to make the parties restore themselves to the positions they were in before the contract. Article 58 also regulates other remedies such as monetary compensation.[197]

4.5.3 EU Law

4.5.3.1 The Unfair Contract Terms Directive

4.5.3.1.1 Introduction

Article 3(1) of the Unfair Contract Terms Directive provides two criteria for determining whether a contract term is unfair: (1) good faith; (2) a significant imbalance in the parties' rights and obligations.[198] Before the final version of this directive was laid down, there was a challenge about whether to adopt the concept 'good faith'. In the Commission's 1990 proposal, good faith was one of the four alternative criteria for the assessment of fairness – failure of a term to comply with just one of the criteria would lead to unfairness and the term would be unenforceable.[199] But in the 1992 Proposal, the criteria were reduced to just two which were to be applied in

---

exercise the right within one year from the day that it knows or ought to know the causes of avoidance; (2) A party having the right to avoid the contract explicitly expresses or conducts an act to waive the right after it knows the causes of avoidance.'

[196] Article 58 states: 'The property acquired as a result of a contract shall be returned after the contract is confirmed to be null and void or has been avoided; where the property cannot be returned or the return is unnecessary, it shall be reimbursed at its estimated price. The party at fault shall compensate the other party for losses incurred as a result therefrom. If both parties are at fault, each party shall respectively be liable.'

[197] More specific descriptions, see Zhang 2006, p. 194.

[198] Article 3(1) reads: 'A contractual term which has not been individually negotiated shall be regarded as unfair if, contrary to the requirement of good faith, it causes a significant imbalance in the parties' rights and obligations arising under the contract, to the detriment of the consumer.'

[199] According to this proposal, a term could be unfair in the following cases: (1) it caused, to the detriment of the consumer, a significant imbalance in the parties' rights and obligations arising under the contract; or (2) it caused the performance of the contract to be unduly detrimental to the consumer; or (3) it caused the performance of the contract to be significantly different from what the consumer could legitimately expect; or (4) it was incompatible with the requirement of good faith. See Proposal for a Council Directive on unfair terms in consumer contracts, COM(90) 322 final.

combination. Good faith lost its independent character and it had to be applied in combination with two other criteria. According to the 1992 Proposal, a term would be regarded as unfair if, contrary to the requirements of good faith, it causes to the detriment of the consumer a significant imbalance in the parties' rights and obligations arising under the contract, or it causes the performance of the contract to be significantly different from what the consumer could legitimately expect.[200] It is suggested that the reason why good faith as an independent criterion was removed is that there was a lack of recognition of this principle in certain Member States, in particular the UK. In order to 'save' this principle, the Commission had to add a recital clarifying the values underlying it and showing that this principle closely resembles the 'reasonableness' criteria regulated by the statutes with which common lawyers are familiar, in particular the UCTA 1977.[201] Thus, with some compromises, the Unfair Contract Terms Directive retained the principle of good faith. When applying the fairness test of Article 3, the courts are required to take all the circumstances with respect to the conclusion of contract into account, including the nature of the goods and services provided (Article 4(1)).

In this part, the issue of exemption clauses, which has not been regulated explicitly by the main body of the directive, is addressed first (Sect. 4.5.3.1.2). Then the fairness test is discussed and its two criteria are analysed separately (Sects. 4.5.3.1.3.1, 4.5.3.1.3.2 and 4.5.3.1.3.3). This is followed by the consideration of the relationship between the fairness test and the requirement of transparency (Sect. 4.5.3.1.3.4), and an introduction of the Annex (Sect. 4.5.3.1.3.5). Finally, the legal consequences for unfair terms are discussed (Sect. 4.5.3.1.4).

4.5.3.1.2 Exemption Clauses

In the context of the Unfair Contract Terms Directive, 'exemption clauses' are not dealt with explicitly. The main body of the directive does not include an article that provides a specific regulation for this type of clause. There is a logical explanation for this: the directive deals with unfair terms in general and 'exemption clauses' are just one type of unfair terms which should be assessed under the fairness test. This means, in order to evaluate whether an exemption clause is enforceable, the general criteria in Article 3(1) with regard to good faith and significant imbalance should be applied.

One specific type of exemption clauses has been mentioned in the examples lying in the Annex to the directive. Under example (a), terms which have the object or effect of excluding or limiting the legal liability of a seller or supplier in the event of the death of a consumer or personal injury to the latter resulting from an act or omission of that seller or supplier will be deemed to be unfair in accordance with Article 3(1).[202]

---

[200] See Amended proposal for a Council Directive on unfair terms in consumer contracts, COM(92) 66 final.

[201] See Nebbia 2007, p. 144.

[202] Example (a), Annex of the Unfair Contract Terms Directive.

4.5.3.1.3 Unfair Contract Terms

4.5.3.1.3.1 'Good Faith' in General

An introduction of the fairness test laid down in the Unfair Contract Terms Directive can start with one of the most significant concepts 'good faith', since it is one of the two criteria used to assess the fairness of a term. To most civil lawyers, 'good faith' is a familiar concept, although the different terminology used in different national laws can make it remarkably unfathomable. As Martijn Hesselink describes, 'Good faith is said to be a norm, a (very important) principle, a rule, a maxim, a duty, a rule or standard for conduct, a source of unwritten law, a general clause.'[203] That being said, a common core of good faith is still widely acknowledged in the civil law jurisdictions.

The specific approaches to applying this concept, as well as the methods to deal with cases, are different from country to country for at least two reasons. Firstly, the meaning of 'good faith' is considerably vague. The legislative objective for including a principle of good faith to settle issues which are not precisely dealt with in the code causes that its denotation cannot be laid down precisely. This means that the content fluctuates with time. The second reason is that each jurisdiction has developed its own understanding of good faith from the moment it was introduced. Jurisdictions have developed different ways to apply this concept in their case law.[204]

Looking at the nature of the good faith principle, a number of observations can be made. Firstly, it can be observed that the concept of 'good faith' is linked with moral standards. Secondly, some jurisdictions make a distinction between 'subjective good faith' and 'objective good faith'. The former is usually defined as a subjective state of mind: not knowing nor having to know of a certain fact or event. It is of relevance particularly in property law (bona fide acquisition). The latter, which is the concept that the general good faith clauses in codification refer to, is usually regarded as a norm for the conduct of contracting parties: 'acting in accordance with or contrary to good faith'.[205] This means, the law requires that the contracting parties should take the interests of the other party into account to meet the requirements of the value of fairness and reasonableness. Thirdly, 'good faith' is an open norm, which refers to the authority given by the legislator to the courts to decide how it is to be applied. Depending on different circumstances and times, civil law judges

[203] And he also gives the relevant references on the basis of the doctrines and legislation provided by the European scholars and legislators. See Hesselink 2011, p. 622.

[204] As a result of this, the extension, which is displayed as the expression of specific article and the application in cases, of 'good faith' used to be omnifarious in the European Union – in some civil codes, a concept of 'good faith' refers to a requirement in terms of the party's performance or the interpretation of contract while some civil codes have proclaimed clearly that it is an important criterion of unfairness assessment. For instance, Article 1143(3) of the French Civil Code which reads 'Contracts (…) must be performed in good faith' could be the representative of the former and Article 16 of the Portuguese Law of 1985 on Contract Terms which provides 'general contractual terms which are contrary to good faith shall be prohibited' could be the example of the latter.

[205] Even some jurisdictions have applied a separate terminology for objective good faith. See Hesselink 2011, pp. 619–620.

have used good faith to set aside grossly unfair contract terms or to supplement the contract with additional obligations.[206]

Regarding the functions of objective good faith, it is elaborated that good faith can have a supplementing function, an interpretative function and a limiting (restrictive) function.[207] To be more specific, the supplementing function concerns the collateral duties that may arise to meet the demand of good faith, for example, duties of information, co-operation, protection, loyalty, disclosure, and so on.[208] The courts are able to read various types of duties into the contract.[209] These duties which require a contracting party to take the other party's interests into account exist in the pre-contractual stage and extend after the contract has been performed. Thus, good faith is the source of these duties. The interpretative function refers to the situation that the interpretation of a contract should be in accordance with good faith.[210] With respect to the limiting function, good faith often serves to limit the exercise of contractual rights. The most common application of this function is to avoid grave injustice as the result of the initial allocation of rights and obligations. It allows the court to invalidate for instance an exemption clause invoked by one party to escape from its liability when this exemption clause would violate the interests protected by good faith. Furthermore, good faith can also provide the legal basis to allow one party to end or adapt the contractual relationship without any liability in case its performance would be excessively onerous due to an unforeseen change in circumstances.[211]

Although most civil law jurisdictions share the core elements and understanding of good faith and have a long history of applying this principle in private law, there are also some jurisdictions that are unfamiliar with it. English law, for example, did not recognise a general principle of good faith. Before the implementation of the directive, the function that 'good faith' plays in civil law jurisdictions was achieved

---

[206] The legitimacy for judges' work here, to Jan Smits, is that the legislator is never able to foresee all situations that end up in the courts – and if it would be, it is seldom on time or even willing to enact a new statute. Courts can then use the good faith provision to keep the law in sync with societal developments. See Smits 2014, p. 138.

[207] See Smits 2014, pp. 138–140.

[208] For example, Article 1:202 PECL reads: 'Each party owes to the other a duty to co-operate in order to give full effect to the contract.'

[209] See Kornet 2006, pp. 260–263.

[210] For example, § 157 BGB reads: 'Contracts are to be interpreted as required by good faith, taking customary practice into consideration.'

[211] For example, the first paragraph of Article 6:258 of Dutch Civil Code provides: 'Upon a right of action (legal claim) of one of the parties to an agreement, the court may change the legal effects of that agreement or it may dissolve this agreement in full or in part if there are unforeseen circumstances of such a nature that the opposite party, according to standards of reasonableness and fairness, may not expect an unchanged continuation of the agreement. The court may change or dissolve the agreement with retroactive effect.'

in English law by other rules,[212] or good faith was explicitly treated as an essential norm only in certain contractual relationships.[213]

The Unfair Contract Terms Directive attempts to provide a uniform solution for the EU to establish a common understanding of good faith for determining the fairness of terms in consumer contracts. It has adopted some elements from the jurisdictions which are not that familiar with 'good faith', in order to make it more understandable and acceptable. Specifically, the directive provides in its recitals that the assessment of good faith should consider the bargaining positions of the parties, whether the consumer had an inducement to agree to the term and whether the goods or services were sold or supplied to the special order of the consumer. The common lawyers are indeed familiar with this part because it resembles Schedule 2 of the UCTA 1977.[214]

4.5.3.1.3.2 'Good Faith' in the Context of the Unfair Contract Terms Directive

Pursuant to the Unfair Contract Terms Directive, good faith is the first criterion to assess the fairness of a contract term.

In line with Recital 16 and Article 3(1), the assessment of a contract term must be supplemented by an overall evaluation of the different interests involved in light of the requirements of good faith. The assessment of good faith includes whether the consumer had an inducement to agree to the terms, and whether the goods and services were sold or supplied to meet the special requirements of the consumer. During this assessment, the parties' bargaining position should also be considered. Recital 16 provides an abstract guideline that 'the requirement of good faith may be satisfied by the seller or supplier where he deals fairly and equitably with the other party whose legitimate interests he has to take into account.' The CJEU further clarified in *Mohamed Aziz v Caixa d'Estalvis de Catalunya, Tarragona i Manresa (Catalunyacaixa)* that the assessment must be determined whether the seller or supplier 'could reasonably assume that the consumer would have agreed to the term concerned in individual contract negotiations'.[215]

Some scholars suggest that whether the terms were expressed in plain and intelligible words should be taken into account under the requirement of good faith, under Article 3(1), distinguishing between 'procedural good faith' and 'substantive good faith'. It is argued that procedural good faith aims at remedying any possible market failure in the form of lack of information and lack of choice and substantive good faith is related to the contractual terms themselves and focuses on whether and

---

[212] The interpretation of contracts on the basis of 'how reasonable parties would understand it' is a good example.

[213] This situation usually occurs in the contractual relationship of insurance. The core is the requirement that the parties must disclose information to their counterpart. Certain contracts are regarded as contract 'uberrimae fidei' (of utmost good faith).

[214] See Recital 16 of the Unfair Contract Terms Directive.

[215] Case C-415/11 [2013] ECLI:EU:C:2013:164.

to what extent the term realises the interests of the consumer.[216] In this respect, the relation between 'procedural good faith' and the 'incorporation problem' becomes confused. On the one hand, providing transparent and sufficient information is definitely relevant to the issue of the incorporation problem, which we have just discussed in the previous part. On the other hand, (procedural) good faith also requires the consumer to be given the opportunity to examine the contractual terms. The inevitable consequence is that (procedural) good faith also requires that the contractual language should be plain and intelligible. This raises the question in which domain does this 'procedural good faith' fall: an assessment of fairness under Article 3(1) or as a matter of incorporation.

Indeed, the concept 'good faith' used by Article 3(1) contains some procedural elements. Other than the language requirement, the assessment of whether the consumer had an 'inducement' to agree to the terms is relevant to the question of consent and not only the substance of the contractual terms. In my view, this problem could be explained in light of the relation between good faith and the other criterion of the fairness test, significant imbalance, and the relation between the fairness test and the requirement of transparency. This is discussed below.[217]

4.5.3.1.3.3 Significant Imbalance

'Significant imbalance' is the second criterion of the fairness test, or another requirement for a term to be policed as 'unfair', pursuant to Article 3 of the Unfair Contract Terms Directive. Unlike good faith, which is explained by Recital 16, there is no Recital elaborating on what is regarded as a 'significant imbalance'. Thus, it is similarly difficult to define the exact meaning and applicable approach through observing the text of the directive. Some scholars claim that 'significant imbalance' involves a lack of symmetry in the parties' rights and obligations, or that the seller's or supplier's rights or remedies are excessive and disproportionate. The 'balance' here means that the consumer bears a greater risk than the seller or supplier.[218]

In the aforementioned *Mohamed Aziz v Caixa d'Estalvis de Catalunya, Tarragona i Manresa (Catalunyacaixa)*, the CJEU ruled that the concept of 'significant imbalance' must be assessed 'in the light of an analysis of the rules of national law applicable in the absence of any agreement between the parties, in order to determine whether, and if so to what extent, the contract places the consumer in a less favourable legal situation than that provided for by the national law in force'.[219] Thereafter, the assessment of 'legal situation' was emphasised and elaborated by *Constructora*

---

[216] See Nebbia 2010, pp. 222–223.

[217] See Sects. 4.5.3.1.3.3 and 4.5.3.1.3.4.

[218] See Nebbia 2010, pp. 223–224. For example, 'a customer may buy goods which appear to carry a full warranty but find that the clause makes the supplier sole judge of whether or not the goods are defective. The imbalance is that the seller can invoke a legal remedy against the buyer if the latter does not pay, but the buyer has no legal redress against the seller if the seller denies that the goods are faulty.' The illustration can be found in Beale 1989, p. 205.

[219] Case C-415/11 [2013] ECLI:EU:C:2013:164.

Principado SA v José Ignacio Menéndez Álvarez. The CJEU further clarified that the existence of a 'significant imbalance' does not necessarily require that the costs charged to the consumer by a contractual term have a significant economic impact having regard to the value of the transaction in question, 'but can result solely from a sufficiently serious impairment of the legal situation in which that consumer, as a party to the contract, is placed by reason of the relevant national provisions, whether this be in the form of a restriction of the rights which, in accordance with those provisions, he enjoys under that contract, or a constraint on the exercise of those rights, or the imposition on him of an additional obligation not envisaged by the national rules.'[220] According to the CJEU, the assessment of significant imbalance also requires the court to 'take into account the nature of the goods or services for which the contract was concluded by referring to all the circumstances attending the conclusion of that contract, as well as all the other terms of contract'.[221]

As aforementioned, the relationship between good faith and significant imbalance is a contested question. Due to the vague and open nature of good faith, it is difficult to separate it, particularly from a substantive perspective, from significant imbalance. In some Member States' implementation, it can be discovered that these two elements are treated as two separate but equal requirements. A contractual term would be ruled as 'unfair' only if it is evident that in substance the term produced an imbalance between parties' rights and obligations and the process by which the contract was made was contrary to good faith.[222] Nevertheless, the general view throughout Europe is that the two requirements are 'cumulative'.[223] Put differently, it is suggested that the directive indicates that 'good faith' and 'significant imbalance' are separate, but not alternative elements of a two-stage test, the latter being dominant. This means the first stage of the fairness test is to find out whether a significant imbalance exists in the substance of the term, and the second stage occurs when the answer to the former question is affirmative. It then becomes necessary to determine whether the requirement of good faith has been met. On the basis of the introduction given in the previous part, good faith requires the European judges to evaluate whether the consumer had an inducement to agree to the terms and whether the goods and services sold or supplied meet the special requirements of the consumer, but, as mentioned, all these factors should be considered only after a significant imbalance has been established.

---

220 Case C-226/12 [2014] ECLI:EU:C:2014:10.

221 Case C-226/12 [2014] ECLI:EU:C:2014:10.

222 The discussion can be found in Unfair Terms in Contracts: A Joint Consultation Paper, the Law Commission Consultation Paper no 166 and the Scottish Law Commission Discussion Paper No 119, paras 3.57–3.62, pp. 42–45.

223 See Nebbia 2007, p. 150. It is suggested that, from a literal interpretation, 'the four conditions (non-individually negotiated term; contrary to good faith; causing significant imbalance; and bring a detriment to the consumer) are cumulative. 'Goanta 2016. Furthermore, it is mentioned that 'the cumulative use of "good faith" and "substantial imbalance" as criteria for determining the unfairness of a pre-formulated clause is said to result from a compromise between a French/German coalition arguing in favour of good faith and the English plea for significant imbalance'. Micklitz and Reich 2014, p. 786.

Thus, the function of good faith is only to supplement the test of significant imbalance.[224] This means procedural elements play an important role in the requirement of good faith, because, if it is understood from a substantive perspective, which means it also deals with 'imbalance' or 'unduly advantageous' transactions, 'good faith' will inevitably overlap with the test of significant imbalance.

4.5.3.1.3.4 The Relation Between the Fairness Test and the Requirement of Transparency

Since the EU concept of 'good faith' in Article 3 contains procedural elements, which focus on improprieties and defects in the negotiation and conclusion of the contract,[225] it is necessary to discuss whether the requirement of transparency should also be taken into account in the context of the fairness test.

As mentioned before, Article 5 of the Unfair Contract Terms Directive implies two different levels of the requirement of transparency. The first level points to the language. It regulates that the consumer should be provided with a real opportunity to become acquainted with the contract terms, and this requires that the terms have to be drafted in plain and intelligible language. Although there is no clear expression in the directive of the specific legal consequence when the terms are not plain and intelligible, this requirement should be seen to fall into the scope of the 'incorporation problem' and it is a separate requirement from the fairness test. The second level of transparency refers to the situation where the contractual term has been incorporated but is ambiguous. In that case, the meaning more favourable to the consumer will prevail. This is the effect of the interpretative function of good faith. What should be noticed is that even though the *contra proferentem* rule accords with the legal spirit underlying good faith, it is still an issue of formal control derived from a consent-oriented approach. Both levels – incorporation and interpretation – are pre-requisites for substantive control, since logically it is possible to conduct the fairness test only after the incorporation and meaning of the terms has been ascertained. Article 5 should be applied before, and not as part of the fairness test. Thus, this study considers that the requirement for plain and intelligible language and the interpretation rule of *contra proferentem* should be regarded as being separate from the fairness test. They deal with different phases of the assessment of contract terms.[226]

Nevertheless, although in theory it can be deduced that the fairness test and the requirement of transparency provide separate and independent rules to assess contract terms, and this is also supported by the wording of the directive since they are separately regulated in different articles, the boundary between these rules is not clear: Article 5 provides the self-standing requirements on language and interpreta-

---

[224] See Nebbia 2007, pp. 150–151.

[225] See Nebbia 2010, p. 222.

[226] The incorporation problem, the interpretation problem and the fairness problem are deemed as three separate problems under the topic of general controls of unfair contract terms. See Smits 2014, pp. 148–149.

tion, while it also needs to be taken into account when applying the criteria regulated by Article 3(1). When the Unfair Contract Terms Directive was implemented at the national level,[227] this boundary becomes even more obscure, since some Member States explicitly regulate that a term may be regarded as unfair from the provision not being clear and comprehensible.[228] Furthermore, even the CJEU, which is responsible for interpreting EU law to ensure unified application, does not intend to make the boundary clear. It has refrained from clarifying the precise meaning of the fairness test, since it is believed that the interpretation of the fairness test should be a matter for each Member State.[229] Therefore, it is possible that the requirement of transparency also constitutes part of the fairness test in national law.

4.5.3.1.3.5 The Annex

Since the abstract criteria may lack sufficient accuracy and precision to be applied in a uniform way throughout the Member States, the Unfair Contract Terms Directive provides an Annex with an indicative and non-exhaustive list of unfair terms. As stated previously, this list is a grey list. 'Indicative' and 'non-exhaustive' imply that a contract term corresponding to one of the model terms is not automatically unfair, and a term not included in the list is not automatically fair.[230] National legislators need to decide how to regulate these terms in their domestic law. Therefore, it is possible that a term enumerated in the EU Annex is strictly prohibited on the national level, and it is also possible this term still needs further specific evaluation.

For the content, the Annex contains a list of 17 model terms. Scholars provide a summary that these terms can be categorised according to the following criteria: (1) terms giving the user the control of the terms or of the performance of the contract (e.g. example (j) of the Annex: terms which enable the seller or supplier to alter the terms of the contract unilaterally without a valid reason which is specified in the contract; see also examples (i), (k), (l), (m), (p)); (2) terms determining the duration of the contract (e.g. example (g): terms enabling the seller or supplier to terminate a contract of indeterminate duration without reasonable notice; see also example (h)); (3) terms restraining the counterparty from having the same rights as the user (e.g. example (c): terms making an agreement binding on the consumer whereas provision of services by the seller or supplier is subject to a condition whose realisation depends on his will alone, see also examples (d), (f), (o)); (4) exemption and limitations clauses (e.g. example (a), terms excluding or limiting the legal liability of a seller or supplier in the event of the death of a consumer or personal injury to the

---

[227] The general criteria on fairness test provided by Article 3(1) was transposed in a number of very different forms in the Member States. See Micklitz et al. 2010, p. 289.

[228] German law is a good example. This is further discussed in Sect. 4.5.3.2.2.

[229] See Micklitz et al. 2010, p. 289; Nebbia 2010, pp. 224–225.

[230] See Nebbia 2010, p. 221.

latter resulting from an act or omission of that seller or supplier, see also examples (b), (e), (n), (q)).[231]

4.5.3.1.4 Consequences of Unfairness

Within the context of the directive, if a contractual term does not comply with the requirement of fairness, Article 6 provides that it will not be 'binding on the consumer'.[232] If it can be established that the other terms in the contract can still exist and be meaningful without the unfair term, they will continue to be binding.[233]

In its case law, the CJEU has developed a set of more detailed rules on the interpretation of Article 6. For example, in *Jana Pereničová, Vladislav Perenič v SOS financ spol. s r. o.*, the CJEU held that a Member State's national law may provide that the whole contract which contains one or more unfair terms be void if that better serves the protection of the consumer.[234] In the same case, it was also stated that, as regards the criteria for assessing whether a contract can continue to exist without the unfair terms, the national court cannot base its decision solely on a possible advantage for the consumer, but rather should adopt an objective point of view.[235] In addition, the CJEU stated in *Banco Español de Crédito SA v Joaquín Calderón Camino* that a Member State's legislation should not allow a national court, in the case where it finds that an unfair term in a contract is void, to modify the contract by revising the content of that term.[236]

It is noteworthy that, in the context of the Unfair Contract Terms Directive, the CJEU has developed an obligation of national courts to apply EU consumer law on their own motion in order to protect the weaker party. This obligation is described as '*ex officio* application'.[237] The CJEU firstly held in *Océano* that the consumer protection provided by the Unfair Contract Terms Directive entails the national court being able to determine of its own motion whether a term of a contract term before it is unfair when making its preliminary assessment as to whether a claim should be allowed to proceed before the national courts.[238] This competence to review was

[231] R Brownsword, G Howells and T Wilhelmsson, 'The EC Unfair Contract Terms Directive and Welfarism' in Brownsword, Howells, and Wilhelmsson (eds.), Welfarism in Contract Law, Aldershot, Dartmouth, 1994, pp. 275–284. Quoted in Nebbia 2007, p. 4.

[232] Article 6(1) of the Unfair Contract Terms Directive.

[233] See Article 6(1) of the Unfair Contract Terms Directive.

[234] See Case C-453/10 [2012] ECLI:EU:C:2012:144.

[235] See Case C-453/10 [2012] ECLI:EU:C:2012:144, paras. 26–36.

[236] See Case C-618/10 [2012] ECLI:EU:C:2012:349. This viewpoint was also affirmed by the aforementioned case Dirk Frederik Asbeek Brusse, Katarina de Man Garabito v Jahani BV, C-488/11 [2013] ECLI:EU:C:2013:341.

[237] For a summary of the development of this obligation in CJEU case law, see Micklitz and Reich 2014, pp. 780–784.

[238] See Joined Cases C-240/98 to C-244/98 [2000] ECR I-04941.

further extended by *Cofidis*[239] and *Mostaza Claro*.[240] In *Pannon GSM Zrt. v Erzsébet Sustikné Győrfi*, the CJEU affirmed its previous position on this issue, and held that an unfair contract term is not binding on the consumer, regardless of whether the consumer has successfully contested the validity of such a term beforehand. The national court is required to examine, of its own motion, the unfairness of a contractual term where it has available to it the legal and factual elements necessary for that task.[241] Where a national court considers a contract term to be unfair, it must not apply it, unless the consumer opposes that non-application.[242] Nevertheless, it is also pointed out by some scholars that this obligation to invoke of their own motion the unfairness of a contractual term is not really helpful in practice.[243]

At last, the specific approach of implementing 'not binding' is left to the Member States to deal with in the context of their national law, which means Member States can use their own conceptual framework to translate 'not binding'.[244] This is addressed in the following sections.

4.5.3.2 German Law

4.5.3.2.1 Exemption Clauses

German law regulates exemption clauses in § 276(3) BGB, which provides that 'The obligor may not be released in advance from liability for intention.' In the context of consumer protection, § 309 no. 7 BGB enumerates two types of terms which are invalid even to the extent that a deviation from the statutory provisions is permissible. The first category concerns the terms that exempt the user's liability for injury to life, body or health. It provides: 'any exclusion or limitation of liability for damage from injury to life, body or health due to negligent breach of duty by the user or intentional or negligent breach of duty by a legal representative or a person used to perform an obligation of the user'. The second category concerns gross fault. It provides: 'any exclusion or limitation of liability for other damage arising from a grossly negligent breach of duty by the user or from an intentional or grossly negligent breach of duty by a legal representative of the user or a person used to perform an obligation of the user'. It should be noticed that the prohibition of the aforementioned terms does not apply to limitations of liability in some specific areas, such as transport and tariff rules of trams, trolley buses and motor vehicles in regular public transport services, to the extent that they do not deviate to the disadvantage of the passenger.[245]

[239] See Case C-473/00 [2002] ECR I-10875.

[240] See Case C-168/05 [2006] ECR I-10421. For details, see Ebers 2010, pp. 828–831.

[241] See Case C-243/08 [2009] ECLI:EU:C:2009:350.

[242] See Case C-243/08 [2009] ECLI:EU:C:2009:350.

[243] See Steennot 2015.

[244] For example, in Belgium, the concept of nullity is used to transpose the EU requirement of non-bindingness. See Cauffman 2012, p. 1326.

[245] See the second paragraph of § 309 no. 7 BGB.

4.5.3.2.2 Unfair Contract Terms

In German law, the general provision for substantive control of standard terms can be found in § 307 BGB. § 307(1) BGB provides that the provisions in standard terms are ineffective if, contrary to the requirement of good faith, they unreasonably disadvantage the other party to the contract with the user. From the wording used by the German legislator, it can be observed that the status of the principle of good faith has been emphasised and the requirement of 'significant imbalance' regulated by the directive is phrased as 'unreasonable disadvantage'. It is noteworthy that, in German law, it is clearly stated that the transparency requirement constitutes part of the substantive fairness test: 'An unreasonable disadvantage may also arise from the provision not being clear and comprehensible'.[246] § 307(2) BGB regulates the two kinds of circumstances in which it will be presumed that an unreasonable disadvantage exists, in particular where a term is incompatible with an essential principle of the statutory provision from which it deviates, or where it limits essential rights or duties inherent in the nature of the contract to such an extent that the attainment of the purpose of the contract is jeopardised. It should be noted, however, that this general provision is mainly applied to the commercial contracts and unfair contractual terms that are not included in the lists laid down in §§ 308, 309 BGB.[247]

Besides the general provision, a grey list (§ 308 BGB, prohibited terms with the possibility of evaluation) and a black list (§ 309 BGB, prohibited terms without the possibility of evaluation) are laid down in the BGB. The list in § 308 BGB is supposed to be an indicative one, whereas the list in § 309 BGB is much stricter. However, in practice the difference is not so great because the expression in § 308 BGB is rather precise. In contrast, there are many abstract formulations using for instance a 'reasonable' standard in § 309 BGB, which makes it necessary to conduct an individual assessment rather than rely on a solely technical operation of the provision.[248] In the BGB, the examples (a), (b), (d), (e), (f), (h), (i), (l), (n), (p), (q) of the Unfair Contract Terms Directive's Annex are laid down in the black list while the examples (c), (k), (o) are supposed to be within the scope of the grey list. In addition, (g), (j), (m) have not been adopted explicitly in the domestic law.

4.5.3.2.3 Consequences of Unfairness

In the light of §§ 307–309 BGB, where a term violates the general or indicative rules provided by the BGB, it will be regarded as an unfair term and held to be null and void. The consequences of an invalid term in this context are regulated by § 306, which mentions the issue of gap-filling when a contractual term is no longer binding.

---

[246] It is mentioned that whether this adds anything beyond the requirement of clear wording with regard to the requirement of transparency or incorporation is doubtful. See Markesinis et al. 2006, p. 177.

[247] See Markesinis et al. 2006, p. 178.

[248] See Markesinis et al. 2006, p. 178.

On the grounds of the first paragraph of § 306 BGB, the rest of the contract will remain effective. The second paragraph elaborates that the gap created by the invalid unfair term should be filled in by means of applying rules contained in the BGB or other statutory sources. If this alteration leads to unreasonable hardship for one party, the contract will be ineffective as a whole.[249] In practice, the optimal approach to gap filling is disputed. Alternative approaches are to search for the hypothetical intentions of the parties to identify a new term that fits best with the previous term or to adjust the unfair term to a reasonable level on the basis of the default rules.[250] Indeed, it should be noted that the main approach of the courts is to fill the gap 'by having recourse to the rules contained in the German Civil Code'.[251]

4.5.3.3 English Law

4.5.3.3.1 Exemption Clauses

4.5.3.3.1.1 The Rules Provided by the UCTA

As mentioned before, the UTCCR 1999 used to be an important piece of legislation since it implemented the EU directive, and now the CRA 2015 provides the newest regulation on consumer contracts. Prior to these statutory instruments, the UCTA 1977, which has a broader scope of application, has provided the basic rules to regulate exemptions clauses and unfair terms. An introduction to the substantive control in English law should therefore start with this specific piece of legislation, since the UCTA may help to understand the newest rules although itself does not apply to consumer contracts anymore.

The UCTA 1977 mainly focuses on contract terms which involve the exclusion or limitation of the supplier's liabilities, namely exemption clauses. The UCTA renders the terms in dispute either totally invalid in the regulated circumstances or valid only if shown to be reasonable. Considering its broad applicable scope, the reasonableness test differs depending on the situation especially in terms of the operation of clauses in the commercial and consumer contexts.

Section 2 UCTA 1977 provides two types of exemption clauses that are governed by this statute. Among these categories, only the first type of exemption clause regarding exclusion of liability for death or personal injury resulting from negligence, is always unenforceable.[252] The second category concerning terms relating to

---

[249] See the third paragraph of § 306 BGB.

[250] It is stated that some courts suggest the judges should not design terms for the parties and this will encourage the civil actors to use standard terms because even if the terms are policed to be unfair and not binding they can still rely on the adjustment of courts. The others hold that in some cases the judges do create terms by means of determining the parties' intentions and treat this approach prior to applying the rules provided by § 306(3). See Markesinis et al. 2006, p. 179.

[251] Markesinis et al. 2006, p. 179.

[252] Section 2(1) UCTA 1977 reads: 'A person cannot by reference to any contract term or to a notice given to persons generally or to particular persons exclude or restrict his liability for death or personal injury resulting from negligence.'

exemption for other types of loss or damage, is not as strict. These exemption clauses are unenforceable unless they meet the requirement of reasonableness.[253] Other than the types of exemption clauses which are mentioned, Section 2 also provides that 'where a contract term or notice purports to exclude or restrict liability for negligence a person's agreement to or awareness of it is not of itself to be taken as indicating his voluntary acceptance of any risk.'[254] This means a term is not simply reasonable because the other party agreed to it or was aware of it. Furthermore, the concept of 'negligence' referred to in Section 2, is defined in the first paragraph of Section 1.[255]

In the context of consumer contracts, the UCTA 1977 provides that if one of the parties deals as consumer the other party cannot by reference to any contract term when himself in breach of contract, exclude or restrict any liability in respect of the breach, claim to be entitled to render a contractual performance substantially different from that which was reasonably expected of him or to render no performance at all in respect of the whole or any part of his contractual obligation except in so far as the term satisfies the requirement of reasonableness.[256] This section was also regarded as 'the most potent provision' in the UCTA 1977.[257] Furthermore, Section 4 provides that a consumer cannot by reference to any contract term be made to indemnify another person in respect of liability that may be incurred by the other for negligence or breach of contract, except in so far as the contract term satisfies the requirement of reasonableness.

It can be observed that the assessment of 'reasonableness' is central to the rules on exemption clauses in the context of the UCTA 1977, because some clauses will only remain binding if they pass the reasonableness test. Section 11(1) provides that, for determining whether a term is reasonable, 'the circumstances which were, or ought reasonably to have been, known to or in the contemplation of the parties when the contract was made' should be taken into account. In addition, Schedule 2 enumerates further elements for the test, such as the relative bargaining strength of the parties, whether the customer received an inducement to agree to the term, whether the customer knew or ought reasonably to have known of the existence and extent of the term, etc. The courts have also referred to this list when assessing the reasonableness of other exemption clauses.[258]

---

[253] Section 2(2) UCTA 1977 provides: 'In the case of other loss or damage, a person cannot so exclude or restrict his liability for negligence except in so far as the term or notice satisfies the requirement of reasonableness.'

[254] Section 2(3) UCTA 1977.

[255] Section 1(1) states: 'For the purposes of this Part of this Act, "negligence" means the breach: (a) of any obligation, arising from the express or implied terms of a contract, to take reasonable care or exercise reasonable skill in the performance of the contract; /(b) of any common law duty to take reasonable care or exercise reasonable skill (but not any stricter duty); /(c) of the common duty of care imposed by the M1 Occupiers' Liability Act 1957 or the M2 Occupiers' Liability Act (Northern Ireland) 1957.'

[256] See Section 3(2) UCTA 1977.

[257] Twigg-Flesner 2007, p. 3.

[258] See Twigg-Flesner 2007, p. 4.

4.5.3.3.1.2 The Rules Provided by the UTCCR and the CRA

Following the Directive's approach, the UTCCR 1999 contains an indicative list and regulations 1(a) and 1(b) deal specifically with exemption clauses. It should be noted that the adoption of the UTCCR brought some difficulties of consistency into English law in relation to consumer contracts, since the consequences of exemption clauses provided by the UTCCR could be different from the UCTA 1977.[259]

Nevertheless, this situation has been changed since the CRA 2015. With the CRA, the UCTA is no longer applicable to consumer contracts. The CRA contains a separate provision, Section 65, barring exclusions or restrictions of liability for death or personal injury resulting from negligence. In addition, the CRA 2015 also contains a Schedule, which provides that a term which has the object or effect of excluding or limiting the trader's liability in the event of the death of or personal injury to the consumer resulting from an act or omission of the trader may be regarded as unfair.[260] Consequently, it should be noted that the terms that exclude or limit the users' liability for death or personal injury may have different fates depending on the nature of the trader's act or omission. If a term is to exclude the liability for death or personal injury resulting from negligence, it is an absolutely void term; If it is resulting from an act or omission of the trader except negligence, it 'may be' regarded as unfair, which requires the evaluator's discretion in every individual circumstance.[261] Section 65(2) makes it clear that where a trader uses a clause that purports to exclude or restrict its liability for negligence, 'a person is not to be taken to have voluntarily accepted any risk merely because the person agreed to or knew about the term'. Section 65(4) provides a definition of 'negligence' that is for the most part the same as the one previously provided in the UCTA 1977.[262] Finally, the application of Section 65 is limited by Section 66 which lays down that it does not apply to, for example, a contract of insurance, or a contract which relates to the creation of an interest in land.[263]

4.5.3.3.2 Unfair Contract Terms

The UTCCR 1999 implemented the Unfair Contract Terms Directive in English law. The formulation in the regulations is essentially the same as the directive. It included an Annex, which provides an indicative and non-exhaustive list of the terms which may be regarded as unfair. This Annex is also an exact copy of the Unfair Contract Terms Directive. For the general criteria, Regulation 5(1) provides

[259] For instance, on a contractual term excludes the liability for a personal injury from negligence, which is regulated by Section 2(1) UCTA 1977 and Schedule 2 paragraph 1(a) UTCCR 1999, under UCTA it will be regarded as a void one but under UTCCR it is only indicatively unfair.

[260] See Schedule 2 Part I paragraph (1) CRA 2015.

[261] See Section 65(1) and Schedule 2 Part I paragraph (1) CRA 2015.

[262] See Section 65(4) CRA 2015.

[263] See Section 66(1) CRA 2015.

that a non-individually negotiated term is unfair if 'contrary to the requirement of good faith, it causes a significant imbalance in the parties' rights and obligations arising under the contract, to the detriment of the consumer.' The UTCCR 1999 thus imports the notion of 'good faith', which was unfamiliar to academics and practitioners into English law. This led the courts to question whether good faith and significant imbalance are two requirements concerning procedural and substantive elements separately, or simply one combined criterion.

In *Director General of Fair Trading v First National Bank*,[264] which is the leading case on the application of this test, whether 'significant imbalance' exists in the parties' respective rights and obligations is assessed by having regard to the context of the agreement. In deciding whether a term by which a bank could charge further interest on the outstanding part of a loan even after a judgment is unfair, the House of Lords held that the court was required to consider whether the supplier had dealt openly and fairly in assessing the fairness of a term. Whether the wording in the agreement which sets out the distribution of rights and obligations is clear and unambiguous and whether the fact that this specific type of contractual term is prohibited by law should also be taken into account. Furthermore, Lord Bingham provided guidance to interpret the fairness test in general and points out that the fairness test provided by the UTCCR 1999 is a measure inspired by EU legislation and it 'should be interpreted free from any shackles of pre-existing domestic notions of fairness'.[265] He also demonstrated the two requirements of the fairness test. On 'significant imbalance', he mentioned the requirement is met if a term is so weighted in favour of the supplier as to tilt the parties' rights and obligations under the contract significantly in his favour. On 'good faith', he restated the opinion held in *Interfoto Library Ltd v Stiletto Visual Programmes Ltd*[266] that 'this does not simply mean that they should not deceive each other, a principle which any legal system must recognise; its effect is perhaps most aptly conveyed by such metaphorical colloquialisms as "playing fair", "coming clean" or "putting one's cards face upwards on the table." It is in essence a principle of fair and open dealing.' Lord Bingham held that 'openness requires that the term should be expressed fully, clearly and legibly, containing no concealed pitfalls or traps. (…) Fair dealing requires that a supplier should not, whether deliberately or unconsciously, take advantage of the consumer's necessity, indigence, lack of experience, unfamiliarity with the subject matter of the contract, weak bargaining position or any other factor listed in or analogous to those listed in Schedule of the Regulations.'[267] Although Lord Steyn pointed out the general fairness test is primarily a substantive one by stating that 'any purely procedural or even predominantly procedural interpretation of the requirement of good faith must be rejected',[268] the procedural elements of the fairness test should never be ignored. This is particularly the case since terms concerning the price and defining

---

264 Director General of Fair Trading v First National Bank [2002] 1 A.C. 481.

265 Twigg-Flesner 2007, p. 12.

266 Interfoto Library Ltd. v Stiletto Ltd. [1988] 2 W.L.R. 615.

267 Director General of Fair Trading v First National Bank [2002] 1 A.C. 481, at [17].

268 Director General of Fair Trading v First National Bank [2002] 1 A.C. 481, at [36].

the main subject matter are excluded from the fairness test. This is because these terms are usually central to substantive fairness. If they are excluded from the test, the test will to a greater extent depend on the procedural consideration.[269] As stated by Lord Bingham, in the context of English law, the procedural elements should also be taken into account when assessing the unfair term.[270]

In subsequent cases this suggestion, that the seller or supplier will be deemed to have satisfied the requirement of good faith if he takes the time to explain the important terms to the consumer, has been followed.[271]

The UTCCR 1999 have now been replaced by the CRA 2015. Pursuant to Section 62(4) and (6), a contract or a notice is unfair if, contrary to good faith, it causes a significant imbalance in the parties' rights and obligations under the contract to the detriment of the consumer. The wording is exactly the same as the UTCCR 1999. However, it should be noticed that Schedule 2 of the CRA 2015, which offers the non-exhaustive and indicative list, provides three more categories of terms which should be examined under the fairness test, compared with the list provided by the UTCCR 1999.[272]

4.5.3.3.3 Consequences of Unfairness

In English law, a contractual term should not bind the consumer if it is unfair,[273] but the contract should continue to be effective if it is able to survive without the unfair term.[274] Although the term is not binding on the consumer, the consumer is not prevented from relying on the term if he or she chooses to do so.[275] Thus, the term can be enforced by, but not against, the consumer. When the term is regarded as unfair, the court is not entitled to re-write the term in order to make it comply with the fairness requirement.[276] However, the general rules on contract gap filling still apply. The court can read default rules into the contract to fill the gap.

---

[269] See Beatson et al. 2016, p. 230.

[270] Director General of Fair Trading v First National Bank [2002] 1 A.C. 481, at [17].

[271] For instance, see Westminster Building Co Ltd. v Beckingham [2004] EWHC 138 (TCC).

[272] They are the terms (1) which require the consumer to pay disproportionately high charges where the consumer decides not to conclude or perform the contract or for services which have not been supplied, even where the consumer cancels the contract; (2) which allow the trader to determine the characteristics or subject matter after the consumer has become bound by it; and (3) which give the trader the discretion to determine the price after the consumer is bound. See Schedule 2 Part I paragraphs (5), (12) and (14).

[273] See Section 62(1) CRA 2015.

[274] See Section 67 CRA 2015.

[275] See Section 62(3) CRA 2015.

[276] See McKendrick 2016, p. 461.

4.5.4 Comparative Review

When dealing with unfair terms, the substantive control is undoubtedly of crucial importance. In this comparative review, observations from three aspects are made.

Firstly, with respect to exemption clauses, it can be observed that the clauses that exempt the party from liability for death and personal injury are regulated in all the jurisdictions under review. Article 53 of the Chinese Contract Law 1999, example (a) of the Unfair Contract Terms Directive's Annex, § 309 no. 7 BGB and Section 65(1) CRA 2015 all deal with this type of exemption clauses. However, there are still some differences: in Chinese law, these clauses are strictly prohibited, while in the EU directive they need to be examined under the fairness test, and in German law and English law they are prohibited when they exempt liability for death or personal injury resulting from negligence. With regard to the clauses that exempt the user's liability for other damage from negligence, the legislators in China, Germany and England have all addressed this issue in their statutes: in China and Germany, these clauses are null and void if they exempt or limit the user's liability for damage from gross negligence, and English law provides that the counterparty is not deemed to have voluntarily accepted any risk merely because he agreed to or knew about the clause. Apart from these two types, other types of exemption clauses need to be considered under the general fairness test, which is discussed below.

Secondly, with respect to the general fairness test, it can be observed that both the Chinese and EU legislators adopt a similar approach by defining a general criterion and identifying a number of terms that are regarded as unfair.

In China, the core concept used to assess contract terms is 'fairness'. It contains two levels. The first is found in Article 54 of the Contract Law 1999, which provides that obviously unfair terms are voidable in all circumstances. The second is based on Article 39 of the Contract Law 1999, which regulates that the user of the standard terms shall abide by the principle of fairness when defining the rights and obligations. In practice, although Article 39 does not provide the specific criteria and consequences for assessing unfair terms, people's courts are highly likely to cite Article 39 as the basis for their ruling.[277] In the EU, the general criterion for the fairness test comprises two concepts: 'good faith' which supplements the assessment of 'significant imbalance' (Article 3(1) of the Unfair Contract Terms Directive, Section 62 CRA, in German it is described as 'unreasonable disadvantage', § 307 BGB). Although the EU fairness test is primarily a substantive one, which focuses on whether and to what extent the contract realises the consumer's interests, the directive regulates that some procedural elements on how the contract is negotiated and concluded should also be taken into account. On the national level, it is further regulated in German and English law that the requirement of transparency should constitute part of the fairness test. The general criteria regulated by the Chinese and EU

[277] This can be observed from the aforementioned case, Gu Jun v the Shanghai Branch of Bank of Communication. See also Guangdong Zhitong Telecom Ltd. Co v Fenming Hong (广东直通电讯有限公司诉洪分明电话费纠纷案), Gazette of the Supreme People's Court of the People's Republic of China, 2001(6) (《中华人民共和国最高人民法院公报》2001年第6期).

legislators are rather similar. Both 'fairness' and 'good faith significant imbalance' are abstract, and need further interpretation. In addition, they all focus on the substantive content of parties' rights and obligations. It is noteworthy that the procedural elements emphasised by the EU fairness test could help to interpret Article 54 of the Chinese Contract Law 1999 and to make a choice between the 'single-element approach' and the 'dual-element approach'. Indeed, 'significant imbalance' or 'unreasonable disadvantage' are objective requirements to define an unfair term, but in practice it is found that a single objective element is not enough. Good faith adds a test of whether the consumer had a real opportunity to examine or influence the terms and whether he had been able to exercise any choice in agreeing to the terms. This EU approach may inspire the Chinese legislator that, when assessing whether a term is obviously unfair, it is not enough to only look at the definition of rights and interests. How the contract is negotiated and concluded should also be taken into account: a dual-element approach should prevail.

Besides the general criterion, all the jurisdictions under review also provide a list of terms regarded as unfair. In China, Article 40 of the Contract Law 1999 and Article 26 of the Consumer Protection Law 2013 clarify that fairness requires that standard terms do not exempt the user from its liability, increase the liability of the other party, and deprive the other party of their material rights.[278] The EU legislators also use the legislative technique of introducing lists that indicate examples of unfair terms (the Annex to the Unfair Contract Terms directive, § 308 and § 309 BGB, Schedule 2 of the CRA 2015). It can be observed that attention is paid to whether the term gives the user control over the terms or the performance, whether the term determines the duration of the contract, whether the term restrains the counterparty from having the same rights as the user, etc. It is noteworthy that there are two types of lists: the lists provided by the Annex to the directive, § 308 BGB and Schedule 2 of the CRA 2015 are grey lists, which enumerate the contract terms that 'may be regarded as unfair' or 'prohibited with the possibility of evaluation', while the list provided by § 309 BGB is a black list, which means the enumerated contract terms are prohibited without the possibility of evaluation. These lists supplement to a great extent the general test and offer a more workable approach to assess unfair terms. This is especially the case for those national jurisdictions that are unfamiliar with the abstract concept of good faith, e.g. English law. If we compare the lists in the different jurisdictions, it can be observed that the lists provided by the EU directive, German law and English law are more precise and concrete than by Chinese law. The three types of terms enumerated by the Chinese list are still broad and abstract. This may require judges to provide further interpretation in individual situations.

[278] As aforementioned, the new Article 26 replaces the previous concept 'standard contracts' with the concept 'standard terms', and changes the previous wording from 'reduce or escape their civil liability for their infringement of the legitimate rights and interests of consumers' to 'exclude or restrict consumer rights, reduce or waive the responsibilities of business operators, or aggravate the responsibilities of consumers'. These changes cause the wording of the Consumer Protection Law 2013 to be now totally consistent with the Contract Law 1999 on the fairness test of standard terms.

Thirdly, there is a difference in approach with respect to the consequence of unfairness. The Chinese Contract Law 1999 and the Consumer Protection Law 2013 provide several different consequences depending on the different causes of unfairness. Where judges support the claim of a consumer that a term in the contract is obviously unfair, the consumer can uphold the contract or avoid it. If the term is an enumerated exemption or standard term, it is null and void. The EU directive provides that an unfair term is 'not binding'. The reason is to provide flexibility for the national jurisdictions to decide how to implement the consequences of fairness in a way that fits their domestic law. At the national level, English law follows the formulation of the directive and German law regulates that an unfair term is null and void. In terms of the gap left by a term that has been invalidated, only German law explicitly provides a method to fill such a gap which points to the rules contained in BGB or other statutory sources. Other jurisdictions just provide that the invalidity of a term does not influence the rest of the contract, with some exceptions, but ordinary contract law will apply to fill the gap (Table 4.3).

4.6 Public Mechanisms for Controlling Unfair Terms

4.6.1 Introduction

To counteract the use of unfair terms in practice, in most jurisdictions there are not only approaches which allow consumers to initiate litigation but also administrative bodies or consumer organisations that protect individual consumers against the use of unfair terms. It is assumed that individual consumers typically do not have sufficient knowledge and expertise to exercise their rights,[279] and in most cases, are unwilling to initiate legal proceedings.[280] Furthermore, even if one consumer wins in litigation, the impact of the individual decision is relatively limited and little actual pressure will be put on the business to stop using its unfair terms. When another consumer encounters the same situation, he will need to initiate his own proceedings. This leads to unnecessary additional judicial proceedings and costs for consumers. Public enforcement could consequently be more popular, reliable and efficient than private enforcement.[281]

[279] See Micklitz et al. 2010, p. 499.

[280] See Bright 2000, p. 333.

[281] Reinhard Steennot distinguishes the enforcement mechanisms of rules on unfair contract terms into three categories: civil remedies in the individual relation between a seller or supplier on the one hand and a consumer on the other hand, which ensure that an unfair contract term does not bind the consumer (private enforcement); remedies preventing the further use of unfair contract terms (private or public enforcement, depending on the identity of the entity applying for an injunction (e.g., private consumer protection associations versus governmental protection authorities)); administrative and/or penal sanctions for the use of unfair contract terms (public enforcement). See Steennot 2015, p. 594. This study also adopts this classification: whether an enforcement mechanism is private or public depends on who invokes the specific remedy.

Table 4.3 Substantive control

	Exemption clauses	Legal consequences	Unfair contract terms	Legal consequences
Chinese Contract Law	Article 53 (1. Personal injury; 2. Intention or gross fault)	Article 53 (null and void)	Article 54 (obviously unfair)	Article 54 (voidable)
	Article 40 (exempt the supplier from its liabilities)	Article 40 (null and void)	Article 40 (weights the liabilities of the other party, or excludes the rights of the other party)	Article 40 (null and void)
Chinese Consumer Protection Law	Article 26 (reduce or waive the responsibilities of business operators)	Article 26 (null and void)	Article 26 (impose unfair or unreasonable rules… exclude or restrict consumer rights, … or aggravate the responsibilities of consumers	Article 26 (null and void)
EU Unfair Contract Terms Directive	Annex: Example (a)	Article 6 (not binding)	Article 3(1) (1. Good faith; 2. Significant imbalance; annex)	Article 6 (not binding)
GERMAN LAW	§ 276 BGB (intention)	§ 309 BGB (null and void)	§ 307 BGB (1. Good faith; 2. Unreasonable disadvantage)	§ 308 BGB
	§ 309 BGB, no. 7 (1. Injury to life, body or health; 2. An intentional or grossly negligent breach)	§ 306 BGB	§ 308 BGB (Grey list)	§ 309 BGB (null and void)
			§ 309 BGB (black list)	§ 306 BGB
English Law	Section 65 CRA 2015 (exclusion or restriction of negligence liability)	Section 62 CRA 2015 (not binding)	Section 62 CRA 2015 (1. Good faith; 2. Significant imbalance)	Section 62 CRA 2015 (not binding)
	Schedule 2 paragraph 1 CRA 2015		Schedule 2 CRA 2015 (Grey list)	

In China, as aforementioned, despite the existence of three enumerated unfair terms, the provisions provided by the Contract Law 1999 and the Consumer Protection Law 2013 are imprecise and require case-by-case examination. The process of litigation is complicated, costly, and lengthy, for which reason, in most cases, it is believed that consumers feel it is not worth suing a business where the damage is relatively insignificant.[282] Consequently, some administrative organs and local governments provide alternative approaches to control unfair terms. The common feature of these approaches is the intervention of public authorities. For example, the State Administration for Industry and Commerce has provided more detailed

[282] See Wu (吴志勇) 2004, p. 29.

criteria to examine the fairness of terms and authorises its local branches to give a warning or impose a fine where unfair terms are used. Some local administrations for industry and commerce have developed their own mechanisms, such as requiring business operators to register their standard terms for further examination, or inviting business operators for an 'administrative talk' about their standard terms. Apart from the intervention by these public authorities, consumer associations also help individual consumers to strike down unfair terms. They expose unfair terms, by publishing 'comments on unfair terms' on their website to warn consumers as well as to put pressure on businesses.

The situation in the EU is rather similar, since the consumer protection rules are mostly enforced and exercised by administrative bodies and consumer organisations. Article 7 of the Unfair Contract Terms Directive requires Member States to take adequate and effective measures to protect consumers from unfair terms. In most Member States, it is possible to find different approaches that help consumers to permanently strike down unfair terms. However, the scope and duties of the authorities differ considerably from one jurisdiction to another. For example, in some countries, administrative bodies are relatively powerful and they have the primary role to enforce consumer law. In contrast, in other countries the power of administrative bodies is limited and consumer organisations fulfil the responsibility to protect consumers.

This section addresses the mechanisms that can be used to strike down unfair terms apart from litigation before the courts. The public mechanisms for controlling unfair terms in China (Sect. 4.6.2) and the representative EU jurisdictions, Germany (Sect. 4.6.3.2) and England (Sect. 4.6.3.3), are introduced and subsequently compared (Sect. 4.6.4). In each subsection, the methods adopted by administrative bodies and consumer organisations are dealt with separately.

4.6.2 Chinese Law

4.6.2.1 Administrative Bodies

There are several articles in Chap. 4 of the Consumer Protection Law 2013 regulating the responsibilities of the government to protect consumers' lawful rights and interests. Besides the general requirement that the State and the people's governments at all levels should endeavour to protect consumers,[283] a specific governmental organ, the Administration for Industry and Commerce, has been given a special

[283] Article 30 regulates that the State shall hear the opinions of consumers and their association when developing laws, regulations, rules and mandatory standards which are related to consumer rights and interests. Article 31 provides that 'the people's governments at all levels shall strengthen their leadership, organise, coordinate and supervise the relevant administrative departments in satisfactorily protecting the lawful rights and interests of consumers, and fulfil their duties in protecting the lawful rights and interests of consumers.'

responsibility for consumer protection.[284] On the basis of item 4 of the 2008 Provisions of the State Administration for Industry and Commerce on Main Functions, Internal Bodies and Staffing,[285] protecting consumers' lawful rights and interests falls under the scope of this governmental department's duties. The department administers a hotline, identified as '12315', which has dealt with a vast number of complaints, consultations and reports over the past decades. It is believed that this platform has been playing an essential role in supporting consumers.[286]

The State Administration for Industry and Commerce, which is the head of all administrations for industry and commerce in China, published a set of administrative rules, the 'Measures for the Supervision and Handling of Contract-related Violations' (hereinafter 'Measures 2010'), in 2010 that relate to unfair terms.[287] These measures give more detailed criteria for examining whether a standard term meets the requirement of fairness. In particular, Articles 9, 10 and 11 illustrate specific situations of the three enumerated types of unfair terms mentioned in Article 40 of the Contract Law 1999 and Article 26 of the Consumer Protection Law 2013. With respect to the first type of term dealt with in Article 40 of the Contract Law – exemption terms – Article 9 of the Measures 2010 provides that the business operator should not be exempted by standard terms in a consumer contract for: '(1) the liability for any personal injury to the consumer; (2) the liability for the consumer's property loss caused deliberately or by gross negligence; (3) the guarantee liability legally assumed for the commodities or services provided; (4) the liability legally assumed for breach of contract; and (5) other liabilities legally assumed.' In terms of the second category in Article 40 of the Contract Law – terms that increase the liabilities of the other party – Article 10 of the Measures 2010 provides that the business operators should not increase the consumer's liability '(1) by setting an amount of liquidated damages or compensatory damages which exceeds the statutory or reasonable amount; (2) by requiring the consumer to assume any operational risk that shall be assumed by the provider of the standard clauses; or (3) by imposing on the consumer any liability that shall not be assumed by the consumer in accordance

[284] See Article 32. It reads: 'The administrative departments for industry and commerce of the people's governments at all levels and other relevant administrative departments shall take measures to protect the lawful rights and interests of consumers within their respective functions in accordance with the provisions of laws and regulations. /The relevant administrative departments shall hear the opinions of consumers, consumer associations, and other organisations on issues concerning the transactions of business operators and the quality of commodities and services, and investigate and address such issues in a timely manner.'

[285] Provisions of the State Administration for Industry and Commerce on Main Functions, Internal Bodies and Staffing (《国务院办公厅关于印发国家工商行政管理总局主要职责内设机构和人员编制规定的通知》), No. 81 [2009] of the State Administration for Industry and Commerce (国办发[2008]88号).

[286] See Jia (贾东明) 2013, p. 150. Apart from this, there is also a well-known TV program called '3.15 Gala' exposing typical business operators' unlawful behaviour which may harm consumers.

[287] Measures for the Supervision and Handling of Contract-related Violations (《合同违法行为监督处理办法》), Order No. 51 of the State Administration for Industry and Commerce (国家工商行政管理总局令(第51号)).

with laws and regulations'. Article 11 of the Measures 2010 deals with the third type of terms enumerated by Article 40, and regards as unfair standard terms that deprive the material rights of the other party, such as '(1) the right to modify or rescind the contract in accordance with law; (2) the right to claim for payment of liquidated damages; (3) the right to claim for compensation for damages; (4) the right to interpret the standard clauses; (5) the right to lodge a lawsuit for disputes over the standard clauses; and (6) other rights enjoyed by the consumer in accordance with law.' Article 12 of the Measures 2010 gives the administrations for industry and commerce, depending on the seriousness of the case, the power to 'give a warning, impose a fine of not more than 3 times the illegal income but not more than 30,000 yuan or in the absence of illegal income, a fine of not more than 10,000 yuan upon the party.'[288] Where the violation is not significant or no harmful consequences occurred, exceptions have been provided in Article 13 of the Measures.[289]

In practice, along with the viewpoint that the level of the punishment always depends on the severity and social consequence of the violation, in general, the actions taken by the administrations are initiated by consumers' reports and complaints. For example, the Chongqing Administration for Industry and Commerce started a supervision campaign on unfair terms used by Apple Inc. in order to

[288] Article 12 of the Measures 2010. In each province, the determination of the amount of fine is subject to the local administrative rules decided by local branches of the administrative department. For example, the Shanghai Administration for Industry and Commerce provides that: (1) A warning will be given if the duration of the employment of unfair terms are not long and they have been immediately amended after being discovered by examination; (2) in case the unfair terms did not cause complaints by consumers, the result of employment is not harmful, the influence is not big and the unfairness has been rectified in time, a fine equivalent to the illegal income shall be imposed or in the absence of illegal income, a fine of 2000 yuan upon the party; (3) if the employment of unfair terms caused the report by consumers, this violation occurred repeatedly or it led to big social influence, a fine of 2 times the illegal income shall be imposed or in the absence of illegal income, a fine of 8000 yuan upon the party; (4) in the event of a intervenient circumstance of item (2) and (3), a fine of 1.5 times the illegal income shall be imposed or in the absence of illegal income, a fine of 5000 yuan upon the party; (5) if the employment of unfair terms caused mass complaints by consumers, it aroused tremendous repercussions in society and the business operator refused to correct after repeated warnings, a fine of 2.5 times the illegal income shall be imposed or in the absence of illegal income, a fine of 10,000 yuan upon the party. See the Notice of the Shanghai Administration for Industry and Commerce on Issuing the 'Discretionary Standards of the Shanghai Administration for Industry and Commerce for Administrative Penalties for Violations of the "Measures for the Supervision and Handling of Contract-Related Violations" and the "Provisions of Shanghai Municipality on the Supervision of Standard Contract Clauses"' (上海市工商行政管理局关于印发《上海市工商行政管理局关于违反〈合同违法行为监督处理办法〉、〈上海市合同格式条款监督条例〉行政处罚裁量基准》的通知), No. 194 [2014] of the Shanghai Administration for Industry and Commerce (沪工商合(2014)194号).

[289] It reads: 'Where the contract-related violation committed by a party is insignificant and is rectified by the party in a timely manner and no harmful consequences are caused, the party shall be exempted from administrative punishment in accordance with law. If the harmful consequences are eliminated or mitigated by the party voluntarily, the party shall be given a lighter or reduced administrative punishment in accordance with law. If the party rectifies voluntarily or discontinues in a timely manner the contract-related violation under supervision or direction, the party may be given a lighter administrative punishment in accordance with law.'

'respond to society's concern' in 2013. It is said that 'the society's concern' arose because the 12,315 hotline centre of the Chongqing Administration for Industry and Commerce received 23,123 reports, complaints and investigations in 2012 and 7.92% were directed at Apple products, which led to Apple taking the top spot in the category of complaints about 'telecom products'.[290] Although in this case a particular business was targeted, sometimes the action taken, for instance by publishing a number of unfair terms, is not targeted at a particular entity, but only responds to addressing a general public interest. That means consumers can directly request the administration to intervene and take further action if they encounter unfair terms in their consumer contract.[291]

It should be noted that, giving warnings or fines is not always the first priority for the local administrations for industry and commerce. In many provinces, holding an 'administrative talk' is often preferred to warnings or fines and it is seen to be effective. For example, in 'the first case of *bawang tiaokuan* ('霸王条款', which literally means 'hegemon clause' as aforementioned) in Harbin', a restaurant's term that stated 'customers are not allowed to bring their own food and drinks otherwise the discount, coupon or even the invoice would not be provided' was revoked and the non-provided invoice was sent to the consumer, after the owner of the restaurant had an administrative talk with the Harbin Administration for Industry and Commerce.[292] Although the legal status of the 'administrative talk' is still in dispute,[293] considering the strong status of the government and the power of public voice in China, it is highly likely that businesses are willing to amend their contractual terms if they are being monitored by administrations for industry and commerce in order to avoid greater losses as a result of fines or adverse effects on their business reputation. In the aforementioned Apple Inc. case, just half a month after the press conference held by the Chongqing Administration for Industry and Commerce during which 10 unfair standard terms and comments on these terms were published, 34 authorised service providers and franchisers of Apple promised that they would comply with the legal provisions and rules to provide consumers with the required maintenance services even if the contract supplied by Apple Inc. had not yet been amended.[294] Considering that taking action without punishment could 'show the impression of weakness' or 'compromise to violation',[295] if the business refuses to amend its terms, a warning or a fine may ensue. For instance, in 2013, the legal department of Shanxi Administration for Industry and Commerce published a collection of seven

[290] See Zhou (周哲) 2013a.

[291] For example, Beijing Administration for Industry and Commerce published 6 types of unfair terms in the area of catering industry in December 2012 that requires the sellers and suppliers to amend these terms in 1 month and after that they would take actions to punish the sellers and suppliers who refused to do so on the basis of the Measures. See Yao (姚敏) 2013.

[292] See Zuo (左靓) 2014. In the mentioned case of Apple Inc's unfair terms, the method of administrative talk was also applied. See Zhou (周哲) 2013b.

[293] For the latest research, see Meng (孟强龙) 2015.

[294] See Zhou (周哲) 2013b.

[295] See Fan (范子军) 2014.

cases concerning different types of standard-terms-related violations in the China Industry and Commerce News, a newspaper sponsored by the State Administration of Industry and Commerce. For example, a fine of 500 yuan was imposed on the owner of a pharmacy on the grounds of Article 11 and 12 of the Measures 2010 because an unfair term which declares 'our company is entitled to alter and terminate the employment of this card at any time and the ultimate right to interpret is reserved' was found in their membership contract.[296]

Local administrations have also developed some regional approaches to protect consumers from unfair terms. The Zhejiang Administration for Industry and Commerce requires, for instance, that the users of several specific types of contracts, such as estate sale, estate management, travel, public service, telecom, etc.,[297] register their standard terms, which is stated in Article 13 of the Provisions of Zhejiang Province on Administration and Supervision on Contracts adopted by the Standing Committee of Zhejiang Province.[298] Afterwards, a professional committee, whose members include the invited experts such as scholars and practitioners, examine the fairness of these terms.[299] In the case where a term is deemed as 'unfair', the user has to rectify it within 15 days.[300] If the user challenges the decision, a public hearing is held to solve the dispute.[301] If the term is still deemed to be unfair, the user is compelled to amend the term within 30 days after he received the reply for the administration.[302] The situation in Shanghai is rather similar and the relevant rules can be found in the Regulations of Shanghai on Supervision on Contractual Standard Terms adopted by the Standing Committee of Shanghai.[303] It is noteworthy that some more detailed information on the procedure of the public hearing is provided by the Provisions of Shanghai on Public Hearing of Standard Terms.[304]

[296] See Legal Department of Shanxi Administration for Industry and Commerce (山西省工商局法制处) 2013.

[297] It is introduced that these contract terms are stressed because most reports and complaints had arisen in these areas. See Zhang and Lu (张红勤、陆立权) 2004, p. 24.

[298] Provisions of Zhejiang Province on Administration and Supervision on Contracts (《浙江省合同行为管理监督规定》).

[299] See Zhang and Lu (张红勤、陆立权) 2004, p. 24.

[300] Article 16 of the Provisions of Zhejiang Province on Administration and Supervision on Contracts.

[301] Article 17 of the Provisions of Zhejiang Province on Administration and Supervision on Contracts.

[302] Article 18 of the Provisions of Zhejiang Province on Administration and Supervision on Contracts.

[303] Regulations of Shanghai on Supervision on Contractual Standard Terms (《上海市合同格式条款监督条例》).

[304] Provisions of Shanghai on Public Hearing of Standard Terms (上海市工商行政管理局关于印发《上海市合同格式条款听证规定》的通知), No. 324 [2010] of the Shanghai Administration for Industry and Commerce(沪工商合(2010)324号).

4.6.2.2 Consumer Organisations

The China Consumers' Association[305] and its branches (regional consumer protection committees) are the national consumer protection watchdog.[306] Chap. 5 of the Consumer Protection Law 2013 regulates their powers and duties. Article 36 provides that 'Consumer associations and other consumer organisations are social organisations legally formed to exercise social supervision over commodities and services and protect the lawful rights and interests of consumers.' In light of Article 37(1), consumer associations should perform a number of functions,[307] of which 'reporting or inquiring about issues' (item (4)), 'accepting and investigating or mediating complaints' (item (5)), 'filing lawsuits' (item (7)) and 'exposing and criticizing through mass media' (item (8)) are most relevant to the topic of this chapter.

Firstly, items (5) and (8) can be considered as a whole. In the area of unfair terms, the China Consumers' Association and its branches are entitled to intervene in disputes between consumers and business operators. Where a term is considered to be 'unfair' and the user refuses to rectify it, the consumer association can expose and criticise the use of this unfair term to put pressure on the user by challenge this term by complaining to administrations for industry and commerce or by initiating a lawsuit. In this context, the 'comments on standard unfair terms'[308] promulgated by the China Consumers' Association should be taken into account.

In order to realise the functions mentioned in the Consumer Protection Law 2013, the China Consumers' Association from time to time publishes contract terms that are in use in its 'comments on standard unfair terms'. These terms are sometimes reported by its branches and the association generally lists and comments on unfair terms in specific areas. The comments inform consumers and instruct them about the kinds of terms that are unfair and how they can take action to protect their rights and interests.

---

[305] China Consumers' Association (中国消费者协会).

[306] Zhang 2006, p. 140.

[307] Article 37 reads: '(1) Providing consumption information and consultation services to consumers, increasing consumers' ability to protect their lawful rights and interests, and guiding consumption in a civilised, healthy, resource conservation, and environmental protection manner; (2) Participating in the development of laws, regulations, rules, and mandatory standards related to consumer rights and interests; (3) Participating in the supervision and inspection of commodities and services conducted by the relevant administrative departments; (4) Reporting or inquiring about issues concerning the lawful rights and interests of consumers to the relevant authorities and providing recommendations; (5) Accepting complaints of consumers and investigating or mediating complaints; (6) When necessary, authorizing an appraisal by a qualified appraiser, which shall issue an appraisal opinion, if a complaint involves any quality problems of commodities or services; (7) For infringement upon the lawful rights and interests of consumers, supporting the victims in filing lawsuits or, in accordance with this Law, filing lawsuits; (8) Exposing and criticizing through mass media the acts infringing upon the lawful rights and interests of consumers.'

[308] See China Consumers' Association (中国消费者协会), 'Comments on standard unfair terms' (《点评不公平格式条款》), available at: <http://www.cca.org.cn/web/dcjd/newsList.jsp?id=313>, last visited: 2013/10/4.

Recently, the association has published comments on unfair terms in Apple Inc's maintenance contracts.[309] Since 2012, the China Consumers' Association has been concerned with the unfair terms in Apple Inc's maintenance contracts and pressing Apple Inc. to comply with Chinese law, to respect the rights and interests of Chinese consumers, and to rectify the terms that violate Chinese law and damage the rights and interests of Chinese consumers. For instance, they commented on Article 4 of the Apple Maintenance Terms and Conditions as follows[310]:

> *Problem No. 1: Old Component which has been Replaced Belongs to Apple Inc but not Owner.*
>
> *Terms: Article 4 of the Apple Maintenance Terms and Conditions reads: 'If the maintenance service is not within the scope of maintenance... Apple Inc will reserve the replaced component as its property. Meanwhile, the renewed component will be your property. The replaced component can generally be repaired and Apple Inc will replace it or maintain it for you at the same price. If the relevant laws request Apple Inc to restitute the replaced component, you agree to pay the extra fee to replace the component.*
>
> *Comments: Consumers are entitled to the rights to possess, use, seek profits from and dispose of the product and its components since they have purchased a product provided by Apple Inc, regardless of whether it is within the time period of the 'three guarantees'(translated from the Mandarin phrase 'san bao' (三包), it refers to three methods of guarantee – which are guarantee of maintenance, guarantee of replacement and guarantee of return – within a certain time period regulated by Chinese law). Within the time period of the 'three guarantees', it is the legal duty of the business operator to maintain the product for free. Even if the business operator has replaced the component for the consumer, it will not change the fact that the replaced component is owned by the consumer. Thus, the replaced component belongs to the consumer and Apple Inc has no right to take it back. Outside the time period of the 'three guarantees', if the consumer has paid for maintenance or replacement, Apple Inc shall not keep the replaced component as its certain property. The replaced components still have value. If Apple Inc wants to obtain the old component, they can negotiate with the consumer and buy it back. Therefore, Article 4 in the maintenance contract violates the Property Law 2007[311] and the Consumer Protection Law 2013. It violates the right of ownership, the right of free choice and the right of fair trade.*
>
> *Legal basis: Articles 4 and 39 of the Property Law 2007, Articles 9 and 10 of the Consumer Protection Law 2013.*[312]

---

[309] See China Consumers' Association (中国消费者协会), 'Special Report: Comments on Standard Unfair Terms in Apple Inc's Maintenance Contracts' (《专题报道:点评苹果维修不公平格式条款》), available at: <http://www.cca.org.cn/web/ztbd/newsList.jsp?id=3581>, last visited: 2013/10/4.

[310] See China Consumers' Association (中国消费者协会), 'Problem No. 1 of Comments on Apple Maintenance Terms: Old Component which has been Replaced Belongs to Apple Inc. but not Owner, published on 30 August 2012' (《再评苹果维修条款问题1:更换旧件归公司财产不容自处分》(2012年8月30日发布)), available at: <http://www.cca.org.cn/web/ztbd/newsShow.jsp?id=61840&cid=3581>, last visited: 2013/10/4.

[311] Property Law of the People's Republic of China (《中华人民共和国物权法》).

[312] Article 4 of the Property Law provides: 'The real rights of the state, collectives, individuals or any other right holder shall be protected by law and shall not be infringed by any entities or individuals.' Article 39 reads: 'The owner of a real property or movable property has the rights to possess, use, seek profits from and dispose of the real property or movable property according to law.' Article 9 of Consumer Protection Law provides: 'Consumers shall enjoy the right of free

However, it is argued that in China the consumer protection provided by social supervision of the China Consumers' Association is less effective than exerting administrative power. Scholars point out that although publishing 'comments' raises public awareness, the targeted users still persist in their old ways and refuse to amend their terms.[313] This could be related to the function mentioned in item (4). Since consumer associations are considerably weak, they can seek assistance from the people's governments at various levels and the latter are required to give support to consumer associations in the performance of their functions. In practice, it is likely that there are many circumstances in which they work together to protect consumers.

With regard to item (7), the new Consumer Protection Law 2013 grants consumer associations standing to initiate lawsuits, which is also a significant change in Chinese consumer law. Article 47 of the Consumer Protection Law 2013 provides: 'For infringement upon the lawful rights and interests of vast numbers of consumers, the China Consumers' Association and the consumer associations formed in provinces, autonomous regions, and municipalities directly under the Central Government may file lawsuits in the people's courts.' In a juridical interpretation promulgated in 2016, the Interpretation of the Supreme People's Court on Several Issues concerning the Application of Law in the Conduct of Consumer Civil Public Interest Litigations,[314] the Supreme People's Court confirms that Article 47 is applicable where the business operator uses standard terms and conditions, notices, declarations, on-site posters, or other means to exclude or restrict consumer rights, reduce or waive the responsibilities of business operators, or aggravate the responsibilities of consumers.[315] Consequently, if a contractual standard term harms the lawful rights or interests of a vast number of consumers, the local consumer association is able to sue the user under the new Consumer Protection Law.[316] In late 2016,

choice of commodities or services. /Consumers shall have the right to make a free choice of business operators for supply of commodities or services, select freely among varieties of articles or forms of services and decide independently to buy or not to buy any kind of commodities, or to accept or not to accept any item of services. /Consumers shall have the right to make comparisons, differentiations and selections when they make a free choice of commodities or services.' Article 10 reads: 'Consumers shall enjoy the right of fair deal. /Consumers shall, in their purchasing commodities or receiving services, have the right to obtain fair deal prerequisites such as guarantee of quality, reasonable prices and correct measurement, and have the right to refuse any compulsory transaction of business operators.' What should be noticed is that the Consumer Protection Law mentioned here is the old version before the amendment, which is the Consumer Protection Law 1993.

[313] See Wu (吴志勇) 2004, p. 29.

[314] Interpretation of the Supreme People's Court on Several Issues concerning the Application of Law in the Conduct of Consumer Civil Public Interest Litigations (《最高人民法院关于审理消费民事公益诉讼案件适用法律若干问题的解释》), No. 10 [2016] of the Supreme People's Court (法释[2016]10号).

[315] See item (4) of Interpretation No. 10 [2016] of the Supreme People's Court.

[316] Only two judicial decisions can be found. The Shanghai Consumers' Association sued Tianjin Samsung Communication Technology Co Ltd. and the Guangdong Oppo Mobile Communication Co Ltd. respectively for their non-disclosure of important information on preloaded applications.

the Jiangsu Consumers' Association brought a lawsuit against the Nanjing Tap Water General Company, which is a state-owned enterprise in charge of the whole Nanjing city's tap water production and supply. The Jiangsu Consumers' Association claimed that the standard term which states 'if the consumer delayed in paying the water rate, he should pay 0.5% of the water rate per day as liquidated damage' is unfair, since 0.5% is much higher than the bank interest. This case has drawn wide attention, because this contract term is closely related to people's daily life and public welfare. Since individual consumers cannot vote with their feet since the defendant is a monopolistic company, it is necessary for the Jiangsu Consumers' Association to take the action. Although the trial is still in session, this case is already regarded as a template for the public interest litigation in the area of consumer law.[317]

4.6.3 EU Law

4.6.3.1 The Unfair Contract Terms Directive

Article 7 of the directive requires Member States to introduce 'adequate and effective' means to prevent the use of unfair terms.[318] This means that national jurisdictions have to ensure consumers' rights and interests are protected against unfair terms. Within this context, it is of considerable importance to create a clear path for consumers to address national courts or administrative bodies.[319] To meet this

Since the cell phone companies were both willing to rectify their contracts and provide the consumer with more sufficient information, the Shanghai Consumers' Association withdrew the lawsuits. See Shanghai Consumers' Association v Guangdong Oppo Mobile Communication Co Ltd. (上海市消费者权益保护委员会诉广东欧珀移动通信有限公司侵权责任纠纷案), Civil Ruling [2015] No. 10 of the Shanghai No. 1 Intermediate People's Court (上海市第一中级人民法院(2015)沪一中民一(民)初字第10号民事裁定书), and Shanghai Consumers' Association v Tianjin Samsung Communication Technology Co Ltd. (上海市消费者权益保护委员会诉天津三星通信技术有限公司侵权责任纠纷案), Civil Ruling [2015] No. 10 of the Shanghai No. 1 Intermediate People's Court (上海市第一中级人民法院(2015)沪一中民一(民)初字第10号民事裁定书).

317 See Yan (晏扬) 2016.

318 The CJEU will examine whether the forms and methods adopted by Member States are enough. In Commission of the European Communities v Kingdom of the Netherlands, the court considered the chosen form and method was sufficient. See Case 144/99 [2001] ECR I-3541. In this case, the Netherlands government claimed that the existing provisions of the 1992 Burgerlijk Wetboek (DBW) had already given sufficient basis for protection of consumers against unfair contract terms so the implementation of the Unfair Contract Terms Directive is not necessary. The Netherlands government invoked Article 3:35, 6:231, 6:233 and 6:248 of the DBW. However, the Commission maintained that the transposition is incomplete because of the insufficiency of the form, method and effect. See Hondius 1997, p. 193.

319 Being limited by its competence, the CJEU cannot do anything in a specific fairness assessment. It is only entitled to interpret the Unfair Contract Terms Directive. This is clearly stated in the Case 237/02 Freiburger Kommunalbauten GmbH Baugesellschaft & Co KG v Ludger Hofstetter and

requirement, Member States use various methods to help consumers address a public body, such as the Competition and Markets Authority (hereinafter 'CMA') in the United Kingdom.

It should be noted that the rationale behind Article 7 is that preventing the continued use of unfair terms should be dealt with by public authorities, and not solely rely on individual consumers. Consequently, Member States have introduced diverse 'public reviews' to control unfair terms. In addition, in case the collective interests of consumers in the internal market are infringed, the Injunctions Directive[320] provides means to bring action for the cessation of infringement. The Injunctions Directive allows a qualified entity from one Member State, which could be a consumer representative body or a recognised independent public body, to seek an injunction in the other Member State where the infringement originated.[321] To the nature of infringements addressed by the directive includes the use of unfair terms.[322] Regulation 2006/2004[323] provides that the public authorities responsible for enforcing consumer protection law, which are designated by each EU Member State, will join the mutual assistance network, which enables national authorities to exchange information and cooperate with their counterparts in other Member States. Through this network, it becomes easier to stop consumer regulation violations even if the trader and consumer are located in different countries.

The following sections introduce the instruments available to administrative bodies and consumer organisations under German law and English law.

4.6.3.2 German Law

4.6.3.2.1 Administrative Bodies

In Germany, it must be pointed out that the power of administrative bodies to protect consumers from unfair terms is restricted. It is argued that this standpoint has been adopted on the grounds that the intervention of administrative bodies challenges the principle of freedom of contract. As a result, in Germany, public bodies simply have

---

Ulrike Hofstetter [2004] ECR I-3403, where the Court reasoned that it is for the national court to decide whether a contractual term in a building contract requiring the whole of the price to be paid before the performance by the seller or supplier of its obligations and provision by the latter of a guarantee satisfies the requirements for it to be regarded as unfair under Article 3(1). See Gavrilovic 2013, p. 176.

[320] Directive 2009/22/EC of the European Parliament and of the Council of 23 April 2009 on injunctions for the protection of consumers' interests [2009] OJ L110/30.

[321] A whole list of the qualified entities can be found in Notification from the Commission concerning Article 4(3) of Directive 2009/22/EC of the European Parliament and of the Council on injunctions for the protection of consumers' interests, which codifies Directive 98/27/EC, concerning the entities qualified to bring an action under Article 2 of this Directive, [2016] OJ C 361/1.

[322] See Annex I, item (5) of the Injunctions Directive.

[323] Regulation (EC) No 2006/2004 of the European Parliament and of the Council of 27 October 2004 on cooperation between national authorities responsible for the enforcement of consumer protection laws (the Regulation on consumer protection cooperation) [2004] OJ L364/1.

supervisory tasks[324] and administrative enforcement is not a duty or power which should be performed by the government. For example, the Federal Ministry of Justice and Consumer Protection (*Bundesministerium der Justiz und für Verbraucherschutz*, hereinafter 'BMJV') primarily serves to draft legislation and to advise the other Federal Ministries in the preparation of legislative proposals. It also aims to establish the conditions for safe and self-determined consumer activity.[325]

4.6.3.2.2 Consumer Organisations

In Germany, in contrast to the relatively weak administrative bodies, consumer organisations are expected to do more in the context of combatting unfair terms. It is even suggested that 'consumer organisations are more or less the sole players in such areas as unfair terms and unfair commercial practices'.[326] German law relies on private organisations to file actions for an injunction in order to protect the common interest and the freedom of contract of consumers in general. Pursuant to §13 AGBG, consumer organisations and other qualified bodies are entitled to petition the courts for a cease and desist order (*Unterwerfungserklärung*) to stop the use of unfair terms. This rule was subsequently replaced by the UKlaG: § 1 reiterates the right for these qualified bodies to seek injunctive relief against the use of unfair standard contract terms.

As for 'qualified bodies', a complete list can be found in the Notification from the Commission concerning Article 4(3) of Directive 2009/22/EC of the European Parliament and of the Council on injunctions for the protection of consumers' interests, which codifies Directive 98/27/EC, concerning the entities qualified to bring an action under Article 2 of this Directive.[327] Among all these qualified bodies, the Federation of German Consumer Organisations (Verbraucherzentrale Bundesverband, hereinafter 'VZBV') as a non-governmental organisation acts as an umbrella for 41 German consumer associations.[328] VZBV devotes itself to protecting and empowering consumers, by lobbying and campaigning at national and European levels, by providing information and advice, by taking collective legal action on behalf of consumers, by ensuring that its message receives broad media coverage, and by providing professional training for the staff of consumer organisations.[329]

---

[324] In particular, it is restricted to superintending consumer organisations receive public funding. See Cafaggi and Micklitz 2007, p. 7.

[325] See Tasks of the Federal Ministry of Justice and Consumer Protection, available at: <http://www.bmjv.de/EN/Ministry/StructureOrganisation/Tasks/tasks_node.html; jsessionid=D0EC846058CDF5B72045B8BD5C3EF4F8.1_cid324>, last visited: 2017/3/5.

[326] Cafaggi and Micklitz 2007, pp. 6–7.

[327] See Notification from the Commission concerning Article 4(3) of Directive 2009/22/EC of the European Parliament and of the Council on injunctions for the protection of consumers' interests, which codifies Directive 98/27/EC, concerning the entities qualified to bring an action under Article 2 of this Directive, [2016] OJ C 361/5.

[328] See Verbraucherzentrale Bundesverband, 'Welcome to the VZBV', available at: <http://en.vzbv.de/>, last visited: 2017/3/8.

[329] See Verbraucherzentrale Bundesverband, 'What we do', available at: <http://en.vzbv.de/1578.htm>, last visited: 2017/3/8. See also, Notification from the Commission concerning Article 4(3)

4.6.3.3 English Law

4.6.3.3.1 Administrative Bodies

In the United Kingdom, the Office of Fair Trading (hereinafter 'OFT') and its Unfair Contract Terms Unit used to play an important role in protecting consumers from unfair terms. Regulation 10 to Regulation 15 UTCCR 1999 outlined how this system works. This has now been replaced by Schedule 3 of the CRA 2015. This function of the OFT is now performed by the CMA. This section introduces both the old and new system.

The actions taken by the OFT were usually initiated by a complaint from consumers. In the UTCCR 1999, the Director General of Fair Trading[330] had the duty to consider any complaint that the target contract term drawn up for general use is unfair.[331] There were two exceptions provided: (a) if the complaint is frivolous or vexatious; or (b) if a qualifying body has notified the Director that it agrees to consider the complaint, the OFT is no longer bound by the aforementioned duty. Apart from the OFT, other qualifying bodies, such as the Director General of Electricity Supply, the Director General of Gas Supply, etc.,[332] were also entitled by the UTCCR 1999 to consider consumers' complaints and interfere in disputes. After the introduction of the UTCCR 1999, the Enterprise Act 2002 further extended the scope of 'qualifying bodies' to include local weights and measures authority in Great Britain and the Department of Enterprise, Trade and Investment in Northern Ireland as 'general enforcers'. It is also possible for the Secretary of State to designate enforcers.[333] In the CRA 2015, the aforementioned rules are integrated in Schedule 3, which provides that a regulator may consider a complaint about a term or notice.[334] The foregoing qualifying bodies are enumerated in paragraph 8 as 'regulators'.[335]

---

of Directive 2009/22/EC of the European Parliament and of the Council on injunctions for the protection of consumers' interests, which codifies Directive 98/27/EC, concerning the entities qualified to bring an action under Article 2 of this Directive, [2016] OJ C 361/14.

[330] Regulation 3 UTCCR 1999. It is noteworthy that the Enterprise Act 2002 replaces the Director General by the OFT to materialise these functions. In the following introduction 'OFT' will be directly applied although in the original text it should be 'the Director General'. See Section 2(1) of the Enterprise Act 2002. It reads: 'The functions of the Director General of Fair Trading (in this Act referred to as "the Director"), and his property, rights and liabilities, are transferred to the OFT.'

[331] See Regulation 10(1) UTCCR 1999.

[332] On the grounds of Part 1, Schedule 1 of the UTCCR 1999, the qualifying bodies are: (1) The Data Protection Registrar; (2) The Director General of Electricity Supply; (3) The Director General of Gas Supply; (4) The Director General of Electricity Supply for Northern Ireland; (5) The Director General of Gas for Northern Ireland; (6) The Director General of Telecommunications; (7) The Director General of Water Services; (8) The Rail Regulator; (9) Every weights and measures authority in Great Britain; (10) The Department of Economic Development in Northern Ireland; (11) Consumers' Association.

[333] Section 213, 'Enforcers', the Enterprise Act 2002, Part 8.

[334] Paragraph 2(1) of Schedule 3 CRA 2015.

[335] They are: (a) the CMA; (b) the Department of Enterprise, Trade and Investment in Northern Ireland; (c) a local weights and measures authority in Great Britain; (d) the Financial Conduct

Although these regulators are all entitled to consider a complaint, the CMA remains of primary importance since the other bodies are required to notify the CMA if they intend to consider a complaint.[336] A regulator must provide reasons to the person who made the complaint, if an application for the specific action is not made.[337]

The 'specific action' that the OFT or other qualifying body could take was to petition the court for an injunction, on the grounds of Regulation 12 UTCCR 1999, where it considered a term to be unfair in order to stop the use of the term.[338] Under this provision, the court may grant an injunction on such terms as it thinks fit.[339] The OFT was required to provide reasons and ask the business to provide undertakings concerning the continued use of such a term.[340] In practice, an injunction was not often needed because the Unfair Contract Terms Unit usually required the business to provide an undertaking to discontinue the use of the unfair term. Since the majority of businesses involved are willing to give such an undertaking and abandon or amend their terms, most disputes are solved by this sort of approach. Court action is a last resort and has been rarely initiated.[341] It is suggested that businesses are willing to make such undertakings for two main reasons. First, the OFT was under a duty to publish the details of the unfair terms it identified on the grounds of Regulation 15 and businesses fear bad publicity. Secondly, there are cost savings if an unfair term is amended since it can then still be used in contrast to the situation where an injunction is granted and the whole term is struck down.[342] In the CRA 2015, the injunction is still the primary instrument to stop the use of an unfair term. The application by a regulator and the determination by the court are regulated by paragraphs 3 and 5 of Schedule 3. The CRA 2015 also includes the mechanism of requiring businesses to give 'undertakings' concerning the continued use of unfair terms.[343] The contents of these paragraphs are for the most part the same as the provisions in the UTCCR 1999.

It should be noticed that dealing with trade associations is also recognised as 'an efficient way' to change contract practices. It is argued that agreements reached at

Authority; (e) the Office of Communications; (f) the Information Commissioner; (g) the Gas and Electricity Markets Authority; (h) the Water Services Regulation Authority; (i) the Office of Rail Regulation; (j) the Northern Ireland Authority for Utility Regulation, or (k) the Consumers' Association.

336 See paragraph 2(2) of Schedule 3 CRA 2015.

337 See paragraph 2(3) of Schedule 3 CRA 2015.

338 It should be noticed that if a qualifying body purports to apply for an injunction, it must give the Director General notice. Furthermore, unless a shorter period is permitted, they cannot commence an action within 14 days. Regulation 12 UTCCR 1999.

339 Regulation 12(3) UTCCR 1999.

340 Regulation 10(2), (3) UTCCR 1999.

341 Susan Bright provides that although the Director General of Fair Trading has power to apply for an injunction, this had occurred only once by the end of the time that she wrote her contribution. See Bright 2000, p. 334.

342 See Bright 2000, p. 335.

343 See paragraph 6 of Schedule 3 CRA 2015.

this level will be passed down to the businesses through the use of the association's standard terms. Susan Bright provides an example that the agreement concluded between the OFT and the British Vehicle Rental and Leasing Association on revision of the model contract for use has affected 85% of the companies in the industry because they all belong to this association.[344]

4.6.3.3.2 Consumer Organisations

The Consumers' Association is also recognised as a qualifying body to consider complaints from individual consumers and apply for an injunction on the ground of Part 2 of Schedule 1 of the UTCCR 1999. This can now also be found in paragraph (k) of Schedule 3 of the CRA 2015. The Consumers' Association is also under a duty to report all undertakings it receives and the result of any application for an injunction. After the introduction of the Enterprise Act 2002, the Secretary of State also recognised the Consumers' Association as a designated enforcer to initiate special proceedings in the area of consumer protection.

Section 11 of the Enterprise Act 2002 authorises the Consumers' Association and other designated enforcers to make a complaint to the OFT that 'any feature, or combination of features, of a market in the United Kingdom for goods or services is or appears to be significantly harming the interests of consumers'. This is recognised as a 'super complaint'. The OFT must react within 90 days by publishing a response and declaring how it intends to deal with the complaint as well as provide reasons.[345] The CMA is now the official body in charge of super complaints.

4.6.4 Comparative Review

On the basis of the above analysis, we can conclude that public mechanisms operated by administrative bodies and consumer organisations play a crucial role in enforcing consumer protection laws in many jurisdictions. However, it is possible to observe a tension between these two public mechanisms: there is invariably one institution that is in charge. In China and England, although consumer organisations are entitled to accept and consider complaints, they have the duty to report to the administrative bodies and the arrangements will be always made by the administrative bodies (the Administrations for Industry and Commerce and the CMA). In particular, the administrations in China have more authority and they can take actions which cannot be taken by consumer organisations, and in England it is believed that the administrative mode 'is a much more effective way of preventing the continuing use of unfair terms and changing contracting practice.'[346] In contrast, in Germany,

[344] See Bright 2000, p. 335.

[345] Section 11(2), (3), the Enterprise Act 2002.

[346] Bright 2000, p. 333.

the consumer organisations are relied on to petition the courts for an injunction to protect consumers in general. Generally speaking, 'consumer organisations play a less important role in countries with a strong consumer agency and vice versa. The interaction between the two players therefore depends on who is taking the lead in enforcing consumer law.'[347]

Amongst the jurisdictions in which administrative bodies play the dominant role in protecting consumers from unfair terms, the instruments that are applied or the specific approach taken can still differ. In China, the most effective instrument adopted by the administrations for industry and commerce is the imposition of a fine. In contrast, in England, the CMA only has the power to apply for an injunction. This difference could be explained by the different role of government in the two countries: in China, the government is a strong watchdog that supervises businesses closely, and the market economy in the United Kingdom requires more freedom. This difference also influences the approach taken prior to imposing a fine or petitioning the court for an injunction. In China, an administrative talk can be characterised as an action of market control or management, rather than a negotiation between two equal parties. This issue is further discussed in the last section of this chapter.

Furthermore, in China, the administrative bodies have the ultimate decision-making power to determine whether a term is fair, whereas in England, even if an injunction is sought, it is still for the court to assess whether it is 'appropriate' to grant the injunction. Since the determination whether a term is fair is a legal issue, it makes sense that this decision is taken by a judge. In this light, the Chinese approach could be subject to criticism. However, if the specific officials dealing with these matters have a legal background, and are more experienced in this specific field, this difference in approach may not be that significant. Nevertheless, even if they are well-trained and experienced, it is still possible to challenge their neutrality when dealing with disputes between consumers and state-owned enterprises. In recent years, the administrations for industry and commerce have been suspected of regional protectionism since many enterprises that have been punished are large-scale multinational enterprises even though their violations are often not that severe (Table 4.4).

4.7 Concluding Remarks

4.7.1 Comparison Between China and the EU

This chapter describes how Chinese law and EU law deal with 'unfair terms' in consumer contracts, in particular when contractual terms contravene the principle of 'fairness'. Standard terms are usually designed and provided by one party and the other party can scarcely influence their content. Sometimes the terms are

[347] Cafaggi and Micklitz 2007, p. 7.

Table 4.4 Public mechanisms for controlling unfair terms

	Administrative bodies and their measures	Consumer organisations and their measures
Chinese Consumer Protection Law	Administrations for industry and commerce; Accepting and hearing complaints Administrative talk; Publishing unfair terms; Giving warnings; Imposing fines	China consumers' association and its branches accepting and investigating or mediating complaints; Exposing and criticizing through mass media; (e.g. comments on unfair terms)
		Reporting or inquiring about issues to administrations; Filing lawsuits
EU Unfair Contract Terms Directive	Article 7	
German Law	BMJV; Draft legislation; Advise the other Federal Ministries in the preparation of legislative proposals, etc	AGBG § 13 Consumer Organisations and trade Organisations; Filing lawsuits; Applying injunctions
English Law	Competition and markets authority; Other regulators; Considering complaints; Requiring undertakings; Applying injunctions; Publishing details and information about unfair terms Dealing with trade associations	Consumers' association; Considering complaints; Applying injunctions; Super complaint

incorporated even without the other party's explicit awareness. Holding the other party strictly bound by them, like in the case of individually negotiated terms, could lead that party to suffer great disadvantage. Thus, legislators consider it necessary to intervene and provide rules to police these terms. The emphasis in this chapter has been on understanding the standard against which standard contract terms are evaluated. Although there are commonalities in the rules of the different jurisdictions, there are also differences. The findings of this chapter can be presented as follows.

Firstly, it is observed that each national jurisdiction adopts a 'double-decker structure': there are rules designed for contracts in general and rules devised for consumer contracts only. However, on the EU level, because of the restriction on the EU's legislative competence, the directive is solely applicable to B2C contracts.

Secondly, a further distinction is made with respect to the type of contract term that is assessed. In the EU, only non-individually negotiated terms can be evaluated under the directive. A contract term is regarded as 'non-individually negotiated' if it was drafted in advance and the consumer was not able to influence the substance of the term. On the national level, the German approach focuses on standard terms and the English CRA 2015 applies to all consumer contract terms. In contrast, although Chinese law also contains provisions directed at standard terms, there are provisions that are applicable to all contract terms. In terms of the concept of 'standard terms', the Chinese Contract Law 1999 defines it as '(the terms which) were prepared in advance for the purpose of repeatable use and which were not negotiated with the other party'. It can be observed that this Chinese definition is very similar to the EU definition of 'non-individually negotiated terms', except that the terms have to be reused. This requirement of repeatable use makes the scope of the Chinese rules narrower than the EU Unfair Contract Terms Directive, because the EU rules also apply to one-off transactions provided the terms were not individually negotiated. In practice, the difference is negligible. German law explicitly provides that the terms prepared for a one-off trade also need to undergo the fairness test, and English law provides the broadest applicable scope. With regard to the applicable scope, there is a conspicuous difference between Chinese law and EU jurisdictions. The Unfair Contract Terms directive, German law and English law all provide that 'core terms' regarding the description of the main subject matter of the contract or the quality/price ratio of the goods or services supplied shall be excluded from the fairness test, whilst in China no such rule can be found. We can therefore see that the jurisdictions make different choices concerning the type of contract terms that can be policed.

Thirdly, it is pointed out that in all the jurisdictions under review, the control of standard terms can be divided into two steps: formal control and substantive control. The formal control focuses on the improprieties and defects in the negotiation and conclusion of the contract. It requires that the consumer should be given an actual opportunity to become acquainted with the term and agree to it sincerely. The duty to draw attention and the requirement of transparency regarding language and the interpretation rule *contra proferentem* all fall within this step. The substantive control, on the other hand, concerns the substance of the term, in particular the fairness of the rights and obligations of the parties.

The formal control of standard terms includes two layers of legal mechanisms. The first layer is to evaluate whether the term is incorporated. In Chinese, German and English law, if a consumer claims he is not acquainted with a standard term in the contract, the law examines whether the trader has drawn attention to the term. If the trader has not done so appropriately, the term will not be binding. Apart from this similarity, there is a difference in the approach of these three jurisdictions. In Chinese law, it is provided by a judicial interpretation that the consequence of the failure to draw attention to the term – or information duty – is that the term is incorporated but it can be avoided by the other party. In sharp contrast, the consequence in German and English law is that the term has not been incorporated because of a lack of consensus. The second layer of formal control is to determine how the standard term should be interpreted. Specifically, the *contra proferentem* rule whereby the interpretation that is most favourable to the consumer prevails can be found in all investigated jurisdictions. In addition, the EU directive requires that the terms be drafted in plain and intelligible language. However, the consequence of violating this duty is not provided in the directive, and is left to the Member States. Consequently, in English law the term will not be binding, while in Germany the duty supplements the substantive fairness test. In contrast, in China, there is no statutory requirement to use plain and intelligible language. It can be observed therefore that EU jurisdictions place more emphasis on formal control, since the EU directive, and national law consequently, include a duty to use plain and intelligible language. And the duty to draw attention is also regulated in a more precise and detailed way. In contrast, the incorporation rule on surprising terms or the 'red hand rule' can only be found in Chinese doctrine and court decisions, but no such rule can be found in national statutes.

The substantive control of standard terms addresses whether the terms that pass the formal control and thus form part of the consumer contract are fair. From the investigation of the relevant rules in the target jurisdictions, the first conclusion to be drawn is that terms that exempt a party's liability for death or personal injury are always prohibited. In China, Germany and England, this is also the case for terms that exempt the provider of the terms from liability for gross negligence, but this type of term is not enumerated in the EU directive. Apart from these two specific types of exemption terms, Chinese law and EU law (and consequently the national laws of the Member States) adopt a similar approach to regulate the substantive assessment of standard terms. It includes two parts: a general and abstract criterion and lists that provide examples of unfair terms.

In Chinese law, standard terms first undergo the general assessment of whether they create an obviously unfair situation. As previously mentioned, some Chinese scholars and judges suggest that only assessing the unbalanced allocation of rights and obligations in substance is not sufficient to meet the requirements of an obviously unfair term, and also require that the (consumer) contract be concluded under a situation of urgency or inexperience. This is still a controversial issue. Regarding the special rules which are only applicable to standard terms, the Chinese Contract Law 1999 first provides that the standard terms should comply with the general principle of fairness. In practice, judges even sometimes apply the principle of fairness directly as the basis for ruling on whether the terms are fair. With regard to the list, standard terms are not permitted to exempt the user's liability, increase the other party's liability, or exclude the material rights of the other party.

In EU law, the fairness of non-individually negotiated terms needs to be evaluated according to two criteria: significant imbalance and good faith. To be specific, the Unfair Contract Terms Directive starts with an assessment of whether there is a significant imbalance in the allocation of the parties' rights and obligations. If so, the law continues to evaluate whether the consumer had an inducement to agree to the terms, and whether the goods and services were sold or supplied to meet the special requirements of the consumer. This is required by good faith. Apart from the abstract criteria, the EU legislator has provided an indicative list of terms that are regarded as unfair in the Annex of the Unfair Contract Terms Directive. Considering the fact that common law judges and scholars were not familiar with the concept of 'good faith' when the directive was introduced, the indicative list contributed to establishing a consistent understanding of 'unfair terms' in the EU. English legislation has incorporated both the general criteria and the indicative list, while German law, besides the general criteria, has made a more detailed distinction between a black list, which contains the terms that are prohibited without the possibility of evaluation, and a grey list, which contains the terms that allow further evaluation.

In comparison, it can be observed that the core of the fairness tests in different jurisdictions is rather similar. Legislators in China, the EU, Germany and England all require that the rights and interests of the consumer need to be taken into account when the term is drafted. The European jurisdictions, however, focus more on the procedural elements of the fairness test. The criterion of good faith to a great extent concerns the process of the negotiation and conclusion of the contract. In contrast, Chinese law even contains a rule that a contract term should not be obviously unfair, and this rule, from the literal interpretation, only concerns the definition of rights and obligations in substance.

A fourth finding of this thesis is that the jurisdictions are similar in terms of the consequences attached to the determination that a term is unfair. The EU legislator has provided that unfair terms are 'not binding'; however, it has left it to the national legislators to establish the consequences, because the rules, in the end, have to fit the national contract law system. In German law, unfair terms are 'null and void', whilst in English law the legislator has chosen to still use the wording 'not binding'. In Chinese law, if a term violates the special rules on standard terms, it is null and void. If a standard term only creates an obviously unfair situation, for example there is a wide gap between the value of the consumer's and trader's performances, the consumer is entitled to avoid the contract. Although the legal effect of 'null and void' and 'voidable' may differ because in the latter case the consumer is bound by the rule on expiration period etc., the viewpoints behind the rules are similar: the unfair term should only be enforced by the consumer, but not against the consumer.

Fifthly, in addition to the substantive rules, this chapter also looked into the public mechanisms for controlling unfair terms at the national level. It is observed that in China and England, administrative bodies play a more important role in enforcing the legal rules, whilst in Germany the consumer organisations are more active. Compared with the other two jurisdictions, it is noteworthy that the Chinese administrations for industry and commerce are entitled to use more powerful actions, for example imposing a fine or demanding an 'administrative talk'. Besides, only in China can the administrative bodies make the ultimate decision on whether a term is fair. Even in England, the administrative bodies are only entitled to apply for an injunction and they cannot make a final decision on whether a term is fair themselves. Furthermore, the power of mass media in China is also noteworthy: the exposure of the use of unfair terms may severely harm the reputation of the enterprise and lead to a reduction in profits.

To conclude, a comparison of the legal rules and their enforcement in the target jurisdictions reveals that the rules on unfair terms are rather similar. Firstly, in China and the EU, the focus is directed at non-individually negotiated terms (standard terms); Secondly, the rules on assessing standard terms have two parts, which are the process of negotiation and conclusion of the contract (formal control) and the substantive definition of rights and obligations (substantive control). The former requires the user of standard terms to provide the consumer with an actual opportunity to become acquainted with the terms and agree to them. It also requires the judge or the administrator to adopt the interpretation against the user when the term is ambiguous. The latter also includes two steps: the general criteria that apply to all circumstances and the lists that provide the examples of unfair terms. For the general criteria, the jurisdictions usually use abstract concepts or principles such as 'fairness' and 'good faith'. For the lists which provide examples of unfair terms, attention is paid to whether the allocation of rights and obligations creates an imbalance which is prohibited by law. For example, it concerns whether the user of the terms is given control over the terms or performance, whether the statutory rights of the consumer are restrained, etc. Thirdly, the consequences for unfairness are also similar: the unfair term cannot be enforced against the consumer.

Although most of the rules are similar, two significant differences can be found. Firstly, procedural elements play a much more important role in the EU approach. The requirement of transparency not only constitutes part of the formal control, but also supplements the substantive control. The Unfair Contract Terms directive, German law and English law provide the requirement that the language of the term needs to be clear and intelligible. In contrast, the significance of substantive elements is decreased, because the exclusion of core terms makes it impossible to assess the most substantive part of the contract. The principle of good faith further adds procedural elements to the substantive test. In comparison, in China, neither the exclusion of core terms nor procedural elements in the substantive test can be found. Secondly, in the area of enforcement, the Chinese administrative bodies play a more significant role in the market when compared with their European counterparts, which refers to Germany and England in this context. The administrations for industry and commerce can be the final evaluator of the fairness test, and use powerful approaches to strike down unfair terms, such as the imposition of a fine and 'administrative talks'. In Germany and England, the final decision needs to be made by the court, and the administrative punishment does not play a dominant role in fighting unfair terms. It should be noted that the second difference may not be applied to other EU Member States, since the Unfair Contract Terms Directive only gives the guideline and leaves the issue of enforcement to the national level, and only Germany and England have been looked into by this study.

4.7.2 Explanatory Analysis

To explain these two main differences, attention should be paid to the distinction between the different types of markets as illustrated in Chap. 1. Hypothesis (2) may explain the reason why the Chinese and EU consumer contract rules place different emphasis on the different ways to assess the 'unfairness' of the contractual terms. This hypothesis concerns the different orientation in assessing misconduct in different types of markets and posits that 'the criteria employed by the Chinese consumer law to assess misconduct are more substantive, whereas the assessment of misconduct in the EU context is of a more procedural nature'. Hypothesis (4) may help with understanding the reason why the ways of enforcement are rather dissimilar. This hypothesis posits that 'the public enforcement of consumer protection law is more important in China than in the EU, which focuses more on private enforcement'. In China, enforcement of the unfair contract terms legislation to a large extent depends on the administrative bodies. The measures such bodies are able to adopt are more powerful than the measures that can be adopted by individual consumers and consumer organisations. From the comparative analysis, it can be seen that private enforcement is more crucial in Germany and England.

Turning to the first main difference – the different weight given to the formal and substantive control – it was seen that the EU fairness test is a more procedural one because the legislator believes that the substantive issues, especially the substantive value of the performance, should be decided by the market itself. This fits in well with the requirements of a competitive market. Thus, the rules regarding unfair terms control are not applicable to core terms, and the procedural elements focusing on how the contract is negotiated and concluded play a more important role. In China, this is not the case because the Chinese market is more regulated. The state has its own interest in the market and there is less certitude that the market can handle the issue of fairness itself. An immense disparity between the parties' obligations is not permitted because the government regards the value of equality as the cornerstone of the society. In these circumstances, because of the severe imbalance of bargaining power, party autonomy could lead to a significant inequality in the distribution of wealth and consequently to unrest in society. Thus, unlike in the European setting, where the parties are allowed to determine the 'fair' value of their performance themselves, in China, the idea of equality constitutes a significant component of the idea of fairness. An important part of the Chinese fairness test is to inspect the substantive allocation of rights and obligations. The rule that provides that the contractual terms cannot create an obviously unfair situation is purely concerned with the distribution of the parties' interests and wealth. In a competitive market, this would usually be left to the market. Thus, hypothesis (2) may successfully explain the first difference.

In relation to the second main difference identified in the comparative analysis, the influence of the market type on the enforcement mechanism is even more apparent. In China, a regulated market means that the market is still sometimes dominated by state-owned enterprises. This is particularly the case in the areas of transportation and telecommunication. In these areas, standard terms are widely used, and not all of them are fairly drafted. However, even though consumers are affected by these unfair terms, they lack the motivation to take action themselves. This is because they are not dealing with pure market actors. Rather, they are facing market giants with state backing. Due to the large scale of enterprises such as *China Telecom* and *China Unicom*, a single consumer usually does not have the incentive to initiate a lawsuit or to invoke other private enforcement measures. The cost he would incur would usually not match the potential benefit he would gain from such an action. Besides, group litigation and public interest litigation are not well developed in China. Therefore, the only solution to deal effectively with unfair terms is the intervention of another governmental actor: the Administration for Industry and Commerce and its branches undertake the responsibility to combat unfair terms. Compared with individual consumers, they have weapons that are granted by the government and they can bear the costs and risks associated with dealing with state-owned enterprises. Public enforcement in this sense is more effective and favourable to society as a whole in comparison with private enforcement. In contrast, the roles played by German and English administrative bodies are not as significant, since their methods for fighting unfair terms are rather indirect (German law). Even in England, where administrative bodies are heavily relied upon, they do not have the same authority as their Chinese counterparts. Specifically, in China, the most effective instrument adopted by the administrations for industry and commerce is the imposition of a fine, while in England the CMA only has the authority to apply for an injunction. In addition, the Chinese administrative bodies can also decide whether a term is fair on their own discretion, while this is not the case in Germany and England: it is always for the court to make that determination. As aforementioned, this difference shows that the Chinese government serves as a strong watchdog that supervises businesses closely in a regulated market, and the competitive markets in Germany and England require more freedom so the government's power is more limited. Thus, hypothesis (4) is confirmed, if China, Germany and England are compared.[348]

References

(Beale 1989) Hugh Beale, 'Unfair Contracts in Britain and Europe', 42 *Current Legal Problems* 1, 1989, p. 197–215.

(Beale 1999) Hugh Beale (ed.), *Chitty on Contracts, vol.1*, 28th edition, London: Sweet & Maxwell, 1999.

(Beale, Fauvarque-Cosson, Rutgers, Tallon & Vogenauer 2010) Hugh Beale, Bénédicte Fauvarque-Cosson, Jacobien Rutgers, Denis Tallon & Stefan Vogenauer, *Cases, Materials and Text on Contract Law*, 2nd edition, Portland: Hart Publishing, 2010.

(Beatson, Burrows & Cartwright 2016) Jack Beatson, Andrew Burrow & John Cartwright, *Anson's Law of Contract*, 30th edition, Oxford: Oxford University Press, 2016.

(Brandner & Ulmer 1991) Hans Erich Brandner & Peter Ulmer, 'The Community Directive on Unfair Terms in Consumer Contracts: Some Critical Remarks on the Proposal Submitted by the EC Commission', 28 *Common Market Law Review*, 1991, p. 647–662.

(Bright 2000) Susan Bright, 'Winning the Battle against Unfair Contract Terms', 20 *Legal Studies* 3, 2000, p. 331–352.

(Cauffman 2012) Caroline Cauffman, 'The Impact of EU Law on Belgian Consumer Law Terminology', 20 *European Review of Private Law* 5/6, 2012, p. 1325–1351.

(Chen 2010) Lei Chen, 'Private Property with Chinese Characteristics: A Critical Analysis of the Chinese Law on Property of 2007', 18 *European Review of Private Law* 5, 2010, p. 983–1004.

(Cherednychenko 2015) Olha O. Cherednychenko, 'Public and Private Enforcement of European Private Law: Perspectives and Challenges', 23 *European Review of Private Law* 4, 2015, p. 481–489.

(Civil Law Office of the Legislative Affairs Commission of the Standing Committee of the National People's Congress (全国人大法制工作委员会民法室) 1999) 全国人大法制工作委员会民法室编著[Civil Law Office of the Legislative Affairs Commission of the Standing Committee of the National People's Congress (eds.)]: 《〈中华人民共和国合同法〉立法资料

[348] It should be noticed that this conclusion may be achieved only in the context of fighting against unfair contract terms, based on the comparison between China, Germany and England. This is because, recently, 'the EU has promoted reliance on public supervision and enforcement in the realm of European private law with a view to achieving specific public goals, such as market integration and consumer protection.' Cherednychenko 2015, p. 485. It is pointed out that 'enforcement is undergoing a deep and substantive change.' Micklitz 2015, p. 492.

选》[The Selection of Legislative Materials of the Contract Law of the People's Republic of China],法律出版社1999年版[Law Press, 1999]

(Cseres 2008) KJ Cseres, 'What Has Competition Done for Consumers in Liberalised Markets?', 4 *The Competition Law Review* 2, p. 77–121.

(Cui (崔建远) 2007) 崔建远主编[Jianyuan Cui (ed.)]:《合同法》[Contract Law],法律出版社2007年第4版[Law Press, 2007, 4th Edition]。

(Cui (崔建远) 2008) 崔建远[Jianyuan Cui]:《合同法总论》(上卷)[General Introduction to Contract Law (Vol. 1)],中国人民大学出版社2008年版[China Renmin University Press, 2008]。

(Cui (崔建远) 2014) 崔建远[Jianyuan Cui]:"编纂民法典必须摆正几对关系"[The Need For Straightening Several Relations When Enacting the Chinese Civil Code],《清华法学》2014年第6期[Tsinghua University Law Journal, 2014(6)],第43—53页[p. 43–53]。

(Ebers 2010) Martin Ebers, 'ECJ (First Chamber) 6 October 2009, Case C-40/08, Asturcom Telecomunicaciones SL v. Cristina Rodríguez Nogueira – From Océano to Asturcom: Mandatory Consumer Law, Ex Officio Application of European Union Law and Res Judicata', 18 *European Review of Private Law* 4, 2010, p. 823–846.

(Fan (范子军) 2014) 范子军[Zijun Fan]:"'约谈执法'弹不动'霸王条款'"[Administrative Talk Cannot Deal with Unfair Terms],《人民法院报》2014年3月28日第02版[People's Court Daily, 2014/3/28, Page 02]。

(Faure & Luth 2011) Michael G. Faure & Hanneke A. Luth, 'Behavioural Economics in Unfair Contract Terms: Cautions and Considerations', 34 *Journal of Consumer Policy* 3, 2011, p. 337–358.

(Gavrilovic 2013) Nenad Gavrilovic, 'The Unfair Contract Terms Directive through the Practice of the Court of Justice of the European Union Interpretation or Something More', 9 *European Review of Contract Law* 2, 2013, p. 163–180.

(Goanta 2016) Catalina Goanta, *Convergence in European Consumer Sales Law: A Comparative and Numerical Approach*, Cambridge: Intersentia, 2016.

(Han (韩世远) 1994) 韩世远[Shiyuan Han]:"免责条款研究"[Research on Exemption Clauses], 载梁慧星主编[Huixing Liang (ed.)]:《民商法论丛》(第2卷)[Civil and Commercial Law Review, Vol. 2],法律出版社1994年版[Law Press, 1994]。

(Han (韩世远) 2011) 韩世远[Shiyuan Han]:《合同法总论》[The Law of Contract],法律出版社2011年第3版[Law Press, 2011, 3rd Edition]。

(Hesselink 2011) Martijn W. Hesselink, 'The Concept of Good Faith', in Arthu Hartkamp, Martijn Hesselink, Ewoud Hondius, Chantal Mak, Edgar du Perron (eds.), *Towards a European Civil Code*, Fourth revised and expanded edition, Alphen aan den Rijn: Kluwer Law International, 2011.

(Hondius 1997) Ewoud Hondius, 'Non-implementation of the Directive on Unfair Contract Terms: the Dutch case', 5 *European Review of Private Law* 2, 1997, p. 193–196.

(Hu (胡康生) 2013) 胡康生主编[Kangsheng Hu (ed.)]:《中华人民共和国合同法释义》[Paraphrase on the Contract Law of the People's Republic of China],法律出版社2013年第3版[Law Press, 2013, 3rd edition]

(Jia (贾东明) 2013) 贾东明主编[Dongming Jia (ed.)]:《中华人民共和国消费者权益保护法解读》[Understanding on the Law of the People's Republic of China on the Protection of Consumer Rights and Interests],中国法制出版社2013年版[China Legal Publishing House, 2013]。

(Kornet 2006) Nicole Kornet, *Contract Interpretation and Gap Filling: Comparative and Theoretical Perspectives*, Antwerpen: Intersentia, 2006.

(Legal Department of Shanxi Administration for Industry and Commerce (山西省工商局法制处) 2013) 山西省工商局法制处[Legal Department of Shanxi Administration for Industry and Commerce]:"山西省工商系统查办的典型格式条款违法案件"[Typical Cases Regarding Violations by Standard Terms Handled by the Shanxi Administrative System for Industry and Commerce],《中国工商报》2013年7月4日第A03版[China Industry and Commerce News, 2013/7/4, Page A03]。

(Liang (梁慧星) 1993) 梁慧星[Huixing Liang]:《民法学说判例与立法研究》[Research on Civil Law's Theories, Cases and Legislation],中国政法大学出版社1993年版[China University of Political Science and Law Press, 1993]。

(Liang (梁慧星) 1995) 梁慧星[Huixing Liang]:《民法解释学》[Civil Law Hermeneutics],中国政法大学出版社1995年版[China University of Political Science and Law Press, 1995]。

(Liang (梁慧星) 1999) 梁慧星[Huixing Liang]:《民法学说判例与立法研究》(第2册) [Research on Civil Law's Theories, Cases and Legislation (Vol. 2)],国家行政学院出版社1999年版[China National School of Administration Press, 1999]。

(Liang (梁慧星) 2000) 梁慧星[Huixing Liang]:"中国的消费者政策和消费者立法"[On Chinese Consumer Policies and Consumer Legislation],《法学》2000 年第5期[Law Science, 2000(5)],第20—26页[p. 20–26]。

(Liang (梁慧星) 2002) 梁慧星[Huixing Liang]:《为中国民法典而斗争》[Fighting for China's Civil Code],法律出版社2002年版[Law Press, 2002]。

(Liang (梁慧星) 2007) 梁慧星[Huixing Liang]:《民法总论》[General Introduction to Civil Law],法律出版社2007年第3版[Law Press, 2007, 3rd Edition]。

(Markesinis, Unberath & Johnston 2006) Basil Markesinis, Hannes Unberath & Angus Johnston, *The German Law of Contract: A Comparative Treatise*, 2nd edition, Oxford: Hart Publishing, 2006.

(McKendrick 2016) Ewan McKendrick, *Contract Law: Text, Cases, and Materials*, 7th edition, Oxford: Oxford University Press, 2016.

(Meng (孟强龙) 2015) 孟强龙[Qianglong Meng]:"行政约谈法治化研究"[On the Institutionalisation of Administrative Talk],《行政法学研究》2015年第6期[Administrative Law Review, 2016(6)],第99—118页[p. 99–118]。

(Micklitz, Stuyck & Terryn 2010) Hans-W. Micklitz, Jules Stuyck, Evelyne Terryn (eds.), *Cases, Materials and Text on Consumer Law*, Portland: Hart Publishing, 2010.

(Micklitz & Reich 2014) Hans-W. Micklitz & Norbert Reich, 'The Court and Sleeping Beauty: The Revival of the Unfair Contract Terms Directive (UCTD)', 51 *Common Market Law Review* 3, 2014, p. 771–808.

(Micklitz 2015) Hans-W. Micklitz, 'The Transformation of Enforcement in European Private Law: Preliminary Considerations', 23 *European Review of Private Law* 4, 2015, p. 491–524.

(Nebbia 2007) Paolisa Nebbia, *Unfair Contract Terms in European Law: A Study in Comparative and EC Law*, Portland: Hart Publishing, 2007.

(Nebbia 2010) Paolisa Nebbia, 'Unfair Contract Terms', in Christian Twigg-Flesner (ed.), *The Cambridge Companion to European Union Private Law*, New York: Cambridge University Press, 2010, p. 216–228.

(Novaretti 2010) Simona Novaretti, 'General Clauses and Practice: The Use of the Principle of Good Faith in Decisions of Chinese Courts', 18 *European Review of Private Law* 5, 2010, p. 953–981.

(Peel & Treitel 2007) Edwin Peel & G. H. Treitel, *Treitel on the Law of Contract*, 12th edition, London: Sweet & Maxwell, 2007.

(Poole 2012) Jill Poole, *Textbook on Contract Law*, 11th edition, Oxford: Oxford University Press, 2012.

(Research Office of the Legislative Affairs Commission of the Standing Committee of the National People's Congress (全国人大法工委研究室编写组) 1999) 全国人大法工委研究室编写组[Research Office of the Legislative Affairs Commission of the Standing Committee of the National People's Congress]:《中华人民共和国合同法释义》[Paraphrase on Contract Law of People's Republic of China],人民法院出版社1999年版[People's Court Press, 1999]。

(Research Office of the Supreme People's Court (最高人民法院研究室) 2009) 最高人民法院研究室编著[Research Office of the Supreme People's Court (eds.)]:《最高人民法院关于合同法司法解释(二)理解与适用》[Interpretation and Application of the Interpretation II of the Supreme People's Court of Several Issues concerning the Application of the Contract Law of the People's Republic of China],人民法院出版社2009年版[People's Court Press, 2009]。

(Rougier-Brierre 2007) Guillaume Rougier-Brierre, 'The Particularities of Contractual Negotiation and Practice in China', 2007 *International Business Law Journal* 2, 2007, p. 151–170.

(Smits 2014) Jan M. Smits, *Contract Law: A Comparative Introduction*, Cheltenham: Edward Elgar Publishing, 2014.

(Steennot 2015) Reinhard Steennot, 'Public and Private Enforcement in the Field of Unfair Contract Terms', 23 *European Review of Private Law* 4, 2015, p. 589–619.

(Su (苏号朋) 2004) 苏号朋[Haopeng Su]:《格式合同研究》[A Study on Standard Contract Clauses],中国人民大学出版社2004年版[China Renmin University Press, 2004]。

(Suli (苏力) 2003) 苏力[Suli]:"司法解释、公共政策和最高法院——从最高法院有关'奸淫幼女'的司法解释切入"[Judicial Interpretation, Public Policy and the Supreme People's Court – Judicial Interpretation on the Crime of Fornication with an Underage Girl as Cutting Point],《法学》2003年第8期[Law Science, 2003(8)],第3—29页[p. 3–29]。

(Tan & Hu (谭振亚、胡建) 2012) 谭振亚、胡建[Zhenya Tan, Jian Hu]:"论格式条款之订入合同及其效力——以中国大陆与德国、中国台湾地区立法之比较为视角"[On Incorporation and Effectiveness of Standard Terms – On the basis of the Comparison among Mainland China, Germany and Chinese Taipei],《云南财经大学学报(社会科学版)》2012年第1期[Yunnan Finance & Economics University Journal of Economics & Management, 2012(1)],第137—142页[p. 137–142]。

(Wang & Cui (王利明、崔建远) 2000) 王利明、崔建远[Liming Wang, Jianyuan Cui]:《合同法新论•总则》[New Theory on Contract Law: General Principles],中国政法大学出版社2000年修订版[China University of Political Science and Law Press, 2000, revised Edition]。

(Wang (王利明) 2002a) 王利明[Liming Wang]:"消费者的概念及消费者权益保护法的调整范围"[The Concept of Consumer and the Applicable Scope of the Consumer Protection Law],《政治与法律》2002年第2期[Political Science and Law, 2002(2)],第3—12页[p. 3–12]。

(Wang (王利明) 2002b) 王利明[Liming Wang]:《合同法研究》(第1卷)[Research on Contract Law (Book 1)],中国人民大学出版社2002年版[China Renmin University Press, 2002]。

(Wang (汪世荣) 2000) 汪世荣[Shirong Wang]:"司法解释批复四题"[Four Problems on the Written Reply of Judicial Interpretation],《法律科学(西北政法学院学报)》2000年第4期[Law Science (Journal of Northwest Institute of Political Science and Law), 2000(4)],第16—28页[p. 16–28]。

(Wang (王利明) 2011b) 王利明 [Liming Wang]:《侵权责任法研究(上卷)》 [Research on Tort Liability Law(Book 1)], 中国人民大学出版社2011年版 [China Renmin University Press, 2011]。

(Wilhelmsson 2011) Thomas Wilhelmsson, 'Standard Form Conditions', in Arthu Hartkamp, Martijn Hesselink, Ewoud Hondius, Chantal Mak & Edgar du Perron (eds.), *Towards a European Civil Code*, Fourth revised and expanded edition, Alphen aan den Rijn: Kluwer Law International, 2011, p. 571–586.

(Wu (吴志勇) 2004) 吴志勇[Zhiyong Wu]:"浅议合同格式条款的行政监管"[On the Administrative Supervision on Contractual Standard Terms],《工商行政管理》2004年第16期[Biweekly of Administration for Industry and Commerce, 2004(16)],第29—30页[p. 29–30]。

(Yan (晏扬) 2016) 晏扬[Yang Yan]:"'消协起诉水务'堪称公益诉讼样本"[Consumers' Association sue Tap Water Company: A Template for Public Interest Litigation],《检察日报》2016年11月2日第5版[Procuratorate Daily, 2016/11/02, Page 5]。

(Yao (姚敏) 2013) 姚敏[Min Yao]:"6种餐饮霸王条款被北京工商局叫停"[Six Types of Unfair Terms Are Prohibited by the Beijing Administration for Industry and Commerce],《中国消费者报》2013年12月16日第B01版[China Consumer News, 2013/12/16, Page B01]。

(Yin (尹田) 1995) 尹田[Tian Yin]:《法国现代合同法》[French Modern Contract Law],法律出版社1995年版[Law Press, 1995]。

(Yin (尹华广) 2005) 尹华广[Huaguang Yin]:《论我国格式条款立法规制的不足与完善》[Drawbacks of China's Legislative Regulation on Standard Terms and the Improvement],《黑龙江省政法管理干部学院学报》2005年第6期[Journal of Heilongjiang Administrative Cadre Institute of Politics and Law, 2005(6)],第48—50页[p. 48–50]。

(Zhang & Lu (张红勤、陆立权) 2004), 张红勤、陆立权[Hongqin Zhang, Liquan Lu]:"加强格式条款行政监管,拓展合同执法新领域"[Enhancing Supervision on Standard Terms and Expanding Domains of Executing Contract Regulations],《工商行政管理》2004年第16期[Biweekly of Administration for Industry and Commerce, 2004(16)],第23—25页[p. 23–25]。

(Zhang 2006) Zhang Mo, *Chinese Contract Law*, Leiden: Koninklijke Brill NV, 2006.

(Zhou (周哲) 2013a) 周哲[Zhe Zhou]:"重庆整治'苹果'不公平合同格式条款——五十一家授权服务商经销商被要求整改"[Chongqing Cleans up Apple Inc's Unfair Standard Terms: 51 Authorised Service Providers and Franchisers are Required to Amend Their Terms],《中国工商报》2013年6月6日第A01版[China Industry and Commerce News, 2013/6/6, Page A01]。

(Zhou (周哲) 2013b) 周哲[Zhe Zhou]:"重庆整治苹果公司不公平条款有进展——三十四家授权服务商经销商承诺先行整改"[Chongqing is Making Progress in Cleaning up Apple Inc's Unfair Terms: 34 Authorized Service Providers and Franchisers Promised to Amend Their Terms],《中国工商报》2013年6月29日第A01版[China Industry and Commerce News, 2013/6/29, Page A01]。

(Zhu (朱岩) 2010) 朱岩[Yan Zhu]:"社会基础变迁与民法双重体系建构"[Transformation of the Social Foundation and Construction of a Dual System of Civil Law],《中国社会科学》2010年第6期[Social Sciences in China, 2010(6)],第151—168页[p. 151–168]。

Research Services, Working Papers, Etc

(Cafaggi and Micklitz 2007) Fabrizio Cafaggi and Hans-W. Micklitz, Administrative and Judicial Collective Enforcement of Consumer Law in the US and the European Community (August 2007), *EUI LAW Working Paper* No. 2007/22, available at SSRN: <http://ssrn.com/abstract=1024103>.

(Twigg-Flesner 2007) Christian Twigg-Flesner, The Implementation of the Unfair Contract Terms Directive in the United Kingdom (November 30, 2007), *Contemporary Issues in Law*, 2006/2007, available at SSRN: <http://ssrn.com/abstract=1399631>.

Chapter 5
Withdrawal Rights

5.1 Introduction

The discussion on withdrawal rights can start with the principle of *pacta sunt servanda*. This principle implies that the contracting parties should strictly comply with the contract and neither of them is allowed to withdraw from the contract at will. It is believed that this principle is the cornerstone of private law, because 'it is a pre-condition for the functioning of contract as a means of social ordering between strangers'.[1] Both in the EU and China, this principle is seen as an important principle in the area of contract law. For example, the Chinese Contract Law 1999[2] regulates that 'no party shall unilaterally modify or terminate the contract'.[3]

However, this principle is not applicable when the consent of contracting parties is defective.[4] In case of a defect of consent, e.g. mistake, fraud or threat, a party is entitled to avoid the contract.[5] In addition, in some specific types of consumer contracts, consumers are conferred to withdraw from the contracts by virtue of their unilateral intention, even if there is no defect such as mistake or fraud. In these cases, the consumer is allowed to reconsider his decision within a set 'cooling-off period'. During this period, the consumer does not even have to prove that his right or interest was harmed or the contract deviated from his actual declaration of intention, but only

[1] Markesinis et al. 2006, p. 265

[2] Contract Law of the People's Republic of China (《中华人民共和国合同法》)

[3] See Article 8 of the Contract Law 1999: 'A lawfully established contract shall be legally binding on the parties thereto, each of whom shall perform its own obligations in accordance with the terms of the contract, and no party shall unilaterally modify or terminate the contract'.

[4] Besides, it is often challenged by the rule of 'change of circumstances'.

[5] See Smits 2014, pp. 159–169.

J. Ge, *A Comparative Analysis of Policing Consumer Contracts in China and the EU*, https://doi.org/10.1007/978-981-13-2989-0_5

by means of notifying the trader that he changes his mind can he extricate himself from the contract. The terminology of this special protection is 'withdrawal right'.[6]

Due to the reason that withdrawal rights allow the consumer to end a concluded contract without a proven defect of consent, it needs to be justified otherwise. Contracts would not be relied on anymore, and a cornerstone of private law would become obsolete. The legitimacy of withdrawal rights can be based on two categories of reasons: (1) reasons that can be generally applied and (2) reasons that are suggested by some jurisdictions to achieve special legislative objectives. These reasons are addressed as follows.

For general reasons, withdrawal rights are regulated because legislators intend to protect the consumer and promote the efficiency of business.

To be specific, firstly, legislators find it necessary to protect the consumer where the seller's negotiating technique is particularly aggressive and the substance of the contract is difficult or even impossible to assess.[7] This phenomenon leads to two specific consequences: 'negotiation status asymmetry' and 'information asymmetry'. These two asymmetries are believed to be the reasons that cause the weaker status of the consumer in both psychological and informational aspects.[8] Therefore, in order to protect consumers, it is suggested that law should interfere where the actual intention of the consumer was severely influenced and the freedom of making decision was restricted. In case a withdrawal right is regulated, consumers in a certain type of transaction are presumed to be protected from making a hasty decision and against aggressive sales techniques.[9] Additionally, consumers are able to examine the goods after delivery to confirm whether the subject matter is indeed what they wanted.[10] It even becomes possible for consumers to obtain much more objective information or advice for complex contracts.[11] In this regard, although some

---

[6] It is noteworthy that in some legislation, this right is also named 'the right of cancellation'. However, in order to keep the consistency of this chapter, 'withdrawal right' or 'the right of withdrawal' is applied as a consistent concept.

[7] See Markesinis et al. 2006, p. 266. As stated by the legislator of the European Union, the consumer should be given a period to assess the obligations arising under the contract where he is unable to compare the quality and price of the offer with other offers when the contract was concluded. See recitals of the Doorstep Selling Directive (Council Directive of 20 December 1985 to protect the consumer in respect of contracts negotiated away from business premises (85/577/EEC) [1985] OJ L 372/31).

[8] See Wang (王洪亮) 2010, pp. 98–99.

[9] Scholars pointed out that cooling-off periods may reflect good examples of 'asymmetric paternalism', which means the regulation creates large benefits for those who make errors, while imposing little or no harm on those who are fully rational, because, in many instances, cooling-off periods impose minimal costs if people are rational – the cost of delaying the purchase of a car by a few days is not plausibly large and at the same time protects those people who make decisions in the heat of the moment. See Camerer et al. 2003, pp. 1239–1240.

[10] See Recital 5 of the Doorstep Selling Directive. It is stated that 'the consumer is often unable to compare the quality and price of the offer with other offers' in the context of this specific approach of selling. Thus, 'the consumer should be given a right of cancellation over a period of at least 7 days in order to enable him to assess the obligations arising under the contract'.

[11] See Loos 2009, pp. 249–250.

scholars recognise the right of withdrawal as an exception to the principle of *pacta sunt servanda*,[12] if we consider 'a free, well considered and informed consent' as a necessary element for a binding contract, withdrawal rights are not an exception but a nuance to the principle.[13] Its legislative aim is to protect the substantive freedom of contract.[14]

Secondly, withdrawal rights can promote online shopping[15] and lead to the efficiency of business because this rule will stimulate sellers to improve the quality of their commodities so as to avoid goods being returned.[16]

For special reasons, withdrawal rights are believed to be a good tool which is conducive to achieving some specific policy objectives. For example, in the context of strengthening cross-border transactions in order to establish and consolidate an EU internal market, a uniform mechanism of withdrawal rights can help with encouraging consumers to deal with traders outside their country and making it easier for foreign companies to enter into new markets. Both these two functions are regarded as 'advantageous' to the growth of cross-border transactions. Therefore, it is believed that withdrawal rights are beneficial to the establishment of the internal market.[17]

In China, the right of withdrawal (usually described as *Xiaofeizhe Chehui Quan* ('消费者撤回权'), which is widely used by academic articles and literally means 'the consumer's right to revoke'; or *Houhui Quan* ('后悔权'), which is frequently used by social media and literally means 'the right to regret'[18]; or *Wu Liyou Tuihuo Quan* ('无理由退货权'), which literally means 'the right to return without reason'),[19] was regulated by an administrative regulation on direct selling for more than 10 years. Furthermore, the right of withdrawal as a voluntary guarantee was provided by many e-commerce platforms or participating online shops to increase their market competitiveness. These voluntary rights of return are not discussed in detail here. The right of withdrawal later became a spotlight in the amendment of the Consumer Protection Law 2013[20] because it was the first time for Chinese legislators to establish a 'withdrawal rights mechanism' in the whole domain of Chinese

[12] See Rott 2010, p. See also Zhang (张学哲) 2009, p. 70.

[13] See Micklitz et al. 2010, p. 240.

[14] See Zhang (张学哲) 2009, p. 70.

[15] See Loos 2009, p. 248.

[16] See Sun (孙良国) 2011, pp. 109–110.

[17] See Recital 4 and 5 of the Consumer Rights Directive (Directive 2011/83/EU of the European Parliament and of the Council of 25 October 2011 on consumer rights, amending Council Directive 93/13/EEC and Directive 1999/44/EC of the European Parliament and of the Council and repealing Council Directive 85/577/EEC and Directive 97/7/EC of the European Parliament and of the Council [2011] OJ L304/64). See also, Micklitz 2005, pp. 574–577.

[18] The use of this phrase is questioned by some scholars because the Chinese characters for 'regret' involve negative connotation which implies that the consumer might be morally criticised. See Sun (孙良国) 2012, p. 58.

[19] See Ge (葛江虬) 2015, p. 99.

[20] Law of the People's Republic of China on the Protection of Consumer Rights and Interests (2013 Amendment) (《中华人民共和国消费者权益保护法(2013修正)》).

consumer law.[21] The significance of establishing the mechanism of the rights of withdrawal in Consumer Protection Law should not be underestimated, because after the recently amended legislation came into effect, the application of withdrawal rights is not limited to the domain of direct selling anymore, and it is not voluntary or alternative. Now it is a mandatory rule.[22] The distinctions among the drafts and the final version can be observed from the table below (Table 5.1).

In Europe, the rules on withdrawal rights can be traced back to German law. A German statute of 1969 entitled the consumer to withdraw from a contract in which he purchased foreign investment shares away from the business premises of the trader.[23] Since then, in order to establish an internal market and promote the interests of consumers, a series of EU directives which regulate withdrawal rights have been adopted and implemented on the national level. It is argued that these harmonised withdrawal rights will take away barriers to cross-border trade.[24] In Germany and England, along with the process of implementing the directives, a number of specialised statutes have been enacted. Now the German ones have been incorporated into the BGB as a result of the reform of the law of obligations in 2002. It is noteworthy that, although there is a lack of consistency in terminology in the EU directives,[25] German law persists in applying the term *Widerruf* (which literally means 'revocation')[26] and English law retains the concept of 'cancellation'. These differences are not essential, because they are merely different ways to implement directives. Thus, in the following introduction, the terms 'rights of withdrawal' or 'withdrawal rights' are used to discuss the relevant rules, while 'the rights of revocation' and 'the rights of cancellation' are only used for directly quoting the articles regarding the rights of withdrawal in German law and English Law, respectively.

---

[21] This is for the purpose of 'protecting the consumers' right of choice' according to the people who were in charge of the lawmaking process. See Li (李适时) 2013, p. 331. The author is the director of the Legislative Affairs Commission of the Standing Committee of the National People's Congress (全国人大常委会法制工作委员会).

[22] In practice, we can learn from a survey provided by the China Consumers' Association that approximately one-fifth of the consumers (2657/14164) have performed their withdrawal rights and 85.66% of them received oral consent by the sellers. See China Consumers' Association (中国消费者协会), 'Survey on the Implementation of Withdrawal Rights in E-Commerce Businesses' (《网购企业落实消费者"后悔权"调查报告》), available at: <http://www.cca.org.cn/web/dcjd/newsShow.jsp?id=67498>, last visited: 2014/6/1.

[23] See German Foreign Investment Law (Auslandsinvestmentgesetz) 1969.

[24] See Loos 2009, pp. 246–247.

[25] It refers to the 'right of cancellation' and 'right of withdrawal' in different directives, which is detailed in the later analysis.

[26] This translation is given by Langenscheidt Translation Service, which is published on BGB's official website. Available at: <http://www.gesetze-im-internet.de/englisch_bgb/index.html>, last visited: 22 October 2014. In some senses it is strange that the German Civil Code applies a concept which is usually employed in the contexts where the legal acts and declaration of intention have not become fully effective, for example, the revocability of a contract concluded by a minor (§ 109), the revocability of a contract concluded by an unauthorised agent (§ 178) and the revocability of a prior offer (§ 183). There is no reason to deny the effectiveness of the contract even though it could come to an end because of the exercise of the withdrawal right.

Table 5.1 Legislative History of Article 25 of the Consumer Protection Law

Title	Article
The Draft of the Amendment of the Law on the Protection of Consumer Rights and Interests (No. 9)[a]	Article 28 Where business operators sell commodities on the Internet, on television, over telephone or by mail order, among others, consumers shall have the right to return the commodities within 7 days of receipt of them, except the commodities unsuitable for return by nature
	Business operators shall, within 7 days of receipt of the returned commodities, refund the payments made by consumers
The Second Draft of the Amendment of the Law on the Protection of Consumer Rights and Interests (No. 10)[b]	Article 28 Where business operators sell commodities on the Internet, on television, over telephone or by mail order, among others, consumers shall have the right to return the commodities within 7 days of receipt of them without cause, except the following commodities:
	(1) Custom-made commodities
	(2) Fresh, live or perishable commodities
	(3) Audio-visual recordings, computer software unpacked by consumers
	(4) Newspapers or periodicals delivered
	(5) Other commodities unsuitable for return by nature
	Consumers shall return the commodities within 7 days of their claims. Business operators shall, within 7 days of receipt of the returned commodities, refund the payments made by consumers for the commodities
Law of the People's Republic of China on the Protection of Consumer Rights and Interests (2013 Amendment) [Effective]	Article 25 Where business operators sell commodities on the Internet, on television, over telephone or by mail order, among others, consumers shall have the right to return the commodities within 7 days of receipt of them without cause, except the following commodities:
	(1) Custom-made commodities
	(2) Fresh, live or perishable commodities
	(3) Audio-visual recordings, computer software and other digital commodities downloaded online or unpacked by consumers
	(4) Newspapers or periodicals delivered
	In addition to the commodities listed in the preceding paragraph, the return without cause shall not apply to commodities unsuitable for return by nature as confirmed by consumers at the time of purchase
	The commodities returned by consumers shall remain intact. Business operators shall, within 7 days of receipt of the returned commodities, refund the payments made by consumers for the commodities. The freight charge for the return of commodities shall be assumed by consumers, except as otherwise agreed upon by business operators and consumers

[a]The whole draft was published on 23 April 2013 by the National People's Congress on its official website (www.npc.gov.cn), soliciting advice and suggestions. See the National People's Congress of the People's Republic of China (全国人民代表大会), 'Articles and Interpretations on the Draft of the Amendment of Law on the Protection of Consumer Rights and Interests' (《消费者权益保护法修正案(草案)条文及草案说明》), available at: <http://www.npc.gov.cn/npc/xinwen/lfgz/flca/2013-04/28/content_1793762.htm, last visited: 2014/9/22

[b]The second draft was published on 6 September 2013 by the National Congress. See the National People's Congress of the People's Republic of China (全国人民代表大会), 'Articles of The Second Draft of the Amendment of the Law on the Protection of Consumer Rights and Interests' (《消费者权益保护法修正案(草案二次审议稿)条文》), available at: <http://www.npc.gov.cn/npc/xinwen/lfgz/2013-09/06/content_1805745.htm, last visited: 2014/9/22

It should be noted that withdrawal rights are often criticised for the excessive protection of consumers – even if 'psychological deficit' and 'information asymmetry' are widely recognised as the rationale for withdrawal rights, it is still doubtful whether these motives justify these rights.[27] In order to respond to these concerns, in most jurisdictions, withdrawal rights are applicable to a limited number of circumstances. The exercise of these rights is also considerably restricted: the cooling-off periods are usually relatively short, and not all categories of commodities can be returned without reason.

In this chapter, the rules on withdrawal rights in China and the EU are addressed. Firstly, the applicable scope of withdrawal rights is discussed (Sect. 5.2). The exceptions are introduced secondly (Sect. 5.3). Thirdly the different rules on the periods of withdrawal rights in different jurisdictions are discussed. Some related topics such as the duty to inform the consumer about withdrawal rights are also touched upon (Sect. 5.4). The fourth part focuses on the exercise of withdrawal rights (Sect. 5.5). The consequences of withdrawal constitute the fifth section (Sect. 5.6). In each section, rules and their interpretation in China law and EU directives, German law and English law are addressed separately for the comparative observations subsequently offered. At the end of this chapter, an overview of all comparative reviews and the possible explanation of the similarities and differences is provided (Sect. 5.7).

In consideration of the length and the core issues which are comparable, emphasis is laid on the area of off-premises selling and distance selling.

5.2 Applicable Scope

5.2.1 Introduction

In most jurisdictions, withdrawal rights are applied to several specified types of transactions. Only in these circumstances are consumers free to escape from being bound by the concluded contract.

In this section, the question of what types of consumer contracts can be withdrawn from is addressed. The focus is firstly on Chinese law (Sect. 5.2.2), EU directives (Sect. 5.2.3.1), German law (Sect. 5.2.3.2) and English law (Sect. 5.2.3.3), and afterwards a comparative review (Sect. 5.2.4) is provided.

[27] To quote Markesinis, 'Invariably, cancelling the contract does not presuppose that the exercise of the free will of consumer was actually impaired'. Markesinis et al. 2006, p. 266.

5.2.2 Chinese Law

5.2.2.1 Withdrawal Rights Regulated by Administrative Regulations and Departmental Administrative Regulations

Mandatory withdrawal rights in Chinese legislation can be traced back to an administrative regulation promulgated in 2005: the Regulations on Direct Selling Administration.[28] The second paragraph of Article 25 provides that consumers are conferred the right of changing or returning the product if it has not been opened within 30 days from the day of purchasing any direct selling product. For the meaning of 'direct selling', Article 3 refers to this phrase as a type of business model, in which 'direct selling companies recruit sales promoters to sell products directly to end consumers outside the companies' fixed outlets'. It should be noted that these direct selling contracts have to be concluded outside the sellers' premises.[29]

Another area where the right of withdrawal is regulated is life insurance. As a piece of regulation of the ministries and commissions under the State Council,[30] the Notice on Life Insurance 2011 promulgated by the China Insurance Regulatory Commission[31] provides that a consumer is entitled to withdraw from a life insurance contract without any reason within a period of 10 days.

---

[28] Regulations on Direct Selling Administration (《直销管理条例》), Order of the State Council, No.443 (国务院令第443号). The motivation of the introduction of this administrative regulation includes that China shall perform the promise to remove the restriction on direct selling within 3 years of its WTO accession.

[29] Besides, whether there is a right of withdrawal entitled to consumers is an important distinction between 'zhixiao' ('直销', which literally means 'direct selling') and another selling approach called 'chuanxiao' ('传销', which refers to 'pyramid schemes selling'), which is prohibited in the People's Republic of China. 'Chuanxiao' as a Chinese word has different meaning in diverse context. In the People's Republic of China, it refers to a kind of economic crime which contains the selling of pyramid schemes. See Regulations on the Prohibition of Pyramid Selling (《禁止传销条例》), Order of the State Council, No. 444 (国务院令第444号). Its Article 2 defines that 'pyramid selling' refers to such an act by which an organiser or operator seeks unlawful interests, disturbs the economic order and affects the social stability by recruiting persons, calculating and paying remunerations to recruiters on the basis of the number of persons a recruiter has directly or indirectly recruited or the sales performance or asking the recruiters to pay a certain fee for obtaining the qualification for participation. Moreover, Article 7 enumerates the types of behaviour which are recognised as 'pyramid selling'.

[30] In terms of the meaning of 'regulations of the ministries and commissions under the State Council' and the discussion on whether it is a source of law, see Chap. 2 of this study.

[31] Notice on relevant matters concerning Regulating Issues of Life Insurance (《关于规范人身保险业务经营有关问题的通知》), No. 36 [2011] of the China Insurance Regulatory Commission (保监发[2011]第36号).

5.2.2.2 Withdrawal Rights Regulated by Local Regulations

Preceding the promulgation of the new Consumer Protection Law 2013, some local regulations contain the provisions regulating withdrawal rights when implementing the old Consumer Protection Law 1993[32] on the local level, although no such rule can be found in the original statute. For example, the Regulations of Shanghai on the Protection of Consumer Rights and Interests 2002[33] provide that a consumer may return the commodity which was purchased by 'doorstep selling' within 7 days and no statement of reason is required.[34] In terms of the meaning of 'doorstep selling', a Chinese phrase *shangmen tuixiao* ('上门推销') is used by the local regulation, and it literally means 'visiting doorstep and selling goods'. It implies that the contract is required to be concluded outside the trader's premises for a doorstep selling transaction. In addition, there is no modifier in front of 'doorstep'. Thus, the applicable scope is not limited to the doorsteps of consumers' home, but the doorsteps of their workplaces are included as well.

However, the local regulation has not provided further explanation on this phrase's meaning and in practice cases regarding this issue can be rarely found. Hence, the relation between 'doorstep selling' and aforementioned 'direct selling' remains unclear. A doorstep selling contract is the result of negotiation with a visiting salesman. If this visiting salesman is a 'sale promoter' hired by the manufacturer and the goods are directly sold to the consumer, it is also a direct selling contract. Therefore, in the context of the Regulations on Direct Selling Administration 2005, the scope of 'doorstep selling' is broader than the scope of 'direct selling', because the administrative regulation requires that direct selling should be accomplished by a sale promoter and has to be done outside the companies' outlets. This means every single direct selling contract is a doorstep selling. Meanwhile, doorstep selling includes not only direct selling but also the case where the visiting salesman is not directly hired by the manufacturer.[35]

[32] Law of the People's Republic of China on the Protection of Consumer Rights and Interests (《中华人民共和国消费者权益保护法》).

[33] Regulations of Shanghai on the Protection of Consumer Rights and Interests 2002 (《上海市消费者权益保护条例》(2002)).

[34] See the third paragraph of Article 28 of Regulations of Shanghai on the Protection of Consumer Rights and Interests 2002.

[35] Based on the aforementioned administrative regulations and local regulations, some scholars further argue that withdrawal rights should be granted to a consumer where (1) the consumer contract is concluded in a special way, such as distance selling and doorstep selling, because consumers in these situations lack information and (2) the transaction will deeply influence the daily life of the consumer, such as immovable property selling and consumer credit contract, due to the reason that it is difficult for normal consumers to predict the risks. See Zhang (张学哲) 2011, p. 46.

5.2.2.3 Withdrawal Rights Regulated by the Consumer Protection Law

Apart from mandatory withdrawal rights in the Consumer Protection Law 2013, providing voluntary withdrawal rights is common in e-commerce business practice in China. For example, the most frequently used e-commerce platform Taobao ('淘宝网', www.taobao.com)[36] provided a service project called 'return in 7 days without reasons'. For the online shops who participate in this specific service project, they get an icon which can be seen by consumers on their website. The icon proves that, according to the agreement which the trader signed with Taobao, the consumer can return the goods in 7 days after the goods were signed for after receipt without giving any reason and without incurring any penalty. Otherwise, Taobao will support the consumer's claim if a dispute emerges.[37]

Based on these business practices, the Consumer Protection Law 2013 focuses on distance selling contracts. Its Article 25 states that consumers are granted the right to return the commodities where business operators sell commodities on the Internet, on television, over telephone, by mail order, etc. It should be noted that the legislation only enumerates several specific types of distance selling, but it does not employ a summarised phrase such as 'distance selling'. In addition, the issue 'whether it is applicable to doorstep selling or other types of selling' is not clarified.[38]

To quote the Understanding of authority provided by the Civil Law Office of the Legislative Affairs Commission of the Standing Committee of the National People's Congress, the incentive of regulating mandatory withdrawal rights is to deal with the impact on parties' actual declaration of intention caused by information asymmetry in some specific circumstances. Thus, the applicable scope of withdrawal rights should be interpreted via a generalised approach. Not only distance selling but also doorstep selling and direct selling fall under the applicable scope of this article.[39] Additionally, the phrase *deng* ('等', which literally means *et cetera*) here

---

[36] On the grounds of the empirical data, 88.1% of the e-commerce consumers have purchased from their online shops. See CNNIC (China Internet Network Information Center) (中国互联网络信息中心), 'Research on Chinese Online Shopping Market in 2012' (《2012年中国网络购物市场研究报告》), available at: <http://www.cnnic.cn/hlwfzyj/hlwxzbg/dzswbg/201304/P020130417543965742695.pdf>, last visited: 2014/4/30.

[37] Taobao.com (淘宝网), 'Agreements on Returning Goods in 7 Days without Reasons' (《7天无理由退货服务协议》),available at: <http://service.taobao.com/support/knowledge-1121954.htm#>, last visited: 2014/5/7.

[38] Even though during the process of revising the law, it was suggested that the new amended Consumer Protection Law should clarify that whether consumers in the context of doorstep selling are granted the right of withdrawal, the final and formal version does not respond to this specific issue. See Opinions of the Local People's Congresses and the Relevant Departments of the Central Government on the Draft of the Amendment of Law on the Protection of Consumer Rights and Interests (《地方人大、中央有关部门和单位对消费者权益保护法修正案(草案)(征求意见稿)的意见》), in Civil Law Office of the Legislative Affairs Commission of the Standing Committee of the National People's Congress (全国人大常委会法制工作委员会民法室) 2013, p. 30.

[39] See Jia (贾东明) 2013, p. 103.

not only provides the space to include doorstep selling and direct selling into the applicable scope, as the Understanding clarifies, but also reserves room for new transactions in the future. It is supposed that as long as the transaction is concluded by means of an approach which is different from the traditional way of on-premises sale, or the consumer's actual declaration of intention is severely affected because of the unbalanced status of information, the consumer will be entitled to the right of withdrawal.[40]

With respect to why 'doorstep selling' is included in the meaning of *deng*, the Understanding of authority provides another reason from a legislative perspective: during the process of lawmaking, legislators manifested that they do not want to exclude doorstep selling from the applicable scope of withdrawal rights. Specifically, legislators were advised that an abstract concept, *fei xianchang gouwu* ('非现场购物', which literally means 'non-presence consumption'), could be used to refer to all distance selling contracts including selling on the Internet, on television, over telephone and by mail in the amendment of the Consumer Protection Law. However, legislators consider that withdrawal rights shall be also applicable to doorstep selling contracts in which consumers do have the opportunity to negotiate with business vis-à-vis and they can see and touch the commodity indeed.[41]

Although the legislator has not precisely regulated doorstep selling in the national statute, the implementation of the Consumer Protection Law 2013 on the local level still considers doorstep selling as an obvious type of transaction to which the withdrawal right should apply. For example, the newly amended Regulations of Shanghai on the Protection of Consumer Rights and Interests 2015[42] states unequivocally in its Article 30 that the right of withdrawal is applicable to 'doorstep selling' contracts.

Since 'direct selling' has been regulated by the Consumer Protection Law 2013 through the interpretation of *deng*, a new problem has emerged: the periods of withdrawal rights and the limitations on exercise are rather different between the national statute and the aforementioned administrative regulation, the Regulations on Direct Selling Administration 2005. With regard to the hierarchy of application, it is difficult to achieve any conclusion since the national statute is newer and of higher priority, but the administrative regulation provides special rules on direct selling. In substance, the restrictions on exercising the withdrawal right are less strict in the new Consumer Protection Law, but the period is also much shorter in comparison with the administrative regulation. Besides, whether the rule stated in the China Insurance Regulatory Commission's Notice has been repealed by the new Consumer Protection Law also needs further demonstration.

---

[40] See Jia (贾东明) 2013, p. 104.

[41] There is another reason why legislators refused to adopt this concept: this concept is regarded as 'not a common Mandarin expression' and 'it is difficult to be understood by ordinary consumers'. See Jia (贾东明) 2013, p. 104.

[42] Regulations of Shanghai on the Protection of Consumer Rights and Interests 2015 (《上海市消费者权益保护条例》(2015))

It is considered that the rule established by Article 79 of the Legislation Law 2015[43] that the hierarchy of national statutes is higher than administrative regulations should be strictly followed.[44] Even from a substantive perspective, although the period offered by the Regulations on Direct Selling Administration is longer, to keep the purchased goods unopened is disadvantageous to consumers. If the consumer is not allowed to inspect and examine the commodity, the legislative objective of protecting consumers from aggressive negotiation will fail. Therefore, after the amendment of the Consumer Protection Law, the article on withdrawal rights provided by this legislation should be the sole effective provision. In terms of life insurance, this issue is discussed in Chap. 3 with the conclusion that currently the Consumer Protection Law 2013 can be applied to the insurance contract. Thus, the rule on withdrawal right provided by the Notice on Life Insurance 2011 should be replaced by the rule provided by the Consumer Protection Law 2013.

5.2.3 EU Law

5.2.3.1 Directives

The right of withdrawal is not a new concept invented by EU directives. In the 1960s and 1970s, a cooling-off period for doorstep selling was firstly regulated in some national jurisdictions, such as German law and Dutch law.[45] Doorstep selling is the first domain where the right of withdrawal was regulated on the EU level.

To be specific, the Doorstep Selling Directive[46] provided in Article 5 that a consumer should have the right to 'renounce the effects of his undertaking by sending notice within a period of not less than seven days' which leads to the effect of releasing the consumer from any obligations under the cancelled contract. With regard to the definition of 'doorstep selling', a detailed demonstration of applicable scope can be found in Article 1.[47] This article revealed that the consumer is

[43] Legislation Law of the People's Republic of China (2015 Amendment) (《中华人民共和国立法法(2015修正)》)

[44] It reads: 'The effect of laws is higher than that of administrative regulations, local regulations, and rules'.

[45] See Micklitz et al. 2010, p. 241. For more details, see Loos 2009, p. 239.

[46] Council Directive of 20 December 1985 to protect the consumer in respect of contracts negotiated away from business premises (85/577/EEC) [1985] OJ L 372/31

[47] Article 1 of the Doorstep Selling Directive read: '1. This Directive shall apply to contracts under which a trader supplies goods or services to a consumer and which are concluded: /– during an excursion organised by the trader away from his business premises, or /–during a visit by a trader (i) to the consumer's home or to that of another consumer; (ii) to the consumer's place of work; where the visit does not take place at the express request of the consumer. 2. This Directive shall also apply to contracts for the supply of goods or services other than those concerning which the consumer requested the visit of the trader, provided that when he requested the visit the consumer did not know, or could not reasonably have known, that the supply of those other goods or services formed part of the trader's commercial or professional activities. 3. This Directive shall also apply

recognised as not ready for concluding a contract whether it is away from the trader's premises, at the consumer's home or working place or even if the trader was invited by the consumer but the consumer is not aware of the relation between the supplied goods and the further commercial or professional activities. In these circumstances, the right of withdrawal is granted.

The right of withdrawal is also an important part of the Timeshare Directive.[48] Its Article 6 provides that consumers in the EU Member States shall be given a period of 14 calendar days to withdraw from a timeshare, long-term holiday product and resale or exchange contract, without giving any reason.[49]

According to the Distance Selling Directive,[50] consumers should have a period of at least 7 working days to withdraw from a distance contract without penalty and without giving any reason. In respect of the meaning of 'distance contract', Article 2 of this directive gave the demonstration. It was stressed that the contract has to be concluded under an organised distance sales or service-provision scheme, which contains one or more means of distance communication, run by the seller.[51]

Furthermore, consumers in the context of life insurance,[52] distance selling of financial services[53] and consumer credit[54] are entitled to withdrawal rights on the grounds of the relevant provisions.

Of all these directives, the Doorstep Selling Directive and the Distance Selling Directive have been replaced by the Consumer Rights Directive.[55] On the basis of

---

to contracts in respect of which an offer was made by the consumer under conditions similar to those described in paragraph 1 or paragraph 2 although the consumer was not bound by that offer before its acceptance by the trader. 4. This Directive shall also apply to offers made contractually by the consumer under conditions similar to those described in paragraph 1 or paragraph 2 where the consumer is bound by his offer'.

[48] Directive 2008/122/EC of the European Parliament and of the Council of 14 January 2009 on the protection of consumers in respect of certain aspects of timeshare, long-term holiday product and resale and exchange contracts [2009] OJ L33/10

[49] The definition of 'timeshare contract', 'long-term holiday product contract', 'resale contract' and 'exchange contract' can be found in Article 2 of the Timeshare Directive.

[50] Directive 97/7/EC of the European Parliament and of the Council of 20 May 1997 on the protection of consumers in respect of distance contracts [1997] OJ L144/19

[51] It stated: '"distance contract" means any contract concerning goods or services concluded between a supplier and a consumer under an organised distance sales or service-provision scheme run by the supplier, who, for the purpose of the contract, makes exclusive use of one or more means of distance communication up to and including the moment at which the contract is concluded'.

[52] See Article 186 of the Insurance and Reinsurance Directive (Directive 2009/138/EC of the European Parliament and of the Council of 25 November 2009 on the taking-up and pursuit of the business of Insurance and Reinsurance (Solvency II) [2009] OJ L 335/1).

[53] See Article 6 of the Distance Marketing Directive (Directive 2002/65/EC of the European Parliament and of the Council of 23 September 2002 concerning the distance marketing of consumer financial services and amending Council Directive 90/619/EEC and Directives 97/7/EC and 98/27/EC [2002] OJ L271/16).

[54] See Article 14 of the Consumer Credit Directive.

[55] Directive 2011/83/EU of the European Parliament and of the Council of 25 October 2011 on consumer rights, amending Council Directive 93/13/EEC and Directive 1999/44/EC of the

Article 31 of the Consumer Rights Directive, the Doorstep Selling Directive and the Distance Selling Directive are repealed as of 13 June 2014. In the Consumer Rights Directive, a cooling-off period of 14 days is regulated by Article 9. Within this period, consumers can withdraw from a distance or off-premises contract.

In terms of the applicable scope, a distance contract refers to 'any contract concluded between the trader and the consumer under an organised distance sales or service-provision scheme without the simultaneous physical presence of the trader and the consumer, with the exclusive use of one or more means of distance communication up to and including the time at which the contract is concluded'.[56] Compared with the old definition on distance contract provided by the Distance Selling Directive, the new one is rather similar except that the requirement of 'without simultaneous physical presence' is emphasised.

Regarding 'doorstep selling', a new concept, 'off-premises contract', is used to describe the following types of contract: '(a) concluded in the simultaneous physical presence of the trader and the consumer, in a place which is not the business premises of the trader; (b) for which an offer was made by the consumer in the same circumstances as referred to in point (a); (c) concluded on the business premises of the trader or through any means of distance communication immediately after the consumer was personally and individually addressed in a place which is not the business premises of the trader in the simultaneous physical presence of the trader and the consumer; or (d) concluded during an excursion organised by the trader with the aim or effect of promoting and selling goods or services to the consumer'.[57] In comparison with Article 1 of the Doorstep Selling Directive, both the language and content are changed. To be specific, the Consumer Rights Directive uses the expression 'concluded in the simultaneous physical presence of the trader and the consumer, in a place which is not the business premises of the trader' instead of referring to the contracts concluded during a visit by a trader to the consumer's home or place of work. This means, as long as the conclusion of contract is away from the trader's business premises, the contract will fall under the applicable scope, regardless of whether the location is the consumer's home or place of work or whether the visit of the trader is voluntary or requested by the consumer. The factor of simultaneous physical presence of both the trader and consumer is stressed. Besides, even if the contract was concluded inside the trader's business premises, if it is the immediately occurring result of consumer being personally and individually addressed outside the business premises, it is still an 'off-premises contract'.

European Parliament and of the Council and repealing Council Directive 85/577/EEC and Directive 97/7/EC of the European Parliament and of the Council [2011] OJ L304/64

[56] See Article 2 of the Consumer Rights Directive (Directive 2008/48/EC of the European Parliament and of the Council of 23 April 2008 on credit agreements for consumers and repealing Council Directive 87/102/EEC [2008] OJ L133/66).

[57] See paragraph 8 of Article 2 of the Consumer Rights Directive.

5.2.3.2 German Law

As mentioned, German law was the first civil law jurisdiction to regulate the right of withdrawal in 1969 by means of setting the provisions on purchasing foreign investment shares away from the business premises of the trader. The related rules are now regulated in § 126 *Investmentgesetz*, BGB1. 2003-I, 2676.[58] Subsequently, a series of specialised statutes whose primary function is to implement the EU directives at the national level had been promulgated, and in 2002 they were integrated into the Civil Code (*Bürgerliches Gesetzbuch*, hereinafter 'BGB') as a result of the reform of the law of obligation. In 2013, in order to implement the Consumer Rights Directive, the German legislators amended the relevant rules in the BGB through the introduction of the Act on the Implementation of the Directive. Up to this day, the conditions and consequences for exercising withdrawal rights are regulated by § 355 et seq BGB, while the applicable scope is clarified by § 312, etc. BGB.

In the light of new § 312 g BGB, a consumer has the right to withdraw from an off-premises or distance contract on the basis of § 355 BGB. It is noteworthy that, in accord with the terminology adopted by the Consumer Rights Directive, the BGB replaced the previously used concept 'doorstep transactions' (*Haustürgeschäft*) by 'off-premises contracts' (*Außerhalb von Geschäftsräumen geschlossene Verträge*). Its § 312b provides that a contract will be defined as an 'off-premises contract' where (1) the contract was concluded with the simultaneous physical presence of the consumer and the trader in a place that is not the business premises of the trader; (2) the consumer has submitted a bid in the circumstances referred to in paragraph 1; (3) the contract was concluded on the business premises of the trader or by means of distance communication, where the consumer was, however, previously addressed directly, personally and individually outside the business premises of the trader in the simultaneous physical presence of the consumer and the trader; or (4) a contract was concluded on an excursion organised by the trader or with his help to promote the consumer for the sale of goods or the provision of services and enter into appropriate contracts with him.[59] As previously mentioned, the rationale for the German legislator granting consumers the right to withdraw from an off-premises contract is that traders may impose 'psychological pressure' on them and they can hardly say no or compare the offer with others.[60]

§ 312c BGB provides the definition of 'distance contracts', where the right of withdrawal under § 355 BGB is granted to consumers as well. This article regulates that distance contracts are contracts which are entered into between a trader and a consumer by the use of means of distance communication, unless the conclusion of contract was not under a sale or service system organised for distance sales.[61] In the previous version of § 312 BGB, it was clearly stated that 'financial services' were

[58] See Markesinis et al. 2006, p. 265.

[59] See § 312b (1) BGB.

[60] See Markesinis et al. 2006, p. 273.

[61] See § 312c BGB.

included in the scope of 'distance contracts',[62] but now only the definition of 'distance communication' is given because contracts of financial services are exempt from the effect of the Consumer Rights Directive.[63] As a result, the BGB regulates that the right of withdrawal is granted in the area of financial services as well, and it provides some special rules on the start of the period and consequences in its §§ 356, 357a. § 312c BGB provides that 'distance communication' refers to 'all means of communication that can be used to initiate or conclude a contract, without the contracting parties' simultaneously and physically present. It is noteworthy that a list is provided to demonstrate that 'distance communication' includes but is not limited to 'letters, catalogues, telephone calls, copies, e-mails sent via the mobile service messages (SMS) and broadcasting and telemedia'.[64] In the old version of the article on 'distance contracts', a particular rule regulated that the rules in terms of withdrawal right and providing information only apply to the first transaction in a series.[65] However, this is not the case anymore.

The rights of withdrawal are also applicable to distance learning contracts (§ 4 of the *Fernunterrichtsschutzgesetz* of 1976), timeshare contracts (§ 485 BGB) and consumer credit contracts (§ 495 BGB).

5.2.3.3 English Law

Withdrawal rights in English law can also be traced back to the 1960s. In the Hire-Purchase Acts of 1964 and 1965, a right to cancel a concluded credit agreement within 4 days of the receipt of that agreement was granted to consumers. Afterwards, this rule was adopted by Section 67 of the Consumer Credit Act 1974.[66] In Section

[62] It reads: 'Distance contracts are contracts for the supply of goods or the rendering of services, including financial services, which are entered into between an entrepreneur and a consumer solely by the use of means of distance communication, except where the entering into of the contract does not take place in the context of a sales or service system organised for distance sales'. With regard to the meaning of 'financial service', it is mentioned in the same article that 'financial services' are 'banking services and services in connection with the granting of a credit, insurance, provision for old age for individuals, investment or payment'.

[63] See Article 3 of the Consumer Rights Directive. It is clarified in Recital 32 that the reason why the European Union does not regulate the contracts of financial services is that the existing Union legislation contains numerous rules on it and the Member States should be encouraged to draw inspiration from these rules.

[64] See § 312c(2) BGB.

[65] It reads: 'In the case of contractual relationships that consist of an initial agreement with transactions following upon it or a series of separate transactions following upon it of the same type that have a temporal connection, the provisions on distance contracts only apply to the first agreement. If such transactions follow one another without such an agreement, the provisions on the duties of an entrepreneur to provide information apply only to the first transaction. However, if no transaction of the same type occurs for longer than one year, the next transaction is deemed to be the first transaction of a new series within the meaning of sentence 2'. See the previous version of § 312b.

[66] It provides: 'A regulated agreement may be cancelled by the debtor or hirer in accordance with this Part if the antecedent negotiations included oral representations made when in the presence of

8 of this Act, it was provided that a consumer credit agreement is an agreement between an individual ('the debtor') and any other person ('the creditor') by which the creditor provides the debtor with the credit of any amount.

In the area of doorstep selling, the Cancellation of Contracts made in a Consumer's Home or Place of Work, etc. Regulations 2008 (hereinafter 'Regulations 2008') and its previous version[67] should be noted. These regulations applied to 'a contract, including a consumer credit agreement, between a consumer and a trader which is for the supply of goods or services to the consumer by a trader and which is made: (a) during a visit by the trader to the consumer's home or place of work, or to the home of another individual; (b) during an excursion organised by the trader away from his business premises; or (c) after an offer made by the consumer during such a visit or excursion'.[68]

Regarding distance contracts, consumers were granted the right of withdrawal based on the Consumer Protection (Distance Selling) Regulations 2000 (hereinafter 'Regulations 2000').[69] This legislation provided that 'distance contract' means 'any contract concerning goods or services concluded between a supplier and a consumer under an organised distance sales or service provision scheme run by the supplier who, for the purpose of the contract, makes exclusive use of one or more means of distance communication up to and including the moment at which the contract is concluded'.[70] For the meaning of 'means of distance communication', it referred to the means 'without the simultaneous physical presence of the supplier and the consumer, may be used for the conclusion of a contract between those parties; and an indicative list of such means is contained in Schedule 1'.[71] Schedule 1 further provided that the stated means of distance communication include 'unaddressed printed matter, addressed printed matter, letter, press advertising with order form, catalogue, telephone with human intervention, telephone without human intervention (automatic calling machine, audiotext), radio, videophone (telephone with screen), videotext (microcomputer and television screen) with keyboard or touch screen, electronic mail, facsimile machine (fax) and television (teleshopping)'.[72]

Besides, withdrawal rights are also granted to consumers in the context of timeshare.[73]

With a view to implementing the Consumer Rights Directive, the Consumer Contracts (Information, Cancellation and Additional Charges) Regulation 2013

---

the debtor or hirer by an individual acting as, or on behalf of, the negotiator'. Afterwards some exceptions are listed in items (a) and (b).

[67] See the Consumer Protection (Cancellation of Contracts Concluded away from Business Premises) Regulations 1987, SI 1997 No 1081.

[68] Regulation 5 of the Regulations 2008

[69] See Regulation 10 of the Regulations 2000.

[70] Regulation 3 of the Regulations 2000

[71] See Regulation 3 of the Regulations 2000.

[72] See Schedule 1 of the Regulations 2000.

[73] See Part 2 of the Timeshare, Holiday Products, Resale and Exchange Contracts Regulations 2010.

(hereinafter 'Regulations 2013') was introduced, while the Regulations 2000 and the Regulations 2008 do not apply in the relevant fields anymore. Part 3 of the Regulations 2013 provides that the right of withdrawal applies to distance and off-premises contracts between a trader and a consumer.[74] Regarding the definition of 'distance contracts' and 'off-premises contracts', it is regulated in Section 5 and no obvious difference can be found if compared with the directive. It is noteworthy that the Regulations 2013 specifically regulate that in some circumstances, for instance, the contracts for passenger transport services and the off-premises contracts the payment of which is not more than 42 pounds, the right of withdrawal is not applicable.[75]

5.2.4 *Comparative Review*

Comparing the applicable scopes of withdrawal rights regulated in Chinese law and the EU jurisdictions, it firstly can be observed that legislators focus in particular on distance selling.[76] In order to facilitate consumers to find out the circumstances under which they can exercise their withdrawal rights, the Chinese Consumer Protection Law does not use an abstract concept such as 'distance selling'. Rather, it regulates the applicable scope of withdrawal rights by enumerating several distance selling means. However, only a few means are enumerated. Other distance selling means are left to be interpreted via the Chinese character *deng*, which refers to the circumstances that are not enumerated and the unpredictable ones that could occur in the future.[77] In contrast, the EU directive, German law and English all provide the abstract concept 'distance contract' and its definition, and German law and English law also provide the enumeration of means of distance communication. Even if we only compare the enumerations provided by different jurisdictions, the number of means listed in German law and English law is more elaborate than in Chinese law. For example, although purchasing via the Internet, television, telephone and mail order are all regulated, other means, such as catalogue, fax and radio, which are regulated by the BGB and the Regulations 2000, are ignored by the

[74] See Regulation 27(1) of the Regulations 2013.

[75] See Regulation 27(2)(3) of the Regulations 2013.

[76] This is to cure the aforementioned 'information asymmetry'. However, both in the EU and China, there are critiques that the information asymmetry cannot provide the legitimacy for withdrawal rights. See, for example, Sun (孙良国) 2011, p. 107. It is argued that information asymmetry also emerges between SMEs and transnational corporations, but SMEs are not entitled to withdrawal rights.

[77] The use of open-ended approach may result in the legal uncertainty. Nevertheless, from another perspective, it will be also understandable why Chinese legislators adopt this approach if it can be evidenced, for example, by virtue of the empirical research on the number of disputes, that the significance of the rights of withdrawal in these specific domains is much more crucial than the others.

Chinese Consumer Protection Law. Nonetheless, from a comparative law perspective, these means can be certainly helpful when interpreting *deng* in practice.

Another type of transaction to which withdrawal rights are applicable is doorstep selling. In China, although the Consumer Protection Law has not precisely mentioned this concept, it is widely accepted that doorstep selling falls into the applicable scope. When interpreting *deng*, doorstep selling is undoubtedly included. It is noteworthy that an administrative regulation provided that the right of withdrawal is applicable to 'direct selling' contracts. Based on the previous description, 'direct selling' in the context of Chinese Law should be a specific type of 'doorstep selling'. Unlike Chinese law, the EU law makes it rather clear that withdrawal rights are applicable to 'doorstep selling' contracts and there is always a rather precise definition attached to the abstract phrase in the EU legislation.

In the EU context, because every single directive has its own applicable scope and, in some circumstances, these applicable scopes overlap, it is possible that two or more withdrawal rights are applicable. The doorstep selling or distance selling of a timeshare is a good example. These withdrawal rights sometimes have different cooling-off periods. The rules on exercise, exceptions or the duty of notification could also be different. Scholars suggest that the lack of coherence may cause legal uncertainty.[78] In the Chinese context, how to decide applicable law could also become a problem where different legislation provides regulation on the same issue, such as direct selling. It calls for a further analysis on the relation between the rules in the Consumer Protection Law 2013 and the previous administrative regulation. However, in China it is not difficult to decide because there are certain rules on the hierarchy of different legal sources. Because the Consumer Protection Law 2013 is 'law' and new, it should be applied prior to the administrative regulation. For the EU counterpart, sometimes it is necessary for the court to decide where two or more rights of withdrawal are applicable. In a case of doorstep selling of a timeshare, the CJEU confirmed that two directives are both applicable.[79] Nevertheless, it is still suggested that the EU rules on withdrawal rights need to be further harmonised. It can be observed that the Consumer Rights Directive has already provided the harmonised rules in the domains of off-premises contracts and distance contracts.

Apart from the similarities, it is noteworthy that the Chinese withdrawal right is only applicable to sales contracts. This can be observed from the wording that 'consumers shall have the right to return the commodities'. No withdrawal right is applicable to service-provision contracts.[80] In the EU context, this is not the case: withdrawal rights are also applicable to service provision. This is regulated in the EU directive, German law and English law (Table 5.2).

---

[78] See Loos 2009, p. 242.

[79] See Travel Vac SL v Manuel José Antelm Sanchi, Case C-423/97 [1999] ECR I-02195.

[80] A leading scholar of civil law in China, Jin Ke-ke, argues that it is not appropriate to exclude service-provision contracts from withdrawal rights' applicable scope. Therefore, when interpreting 'commodities', some tokenised service provision should also be regarded as 'commodities'. See Jin (金可可) 2014, p. 12.

Table 5.2 Applicable scope

	Applicable scope	Means of communication
Chinese Consumer Protection Law	Business operators sell commodities on the Internet, on television, over telephone, by mail order, etc.	Internet, television, telephone, mail order
	(Article 25 of the Consumer Protection Law 2013)	
EU Directives	Timeshare	
	Distance selling of consumer financial services	
	Consumer credit	
	Life insurance	
	Off-premises contracts	
	Distance contracts	
	Others	
German Law	Off-premises contracts	Letters, catalogues, telephone calls, copies, e-mails sent via the mobile service messages (SMS) and broadcasting and telemedia
	Distance contracts	
	Distance learning	
	Consumer credit	
	Timeshare	
	etc.	
English Law	Off premises contracts	Unaddressed printed matter, addressed printed matter, letter, press advertising with order form, catalogue, telephone with human intervention, telephone without human intervention (automatic calling machine, audiotext), radio, videophone (telephone with screen), videotext (microcomputer and television screen) with keyboard or touch screen, electronic mail, facsimile machine (fax) and television (teleshopping)
	Distance contracts	
	Timeshare	
	Consumer credit	
	etc.	

5.3 Exceptions to Withdrawal Rights

5.3.1 Introduction

In both China and the EU, legislators consider that withdrawal rights are not applicable to all commodities or services. In some certain types of transactions, the trader would suffer great loss if the consumer is free to change his or her mind and cancel the contract at will. To balance the reasonable interest between traders and consumers, the law lists the types of contracts to which withdrawal rights are not applicable. This section introduces these rules separately (Sects. 5.3.2 and 5.3.3), and a comparative review is provided (Sect. 5.3.4).

5.3.2 Chinese Law

Before mandatory withdrawal rights were incorporated into the Consumer Protection Law 2013, in business practice, some e-commerce platforms had already provided some terms or bulletins that not all goods can be returned without reason even if the consumer is entitled to voluntary withdrawal rights. For example, the third biggest e-commerce platform Jingdong ('京东商城', www.jd.com)[81] demonstrated in its after-sale policies that, even though there is no defect, the consumer is entitled to return the commodity within 7 days after he has received it, as long as the return will not affect the secondary sale of the goods and the consumer can afford the fee of return. Besides, it was pointed out that this voluntary withdrawal right is not applicable to the following types of commodities: diamond, gold, watches, jewels and personal accessories; food, health products, nursing products, paraphernalia, cosmetics, virtual goods and software and goods which were declared to be nonreturnable when the sale had been concluded.[82]

For mandatory rules, the Consumer Protection Law provides a list of categories of goods to which the right of withdrawal is not applicable.[83] It states: 'the consumers shall have the right to return the commodities within 7 days of receipt of them without cause, except the following commodities: (1) Custom-made commodities; (2) Fresh, live, or perishable commodities; (3) Audio-visual recordings, computer software, and other digital commodities downloaded online or unpacked by consumers[84]; (4) Newspapers or periodicals delivered'. Furthermore, 'in addition to the commodities listed in the preceding paragraph, the return without cause shall not apply to commodities unsuitable for return by nature as confirmed by consumers at the time of purchase'.[85]

---

[81] It reveals that 29.9% of the e-commerce consumers have purchased from their website, which ranks third in all e-commerce platforms in 2012. See CNNIC (China Internet Network Information Center) (中国互联网络信息中心), 'Research on Chinese Online Shopping Market in 2012' (《2012年中国网络购物市场研究报告》), available at: <http://www.cnnic.cn/hlwfzyj/hlwxzbg/dzswbg/201304/P020130417543965742695.pdf>, last visited: 2014/5/31.

[82] See jd.com (京东商城), 'After-sale Policies' (《售后政策》), available at: <http://help.jd.com/help/question-97.html>, last visited: 2014/5/31.

[83] In the first Draft of the Amendment, the enumeration was not included. The only exception was the commodities unsuitable for return by their nature. When the legislator was seeking for advice and suggestions, some people suggested that the circumstances where the commodities are not suitable for return should be clarified, in order to prevent the abuse of this type of right. This suggestion was adopted. See 'Reports of the Legislative Affairs Commission of the Standing Committee of the National People's Congress on the Draft of the Amendment of Law of the People's Republic of China on the Protection of Consumer Rights and Interests' (《全国人民代表大会法律委员会关于〈中华人民共和国消费者权益保护法修正案(草案)〉修改情况的汇报》), in Jia (贾东明) 2013, p. 334.

[84] In the first and second drafts, digital commodities downloaded online have not been mentioned.

[85] See Article 25 of the Consumer Protection Law 2013. During the process of revising the law, some representatives from the local people's congresses and the departments of the central government suggested financial products, credit and loan products and travel products should also be excluded. See 'Opinions of the Local People's Congresses and the Relevant Departments of the

To explain why these types of commodities are not suitable for withdrawal rights, the Understanding of authority elaborates the reason for each category. Firstly, withdrawal rights are not applicable to custom-made commodities because these commodities are considerably difficult to be sold again if they were returned by consumers. Secondly, contracts of selling fresh, live or perishable commodities cannot be withdrawn without reason, because the factor of time has a great influence on the value of goods. When the seller receives the returned commodity, it is rather likely that the goods have already perished or the value has significantly reduced. The third category points to digital commodities. It is alleged that the right of withdrawal is not applicable because these commodities can be copied after being downloaded or unpacked. Allowing the return after being downloaded or unpacked will severely damage the lawful interests of traders, and the copyright owners' legal rights and interests may also be infringed. Finally, newspapers and periodicals cannot be returned without reason because of the time factor: when the time has passed, the value of goods will decrease.

It is noteworthy that the law does not prohibit traders from providing a protection of higher level to attract consumers. If the trader provides a voluntary right of withdrawal, he will be bound by his words even if the commodity is contained in these exceptions.[86]

The categories in the list are not the only exceptions to withdrawal rights. Article 25 also provides a fallback rule that withdrawal rights should not apply to other commodities unsuitable for return by nature as confirmed by consumers at the time of purchase. It is obvious that the list cannot cover all circumstances that withdrawal rights should not apply. Thus, a 'miscellaneous provision' is regulated to deal with the dependent situations. Indeed, apart from the four categories enumerated by law, there are other types of commodities which might not be suitable for return without reason. The luxuries such as golden accessories are good examples: the trader could suffer great loss if the consumer returns a substituted fake golden accessory.[87] In determining whether a type of commodity is 'nonreturnable by nature', three elements can be used for assessment: (1) the value of the commodity, (2) the cost and difficulty of repacking and (3) the difficulty to recognise whether there exists an abuse of withdrawal right.[88] In the Interim Measures for the Return without Reasons of Commodities Purchased Online within 7 Days (hereinafter 'Interim Measures 2017'),[89] the State Administration for Industry and Commerce also provides that

---

Central Government on the Draft of the Amendment of Law on the Protection of Consumer Rights and Interests' (《地方人大、中央有关部门和单位对消费者权益保护法修正案(草案)(征求意见稿)的意见》), in Civil Law Office of the Legislative Affairs Commission of the Standing Committee of the National People's Congress (全国人大常委会法制工作委员会民法室) 2013, p. 30.

[86] See Jia (贾东明) 2013, p. 108.

[87] See Chen (陈玺撼) 2014.

[88] See Ge (葛江虬) 2015, p. 101.

[89] Interim Measures for the Return without Reasons of Commodities Purchased Online within 7 Days (《网络购买商品七日无理由退货暂行办法》), Order No. 90 of the State Administration for Industry and Commerce (国家工商行政管理总局令(第90号))

three types of commodities, according to their nature, may escape the application of the rules on withdrawal rights, as long as consumers confirm at the time of purchase: (1) commodities that are easy to affect personal safety or life and health once unpacked or commodities that are easy to change in quality once unpacked; (2) commodities largely devalued once activated or used on a trial basis; and (3) commodities that customers are aware will soon expire or are flawed before buying them.[90]

During the lawmaking process, there was a worry that this provision is too broad. Buyers and sellers might have dissenting opinions on whether the commodity is suitable for return by nature. As a result, the legislator added that if the seller claims that the specific category of commodities is not returnable, he has to inform the consumer at the time of his purchase and acquire the confirmation by the consumer. Based on the elaboration by the Understanding of authority, the seller putting an announcement on a website merely cannot be recognised as a confirmation of the consumer. It requires a special process to draw the consumer's attention and express that the commodity is not suitable for return. Only in this case, if the consumer still presses the button to confirm his purchase, will the commodity be deemed nonreturnable.[91] In some local regulations to implement the Consumer Protection Law 2013, it is further clarified that the trader needs to inform the consumer via an obvious way and adopt measures for the consumer to confirm.[92]

In the previously mentioned case of Jingdong, the new after-sale policies were adopted to fit the rule regulated by the Consumer Protection Law 2013. Apart from the categories enumerated by law and already existing in the last version, it was announced that luxuries and the commodities which cannot be kept intact after being returned are not returnable.[93] In some other e-commerce platforms, there are more categories of commodities announced to be eliminated from the application of withdrawal rights.[94] Some comments suggest that these additional rules substantively increase the difficulties for consumers to perform their legal rights and even violate the law. However, since the new Consumer Protection Law provides the fallback rule, the core issue becomes whether the business has informed the consumer and obtained the confirmation. This issue would become complicated if the notification of 'the commodity is not suitable for return' is given by standard terms. In some e-commerce platforms, for example, Taobao, the consumer will see a clear statement that the '7-days-return policy does not apply to this commodity' when he

[90] See Article 7 of the Interim Measures 2017.

[91] See Jia (贾东明) 2013, p. 109.

[92] For example, see Article 30 of the Regulations of Shanghai on the Protection of Consumer Rights and Interests 2015 (《上海市消费者权益保护条例》(2015)).

[93] See jd.com (京东商城), 'After-sale service Policies' (《售后服务政策》), available at: <http://help.jd.com/help/question-149.html#help1709>, last visited: 2014/6/1.

[94] See www.china.com.cn (中国网), 'Bawang Tiaokuan Still Exist While the New Consumer Protection Law has been in Effect for One Month; E-commerce Platforms Set Doorsills for Return' (《新消法满月霸王条款不死,京东等电商设退货门槛》), available at: <http://tech.china.com.cn/internet/jjds/20140415/107532.shtml>, last visited: 2014/6/1.

is examining the details with regard to the good's price, quantity, discount and transportation just before accomplishing the payment. Besides, there is even a button next to this statement for the consumer to check why it is not suitable and the specific contents of their withdrawal policy.[95] In this case, it is reasonable for the trader to allege that he has informed the consumer and obtained the confirmation since the consumer clicked on the button of 'I confirm this order'. Besides, there are also some e-commerce platforms which give consumers phone calls to notify the elimination of their rights of withdrawal. This will also lead to the consequence that the withdrawal rights are excluded.[96] Conversely, for example, in the case of Jingdong, even if the consumer gets to the last step before he makes the payment, he can see nothing related to the right of withdrawal, although the commodity could be not suitable for return 'by nature', which has been announced in their after-sale service policies. In this context, these terms cannot be incorporated as a part of the contract because the trader failed to draw the consumer's attention to it.[97]

5.3.3 EU Law

5.3.3.1 Directives

In the area of doorstep selling, the Doorstep Selling Directive (85/577/EEC) regulated that the directive should not apply to (1) the sale of land; (2) the supply of food, drink and other goods intended for current consumption in the household and supplied by regular deliverymen; (3) certain contracts concluded on the basis of a trader's catalogue; (4) insurance contracts; and (5) contracts for securities.[98]

For distance selling contracts, Article 6 of the Distance Selling Directive (97/7/EC) provided a list of exceptions where the consumer may not exercise the right of withdrawal, unless the parties have agreed. The right of withdrawal cannot be exercised in respect of the contracts (1) for the provision of services if performance has begun; (2) for the supply of goods or services the price of which is dependent on fluctuations in the financial market which cannot be controlled by the supplier; (3) for the supply of goods made to the consumer's specifications or clearly personalised or which, by reason of their nature, cannot be returned or are liable to deteriorate or expire rapidly; (4) for the supply of audio or video recordings or computer

[95] This will be further discussed in the last section of this chapter. See Taobao.com (淘宝网), Applicable Scope, Dealing Process and Conditions on '7-days-return' (《"七天退货"支持范围、处理流程及条件》), available at: <http://service.taobao.com/support/seller/knowledge-5701303.htm>, last visited: 2014/10/3.

[96] See Chen (陈玺撼) 2014.

[97] This rule is provided by Article 39 of the Contract law and the first paragraph of Article 26 of the Consumer Protection Law. For the further introduction, see Sect. 4.5 of Chap. 4.

[98] For details, see Article 3(2) of the Doorstep Selling Directive.

software which were unsealed by the consumer; (5) for the supply of newspapers, periodicals and magazines; and (6) for gaming and lottery services.[99]

In the Consumer Rights Directive (2011/83/EU), these old provisions in the area of doorstep selling and distance selling have been replaced by a new list of exceptions, which is set out in Article 16 'Exceptions from the right of withdrawal'. These items are: '(a) service contracts after the service has been fully performed if the performance has begun with the consumer's prior express consent, and with the acknowledgement that he will lose his right of withdrawal once the contract has been fully performed by the trader; (b) the supply of goods or services for which the price is dependent on fluctuations in the financial market which cannot be controlled by the trader and which may occur within the withdrawal period; (c) the supply of goods made to the consumer's specifications or clearly personalised; (d) the supply of goods which are liable to deteriorate or expire rapidly; (e) the supply of sealed goods which are not suitable for return due to health protection or hygiene reasons and were unsealed after delivery; (f) the supply of goods which are, after delivery, according to their nature, inseparably mixed with other items; (g) the supply of alcoholic beverages, the price of which has been agreed upon at the time of the conclusion of the sales contract, the delivery of which can only take place after 30 days and the actual value of which is dependent on fluctuations in the market which cannot be controlled by the trader; (h) contracts where the consumer has specifically requested a visit from the trader for the purpose of carrying out urgent repairs or maintenance. If, on the occasion of such visit, the trader provides services in addition to those specifically requested by the consumer or goods other than replacement parts necessarily used in carrying out the maintenance or in making the repairs, the right of withdrawal shall apply to those additional services or goods; (i) the supply of sealed audio or sealed video recordings or sealed computer software which were unsealed after delivery; (j) the supply of a newspaper, periodical or magazine with the exception of subscription contracts for the supply of such publications; (k) contracts concluded at a public auction; (l) the provision of accommodation other than for residential purpose, transport of goods, car rental services, catering or services related to leisure activities if the contract provides for a specific date or period of performance; (m) the supply of digital content which is not supplied in a tangible medium if the performance has begun with the consumer's prior express consent and his acknowledgment that he thereby loses his right of withdrawal'.

It can be observed that these exceptions are regulated to balance the interests between traders and consumers. If consumers were allowed to withdraw from these contracts, traders might suffer great loss. For example, it would be rather difficult for a trader to resell personalised goods.

[99] See Article 6(3) of the Distance Selling Directive.

5.3.3.2 German Law

On the grounds of § 312g BGB, the right of withdrawal, unless the parties have agreed otherwise, does not apply to the following contracts: (1) contracts for the supply of goods which are not prefabricated and for their manufacture where an individual choice or decision by the consumer is important or which are clearly tailored to the personal needs of the consumer; (2) contracts for the supply of goods that may spoil quickly or whose expiration date has passed quickly; (3) contracts for the supply of sealed goods which are unsuitable for reasons of health or hygiene to be returned when unsealed after delivery; (4) contracts for the supply of goods, if they were mixed after delivery due to their nature inseparably with other goods; (5) contracts for the supply of alcoholic beverages, the price was agreed in the contract that can be delivered earlier than 30 days after the conclusion of the contract, however, and the current value of fluctuations in the market depends on the entrepreneur's control; (6) contracts for the supply of audio or video recordings or computer software in a sealed package, if the seal was removed after delivery; (7) contracts for the supply of newspapers, periodicals or magazines with the exception of subscription contracts; (8) contracts for the supply of goods or provision of services, including financial services whose price depends on fluctuations in the financial market over which the trader has no control and which may occur during the withdrawal period, in particular services related to shares, with shares in open-ended investment assets within the meaning of § 1(4) of the Capital Investment Code (*Kapitalanlagegesetzbuch*) and other tradable securities, foreign currency, derivatives and money market instruments; (9) subject of the sentence than for residential purposes two contracts to provide services in the areas of accommodation for other purposes, carriage of goods, automobile rental, delivery of food and beverages as well as to provide additional services related to leisure activities if the contract provides for a specific date or period of performance[100]; (10) contracts that are concluded in the context of a method of sale where goods or services are offered by the trader to consumers, who attend or are given the possibility to attend the auction in person, through a transparent, competitive bidding procedure run by an auctioneer and where the successful bidder is obliged to purchase the goods or services (publicly accessible auction); (11) contracts for which the consumer has specifically requested the trader to visit him, to make urgent repairs or maintenance; this shall not apply with respect to further services supplied during the visit that the consumer has not expressly requested, or delivered in respect of such goods during the visit that are not necessarily required for the maintenance or repair of replacement parts; (12) contracts for the provision of gaming and lottery services, unless the consumer has given his contact phone or the contract was concluded away from business premises; and (13) notarised contracts; this applies to distance contracts for

[100] According to the last sentence of § 312g(2), it is noteworthy that the exception pursuant to sentence 1 number 9 does not apply to contracts for travel services in accordance with § 651a, if they have been concluded away from business premises, unless the hearings on which the conclusion of the contract is based, have been performed on previous order of the consumer.

financial services only if the notary confirms that the consumer's rights under § 312(2) BGB are respected. Indeed, the list provided by the BGB is rather similar to the Consumer Rights Directive.

5.3.3.3 English Law

In English law, the exceptions to withdrawal rights in the context of doorstep selling and distance selling were laid in the Regulations 2008 and the Regulations 2000.[101] Now the Regulations 2013 provides a list of enumeration as well to regulate the exceptions where the right of withdrawal is not applicable.

To be specific, the rule on the right of withdrawal does not apply as regards the following: '(a) the supply of – (i) goods, or (ii) services, other than supply of water, gas, electricity or district heating, for which the price is dependent on fluctuations in the financial market which cannot be controlled by the trader and which may occur within the cancellation period; (b) the supply of goods that are made to the consumer's specifications or are clearly personalised; (c) the supply of goods which are liable to deteriorate or expire rapidly; (d) the supply of alcoholic beverages, where – (i) their price has been agreed at the time of the conclusion of the sales contract, (ii) delivery of them can only take place after 30 days, and (iii) their value is dependent on fluctuations in the market which cannot be controlled by the trader; (e) contracts where the consumer has specifically requested a visit from the trader for the purpose of carrying out urgent repairs or maintenance; (f) the supply of a newspaper, periodical or magazine with the exception of subscription contracts for the supply of such publications; (g) contracts concluded at a public auction; (h) the supply of accommodation, transport of goods, vehicle rental services, catering or services related to leisure activities, if the contract provides for a specific date or

[101] Schedule 3 of the Regulations 2008 provides a list of categories of commodities which are not suitable for revocation. It includes contracts for the construction, sale or rental of immovable property or contracts concerning other rights relating to immovable property, contracts for the supply of foodstuffs or beverages or other goods intended for current consumption in the household and supplied by a regular roundsman, contracts for insurance and contracts for the supply of goods and services when one of some special conditions is met. For details, see Schedule 3 of the Regulations 2008, 'Excepted contracts'. And Regulation 13 of the Regulations 2000 is a typical provision where exceptions to right of revocation in the context of distance selling can be found. On the basis of this provision, unless the parties have agreed otherwise, 'the consumer will not have the right to cancel the contract by giving notice of cancellation pursuant to Regulation 10 in respect of contracts: (a) for the supply of services if the supplier has complied with Regulation 8(3) and performance of the contract has begun with the consumer's agreement before the end of the cancellation period applicable under Regulation 12; (b) for the supply of goods or services, the price of which is dependent on fluctuations in the financial market which cannot be controlled by the supplier; (c) for the supply of goods made to the consumer's specifications or clearly personalised or which by reason of their nature cannot be returned or are liable to deteriorate or expire rapidly; (d) for the supply of audio or video recordings or computer software if they are unsealed by the consumer; (e) for the supply of newspapers, periodicals or magazines or (f) for gaming, betting or lottery services.

period of performance'.[102] The reasons for excluding withdrawal rights in these contracts are exactly the same as the EU directive and German law.

5.3.4 Comparative Review

Comparing the rules on exceptions to withdrawal rights, the categories of contracts regulated in European jurisdictions are much more than the categories regulated in the Chinese Consumer Protection law, despite the fact that the Chinese legislator particularly mentioned that they had made reference to the European rules when the law was amended.[103] Since the Chinese legislator was aware that other jurisdictions regulate more categories of contracts to which withdrawal rights are not applicable, the reason why these categories are not regulated could be that the legislators do not consider that so many categories should become exceptions or these exceptions should not be specifically regulated in the national statute. The idea is to leave the specific assessment on 'whether the commodity is suitable for return' to practice and provide more protection via granting consumers the right to confirm when the goods are announced to be nonreturnable: in China, even if a trader claims that a commodity is nonreturnable by nature, it still needs to acquire the consumer's confirmation for the subject matter escaping the application of the mandatory withdrawal right.

European jurisdictions usually provide that the situation where the withdrawal right is not applicable can be changed if the parties have other agreements (see § 312d BGB, Regulation 13 of the Regulations 2000). This means that it is possible for the trader to abandon the right to exempt withdrawal rights to increase its commodity or service's attractiveness even if the commodity or service is not suitable for withdrawal rights. But in Chinese law, a similar rule cannot be found.

With regard to the specific categories of contracts, the focus is always on the features which make the commodity or service not suitable for withdrawal rights by nature, for example, the commodity is personalised. In addition to the categories regulated by the Chinese Consumer Protection Law 2013 (custom-made commodities, fresh, live or perishable commodities, digital commodities, newspapers or periodicals), in the European jurisdictions, withdrawal rights are not applicable to the following circumstances: (1) the contract is a service contract, and the service has already begun prior to the consumer's withdrawal; (2) the price of the commodity is dependent on fluctuations in the financial market which cannot be controlled by the seller; (3) the commodity is nonreturnable due to the health protection or hygiene reasons; (4) the commodity is not suitable for return because it will be inseparably mixed with other goods according to its nature after delivery; (5) the contract is about urgent repair or maintenance; (6) the contract is concluded through an auction;

---

[102] Regulation 28 of the Regulations 2013

[103] The Understanding of authority clearly mentions Article 16 of the Consumer Rights Directive and even lists all the 13 categories. See Jia (贾东明) 2013, pp. 106–107.

Table 5.3 Exceptions to withdrawal rights

	Exceptions of withdrawal rights
Chinese Consumer Protection Law	(1) Custom-made commodities; (2) fresh, live or perishable commodities; (3) audio-visual recordings, computer software and other digital commodities downloaded online or unpacked by consumers; (4) newspapers or periodicals delivered
	(Article 25 of the Consumer Protection Law)
EU Directives	Article 16 of the Consumer Rights Directive
German Law	§ 312g BGB
English Law	Regulation 28 of the Regulations 2013

(7) the contract is about betting or lottery; and (8) the contract is relating to immovable property. Among these categories, some of them are regulated by all three European jurisdictions, such as the circumstance where the price cannot be controlled by the seller, and some of them are only regulated by the Consumer Rights Directive or one national jurisdiction, for example, only the EU directive and German law provide that the right of withdrawal is not applicable to the commodities which will be mixed with other goods after the delivery. When the Chinese judges need to decide whether the commodity is suitable for return by nature, these categories can be good references (Table 5.3).

5.4 Periods of Withdrawal Rights

5.4.1 Introduction

This section deals with three questions as follows. In Chinese law and its European counterparts, (1) How long is the consumer permitted to decide whether to escape from a valid contract on the grounds of withdrawal right? (2) After they decide, how long are they allowed to exercise their right? (3) How does the law regulate the start and end of these periods? The relevant rules in Chinese law (Sect. 5.4.2), EU directives (Sect. 5.4.3.1), German law (Sect. 5.4.3.2) and English law (Sect. 5.4.3.3) are introduced, respectively. A summary of comparative observations is provided (Sect. 5.4.4).

5.4.2 Chinese Law

5.4.2.1 Length of the Period

On the basis of Article 25 of the new Consumer Protection Law 2013, consumers should have the right to return the commodities within 7 days of receipt without reason. In the process of amending the law, it was suggested that the period could be 15 days.[104] However, no more official demonstration can be found to explain why the legislator chose 15 days and even why the final version regulates the length of the period as 7 days. Only the Understanding of authority mentions that the period is rather short because this right entitles consumers to change their mind without any reason. In sharp contrast to the rights of avoidance with reasons, such as fraud, significant misconception or obvious unfairness,[105] where the rights can exist for 1 year,[106] only a period of 7 days is granted in this context, because the contract's destiny is solely dependent on the consumer's will.[107] Some scholars provide their assumption to explain why the period is considerably short. For example, Liangguo Sun suggests that the set of 7 days is 'temporarily rational', because the legislator has never regulated the right of withdrawal before and the consequence is unpredictable. Taking a conservative strategy is a wise and safe move at the legislative level.[108]

5.4.2.2 Start and End of the Period

Prior to the era of Consumer Protection Law 2013, the Notice on Life Insurance 2011 provided that the 10-day withdrawal period[109] should begin when the policyholder signs after receiving the policy in a written form. The Consumer Protection Law 2013 adopts the same viewpoint: pursuant to Article 25, the period should start with the receipt of goods.

---

[104] See Opinions of the Representatives of the 11th National People's Congress on Revising Law on the Protection of Consumer Rights and Interests (《十一届全国人大代表议案对修改消费者权益保护法的意见》), in Civil Law Office of the Legislative Affairs Commission of the Standing Committee of the National People's Congress (全国人大常委会法制工作委员会民法室) 2013, p. 22.

[105] Pursuant to the Instrument No. 6 [1988] of the Supreme People's Court (Opinions of the Supreme People's Court on Several Issues concerning the Implementation of the General Principles of the Civil Law of the People's Republic of China (For Trial Implementation) (《最高人民法院关于贯彻执行〈中华人民共和国民法通则〉若干问题的意见(试行)》), Instrument No. 6 [1988] of the Supreme People's Court (法(办)发[1988]6号)), 'fraud' refers to the case that 'any party purposely conveys any false information to the other party, or purposely disguises any fact so as to induce the other party into making any false declaration of will' (Article 68). 'Significant misconception' means 'an actor performs his conduct on the basis of false understanding of the nature of the conduct, the opposite party, the variety, quality, specification and amount of the objects, etc., which leads to the consequence of the conduct going against his own will and results in very serious damages' (Article 71). The definition and interpretation of 'obvious unfairness' have been discussed in Chap. 4 under the topic of unfair terms.

[106] On the grounds of Article 55 of the Contract Law 1999, the right of avoidance will extinguish within 1 year from the day the party who has the right to avoid the contract knows or ought to know the causes of avoidance, if he fails to exercise it.

[107] See Jia (贾东明) 2013, p. 105.

[108] See Sun (孙良国) 2014, p. 83.

[109] See Point 4 of the Notice on Life Insurance 2011.

In terms of the calculation of the period, the Understanding of authority mentions that Article 154 of the General Principles of the Civil Law 1987[110] should be noticed for reference.[111] This is also in line with the systematic interpretation because the General Principles of the Civil Law 1987 provides the general rule with regard to the start and calculation of *Qijian* ('期间', literally means 'periods') in the context of Chinese civil law. On the grounds of Article 154 of the General Principles of the Civil Law 1987, the period should be calculated by the Gregorian calendar. Considering the period of withdrawal right is prescribed in days ('within seven days of receipt'), when the consumer receives the good, that day will not be counted as within the period. The period should start on the second day.[112] The General Provisions of the Civil Law 2017[113] provides the same rule.[114]

Regarding the end of the period, Article 154 states: 'If the last day of a time period falls on a Sunday or an official holiday, the day after the holiday shall be taken as the last day. The last day shall end at 24:00 h. If business hours are applicable, the last day shall end at closing time'.[115] It should be noted that since the last sentence of this article mentions the specific situation where business hours are applicable, the calculation of periods in practice should be different from businesses' opening hours. Only if the shop is open for all year will the period end at 24:00 of the last day.[116]

---

[110] General Principles of the Civil Law of the People's Republic of China (《中华人民共和国民法通则》)

[111] See Jia (贾东明) 2013, p. 106.

[112] See Article 154 of the General Principles of the Civil Law 1987.

[113] General Provisions of the Civil Law of the People's Republic of China (《中华人民共和国民法总则》)

[114] See Article 200, 201 of the General Provisions of the Civil Law 2017.

[115] General Provisions of the Civil Law 2017 provides the same rule. See Article 203 of the General Provisions of the Civil Law 2017.

[116] Although in the Consumer Protection Law 2013 there is no rule on trader's obligation to inform the consumer of the existence of withdrawal right which may affect the start of the period. In the Notice on Life Insurance 2011, it was required that the salesman should inform the policy-holder and insured of the withdrawal right when he is conducting his business as well as sending the policy to them. Besides, the right of withdrawal should be also stated clearly in the policy and its conditions and terms. However, the consequence of non-performance of this obligation was not provided. See Point 2 of the Notice on Life Insurance 2011.

5.4.3 *EU Law*

5.4.3.1 Directives

5.4.3.1.1 Lengths of the Periods

The Doorstep Selling Directive (85/577/EEC) granted consumers a withdrawal right to renounce their undertakings. In terms of the length of the period, the Member States had to prescribe it as not less than 7 days.[117] In the context of distance selling, 'the consumer shall have a period of at least seven working days in which to withdraw from the contract without penalty and without giving any reason'.[118] It should be noted that, even though the lengths of the periods are both 7 days, the Distance Selling Directive (97/7/EC) regulated it as 'seven working days', but the Doorstep Selling Directive did not mention whether it is 7 working days or 7 calendar days.

This aforementioned situation has been changed since the promulgation of the Consumer Rights Directive (2011/83/EU). On the basis of this directive, 'the consumer shall have a period of 14 days to withdraw from a distance or off-premises contract'.[119] Since the approach of maximum harmonisation is adopted, 14 days is not the bottom line, whereas every Member State has to regulate it as 14 days in its national law.[120] Pursuant to Recital 41 of the Consumer Rights Directive, this '14 days' refers to 14 calendar days.[121]

---

[117] See Article 5 of the Doorstep Selling Directive.

[118] Article 6 of the Distance Selling Directive

[119] Article 9 of the Consumer Rights Directive

[120] See Sect. 2.3.2.3.3, Chap. 2.

[121] It reads: '(...) Therefore, all periods contained in this Directive should be understood to be expressed in calendar days'. In other fields, the period for withdrawal rights is usually regulated as 14 days. For example, the Timeshare Directive (2008/122/EC) provides that Member States shall make sure that the consumer is entitled to withdraw from the timeshare contract without giving any reason in 14 calendar days (Article 6(1) of the Timeshare Directive). In the context of life insurance, the policy-holder shall have a period of between 14 and 30 days from the time when they were informed that the contract had been concluded within which to withdraw from the contract (Article 186 of the Insurance and Reinsurance Directive (2009/138/EC)). In terms of distance selling of financial services, the length of the period is similar to the previous two that the consumer should have a period of 14 calendar days to cancel the contract without giving any reason and without penalty (Article 6 of the Distance Marketing Directive (2002/65/EC)). And in the Consumer Credit Directive (2008/48/EC), it is also prescribed that 14 calendar days should be the length of the period of the withdrawal right (Article 14 of the Consumer Credit Directive).

5.4.3.1.2 Start and End of the Periods

Most EU directives regulate a special rule on the start of cooling-off periods that these periods should start when the trader has fulfilled his obligation to inform the consumer of his right of withdrawal if it is later than the conclusion of the contract.

To be specific, in the Doorstep Selling Directive, traders were required to give consumers written notice of their withdrawal right, and the period should start from the receipt by the consumer of this notice if the trader failed to perform this obligation when the contract was concluded. With regard to the content of the notice, the name and address of a person against whom that right may be exercised should be included.[122] In the *Heininger* case, it is established by the CJEU that one consequence of non-compliance with the duty to inform the consumer about his right of withdrawal is that the period for withdrawal is extended indefinitely.[123] This means the calculation of the period will never start before the receipt of trader's notice.

In the case *Annelore Hamilton v Volksbank Filder eG*, the consumer was entitled to withdraw from the contract even years after the contract was concluded. However, in the same case, it is also mentioned that national law may provide that the period ends when a month has passed after both parties have fully performed their obligations.[124]

The rule that the cooling-off period will start only when the trader has fulfilled his information duty can also be found in the contexts of distance financial services,[125] timeshare contracts[126] and consumer credit contracts.[127] Nevertheless, in these directives traders are required to provide the information including but not limited to the withdrawal right, whereas the Doorstep Selling Directive only demanded the trader to give information about the existence of a right of withdrawal. For example, in the Consumer Credit Directive, Article 14 clarifies that the period should begin from the day on which the consumer receives the contractual terms and conditions and information in accordance with Article 10, and it could be easily observed that the information regulated in Article 10 is not restricted to the existence of withdrawal right (point (p)).[128]

---

[122] See Articles 4 and 5 of the Doorstep Selling Directive.

[123] See Case C-481/99 [2001] ECR I-09987.

[124] See Case C-412/06 [2008] ECR I-02383.

[125] Article 6 of the Distance Marketing Directive provides: 'the period of withdrawal shall begin either from the day of the conclusion of the distance contract, except in respect of the said life assurance, where the time limit will begin from the time when the consumer is informed that the distance contract has been concluded, or from the day on which the consumer receives the contractual terms and conditions and the information in accordance with Article 5(1) or (2), if that is later than the date referred to in the first indent'.

[126] See Article 6(2) of the Timeshare Directive.

[127] See Article 14(1) of the Consumer Credit Directive.

[128] For example, the period of the right of withdrawal also will not start if the consumer has not been provided with the information regarding 'the right of early repayment, the procedure for early

In the Distance Selling Directive, it was regulated that all the following information regarding withdrawal right should be provided, otherwise the period should be 3 months: (1) conditions and procedures for exercising the right of withdrawal; (2) the geographical address of the place of business of the supplier to which the consumer may address any complaints; (3) information on after-sales services and guarantees which exist; and (4) the conclusion for cancelling the contract, where it is of unspecified duration or a duration exceeding 1 year.[129] Besides, some distinctions between sale of goods and supply of services are also made on the start of the period: in the case of goods, the period for exercise begins from the day of receipt by the consumer where the information duties have been fulfilled; in the case of services, the period should start from the day of conclusion of the contract or from the day on which the information duties were fulfilled if they are fulfilled after the conclusion of the contract but does not exceed 3 months. With regard to this 3-month limitation, which is different from other directives, it was provided that even though the trader has failed to provide the information, the period should not be infinitely extended but be limited to 3 months.[130] Within the period, if the information has been provided, the 7-day period will start to run.[131]

In the Consumer Rights Directive, Article 9 provides some new rules on the calculation of the withdrawal periods in the context of off-premises and distance contracts. Still, one distinction between service contracts and sales contracts is adopted: for service contracts, the day of the conclusion of the contract should be the start date of the period; for sales contracts, the principle is that 'the period shall begin from the day on which the consumer or a third party other than the carrier and indicated by the consumer acquires physical possession of the goods', while it is also regulated that, in the case of multiple goods ordered by the consumer in one order and delivered separately, the withdrawal period shall start from the day on which the consumer or a third party other than the carrier and indicated by the consumer acquires physical possession of the last goods; in the case of delivery of a good consisting of multiple lots or pieces, the withdrawal period will start from the day on which the consumer or a third party other than the carrier and indicated by the consumer acquires physical possession of the last lot or piece; in the case of contracts for regular delivery of goods during a defined period of time, the withdrawal period will start from the day on which the consumer or a third party other than the

---

repayment, as well as, where applicable, information concerning the creditor's right to compensation and the way in which that compensation will be determined' (point (r)).

[129] See Article 5(1) of the Distance Selling Directive.

[130] See Article 6(1) of the Distance Selling Directive.

[131] Therefore, prior to the promulgation of the Consumer Rights Directive, there are at least four possible moments in which the cooling-off period may start, which is summarised by Marco Loos: (1) when the contract (or a binding pre-contract) is concluded (distance selling of services); (2) when the trader has performed his main obligation under the contract (distance selling of goods); (3) when the trader has performed his information obligation pertaining to the existence of a right of withdrawal (doorstep selling); and (4) when the trader has performed all of his information obligations (distance marketing of financial services; consumer credit; timeshare). See Loos 2009, pp. 251–252.

carrier and indicated by the consumer acquires physical possession of the first goods; in the case of contracts for the supply of water, gas or electricity, where they are not put up for sale in a limited volume or set quantity, of district heating or of digital content which is not supplied on a tangible medium, the withdrawal period will start from the day of the conclusion of the contract.[132] The information duty which is relevant to the calculation of the period is prescribed in Article 10. It provides that the withdrawal period will expire 12 months from the end of the initial withdrawal period if the trader has not provided the information which is relevant to the right of withdrawal as required by point (h) of Article 6(1).[133] Apparently, the Consumer Rights Directive to a large extent follows the rules regulated in the Distance Selling Directive in which the sale of goods and supply of services should be treated differently and the Doorstep Selling Directive in which the information duty influencing the start of the withdrawal period is only related to the information about the existence of the withdrawal right itself.

5.4.3.2 German Law

5.4.3.2.1 Lengths of the Periods

Whenever before or after the implementation of the Consumer Rights Directive, the second paragraph of § 355 BGB provides that the withdrawal period is 14 days in German law. Since the approach of European integration is recognised as 'minimum harmonisation' in the Doorstep Selling Directive and the Distance Selling Directive, Member States are free to regulate a longer cooling-off period than the period prescribed in the directives. After the promulgation of the Consumer Rights Directive, the approach of maximum harmonisation has been adopted, so all Member States have to adjust the lengths of their periods to 14 days in the area of off-premises and distance contracts. Nonetheless, German law does not have to be amended.

Furthermore, pursuant to § 356(3) BGB, a special withdrawal period of 12 months besides the original 14 days should be applied where the trader fails to provide the consumer with the required information regulated by the Introductory Act to the Civil Code (*Einführungsgesetzes zum Bürgerlichen Gesetzbuche*), which is demonstrated in the following part. This means the maximum withdrawal period will now end after 1 year and 14 days.

---

[132] See Article 9(2) of the Consumer Rights Directive.

[133] Point (h) of Article 6(1) states: '(h) where a right of withdrawal exists, the conditions, time limit and procedures for exercising that right in accordance with Article 11(1), as well as the model withdrawal form set out in Annex I(B)'.

5.4.3.2.2 Start and End of the Periods

With regard to the start of the period, § 355(2) BGB provides the general rule that the period begins with the conclusion of the contract, unless otherwise specified. In the areas of off-premises contracts and distance contracts, the sales of goods and supplies of services are treated differently. § 356 firstly provides two rules from both the positive and the negative perspectives to regulate the start of the period of withdrawal in the context of sales contracts.

From the positive perspective, it is regulated that the period begins when the consumer or a third party designated by him, which is not the carrier, has received goods.[134] Furthermore, if the consumer has ordered several products in a single purchase and the goods are delivered separately, the period starts when the consumer or the designated third party has received the last set of goods; if the goods are delivered in multiple pieces, the period starts when the consumer or the designated third party has received the last piece; if the goods are regularly delivered in a specific period, the withdrawal period starts when the first set of goods have been received. Besides, § 356(2) BGB states that the period of withdrawal starts with the conclusion of the contract where it has as its subject matter the supply of water, gas, electricity, district heating or digital content which is not contained in a tangible medium, without the supply having been offered for sale in a limited volume or set quantity.

From the negative perspective, § 356(3) BGB clarifies that the withdrawal period should not begin before the trader has provided the consumer with the information in accordance with the requirements of Article 246a § 1(2) sentence 1 number 1 or of Article 246b § 2(1) of the Introductory Act to the Civil Code. The former regards the information on the conditions, time limit and procedures for exercising withdrawal rights and the possibility that the consumer may need to bear the cost of return, etc. The latter provides that the trader should in a timely manner inform the consumer, prior to the placing of the contract, the following information in a durable medium: (1) the contractual provisions including the terms and conditions and (2) the information referred to in Article 246b § 1(1). However, even though the trader fails to provide the required information, the right of withdrawal will expire no later than 12 months and 14 days after the start of the period which is regulated by § 356(2) BGB or § 355(2) BGB.

5.4.3.3 English Law

5.4.3.3.1 Lengths of the Periods

Prior to the implementation of the Consumer Rights Directive, the lengths laid down in different regulations were rather dissimilar. For instance, in the Consumer Credit Act 1974, a period of 5 days is granted to the consumer,[135] while in the

[134] See § 356(2)(a) BGB.

[135] See Section 68 of the Consumer Credit Act 1974.

Regulations 2000, the period of withdrawal right is 7 working days[136], and the withdrawal period in Timeshare Act 1992 is 14 days.[137]

In the Regulations 2013, the length of period is harmonised to be 14 days in the areas of off-premises and distance contracts. This 14-day period is described as 'normal cancellation period'. For the 'abnormal cancellation period', which is described as 'cancellation period extended for breach of information requirement', Regulation 31 provides that the withdrawal period 'ends at the end of 12 months after the day on which it would have ended under regulation 30'. Compared with the previous rule, the maximum period in English law has been increased from 3 months plus 7 working days[138] to 12 months plus 14 days.

5.4.3.3.2 Start and End of the Periods

The normal cancellation period shall start at the day on which the contract is entered into and ends 14 days after, if the contract is a service contract or a contract for the supply of digital content which is not supplied on the tangible medium.[139] If the contract is a sales contract, the period shall start at the day on which the goods come into the physical possession of the consumer or a person, other than the carrier, identified by the consumer to take possession of them and end 14 days after.[140] For the contracts under which the goods are delivered on different days or goods consisting of multiple lots or pieces, the start of the period will depend on the day when the last of the goods or the last of the lots or pieces come into the possession of the consumer or the person identified by him.[141] In the context of sales contracts for regular delivery of goods during a defined period, the rule of possession will be applied when the first of the goods is delivered.[142]

As mentioned, the period should not start if the trader fails to provide the consumer with the information on the right required by paragraph (l) of Schedule 2, which regards the conditions, time limit and procedures for exercising the withdrawal right,[143] in accordance with Part 2 of the Regulations 2013.[144]

---

[136] See Regulation 11(2) of the Regulations 2000.

[137] See Section 5(3) of the Timeshare Act 1992.

[138] See Regulation 11(4) of the Regulations 2000.

[139] See Regulation 30(2) of the Regulations 2013.

[140] See Regulation 30(3) of the Regulations 2013.

[141] See Regulation 30(4)(5) of the Regulations 2013.

[142] See Regulation 30(6) of the Regulations 2013.

[143] It reads: '(the information referred to in regulations is) where a right to cancel exists, the conditions, time limit and procedures for exercising that right in accordance with regulations 27 to 38'.

[144] See Regulation 31(2) of the Regulations 2013.

5.4.4 Comparative Review

Comparing Chinese law and its European corresponding part, it is obvious that the length of withdrawal period is much shorter in China (7 days vs. 14 days). In Europe, the period was 7 days pursuant to the provisions in the previous directives (e.g. the Doorstep Selling Directive, the Distance Selling Directive), but now it is adjusted to 14 days in the Consumer Rights Directive. The reason why the legislator lengthened the period is not very clear, but it is not difficult to assume that it may be because (1) the European legislator wanted to adopt a higher level of consumer protection and (2) in many directives and national legislation, the periods were already regulated as 14 days, and the objective of harmonisation requires the legislator to unify these periods' lengths.

In general, the periods usually begin once the contract is concluded, but in the context of distance selling and contracts concluded outside of business premises, the period begins with the delivery of the goods. The rationale here is related to the legitimacy of the right of withdrawal that a consumer should have an opportunity to examine the goods, and in the context of distance selling, it always spends some time on the transportation of good. For the cross-border transactions, the transportation could take a long time. If the period starts when the contract is concluded, it even becomes possible that the period has already expired but the consumer has not received the good yet.

The EU directive, German law and English law regulate that the periods only begin when the trader has informed the consumer about the existence of withdrawal rights. In Chinese law, we cannot find a rule which is similar to the requirement of providing consumers with the information related to withdrawal right or other contractual terms and conditions. This means that in China, the withdrawal period simply begins from the second day of the receipt of the goods. In terms of supply of services, it is not even mentioned in the Consumer Protection Law 2013 because its Article 25 only discusses the issues where businesses sell commodities through these specific channels.

In other EU directives, it was sometimes clarified that 14 days should be 14 working days but not 14 calendar days.[145] However, the Consumer Rights Directive regulates 14 days as 14 calendar days. This issue was ignored, although it was mentioned during the process of soliciting advices and suggestions, when the Chinese legislator amended the Chinese Consumer Protection Law.[146] However, on the basis

[145] One may ask: 'If the consumer claims his right of withdrawal in the non-working days, is that still effective?' The answer should be affirmative.

[146] Although it was proposed that the Consumer Protection Law 2013 should also adopt the rule of providing information of withdrawal rights when the law was being revised, the formal text does not contain this kind of obligation. Besides, it was suggested that the Consumer Protection Law 2013 should set '7 working days' instead of '7 days' as well, but this was not adopted either. See Opinions of the Local People's Congresses and the Relevant Departments of the Central Government on the Draft of the Amendment of Law on the Protection of Consumer Rights and Interests (《地方人大、中央有关部门和单位对消费者权益保护法修正案(草案)(征求意见

of the systematic interpretation of Article 25 of the Consumer Protection Law and Article 156 of the General Principles of the Civil Law 1987, '7 days' should be 7 calendar days, but it will extend if the last day is a weekend or holiday.

It is noteworthy that, in the context of Chinese law, if there is a holiday in the middle of the period, sometimes it would be problematic since the period of 7 days is considerably short, and even some holidays, such as the holidays of National Day and Chinese New Year which have a period of 7 days, are not shorter. However, the period is set to limit the exercising of withdrawal rights so only the consumers are influenced by the rule on the length of the period. Because they usually do consumption after work, actually on holidays consumers have more time to make the decision or even perform their rights of withdrawal. Thus, even if a long holiday comes after the start of the period, the period should not be suspended. There is no strong argument for China to abandon the conclusion of systematic interpretation that the '7 days' should be '7 calendar days'.[147]

Another noteworthy issue in terms of EU law is the adoption of 'maximum harmonisation', which means all of the Member States have to strictly regulate that the period is 14 days when they implement the Consumer Rights Directive at the national level. The aim of this change is described to eliminate the barriers of cross-border transactions in order to establish the internal market and provide a higher level of consumer protection.[148] However, the assumption here is rather doubtful. It might be true that different rules exist in different Member States, which is a result of 'minimum harmonisation', and this could bring fragmentation and restrain the consumers from participating in cross-border transactions, and this could indeed result in the barriers and difficulties. Nevertheless, the fragmentation does not only exist on paper. It is further diverse in practice. Even though the EU legislator requires all the Member States to modify their periods of withdrawal rights to a unified length, it has nothing to do with the practice. If a trader wants to, in order to attract more customers probably, he is still allowed to provide the consumer with a longer withdrawal period – that means, there is no reason to restrict the expression of 'the consumer shall have a period of 14 days to withdraw from a distance or off-premises contract' to 'the period should be merely and no longer than 14 days'

稿)的意见》), in Civil Law Office of the Legislative Affairs Commission of the Standing Committee of the National People's Congress (全国人大常委会法制工作委员会民法室) 2013, p. 30.

[147] However, if the consumer can exercise his or her withdrawal right electronically, it may not bring problems, but if the consumer cannot, it may be difficult to get a postal stamp on holiday proving that he or she has sent the letter in time or to phone the business (since nobody will be present).

[148] See Recitals 4, 5, 6 and 7 of the Consumer Rights Directive, especially Recital 7. It is clearly stated that 'full harmonisation of some key regulatory aspects should considerably increase legal certainty for both consumers and traders. Both consumers and traders should be able to rely on a single regulatory framework based on clearly defined legal concepts regulating certain aspects of business-to-consumer contracts across the Union. The effect of such harmonisation should be to eliminate the barriers stemming from the fragmentation of the rules and to complete the internal market in this area. Those barriers can only be eliminated by establishing uniform rules at Union level. Furthermore, consumers should enjoy a high common level of protection across the Union'.

when interpreting Article 9. Therefore, the new approach of harmonisation only reduces the cost to know the law because now consumers can easily acknowledge that the length of period regulated by law is 14 days, but if they want to know the specific rule which is relevant to their transaction, they still have to check the after-sale policy in their individual contexts. Compared with the fact that they knew at least they had 7 days to change their mind, the current situation that they know at least they have 14 days does not make any difference.

In a word, as long as the protection of the higher level is permitted in practice, the effect of achieving policy objectives through maximum harmonisation would be limited (Table 5.4).

Table 5.4 Periods of withdrawal rights

	Length	Start	End	The duty to inform and the consequences of non-performance
Chinese Consumer Protection Law	7 days	The second day after the consumer receives the goods	Where business hour applies: If the last day of a time period falls on a Sunday or an official holiday, the day after the holiday should be taken as the last day	
			Where the shop is open for all year: The period shall end at 24:00 of the last day	
EU Directives	14 days	Service contracts: The day of the conclusion of the contract		Yes
				The period should not start
		Sales contracts: The day on which the consumer or a third party other than the carrier and indicated by the consumer acquires physical possession of the goods		The withdrawal period should expire 12 months from the end of the initial withdrawal period
German Law	14 days	General rule: The conclusion of the contract		Yes
				The period should not start
		Good selling: When the consumer or a third party designated by him, which is not the carrier, has received goods		The right of withdrawal will expire no later than 12 months and 14 days after the start of the period

(continued)

Table 5.4 (continued)

	Length	Start	End	The duty to inform and the consequences of non-performance
English Law	14 days	The day on which the contract is entered into and end 14 days after, if the contract is a service contract or a contract for the supply of digital content which is not supplied on the tangible medium		Yes
		Sales Contract: The day on which the goods come into the physical possession of the consumer or a person, other than the carrier, identified by the consumer to take possession of them		The period should not start
				The cancellation period ends at the end of 12 months after the day on which it would have ended

5.5 Exercise of Withdrawal Rights

5.5.1 Introduction

This section discusses the issues relevant to exercising withdrawal rights. The emphasis is laid on the intactness of the commodity (China) and the notification to be sent to the trader (the EU). In Chinese law, the requirement on intactness is one of the limitations on withdrawal rights to help traders in avoiding undue losses. In the EU context, the rules on notification mainly deal with the formal requirements to facilitate consumers to exercise their rights. For the limitation on withdrawal rights, considering the nature of service contracts and non-tangible digital content contracts, consumers may not maintain their rights of withdrawal once the obligation of contract has been performed.

In this section, two questions are mainly addressed: (1) What are the limitations imposed on consumers when they exercise their rights of withdrawal? (2) How can a consumer claim withdrawal from the contract? The relevant rules in Chinese law (Sect. 5.2), EU directives (Sect. 5.3.1), German law (Sect. 5.3.2) and English law (Sect. 5.3.3) are introduced, respectively. A summary of comparative observations is provided subsequently (Sect. 5.4).

5.5.2 *Chinese Law*

5.5.2.1 'Intactness'

To answer the first foregoing question in the context of Chinese Consumer Protection Law 2013, the interpretation of the word 'intact' is important, because it is regulated by Article 25 that 'the commodities returned by consumers shall remain intact'.

In the Understanding of authority, it is pointed out that the intactness of the commodity is related to the commodity's value – if the value of the commodity has not been decreased apparently due to the reason caused by the consumer, the commodity remains 'intact' regardless of the fact whether the consumer has unpackaged or checked it.[149] In addition, it is further elaborated that the legislative objective of the right of withdrawal is to provide consumers in the context of online shopping with the same opportunities to check and test goods just as they are shopping on site in order to make sure that they can decide whether to purchase on the basis of their free intention. If it were regulated that the goods have to be unfolded, the whole legislative design would become completely meaningless.[150]

In practice, however, the vagueness of 'intact' leaves room for businesses to establish rules which would be beneficial to themselves. Put differently, even though the business complies with the national legislation, where the right of withdrawal is granted, it can still refuse the consumer's claim to return through redefining the concept of 'intact'. For example, the e-platform Jingdong provides in their after-sale-policy that 'we promise that you may return the good and get the refund in seven days, if the goods have not been used and it will not affect the secondary sale of the goods'. In terms of the meaning of 'it will not affect the secondary sale of the goods', it is further demonstrated that 'the following situations shall be considered as "it will affect the secondary sale": (1) in the case of the type of commodity such as a mobile phone, a camera or a laptop, the original package has been unfolded or the power has been turned on; (2) in the case where the type of commodity is clothes, shoes or hats, the package or hangtag is damaged, or the commodity has been worn or washed; (3) in the case where the commodity is sealed up, it has been unfolded; (4) the commodity has been used through being electrified, watered or inserted into a slot'.[151] In this case, the business interprets the scope of 'intact' as 'will not affect the secondary sale', which leads to the result that the exercise of withdrawal rights is considerably restricted because consumers are trapped in a dilemma – where sometimes they cannot unfold the commodity as long as they want to maintain the right of withdrawal but simultaneously they have to unfold the commodity in order

---

[149] See Jia (贾东明) 2013, p. 111.

[150] See Jia (贾东明) 2013, p. 111.

[151] See jd.com (京东商城), 'General Rules on Return or Replace Goods' (《退换货总则》), available at: <http://help.jd.com/help/question-97.html>, last visited: 2014/9/9.

to check and test it.[152] Meanwhile, the ideas of these businesses are rather reasonable as well because, indeed, the value of some commodities is closely linked with their unfolded package.[153]

This paradox brings us back to the discussion of the legitimacy of withdrawal rights at the very beginning. In fact, it is also relevant to the question whether withdrawal rights should be mandatory. The desired rules could break the existing balance in the market where even so the consumers still cannot benefit from these rules.[154]

5.5.2.2 Return of Commodity and the Issue of Notification

In the Second Draft of the Amendment of the Consumer Protection Law, it is regulated that the consumer shall return the commodity within 7 days after he claims to exercise his withdrawal right.[155] A logical deduction here is that the second draft still

---

[152] Some reports mention that consumers can rarely exercise their withdrawal rights successfully because of these limitations. See Beijing Evening (北京晚报), 'Jingdong is Complained in terms of their Withdrawal Policies: Goods cannot be Returned Because They have been Opened' (《京东无理由退货遭投诉:拆开不能退》), 7 July 2013, available at: <http://tech.sina.com.cn/i/2013-07-07/17428515418.shtml>,last visited: 2014/9/9.

[153] For instance, it is of great importance for selling a laptop that whether its package is original since the consumer may doubt whether the laptop is a new one. Indeed, this issue can be also solved in the context of 'exceptions to withdrawal rights': the trader could inform the consumer that the digital devices are not suitable for return without reason before the contract is concluded. See Ge (葛江虬) 2015, p. 113. Pursuant to the Interim Measures 2017, electronic and electrical commodities will loss 'intactness' if use traces in appearance which are difficult to be restored to the original state are left as a result of unauthorised maintenance, modification, destruction or alteration of compulsory product certification marks, indicating stickers or machine serial numbers, among others or use traces concerning data such as retained activation or authorization information or unreasonable personal use data are generated thereby. See Article 9 of the Interim Measures 2017.

[154] In addition, it is not clear who should bear the burden of proof if the commodity failed to remain intact when it reached the consumer, but the business operator alleged that it was intact when it was dispatched. Scholars suggest that this issue needs to be clarified by law. See Jin (金可可) 2014, p. 12. In practice, some judges held that this can be determined by whether the consumer examined the commodity 'in time'. Therefore, if the consumer failed to examine the commodity in 24 h after he had received the commodity, he should bear the disadvantage that the non-intact commodity is no longer returnable. See Yanshen Liao v Guangzhou Jingdong Trading Co Ltd. (廖颜深与广州晶东贸易有限公司等买卖合同纠纷上诉案), Civil Judgment (2015) Sui-Zhong-Fa-Min-Er-Zhong-Zi No. 1064 of the Guangzhou Intermediate People's Court in Guangdong Province (广东省广州市中级人民法院(2015)穗中法民二终字第1064号民事判决书).

[155] This is to respond to the suggestion that the law should be as clear as possible, as specific as possible, to balance the protection of consumers and the development of the new patterns of consumption. See 'Reports of the Legislative Affairs Commission of the Standing Committee of the National People's Congress on the Draft of the Amendment of Law of the People's Republic of China on the Protection of Consumer Rights and Interests' (《全国人民代表大会法律委员会关于〈中华人民共和国消费者权益保护法修正案(草案)〉修改情况的汇报》), in Jia (贾东明) 2013, p. 334.

regulates that the consumer may claim to express the intention to exercise the right and this claim will also determine the fate of his withdrawal right – if he has not sent the goods back within 7 days of making this notification, he is deprived of his right.

In the final version of the amended Consumer Protection Law, however, this rule is abandoned. From a historical perspective, we can assert that now in Chinese consumer law, it is not legally meaningful for the consumer to claim that he decides to return the commodity. The intention of declaration can only be manifested by sending the commodity back while possibly attaching a statement. The distinction is, in the context of the second draft, a consumer is allowed to decide whether he wants to perform the right, for instance, at the 6th day, and as long as he claims his decision to the trader at that time, it is even possible for him to return the commodity at the 12th day after he received the commodity. On the contrary, pursuant to the current law, the consumer has to return the commodity within 7 days of the receipt of the commodities, and the conduct of sending the commodity back is the claim itself. A separate claim or notification is no longer necessary.

Because the Chinese rule of withdrawal right is mainly applicable to distance selling contracts, it is highly possible that there is a gap between the delivery and arrival of the commodity. Thus, it is necessary to make it clear whether it is enough to exercise the right through simply sending the goods back (dispatch principle) or it is necessary for the trader to receive the returned goods (receipt principle). However, this issue is not clarified by the Consumer Protection Law.[156]

Although pursuant to the law there is not much room for the consumer to exercise his withdrawal right via sending a notification to end the contractual relationship, in practice this is different. Many e-commerce platforms grant the consumer the opportunity to withdraw from the contract through informing the trader, instead of sending the commodity back.[157] The specific method to notify is simple: the consumer can click a button of 'return/refund' which is available on the website to deliver a message to the trader that he intends to cancel the deal. Despite the fact that this method of exercising the withdrawal right is not in accordance with the approach regulated by the Consumer Protection Law 2013, it is indeed more preferable, because the trader can be aware of the wish of the consumer immediately and get prepared for the imminent return. It is not only a measure to balance the interests of the parties but also conducive to the consumer because sometimes the trader also provides the service of collecting the commodity to be returned or even bears the cost of return.[158] With a clearer picture, it becomes easier for the parties to arrange

---

[156] In academia there are different opinions. For a scholar who adopts the 'receipt principle', see Yang (杨立新) 2014, p. 35. For a scholar who holds the opposite view, see Ge (葛江虬) 2015, p. 111.

[157] This approach is also supported by the Interim Measures 2017. Its Article 10 states: 'A consumer who chooses to return any commodity without reasons shall issue a goods return notice to the online seller concerned within 7 days of receipt of the commodity'. The department regulations, however, shall not deprive the consumer's right to withdraw from the contract by merely sending the commodity back.

[158] See jd.com (京东商城), 'General Rules on Return or Replace Goods' (《退换货总则》), available at: <http://help.jd.com/help/question-97.html>, last visited: 2014/9/9.

the further return/refund. In terms of the legal basis, the rationale to replace sending back the commodity by sending a notification can be observed from the perspective of systematic interpretation: the withdrawal rights in nature are the rights of termination in the context of Chinese private law.[159] From this, Article 96 of the Contract Law 1999 states that the contract is terminated when the notification of termination reaches the corresponding party. Therefore, although in the context of withdrawal rights the rules contained in the Consumer Protection Law should apply because it is the special law, the parties can still reach an agreement to apply the rule contained in Article 96 of the Contract Law.[160]

Furthermore, although the law deems the return of the goods as the only effective way to exercise withdrawal rights, it does not hold the traders back from offering the consumers more convenient means to exercise their rights. Although the rule provided by Article 25 of the Consumer Protection Law 2015 is a mandatory rule, it is a one-way mandatory rule that only prohibits the agreement which goes against the weaker party. If the agreement concluded in the transaction is different from the mandatory one but it is in favour of the consumer, there is no need for the law to forbid the use of it.[161]

5.5.3 EU Law

5.5.3.1 Directives

5.5.3.1.1 'Intactness'?

There is no provision on the intactness of the good to be returned in the Consumer Rights Directive (2011/83/EU). Put differently, on the EU level, no limitation in terms of the condition of the goods is regulated. Nevertheless, this does not mean that there is no rule on the circumstance where the value of the goods is diminished. Although the consumer may still exercise his withdrawal right, pursuant to Article 14(2) of the Consumer Rights Directive, he may be charged if the diminished value is caused by his behaviour which is beyond the necessary establishment of the good's nature, characteristics and functioning.[162] It is the same case in German law and English law.

---

[159] See Ge (葛江虬) 2015, p. 106–107. This is further discussed in Sect. 5.6.2.

[160] In addition, some judges point out that filing a lawsuit also determines that the right of withdrawal has been successfully exercised. See Ming Yan v Beijing Jingdong Century Information Technology Co Ltd. (阎明诉北京京东世纪信息技术有限公司买卖合同纠纷案), Civil Judgment (2015) Hai-Min-Shang-Chu-Zi No. 18179 of the People's Court of Haidian District of Beijing City (北京市海淀区人民法院(2015)海民(商)初字第18,179号民事判决书).

[161] See Ge (葛江虬) 2015, p. 108.

[162] This is further discussed in Sect. 5.6.3.1.4.

5.5.3.1.2 Notification

Prior to the Consumer Rights Directive, different directives had different rules on the formal requirement for expressing the intention to exercise withdrawal rights. Specifically, three different rules might apply when dealing with the notification of withdrawal in the different contexts. Marco Loos provides a summary as follows: '(1) notification of withdrawal is possible by any means; (2) notification of withdrawal is possible by any means that can be proven in accordance with national law; (3) notification of withdrawal should be in writing or on a durable medium'.[163] The first rule applied to the context of distance selling[164]; the second one applied to the context of distance marketing of financial services and consumer credit[165]; and the third one applied to doorstep selling and timeshare.[166] Among all these rules, Marco Loos pointed out that the second one would not be an optimal rule if it was chosen for applying to all circumstances, because it means in the case of distance selling the consumer had to be governed by the regulation of the trader's national law, which would be unfamiliar to the consumer, then the exercise of withdrawal right would be unreasonably limited. Between option (1) and option (3), option (1) is to be preferred since the scope of 'durable medium' could exclude some frequently used channels such as sending an email in consideration of the related definition in corresponding directives.[167]

Since some Member States also have different regulations on notification[168] and these differences have caused costs for traders selling cross-border,[169] the Consumer Rights Directive (2011/83/EU) harmonises this issue by means of providing that if the consumer intends to withdraw from the contract, he has to inform the trader of his decision before the expiry of the period. With regard to the required form, it is stated the consumer can either 'use the model withdrawal form as set out in Annex I(B)'[170] or 'make any other unequivocal statement setting out his decision to withdraw from the contract', while 'Member States shall not provide for any formal requirements applicable to the model withdrawal form other than those set out in

[163] Loos 2009, p. 260

[164] This is because no formal requirement in terms of notification is regulated in the Distance Selling Directive (97/7/EC).

[165] For example, see point (a) of paragraph 3 of Article 14 of the Consumer Credit Directive (2008/48/EC). It reads: 'In order to give effect to the withdrawal before the expiry of the deadline referred to in paragraph 1, notify this to the creditor in line with the information given by the creditor pursuant to Article 10(2)(p) by means which can be proven in accordance with national law'.

[166] See Article 7 of the Timeshare Directive (2008/122/EC). It provides: 'Where the consumer intends to exercise the right of withdrawal the consumer shall, before the expiry of the withdrawal period, notify the trader on paper or on another durable medium of the decision to withdraw'.

[167] See Loos 2009, p. 263.

[168] See Schulte-Nölke 2008, p. 481.

[169] See Recital 44 of the Consumer Rights Directive.

[170] In terms of a model withdrawal form, Article 5(4) of the Timeshare Directive also points out a separate standard withdrawal form should be provided by the trader to facilitate the exercise of the right of withdrawal. The model of this standard form can be found in Annex V of the directive.

Annex I(B)'.[171] In the third paragraph, the trader is further required to give the consumer the option to electronically fill in and submit either the model withdrawal form or any other unequivocal statement on the trader's website. In these cases, after the receipt of such a withdrawal notification, the trader is also demanded to 'communicate to the consumer an acknowledgement on a durable medium without delay'.

Although in the Consumer Rights Directive it seems the legislator follows the scenario of option (3) that the consumer has to use the model form or other channels to notify the trader, the expression is still rather different: the concept employed in the proposal 'durable medium'[172] was abandoned in the end, and it just regulates that the consumer may 'make any other unequivocal statement' to set out his decision.[173] In this case, 'unequivocal statement' does not rule out any possible channel, even an oral notification, and consumers are free to withdraw in their own words and forms as long as the notification is unequivocal and direct to the trader. 'A letter, a telephone call or returning the goods with a clear statement could meet this requirement'.[174] It is noteworthy that 'the burden of proof of exercising the right of withdrawal in accordance with this Article shall be on the consumer'.[175]

Where a consumer sends a notification to withdraw from the contract, it is questionable whether the notification can discontinue the period of withdrawal right when the consumer dispatches the notification or the trader receives the notification. Whether the principle of dispatch or the principle of receipt should be adopted makes a huge difference since the withdrawal period is usually rather short. Put differently, if the principle of receipt is adopted, the period would be much shorter because in many cross-border cases, the delivery of a letter could take a long time. Besides, it should be allowed 'if the consumer only decides to make use of his right of withdrawal shortly before the end of the cooling-off period'.[176] Therefore, the principle of dispatch should be adopted. In the Consumer Rights Directive, the consumer will be determined to exercise his right of withdrawal successfully if the notification is 'sent by the consumer before that period has expired'.[177]

---

[171] Article 11 of the Consumer Rights Directive

[172] See the first sentence of Article 14(1) of the Proposal for a Directive of the European Parliament and of the Council on Consumer Rights (COM(2008) 614 final). It reads: 'The consumer shall inform the trader of his decision to withdraw on a durable medium either in a statement addressed to the trader drafted in his own words or using the standard withdrawal form as set out in Annex I(B)'.

[173] In the Consumer Rights Directive, 'durable medium' is used in Recital 44 that 'it is in the interest of the consumer to make use of a durable medium when communicating his withdrawal to the trader'.

[174] Recital 44 of the Consumer Rights Directive

[175] Article 11(4) of the Consumer Rights Directive

[176] Loos 2009, p. 264

[177] Article 11(2) of the Consumer Rights Directive. In other directives, see Article 14(3)(2) of the Consumer Credit Directive, the third sentence of Article 7 of the Timeshare Directive. However, there are also some different opinions that the principle of receipt should be adopted. On these arguments, see Bijlage Handelingen Tweede Kamer 1999/2000, 2861, no. 5, pp. 23–24, cited in Loos 2009, p. 265.

As long as the consumer effectively exercises the right of withdrawal, the Consumer Rights Directive regulates that the trader should communicate the consumer 'an acknowledgement of receipt of such a withdrawal on a durable medium without delay'.[178] There was criticism that the use of 'durable medium' excludes e-mail. However, this is not the case anymore, since the legislator changed the way to define this concept – Article 2(10) states that 'durable medium' refers to 'any instrument which enables the consumer or the trader to store information addressed personally to him in a way accessible for future reference for a period of time adequate for the purposes of the information and which allows the unchanged reproduction of the information stored'. Furthermore, Recital 45 of the directive clarifies that in the context of purchasing from the trader's website, sending an e-mail can doubtlessly meet the definition set by Article 10(2).[179] Nevertheless, the consequence of non-performance of this obligation is not provided.

5.5.3.1.3 Supply of Services and Non-tangible Digital Content

On the grounds of Article 14(4)(a) of the Consumer Rights Directive, the consumer should bear no cost for the performance of services during the withdrawal period where the trader has failed to provide the required information or the consumer has not expressly requested performance to begin. This means, if the consumer expressly requested performance to begin and he knew his right of withdrawal, the period expires when the service contract has been fully or partly performed. This rule can also be applied to the area of supplying digital contents not on a tangible medium.

5.5.3.2 German Law

5.5.3.2.1 Notification

Prior to the 2013 amendment of the BGB, it was previously regulated that the notification is necessary for exercising the right of withdrawal, and the notification has to be in 'text form'.[180] The definition of text form can be found in § 126b. It is regulated that 'the declaration must be made in a document or in another manner suitable for its permanent reproduction in writing, the person making the declaration must be named and the completion of the declaration must be shown through the reproduction of a signature of the name or otherwise'.

---

[178] The last sentence of Article 11(3)

[179] It reads: 'As experience shows that many consumers and traders prefer to communicate via the trader's website, there should be a possibility for the trader to give the consumer the option of filling in a web-based withdrawal form. In this case the trader should provide an acknowledgement of receipt, for instance, by e-mail without delay'. This standpoint is repeated in Annex I(A).

[180] See the old version of § 355(3) BGB.

In the new version of § 355 BGB, sending a notice is still the approach to exercise the right of withdrawal. It is noteworthy that the notification does not have to be in 'text form' anymore; the only requirement is that the statement of the decision of the consumer to withdraw must be 'clearly identified', which apparently mirrors the European standard of 'unequivocal'. With regard to the adoption of dispatch principle or receipt principle, it is regulated by § 355(1) BGB that the deadline will be met if the consumer sends the notification in time.

§ 356(1) BGB mentions the obligation of the trader to facilitate the consumer to exercise his withdrawal right. A model withdrawal form is provided in Appendix 2 to Article 246a § 1(2) sentence 1 number 1 of the Introductory Act to the Civil Code. In the context of online shopping, traders are required to offer a withdrawal form on their websites. Furthermore, where the consumer exercises his withdrawal right, the trader must provide the consumer with the confirmation of the receipt immediately on a durable medium.

5.5.3.2.2 Supply of Services and Non-tangible Digital Content

In the context of providing services, § 356(4) BGB provides that the right of withdrawal expires when the service is completed and the parties have started the execution of the contract only after the consumer has given his express consent and at the same time confirmed his knowledge that he loses his right of withdrawal for complete performance of the contract by the contractor. The exception is, in a contract for the provision of financial services, the right of withdrawal expires, notwithstanding sentence 1, if the contract is completely fulfilled by both parties at the express request of the consumer before the consumer exercises his right of withdrawal.

§ 356(5) BGB provides the rule on purchases of intangible digital content. It is regulated that the right of withdrawal expires if the consumer has started the execution of the contract after the consumer (1) has expressly agreed with the execution of the contract to begin before the end of the withdrawal period and (2) has confirmed his knowledge that he loses his right of withdrawal by his agreement with the beginning of the execution of the contract. In this case, as soon as the consumer starts downloading the digital content, the withdrawal right expires.

5.5.3.3 English Law

5.5.3.3.1 Notification

In English law, the consumer has to exercise his withdrawal right through sending a notice to the trader. Section 69(1) of the Consumer Credit Act 1974 and Sections 5 and 12(6) of the Timeshare Act 1992 have already incorporated this rule. On the basis of Regulation 10 of the Regulations 2000, the notice of withdrawal should operate to cancel the contract. Pursuant to its third paragraph, the definition of a notice was provided: 'A notice of cancellation is a notice in writing or in another durable medium available and accessible to the supplier (or to the other person to whom it is given) which, however expressed, indicates the intention of the consumer to cancel the contract'.

In the context of the Regulations 2013, the same approach is followed that the consumer has to inform the trader of the decision to cancel it. To inform the trader, the consumer may either use a form following the model cancellation form in part B of Schedule 3 or make any other clear statement setting out the decision to cancel the contract.[181] On the grounds of the Regulations 2013, the trader not only has to provide a form on his website but also, when he receives the completed and submitted form, communicate to the consumer an acknowledgement of receipt of the cancellation on a durable medium without delay.[182] As to the choice between the dispatch or receipt rule, it is stated that 'the consumer is to be treated as having cancelled the contract in the cancellation period if the communication is sent before the end of the period'.[183] With regard to the burden of proof, it is the consumer who should provide the evidence that he has sent the notification within the period.[184]

5.5.3.3.2 Supply of Services and Non-tangible Digital Content

Pursuant to Regulation 36(2) of the Regulations 2013, if the service has been fully performed, and performance of the service began (a) after a request by the consumer and (b) with the acknowledgement that the consumer would lose that right once the contract had been fully performed by the trader, the consumer ceases to have the right to withdraw from this service contract. It is also regulated that under a contract for the supply of digital content not on a tangible medium, the consumer ceases to have the right to withdraw if the supply of the digital content has begun after the consumer has given the consent and acknowledgement required by Regulation 37(1).

5.5.4 *Comparative Review*

In Chinese law, if the goods do not remain intact, the withdrawal right cannot be exercised. This leaves vast room for traders to define what is 'intactness'. In some senses, the space for consumers to realise their rights is considerably restricted. In the European context, the issue regarding the condition of the commodity is left to the question of who should bear the cost when the goods are diminished. This means there is no limitation regarding the condition of goods on consumers to exercise

[181] See Regulation 32(3) of the Regulations 2013.

[182] See Regulation 32(4) of the Regulations 2013.

[183] Regulation 32(5) of the Regulations 2013

[184] See Regulation 32(6) of the Regulations 2013.

their withdrawal rights. This could reflect a higher level of consumer protection, but it also creates the problem that the seller is in great uncertainty, especially if the period is rather long if the information has not been provided. This makes it possible that the consumer can still withdraw from a contract and get the refund a long period after he has purchased the goods.

In terms of the notification that should be sent by the consumer, the European, German and English legislators make it possible for consumers to deliver an unequivocal statement through any instruments they like, and the only burden is that they have to provide the evidence. In terms of the choice between dispatch principle and receipt principle, the former is chosen by the legislator. Also, the EU legislator requires the trader to provide a channel to help consumers to perform their rights, especially in the area of online shopping. In addition, the formal requirement that limits the performance of withdrawal rights on the national level should be discarded. Although sending a notification is not necessary according to the Chinese Consumer Protection Law, in practice the traders are usually willing to provide buttons on their websites for consumers to deliver notifications. When the message is delivered, the right has been validly exercised.

In Chinese law, whether withdrawal rights are applicable to the supply of services is not clarified. In the EU, the consumer will lose his right to withdraw from a service contract when the services have been fully performed, if he knew he would lose his right and he still consented to the performance. In the context of supplying digital content which is not on a tangible medium, as long as the consumer starts downloading the purchased digital contents, the right of withdrawal expires (Table 5.5).

Table 5.5 Exercise of withdrawal rights

	The requirement of intactness	Specific method to exercise the right and the rule on dispatch/receipt	Instruments for sending the notification
Chinese Consumer Protection Law	Yes	Through the return of the goods	
		(not mentioned)	
EU Directives	No	Through informing the trader of his decision to withdraw	(1) The model withdrawal form
		(dispatch principle)	(2) Any other unequivocal statement
German Law	No	Through the declaration being made to the trader	(1) The model withdrawal form
		(dispatch principle)	(2) Any other unambiguous declaration
English Law	No	Through informing the trader of the decision to cancel	(1) The model cancellation form
		(dispatch principle)	(2) Any other clear statement

5.6 Consequences of Withdrawal

5.6.1 *Introduction*

This section deals with five questions. In a transaction in which the right of withdrawal has been successfully exercised, (1) What are the consequences of the withdrawal? (2) What are the requirements for the consumer to return the good and for the trader to refund the payment? (3) Who should bear the cost of transportation for return? (4) If damage occurs, who should be liable for it? And (5) Who should bear the risk of loss of the goods being returned? These five questions are discussed in Chinese law (Sect. 5.6.2), EU directives (Sect. 5.6.3.1), German law (Sect. 5.6.3.2) and English law (Sect. 5.6.3.3), followed by a comparison (Sect. 5.6.4).

5.6.2 *Chinese Law*

5.6.2.1 Withdrawal of Contract

For the legal consequences of withdrawal, Article 25 of the Consumer Protection Law 2013 provides that the consumer needs to return the good and the trader needs to refund the payment. Thus, the first consequence of exercising a withdrawal right is that the contractual relationship comes to an end. However, the doctrinal nature of the right, for example, whether it is the result of a contract being avoided or terminated, needs further elaboration, because it determines what are the other consequences of withdrawal.

In academia, it is widely accepted that the right of withdrawal is one type of *Gestaltungsrecht* (a legal right to alter a legal act by means of unilateral declaration of intention, its Chinese name is '形成权', which literally means 'the right of formation'). Despite this consensus of its nature of *Gestaltungsrecht*, what kind of *Gestaltungsrecht* the withdrawal right still remains doubtful. The Understanding of authority states that the withdrawal right regulated by the Consumer Protection Law 2013 is a right of avoidance (in Chinese it is '撤销权', which literally means the right to revoke).[185] Nevertheless, in academia, scholars such as Lixin Yang suggest the right to withdraw is a right of termination (in Chinese it is '解除权', which literally means the right to terminate).[186] Similarly, Haopeng Su suggests the consequence of exercise would be similar to the consequence of the exercise of the right of statutory termination.[187] In the context of Chinese contract law, the consequences of exercising the right of statutory termination and the right of avoidance are rather different.

[185] See Jia (贾东明) 2013, pp. 104–105.

[186] See Yang (杨立新) 2014, pp. 32–33.

[187] See Su (苏号朋) 2013, p. 5.

To be specific, the Understanding regards the withdrawn contract as a contract which was avoided. This means, when the consumer exercises his right of withdrawal, the contract will become a null and void one, and the rendered payments should be traced back to the original position as the contract were never concluded. Article 58 of the Contract Law 1999 provides the consequences of an avoided contract.[188] In contrast, the authors who suggest the right of withdrawal should be one type of statutory termination right consider that Article 97 of the Contract Law 1999 provides the consequences if the consumer exercises his withdrawal right.[189] Comparing these two articles, it is not difficult to observe that the legal consequences of these two types of right are rather different: the consequences of an avoided contract focus on the return of the property, while the consequences of a terminated contract lay emphasis on the question of whether the contractual obligation has been performed or not. In the latter case, the performed part may still remain valid, which is definitely not the case in the context of avoidance.

Both sides can establish some arguments to support their opinions. People who suggest that the consequences of withdrawal should refer to the rule on avoidance can argue that (1) the right of avoidance concerns more the defect in declaration of intention, while the right of termination focuses on causes which occurred after the conclusion and effectiveness of the contract. Since the right of withdrawal deals with 'information asymmetry', it is more similar to avoidance than termination. (2) The consequences of avoidance have a retroactive effect, meaning the avoided contract would be deemed a void contract from the very beginning. However, in the context of terminated contracts, whether the retroactive effect exists depends on the willingness of the right holder. In the context of withdrawal rights, in case the withdrawal right is performed, the only consequence is mutual return. It is not possible to validate the performance. (3) The cooling-off period of withdrawal right is more like a scheduled period, (*Ausschlussfrist*, or in Chinese, '除斥期间') which is applied to the right of avoidance since it is regulated by law and it cannot be discontinued. In the context of Chinese law, the scheduled period starts from the day when the party knows or ought to know the cause of avoidance. The aforementioned comparative review also shows that many jurisdictions regulate that the period of withdrawal right should not start until the trader notifies the consumer about the existence of his right. Whether the right holder is aware of the existence of his right should be the core in both circumstances of withdrawal and avoidance. Nevertheless, people who regard the right of withdrawal as the right of termination can also build their

[188] Article 58 reads: 'The property acquired as a result of a contract shall be returned after the contract is confirmed to be null and void or has been revoked; where the property cannot be returned or the return is unnecessary, it shall be reimbursed at its estimated price. The party at fault shall compensate the other party for losses incurred as a result therefrom. If both parties are fault, each party shall respectively be liable'.

[189] Article 97 provides: 'After the termination of a contract, performance shall cease if the contract has not been performed; if the contract has been performed, a party may, in accordance with the circumstances of performance or the nature of the contract, demand the other party to restore such party to its original state or adopt other remedial measures, and such party shall have the right to demand compensation for damages'.

argument as follows: when the legislator, the National People's Congress, published the first Draft of the Amendment, it is clarified that 'in order to protect the right of choice, this draft grants consumers the right to unilaterally terminate the contract within an appropriate period'.[190] Besides, the right of avoidance in Chinese contract law requires the right of the holder to exercise it through requesting the people's court or an arbitration institution,[191] but the right of termination can be simply exercised by sending a notification,[192] which is in line with the practice and other jurisdictions' approach.

In my opinion, the right of withdrawal should be recognised as a special type of right of termination. This is because not only the legislator who published the draft gave a clear demonstration that this is a right to terminate a contract,[193] but the focus should be on the ground of claim itself to build a channel between withdrawal rights provided by the Consumer Protection Law 2013 and the consequences provided by the Contract Law 1999. Indeed, the value of clarifying the nature of withdrawal rights is to find the legal consequences which are prescribed in the Contract Law 1999 while it is not clearly regulated by the Consumer Protection Law 2013. Besides, it is crucial that Article 94 of the Contract Law 1999 provides that one party may terminate a contract under 'other circumstances as provided by law'.[194] This fallback rule makes it possible to apply the relevant rules on termination where the consequence of withdrawal is not very clear, for example, the issue of damage which is discussed in the following parts. In contrast, the statutory right of avoidance should be unequivocally regulated in the legislation. If the right of withdrawal were a right to avoid, there should be an article which is similar to Article 94 that could be found in the Contract Law 1999. Nevertheless, this is not the case because the articles regarding the right of avoidance in the Contract Law 1999 have not provided any space for the interpretation that some other types of civil rights could also be deemed as rights of avoidance.[195]

---

190 See the National People's Congress of the People's Republic of China (全国人民代表大会), 'Articles and Interpretations on the Draft of the Amendment of Law on the Protection of Consumer Rights and Interests' (《消费者权益保护法修正案(草案)条文及草案说明》), available at: <http://www.npc.gov.cn/npc/xinwen/lfgz/flca/2013-04/28/content_1793762.htm>, last visited: 2014/10/17.

191 See Article 54 of the Contract Law 1999.

192 See Article 96 of the Contract Law 1999.

193 Chinese judges also identify the right of withdrawal as a right to terminate. See, for example, Jianhua Cai v Shanghai Oriental TV Shopping Co Ltd. (蔡建华诉上海东方电视购物有限公司电视购物合同纠纷案), Civil Judgment (2015) Yang-Min-Yi-Min-Chu-Zi No. 3098 of the People's Court of Yangpu District of Shanghai City (上海市杨浦区人民法院(2015)杨民一(民)初字第3098号民事判决书).

194 See point 5 of Article 94 of the Contract Law 1999.

195 Furthermore, although there is a type of right of avoidance which is similar to withdrawal rights, the donor's right of avoidance prior to the transfer of rights to the gift property (Article 186 of the Contract Law), the significance of referring to is considerably limited because it does not provide the rules on exercising it either. For a detailed analysis on this issue, see Ge (葛江虬) 2015, pp. 106–107.

5.6.2.2 Return of Rendered Performances

As aforementioned, in the second Draft of the Amendment, the consumer is required to return the commodity within 7 days of claiming that he wants to exercise his right of withdrawal. Nevertheless, in the context of the formal amendment, the consumer is no longer regulated to deliver a notification, but he has to return the goods within the period. Therefore, the conduct of return itself becomes both the exercise of, and one of the consequences of, withdrawal.

If the consumer in a transaction has exercised the right of withdrawal by means of sending back the commodity, the business should, 'within seven days of receipt of the returned commodities, refund the payments made by consumers for the commodities'.[196] However, if the trader failed to refund in 7 days, the consequences are not very clear in the Consumer Protection Law.[197] Besides, regarding the sum of 'the payments', it needs some further elaboration of whether the costs of transport should be refunded. This is discussed in the following section.

5.6.2.3 Cost of Transportation

Especially in the context of distance selling, there are at least two types of costs of transport: the first one refers to the moment when the consumer finishes shopping and the business delivers the goods to him (where occurs the fee of first transportation) and the second one refers to the transport occurring because of the exercise of withdrawal right (the fee of second transportation). Article 25(3) of the Consumer Protection Law 2013 makes it rather clear that the second freight charge should be paid by the consumer: 'The freight charge for the return of commodities shall be assumed by consumers, except as otherwise agreed upon by business operators and consumers'. But in terms of the first freight, it is more complicated since in practice it is not always the consumer, or the trader, who pays for the transportation unilaterally. Sometimes consumers are asked to pay the costs, and sometimes businesses may provide the special offer that the freight will be contained in the total price of the good or 'the transportation fee is exempted'.

On this issue, the Understanding suggests that the first freight should be assumed by the consumer as a principle. This is because in Article 25, it is regulated that the business should only refund 'the payments made by consumers for the commodities'. Put differently, the fee of transportation is not a part of 'payments for the commodities', so it will not be refunded. Only if the business promised that the transportation fee is exempted, the first freight cost should be considered as 'zero',

---

[196] Article 25 of the Consumer Protection Law 2013

[197] Article 31 of the Interim Measures 2017 provides that the online seller shall be punished in accordance with Item (8), paragraph 1, Article 56 of the Law on the Protection of Consumer Rights and Interests, if it fails to refund the payment that has made by a consumer for the commodity within 15 days of receipt of the commodity returned.

and the total amount should be refunded.[198] This viewpoint can be also evidenced from a historical perspective. In the first Draft of the Amendment of the Consumer Protection Law, it was stated that 'the business shall refund the payment', but whether this payment is for the commodity only or for both commodity and the freight was not clarified. During the revising process, it was suggested that it should be clarified that the payment is only for the commodity.[199] From the literal expression of the final amendment and the report provided by the legislator, we can observe that this opinion is accepted.[200]

5.6.2.4 Liability for Damages

The new Consumer Protection Law 2013 does not provide a rule on who should be responsible for the possible damage that may occur when the consumer performs the right of withdrawal. It is described as a 'regretful' issue because it was ignored by the legislator. Scholars suggest that the damage occurred should be paid by the consumer.[201] As aforementioned, Article 97 of the Contract Law 1999 can be applied here. On the basis of this article, the trader should have the right to claim compensation for damage. However, since the withdrawal rule in China requires the 'intactness' of the commodity, it would be not so common where damage can be found.

5.6.2.5 Risk of Loss

In terms of the risk of loss of the commodity being returned, Article 142 of the Contract Law 1999 should be referred to. It provides that the risk of damage to or loss of a subject matter shall be borne by the seller prior to the delivery of the subject matter and by the buyer after delivery, except as otherwise stipulated by law or agreed upon by the parties. This article implies that one should bear the risk of damage or loss if the subject matter is in his control. Thus, in the context of withdrawal, it should be the consumer who bears the risk of loss, since he is in charge of the transportation of return.

---

198 See Jia (贾东明) 2013, p. 109.

199 See 'On Soliciting Advice from the Public in terms of the Draft of the Amendment of Law on the Protection of Consumer Rights and Interests' (《消费者权益保护法修正案草案向社会公众征求意见的情况》), in Civil Law Office of the Legislative Affairs Commission of the Standing Committee of the National People's Congress (全国人大常委会法制工作委员会民法室) 2013, p. 69.

200 See Reports of the Legislative Affairs Commission of the Standing Committee of the National People's Congress on the Draft of the Amendment of Law of the People's Republic of China on the Protection of Consumer Rights and Interests (全国人民代表大会法律委员会关于《中华人民共和国消费者权益保护法修正案(草案)》修改情况的汇报), in Jia (贾东明) 2013, pp. 334–335.

201 See Sun (孙良国) 2014, p. 84.

5.6.3 *EU Law*

5.6.3.1 Directives

5.6.3.1.1 Withdrawal of Contract

In light of Article 12 of the Consumer Rights Directive (2011/83/EU), the first consequence of a contract where the right of withdrawal has been successfully exercised is that the obligations come to an end. It is stated that the obligations of the parties '(a) to perform the distance or off-premises contract; (b) to conclude the distance or off-premises contract, in cases where an offer was made by the consumer' shall be terminated.

5.6.3.1.2 Return of Rendered Performances

Prior to the promulgation of the Consumer Rights Directive, although the principle that 'once the consumer has successfully withdrawn from the contract, performance rendered under the contract must be returned' is widely recognised, directives did not provide precise rules. 'The way it is to be realised is largely left to national law'.[202] For instance, the second sentence of Article 6(1) of the Distance Selling Directive (97/7/EC) only regulates the rule on bearing the transportation cost, but there is no rule related to return itself – no period or other limitation was laid on the consumer's return of the commodity.[203]

In the context of the Consumer Rights Directive, this situation has fundamentally changed. Pursuant to Article 14, the consumer is required to 'send back the goods or hand them over to the trader or to a person authorised by the trader to receive the goods, without undue delay and in any event not later than 14 days from the day on which he has communicated his decision to withdraw from the contract to the trader in accordance with Article 11', unless the trader has offered to collect the goods himself. The proposal of this directive failed to provide the rule on whether it adopted the principle of dispatch or the principle of receipt.[204] This was criticised by scholars that the article 'does not answer the question of whether the seller must have obtained possession of the goods within that period'.[205] In the Consumer Rights Directive, this issue is fixed by regulating that 'the deadline shall be met if the consumer sends back the goods before the period of 14 days has expired'.[206]

[202] Loos 2009, p. 266

[203] It reads: 'The only charge that may be made to the consumer because of the exercise of his right of withdrawal is the direct cost of returning the goods'.

[204] See Proposal for a Directive of the European Parliament and of the Council on Consumer Rights, COM (2008) 614 final.

[205] Loos 2009, p. 267

[206] See the last sentence of Article 14(1) of the Consumer Rights Directive.

For the reimbursement of the payment, Article 6 of the Distance Selling Directive regulated that 'the supplier shall be obliged to reimburse the sums paid by the consumer free of charge' and such reimbursement has to be accomplished as soon as possible and in any event within 30 days. In the context of the Consumer Rights Directive, the trader is required to 'reimburse all payments received from the consumer, including, if applicable, the costs of delivery without undue delay and in any event not later than 14 days from the day on which he is informed of the consumer's decision to withdraw from the contract in accordance with Article 11'.[207]

Besides, it is regulated that the trader has to reimburse the consumer by using the same means of payment as the consumer used for the initial transaction. It is also possible that another channel may be used as long as two requirements can be met: (1) the consumer has expressly agreed to this; (2) the consumer will not incur any fees as a result of this reimbursement.[208]

It should be observed that, since the trader has to bear a high risk as he has to reimburse the consumer without the receipt of good, the right to withhold performance is granted in Article 13(3). It provides: 'Unless the trader has offered to collect the goods himself, with regard to sales contracts, the trader may withhold the reimbursement until he has received the goods back, or until the consumer has supplied evidence of having sent back the goods, whichever is the earliest'.

5.6.3.1.3 Cost of Transportation

In terms of the transportation fee for sending back the goods, the second paragraph of Article 14(1) clearly states that the costs shall be paid by the consumer, 'unless the trader has agreed to bear them or the trader failed to inform the consumer that the consumer has to bear them'.

With respect to the initial transport charge, it will be borne by the trader, because Article 13 of the Consumer Rights Directive states that the trader needs to reimburse 'all payments' but not the payment for the commodity. In order to balance the interests between the trader and the consumer, it is stated if the consumer chose a type of delivery other than the least expensive type of standard delivery, the trader is not required to reimburse the supplementary costs.[209]

5.6.3.1.4 Liability for Damages

On the basis of Article 14(2) of the Consumer Rights Directive, the consumer will not be liable for diminished value if it is necessary to establish the nature, characteristics and functioning of the goods, and it is even mentioned that consumers will in any event not be liable for diminished value where the trader failed to provide notice

---

[207] Article 13 of the Consumer Rights Directive

[208] See the second paragraph of Article 13(1) of the Consumer Rights Directive.

[209] See Article 13(2) of the Consumer Rights Directive.

of the withdrawal right. In terms of the definition of 'establish the nature, characteristics and functioning', it is provided that the consumer should only handle and inspect them in the same manner as he would be allowed to do in a shop. A specific example is that 'the consumer should only try on a garment and should not be allowed to wear it'.[210]

5.6.3.1.5 Risk of Loss

The Consumer Rights Directive has not touched upon the issue of the risk of loss. It is left to national law.

5.6.3.2 German Law

5.6.3.2.1 Withdrawal of Contract

Pursuant to § 355(1) BGB, if the consumer has withdrawn on time, both the consumer and the trader are no longer obliged to perform the contract. § 357 BGB regulates the effects in the contexts of off-premises contracts and distance contracts except contracts for financial services. The latter is mentioned in § 357a BGB, while the effects of withdrawal in timeshare or other types contracts are laid down in § 357b and § 357c BGB. In this section the emphasis is laid on off-premises contracts and distance contracts.

5.6.3.2.2 Return of Rendered Performances

In the contexts of off-premises contracts and distance contracts, once the consumer has successfully exercised his right of withdrawal, it is required that the performance received must be restituted after no later than 14 days.[211] It will be sufficient to meet this deadline by the prompt dispatch of goods.[212] In the context of sales of goods, the consumer does not have to return the goods if the trader agreed to collect them.[213] For off-premises contracts, where the goods have been delivered at the time of concluding the contract at the consumer's home, if the goods are not suitable for return by post, the seller is required to collect them at his own expense.[214]

Pursuant to § 357(2) BGB, the trader must reimburse any payments made by the consumer, including the cost for the initial delivery. In terms of the reimbursement, it is regulated that the trader must use the same currency that is paid by the consumer,

[210] See Recital 47 of the Consumer Rights Directive.

[211] See § 357(1) BGB.

[212] See § 355(3) BGB.

[213] See § 357(5) BGB.

[214] See § 357(6) BGB.

unless otherwise agreed and the consumer will bear no additional costs. In order to prevent excessive risks for traders, § 357(4) BGB states that the trader has the right to withhold the reimbursement until he has received the returned goods or the evidence supplied by the consumer that he has dispatched the goods.

5.6.3.2.3 Cost of Transportation

If the trader has not offered to collect the goods, the consumer should arrange for the return shipment. He is also required to bear the direct cost of returning, if the trader has informed him of this duty in accordance with Article 246a § 1(2), sentence 1 number 2 of the Introductory Act to the Civil Code, unless otherwise specified.[215]

As mentioned, the trader should bear the cost for the initial delivery. However, this does not apply if the additional costs occurred due to the reason that the consumer chose a different type of delivery other than the cheapest standard delivery offered by the trader.

5.6.3.2.4 Liability for Damages

§ 357(7) BGB provides the rules on damage which occurred within the withdrawal period. It is regulated that the consumer has to pay compensation of the loss of value if the loss is not because of the necessary establishing of the nature, characteristics and functioning of the goods and the trader has already informed the consumer in accordance with Article 246a § 1(2), sentence 1 number 1 of the Introductory Act to the Civil Code concerning his right.

5.6.3.2.5 Risk of Loss

In the German Civil Code, it is clarified that the trader will bear the risk of the loss of goods when they are returned.[216]

5.6.3.3 English Law

5.6.3.3.1 Withdrawal of Contract

The first consequence of withdrawal is the cancellation of the contract. Regulation 33(1) of the Regulations 2013 states that 'the cancellation ends the obligations of the parties to perform the contract'. Besides, it should be noticed that, in the context

---

[215] See § 357(6) BGB.

[216] See § 355(3) BGB.

of English law, the right of withdrawal regulated on the EU level is divided into two parts: the right to cancel and the right to 'withdraw' in the English context. The former is applied to the circumstances where the contracts have already been concluded. The latter allows the consumer to withdraw an offer made by the consumer to enter into a distance or off-premises contract. Thus, if an English consumer exercises his right to withdraw, the first consequence would be that he is no longer bound to conclude the contract with the trader.

5.6.3.3.2 Return of Rendered Performances

If a contract is withdrawn by the consumer, the consumer has to send the goods back or hand them over to the trader or a person authorised by the trader to receive them, unless the trader has offered to collect them or, in the case of an off-premises contract, the goods were delivered to the consumer's home when the contract was entered into and by their nature could not be returned by post.[217] The consumer is required to send the goods back without undue delay and in any event not later than 14 days after the day on which the consumer informs the trader of the decision to withdraw.[218]

Similar to German law, the Regulations 2013 also strictly follow the way of the European Directive to regulate the reimbursement of the payment. On the grounds of its Regulation 34(1), the trader must reimburse all payments received from the consumer. The reimbursement should be accomplished without undue delay and in any event within the period of 14 days after the day on which the trader receives the goods back or the day on which the consumer supplies evidence of having sent the goods back, whichever is earlier.[219] In Regulations 34(7) and (8), the trader is required to use the same means of payment as the consumer used for the initial transaction, unless otherwise agreed, and he is not allowed to impose any fee on the consumer in respect of the reimbursement.

5.6.3.3.3 Cost of Transportation

In terms of the transportation cost of sending back the goods, the consumer is required to bear the cost unless the trader agreed to bear those costs or the information duty was not performed by the trader.[220]

---

[217] See Regulations 35(1) and (2) of the Regulations 2013.

[218] See Regulation 35(4) of the Regulations 2013.

[219] See Regulations 34(4) and (5) of the Regulations 2013.

[220] Regulation 35(5)(b) states: '(…) the trader failed to provide the consumer with the information about the consumer bearing those costs, required by paragraph (m) of Schedule 2, in accordance with Part 2'.

With regard to the initial delivery cost, 'unless the consumer expressly chose a kind of delivery costing more than the least expensive common and generally acceptable kind of delivery offered by the trader',[221] the trader also has to reimburse them. In this case, the price of delivery that the consumer would have paid if he had chosen the least expensive common and generally acceptable kind of delivery will be referenced.[222] These rules are just the same as in the EU directive and German law.

5.6.3.3.4 Liability for Damages

In the case where the value of goods is diminished within the period of withdrawal, whether the trader may recover that amount from the consumer depends on whether the handling of the goods by the consumer is beyond what is necessary to establish the nature, characteristics and functioning of the goods and whether the trader has provided the consumer with the information required by paragraph (l) of Schedule 2, in accordance with Part 2 of the Regulations.[223] To recover from the consumer, the trader may deduct from the amount to be reimbursed; otherwise the amount must be paid by the consumer to the trader.[224] In terms of the assessment on 'beyond what is necessary', it is mentioned that the handling is beyond what is necessary if it goes beyond the sort of handling that might reasonably be allowed in a shop.[225]

5.6.3.3.5 Risk of Loss

Similar to the Consumer Rights Directive, the Regulations 2013 have not provided any rule on the risk of loss.

5.6.4 Comparative Review

The fundamental difference between the Chinese and EU rules on consequences of withdrawal is caused by the requirement of notification. Specifically, there are three periods in total regulated by the Consumer Rights Directive: the consumer has to notify the trader of his intention to withdraw in 14 days; the consumer is required to send back the good within 14 days of communicating to the trader that he wants to

---

[221] Regulation 34(2) of the Regulations 2013

[222] See Regulation 34(3) of the Regulations 2013.

[223] See Regulations 34(9) and (11) of the Regulations 2013.

[224] See Regulation 34(10) of the Regulations 2013.

[225] See Regulation 34(12) of the Regulations 2013.

exercise his right of withdrawal; the trader is obliged to reimburse the payments within 14 days once he has received the good or the evidence that the consumer has already sent them back. We can characterise this as a '14-14-14' system. In China, there are only two periods regulated by the Consumer Protection Law 2013: the consumer has to send back the goods within 7 days of receipt of the commodity and the business operator is obliged to refund the payment within 7 days of receipt of the returned commodity. We can call this a '7-7' system. Apparently, both the periods for consumer and trader to perform their legal obligations in the context of withdrawal are rather short in China. Compared with Chinese consumers, the EU consumers have a period of twice the length of the traders' period for them to finish the whole process of exercising their withdrawal rights. They can take their time to send the notification in the first 14 days' period and send back the goods in the second 14 days' period. In China, only a period of 7 days is regulated, and consumers have to finish all they have to do within these 7 days.

In terms of the consequences of mutual return, the trader has to pay more in the context of EU law. For example, in a transaction, the value of the good is 20 EUR, and the fee for delivery is 10 EUR, so the consumer pays 30 EUR in total. If the consumer successfully exercises the right of withdrawal, in China the business operator only has to refund 20 EUR, since the consumer has to pay the costs of delivery, while in the EU, the trader has to reimburse 30 EUR, because the Consumer Rights Directive requires that the trader should reimburse all the payments received from the consumer. It is noteworthy that the Consumer Rights Directive and its German and English implementations regulate that the trader only has to reimburse the payment for delivery up to the amount the consumer would have paid if the consumer had chosen the least expensive kind of delivery.

As mentioned, the Chinese Consumer Protection Law regards 'intactness' as a limitation of the exercise of withdrawal, but the European legislators consider that law 'should not discourage the consumer from exercising his right of withdrawal', so the issue of diminished value is left to the phase of consequences of withdrawal. The general rule is that the consumer does not have to pay for it if the handling of goods is not beyond what is necessary to establish the nature, characteristics and functioning of the goods. It is even provided that the only limitation on examining the goods is not applicable where the trader has failed to provide the notice of the right of withdrawal. In the German context, it could be doubtful whether consumers receive too much protection, because the trader also has to take the risk of loss of the returned goods. However, if the consumer's handling of goods exceeds the level which he is allowed to do in a shop, he will be responsible for the diminished value (Table 5.6).

Table 5.6 Consequences of withdrawal

	Withdrawal of contract	Return of rendered performances	Cost of transportation	Liability for damage and risk of loss
Chinese Consumer Protection Law	Termination of the contract	Consumer: Within 7 days of receipt of the commodity	Cost of the initial delivery: Consumer	
		Trader: Within 7 days of receipt of the returned commodity	Cost of sending back the goods: Consumer	
EU Directives	Termination of the obligations	Consumer: Within 14 days after sending a notification	Cost of the initial delivery: Trader	Consumer does not have to pay for the diminished value if the handling of goods is not beyond what is necessary to establish the nature, characteristics and functioning of the goods
		Trader: Within 14 days once the trader received the goods or the evidence that the consumer has already sent back the goods	Cost of sending back the goods: Consumer	
German Law	Revocation of the declarations of intent	Consumer: Within 14 days after sending a notification trader: Within 14 days once the trader received the goods or the evidence that the consumer has already sent back the goods	Cost of the initial delivery: Trader	Consumer does not have to pay for the diminished value if the handling of goods is not beyond what is necessary to establish the nature, characteristics and functioning of the goods
			Cost of sending back the goods: Consumer	Trader bears the risk of loss
English Law	Cancellation of the contract	Consumer: Within 14 days after sending a notification	Cost of the initial delivery: Trader	Consumer does not have to pay for the diminished value if the handling of goods is not beyond what is necessary to establish the nature, characteristics and functioning of the goods
	Withdrawal of the offer	Trader: Within 14 days once the trader received the goods or the evidence that the consumer has already sent back the goods	Cost of sending back the goods: Consumer	

5.7 Concluding Remarks

5.7.1 Comparison Between China and the EU

Although in some sense it may deviate from the traditional doctrine that contracts are binding, legislators of today grant consumers in certain types of transactions the right to escape the contractual relationship without giving any reason or bearing any damage. These rights are known as 'withdrawal rights'. On the basis of the foregoing introduction and analysis, this chapter provides a picture of how withdrawal rights operate in China and the EU. The findings can be summarised as follows.

Firstly, withdrawal rights are not applicable to all types of transactions. It is noteworthy that both Chinese and EU legislators recognise 'distance selling' as an important area to which the withdrawal right should apply. Regarding the legislative technique, the EU legislator and their Chinese counterparty adopt different approaches. The former uses the model of 'concept and its definition' in the Consumer Rights Directive (2011/83/EU), while the latter provides no abstract definition but a list of means of distance communication in the Consumer Protection Law 2013. However, the list provided by the Chinese legislators is still short when compared with similar lists offered by the domestic legislation of the EU Member States. The very specific method to incorporate the overlooked distance selling transactions into the applicable scope is to interpret the Chinese character *deng* which means 'etc.'. Besides distance selling, doorstep selling is believed to be another area that the right of withdrawal should apply to. In the EU context, this is clear. In contrast, in the Chinese legislation, doorstep selling cannot be found, so the aforementioned method to interpret *deng* has to be used here again.

The second question is to which categories of commodities withdrawal rights are not applicable. It is pointed out that the list provided by the Consumer Rights Directive is long: there is no space for the application of withdrawal rights in 13 types of transactions. In comparison, the Chinese Consumer Protection Law 2013 only mentions four types. Nevertheless, a fallback rule is regulated by this national statute: if there are other commodities which are not suitable to return in nature, the trader is allowed to exclude the application of withdrawal rights as long as he has informed the consumer and obtained the consumer's confirmation before they conclude the contract.

Thirdly, the lengths of cooling-off periods are worth observation. Chinese consumers have a period of 7 days to determine whether they want to withdraw or not. For EU consumers, the Consumer Rights Directive adopts a period of 14 days. It should be noted that the Chinese period starts from the second day of the receipt of the good. Besides, '7 days' stand for '7 calendar days,' and if the last day is a holiday, then the first day after the holiday becomes the last day of the period. In the EU context, the start of the withdrawal period depends not only on the consumer's receipt of the good but also on the fact whether the trader has notified the consumer about the existence of the withdrawal right.

Fourthly, in China if the consumer wants to exercise his right of withdrawal, he has to send back the good within the set period. However, in practice it is usually not the case because the trader always provides a channel for the consumer to inform the trader before sending back the good. This special agreement should be applied prior to the statutory law because it is favourable to the consumer. Furthermore, there is another preliminary condition for the consumer to exercise his right of withdrawal: the goods have to remain 'intact'. It is pointed out that this rule provides much room for the traders to restrict the consumers' withdrawal rights by defining what 'intact' means. In the EU, the intactness of the goods is never a pre-condition for the consumer to exercise his right of withdrawal. The rule on exercising the right is also different from its Chinese counterpart: all the consumer needs to do is to send an unequivocal statement by any means available. The trader is required to provide the tangible channel to facilitate consumers to exercise their rights.

Fifthly, when an EU consumer has exercised his withdrawal right, he has 14 days to send back the commodity. As another consequence of the termination of the contract, the trader is also required to reimburse the payment within 14 days after he has received the commodity itself or the evidence that the consumer has already sent back the goods. In the Chinese context, because the statutory method to exercise the withdrawal rights is to send back the good, there is no further regulation on the 'sending-back period'. Just like the cooling-off period, the length of the reimbursement period in China is also only half of its EU counterpart, which means Chinese traders have to reimburse the consumers within 7 days after they have obtained the returned commodities. Regarding the amount of the reimbursement, there is another discrepancy between the two jurisdictions: in Chinese law the trader only has to reimburse the commodity's value, whereas the EU businesses have to reimburse the whole amount which has been paid by the consumers. Due to the reason that the 'intactness' is a pre-condition of the withdrawal right in China, it is rather difficult for the consumer to exercise his right if the value of the commodity is diminished. In contrast, a EU consumer can still send back the goods if the reduction is caused by an accepted way of inspection.

On the basis of the description of similarities and differences, it is not difficult to observe that the fundamental components of the system of withdrawal rights in the two jurisdictions are relatively similar: in most essential aspects, for example, applicable scope, exceptions, lengths of periods, exercise and consequences; we can always find a Chinese counterpart to the EU directive. Indeed, this is not surprising, because when the Chinese withdrawal rights system was established, the EU legislation was precisely mentioned as a template to which the Chinese legislators had referred. However, there are two important differences.

The first difference is the level of the rules' certainty. The best examples are the legislative techniques adopted to regulate the applicable scope and exceptions. To be specific, it is rather common for the EU legislators to provide a list of definitions on the core terminologies which are employed at the very beginning of each directive. In the context of withdrawal rights, it is still the same case. The European applicable scope of withdrawal rights is not only determined by the semantic analysis of the given abstract concepts, which are 'distance contract' and 'off-premises contract', but also by the detailed definition of these concepts, which is also provided by the directive. To some extent, the list of definitions offers the national legislators and judges a uniformed standard to assess whether a type of transaction should fall into the applicable scope. In the Chinese context, the legislative technique is much more flexible, because only several very specific patterns of transaction are mentioned. To apply withdrawal rights to more situations, it would need to interpret a character with the meaning of 'etc.'. On the national statutory level, no definition is provided nor the guidance to interpret. In terms of the exceptions of withdrawal rights, the Chinese legislators apply this approach again: they provide a list of four items and, which is more important, a fallback rule that the other commodities can also be excluded if their nature renders them unsuitable for return without a reason and the consumer has confirmed with this. On the basis of this fallback rule, the e-commerce platforms have expanded the exception list to a great extent. Besides the four items which are unequivocally written in law, multifarious types of commodities are regulated to be nonreturnable in practice. Compared with this, EU legislators also regulate a list of 13 items, but this list is a complete one. There is no room for the national legislators to add more commodities which they think are not applicable to withdrawal rights.

The second difference is the rules' orientation. Compared with their EU counterpart, the Chinese legislator is more inclined to balance the interests of consumers and traders. In some senses, the Chinese rules on withdrawal rights put more emphasis on protecting the trader's interests, since the consumer's power is restrained. This can be also observed from the first difference: the fallback rule on exceptions leaves great room for traders to regulate their own list. Besides, the period for the consumer to decide whether he wants to cancel the deal is relatively short. Only 7 days is granted. Furthermore, if the trader doesn't voluntarily provide the consumer with another channel, for example, sending a notification, to exercise withdrawal right, the consumer has to send back the goods within the aforementioned 7 days' period. In the EU, consumers have not only 14 days to decide, but another 14 days to send back the goods. Regarding the amount of reimbursement, traders in the EU are required to bear the cost of transportation. In China, the trader is merely required to reimburse the payment for the goods themselves. Moreover, there is another big difference with regard to the situation that the value of the goods is diminished. In the EU, as long as the deduction of value is a consequence of the consumer's normal inspection and examination, he is not required to be responsible for the deduction, and the exercise of withdrawal right is definitely not influenced. In contrast, the Chinese Consumer Protection Law 2013 regulates that the intact state of the commodity is the requirement for the exercise of a withdrawal right. It leads to the consequence that the consumer may lose his statutory right if the commodity is damaged. Even if the damage is caused by the consumer's normal inspection, it makes no difference because the requirement of 'intact' does not take into account the true intention of the consumer. Furthermore, 'intact' is again a concept that needs interpretation. Since there is no elaboration provided by law, the trader can set his own criteria which may have great impact on the consumer's right. In short, the Chinese withdrawal rights mechanism is a more trader-oriented one than the EU mechanism.

5.7.2 Explanatory Analysis

To investigate the reasons behind the foregoing differences, the focus can be put on the fundamental difference regarding different types of markets, which is mentioned in Chap. 1.

Firstly, hypothesis (1) may explain the reason why the Chinese rules regarding withdrawal rights are vaguer and equivocal. It assumes that, with a more regulated market, China has a lower level of demand for consumer law rules and the level of requirement for the clarity and concreteness of the rules is also lower, whereas the demand for consumer law rules and their clarity and concreteness in the EU, which has a more competitive market, should be much higher. In the Chinese context, the consumer protection rules are adopted because they are believed to be beneficial to the sound development of the socialist market economy. However, due to the reason that China does not have a long history of this type of economy, the kind of influence which these legal rules will produce is an open question. It could be too strict if everything is precisely regulated in law. In addition, the Chinese market of consumption has developed so rapidly in recent decades. It is not easy to predict what will happen in the future. Thus, an open-ended way of legislation is supposed to be more safe. The situation of withdrawal rights is therefore rather similar to the situation of the definition of consumer contracts. Just like the intentional design that the definition does not make it clear whether a medical contract is a consumer contract, leaving gaps in the rules regarding withdrawal rights may also help with handling new circumstances which may occur in the future. Providing an enumeration and a fallback rule always creates much space for the necessary interpretation, compared with providing a more precise rule. On these grounds, legal flexibility prevails over legal certainty. Inversely, the EU rules of consumer law are regulated so as to contribute to the establishment of the internal market, which is a relatively competitive market. To the EU legislators, the existing fragmentation is more important. They believe that precise and explicit legal rules will reduce the barriers for traders to do business abroad and enhance consumers' confidence to participate in cross-border transactions. Thus, legal certainty is recognised as a value of higher priority compared with legal flexibility.[226] The clearer the rules are, the less divergence it will create on the national level.

Secondly, as to a more trader-oriented mechanism of withdrawal rights being adopted by Chinese law, the explanation can be started with the feature of the Chinese socialist market economy that manufacturing and export play a significant role, which is demonstrated in Chap. 1.

On the one hand, manufacturing enterprises, especially small and medium-sized manufacturing enterprises, are very important to economic growth in China.[227] If a

---

[226] See Chap. 3, Sect. 3.4.2.

[227] By the end of 2015, the number of industrial SMEs above designated size occupies 97.4% of all industrial enterprises above designated size (industrial enterprises above designated size refers to the enterprises whose prime operating revenue per year is more than 20 million RMB). The total taxation of SMEs accounts for 49.2% of the total taxation of all enterprises. The total profit of SMEs accounts for 64.5% of the total profit of all enterprises. Meanwhile, more than 80% of

consumer-oriented mechanism of withdrawal rights had been adopted, these SMEs would be deeply affected. This is elaborated as follows. Since 2003, the year of the promulgation of the Law of the People's Republic of China on the Promotion of Small and Medium-sized Enterprises,[228] a variety of legislative instruments and state policies have been adopted to improve the business environment and healthy development of SMEs. During the China's 13th Five-Year-Plan (2016–2020) period, the foreign trade of Chinese SMEs is in grave difficulties and the export growth is weaker.[229] Thus, to improve the business environment and healthy development of SMEs becomes even more important. A new plan for promoting the development of SMEs was published by the Ministry of Industry and Information Technology of the People's Republic of China in 2016.[230] In this plan, methods including but not limited to tax reduction, financial support and administrative service support are mentioned.[231] In particular, SMEs are encouraged to use internet and other digital technologies to innovate new modes for production and marketing.[232] However, when the SMEs use these technologies, they could be the enterprises that are most likely to be affected by the relevant legal rules on withdrawal rights. During the process of amending the Consumer Protection Law, many suggestions were submitted to the Legislative Affairs Commission of the Standing Committee of the National People's Congress, stating that the regulation of withdrawal rights could increase

employment are created by the SMEs. See Ministry of Industry and Information Technology of the People's Republic of China (中华人民共和国工业和信息化部), 'the Planning for Promoting the Development of the SMEs (2016–2020)' (《促进中小企业发展规划(2016—2020年)》), Sect 1.1, Chap. 1, available at: http://www.miit.gov.cn/n1146295/n1652858/n1652930/n3757016/c5081157/content.html, last visited: 2017/7/22.

[228] Law of the People's Republic of China on the Promotion of Small and Medium-sized Enterprises (《中华人民共和国中小企业促进法》)

[229] See Ministry of Industry and Information Technology of the People's Republic of China (中华人民共和国工业和信息化部), 'the Planning for Promoting the Development of the SMEs (2016–2020)' (《促进中小企业发展规划(2016—2020年)》), paragraph 1, Chap. 2, available at: http://www.miit.gov.cn/n1146295/n1652858/n1652930/n3757016/c5081157/content.html, last visited: 2017/7/22.

[230] Ministry of Industry and Information Technology of the People's Republic of China (中华人民共和国工业和信息化部), 'the Planning for Promoting the Development of the SMEs (2016–2020)' (《促进中小企业发展规划(2016—2020年)》), available at: http://www.miit.gov.cn/n1146295/n1652858/n1652930/n3757016/c5081157/content.html, last visited: 2017/7/22

[231] Ministry of Industry and Information Technology of the People's Republic of China (中华人民共和国工业和信息化部), 'the Planning for Promoting the Development of the SMEs (2016–2020)' (《促进中小企业发展规划(2016—2020年)》), Sects. 5.2, 5.3 and 5.4, this chapter, available at: http://www.miit.gov.cn/n1146295/n1652858/n1652930/n3757016/c5081157/content.html, last visited: 2017/7/22.

[232] Ministry of Industry and Information Technology of the People's Republic of China (中华人民共和国工业和信息化部), 'the Planning for Promoting the Development of the SMEs (2016–2020)' (《促进中小企业发展规划(2016—2020年)》), Sect. 4.1, Chap. 4, available at: http://www.miit.gov.cn/n1146295/n1652858/n1652930/n3757016/c5081157/content.html, last visited: 2017/7/22

the operating risk of SMEs and that SMEs might be forced to exit the market.[233] It was also cautioned that some traders might employ people to pretend to be consumers and have them return the goods in order to put their competitors out of business. Although the large enterprises in the market might not be influenced, this could bankrupt SMEs.[234] Indeed, if the legal rules on withdrawal rights are more inclined to protect the consumer, it could force traders to bear higher operating costs. It should be noted that Chinese traders already need to take into account the substantive fairness test in the relation to the control of standard terms. If the withdrawal rights are also designed to give consumers increased protection, some enterprises, especially SMEs, would not survive such a high level of consumer protection. Therefore, in order to promote economic growth and facilitate SMEs, the legislator in China also perceives the need to protect business operators. Therefore, although withdrawal rights are incorporated in the Consumer Protection Law 2013, the rules were designed with a view to not overly disadvantaging traders.

On the other hand, while Chinese economic growth heavily relies on manufacturing and export, its consumer market cannot be considered as a mature one.[235] The reason for adopting a trader-oriented mechanism of withdrawal rights can also be observed from the perspective of restraining consumers. Specifically, when the Consumer Protection Law was amended, it was suggested that the social environment needs to be considered when discussing withdrawal rights. In today's China, both citizens' equality and social integrity need to be improved. Since e-commerce in China is increasing, regulating withdrawal rights could encourage irrational consumer practices and cause 'professional returns' and vicious competition.[236] When evaluating the feasibility, timing of the promulgation, social effect and possible problems after the promulgation of the amendment of the Consumer Protection Law, the Legislative Affairs Commission pointed out that the prevention of the

[233] See 'On Soliciting Advices from the Public in terms of the Draft of the Amendment of Law on the Protection of Consumer Rights and Interests' (《消费者权益保护法修正案草案向社会公众征求意见的情况》), in Civil Law Office of the Legislative Affairs Commission of the Standing Committee of the National People's Congress (全国人大常委会法制工作委员会民法室) 2013, p. 69.

[234] See 'Suggestions of Some E-Commerce Enterprises and Relevant Organisations on Revising the Draft of the Amendment of Law on the Protection of Consumer Rights and Interests' (《部分电子商务企业和有关协会对消费者权益保护法修正案(草案)的修改意见》), in Civil Law Office of the Legislative Affairs Commission of the Standing Committee of the National People's Congress (全国人大常委会法制工作委员会民法室) 2013, p. 131

[235] Many authors have mentioned the immaturity of the Chinese market of consumption when discussing withdrawal rights. See, for example, Bai (白江) 2014, p. 39.

[236] See 'On Soliciting Advices from the Public in terms of the Draft of the Amendment of Law on the Protection of Consumer Rights and Interests' (《消费者权益保护法修正案草案向社会公众征求意见的情况》), in Civil Law Office of the Legislative Affairs Commission of the Standing Committee of the National People's Congress (全国人大常委会法制工作委员会民法室) 2013, p. 69.

abuse of withdrawal rights has to be taken into account.[237] As a result, these concerns also stood in the way of the adoption of a highly consumer-oriented withdrawal rights system.

Based on the foregoing reasons, the Chinese legislator adopts a more trader-oriented mechanism of withdrawal rights to balance the interests of both consumers and traders.

References

(Bai (白江) 2014) 白江[Jiang Bai]:《对消费者撤回权立法模式的反思》[Rethinking the Legislative Mode of the Right of Withdrawal],《法学》2014年第4期[Law Science, 2014(4)], 第33—40页[p. 33–40]。

(Chen (陈玺撼) 2014) 陈玺撼[Xihan Chen]:"网购可以后悔,具体如何落实"[You Can Regret in Online Shopping, But How to Materialize It],《解放日报》2014年3月1日第6版[Jiefang Daily, 2014/3/1, Page 6]。

(Civil Law Office of the Legislative Affairs Commission of the Standing Committee of the National People's Congress (全国人大常委会法制工作委员会民法室) 2013) 全国人大常委会法制工作委员会民法室编[Civil Law Office of the Legislative Affairs Commission of the Standing Committee of the National People's Congress (eds.)]:《消费者权益保护法立法背景与观点全集》[Legislative Backgrounds and Viewpoints on the Law on the Protection of Consumer Rights and Interests],法律出版社2013年版[Law Press, 2013]。

(Camerer, Issacharoff, Loewenstein, O'Donoghue & Rabin 2003) Colin Camerer, Samuel Issacharoff, George Loewenstein, Ted O'Donoghue & Matthew Rabin, 'Regulation for Conservatives: Behavioral Economics and the Case for "Asymmetric Paternalism"', 151 *University of Pennsylvania Law Review* 3, 2003, p. 1211–1254.

(Ge (葛江虬) 2015) 葛江虬[Jiangqiu Ge],"论消费者无理由退货权——以适用《合同法》条文之解释论为中心"[On Consumers' Withdrawal Rights: A Focus on the Interpretation through the Application of the Contract Law],《清华法学》2015年第6期[Tsinghua University Law Journal, 2015(6)],第95—116 页[p. 95–116]。

(Jia (贾东明) 2013) 贾东明主编[Dongming Jia (ed.)]:《中华人民共和国消费者权益保护法解读》[Understanding on the Law of the People's Republic of China on the Protection of Consumer Rights and Interests],中国法制出版社2013年版[China Legal Publishing House, 2013]。

(Jin (金可可) 2014) 金可可[Keke Jin]:"浅谈消费者无理由退货权的适用范围"[On the Applicable Scope of Consumers' Withdrawal Rights],《上海人大》2014年第8期[Shanghai Municipal People's Congress],第12页[p. 12]。

(Li (李适时) 2013) 李适时[Shishi Li]:"关于《中华人民共和国消费者权益保护法修正案(草案)》的说明"[Demonstrations on the Draft of the Amendment of the Law on the Protection of Consumer Rights and Interests],载贾东明主编[Dongming Jia (ed.)]:《中华人民共和国消费者权益保护法解读》[Understanding on the Law of the People's Republic of China on the Protection of Consumer Rights and Interests],中国法制出版社2013年版[China Legal Publishing House, 2013],第331页[p. 331]。

(Loos 2009) Marco Loos, 'Rights of Withdrawal', in Geraint Howells & Reiner Schulze (eds.), *Modernising and Harmonising Consumer Contract Law: With Reference to the Planned*

[237] See 'Report on the Evaluation of the Draft of the Amendment of Law on the Protection of Consumer Rights and Interests' (《消费者权益保护法修正案草案论证评估情况报告》), in Civil Law Office of the Legislative Affairs Commission of the Standing Committee of the National People's Congress (全国人大常委会法制工作委员会民法室) 2013, p. 90.

Horizontal Consumer Contract Directive, Munich: sellier. european law publishers, 2009, p. 237–278.

(Markesinis, Unberath & Johnston 2006) Basil Markesinis, Hannes Unberath & Angus Johnston, *The German Law of Contract: A Comparative Treatise*, 2nd edition, Oxford: Hart Publishing, 2006.

(Micklitz 2005) Hans-W. Micklitz, 'The Concept of Competitive Contract Law', 23 *Penn State International Law Review* 3, p. 549–585.

(Micklitz, Stuyck & Terryn 2010) Hans-W. Micklitz, Jules Stuyck, Evelyne Terryn (eds.), *Cases, Materials and Text on Consumer Law*, Portland: Hart Publishing, 2010.

(Rott 2010) Peter Rott, 'Information Obligations and Withdrawal Rights', in Christian Twigg-Flesner (ed.), *The Cambridge Companion to European Union Private Law*, New York: Cambridge University Press, 2010, p. 187–200.

(Schulte-Nölke 2008) Hans Schulte-Nölke, 'Right of Withdrawal', in Hans Schulte-Nölke, Christian Twigg-Flesner & Martin Ebers (eds.), *EC Consumer Law Compendium: The Consumer Acquis and its transposition in the Member States*, Munich: sellier. european law publishers, 2008, p. 471–481.

(Smits 2014) Jan M. Smits, *Contract Law: A Comparative Introduction*, Cheltenham: Edward Elgar Publishing, 2014.

(Su (苏号朋) 2013) 苏号朋[Haopeng Su]:"《消费者权益保护法》修改中若干重大问题研究"[On Several Significant Issues in the Amendment of the Law on the Protection of Consumer Rights and Interests],《西部法学评论》2013年第2期[Western Law Review, 2013(2)],第1—7页[p. 1–7]。

(Sun (孙良国) 2011) 孙良国[Liangguo Sun]:"消费者何以有撤回权"[Why Consumers Are Entitled Withdrawal Rights],《当代法学》2011年第6期[Contemporary Law Review, 2011(6)],第105—112页[p. 105–112]。

(Sun (孙良国) 2012) 孙良国[Liangguo Sun]:"消费者撤回权中的利益衡量与规则设计"[Interest Balancing and Rule Design in Consumers' Right of Withdrawal],《浙江社会科学》2012年第7期[Zhejiang Social Sciences, 2012(7)],第58—64页[p. 58–64]。

(Sun (孙良国) 2014) 孙良国[Liangguo Sun]:"论新《消费者权益保护法》中的主要规制技术"[On New Regulatory Techniques in the New Consumer Protection Law],《当代法学》2014年第4期[Contemporary Law Review, 2014(4)],第79—85页[p. 79–85]。

(Wang (王洪亮) 2010) 王洪亮[Hongliang Wang]:"消费者撤回权的正当性基础"[On the Legal Bases of Withdrawal Rights],《法学》2010年第12期[Law Science, 2010(12)],第96—107页[p. 96–107]。

(Yang (杨立新) 2014) 杨立新[Lixin Yang]:"非传统销售方式购买商品的消费者反悔权及其适用"[On Consumers' Withdrawal Rights in the Non-traditional-sales Contexts and Their Application],《法学》2014年第2期[Law Science, 2014(2)],第30—38页[p. 30–38]。

(Zhang (张学哲) 2009) 张学哲[Xuezhe Zhang]:"消费者撤回权制度与合同自由——以中国民法法典化为背景"[On Withdrawal Rights and the Freedom of Contract – In the Context of the Codification of Chinese Civil Law],《比较法研究》2009年第6期[Journal of Comparative Law, 2009(6)],第62—73页[p. 62–73]。

(Zhang (张学哲) 2011) 张学哲[Xuezhe Zhang]:"论消费者撤回权的构成与行使要件"[On Requirements and the Exercise of Withdrawal Rights],《华东政法大学学报》2011年第1期[Journal of the East China University of Political Science and Law, 2011(1)],第42—51页[p. 42–51]。

Chapter 6
Conclusions

6.1 Introduction

In recent years, more and more consumer contracts have a transnational character. With the development of new business models in particular via the Internet and the logistics industry, consumers are no longer restricted to deal with domestic traders. Now they have more options. For example, if a Chinese consumer is not satisfied with domestic dairy products, she can simply buy milk powder from the Dutch producer Nutrilon through Nutrilon's official e-shop on the e-commerce marketplace Tmall. From a trader's perspective, it is also much easier nowadays to expand business abroad to earn more profits. They may not only set up a branch, which is a traditional way to sell products to foreign consumers, but also use their web-shop or an e-commerce marketplace without leaving their own countries. No matter which approach these traders use, it raises an incentive to become acquainted with the consumer law of the country in which they sell their products. This is because consumers can always claim rights conferred by their domestic consumer law. The domestic law of different jurisdictions may considerably differ from each other, so traders may not take advantage of their old domestic experience to handle new situations. Without the awareness of the target jurisdiction's legal rules on consumer contracts, a trader may suffer great loss due to non-compliance.

Apart from cross-border traders, legislators are also interested in knowing other jurisdictions' consumer contract law, because the alternative solutions provided by other jurisdictions may offer them inspiration. If different jurisdictions regulate the same issue differently, it may show legislators how other solutions could impact traders and consumers or whether other solutions could achieve the same legislative objective in a better way. Even if rules are similar, the reasons for adopting these rules or the objectives they serve could still be diverse. These different reasons or objectives may help legislators to obtain a more comprehensive picture of the situation they are dealing with.

J. Ge, *A Comparative Analysis of Policing Consumer Contracts in China and the EU*, https://doi.org/10.1007/978-981-13-2989-0_6

When observing different jurisdictions' consumer contract law, one might ask: why are the rules regulated in different countries or regions similar or different? This question is important, because the reasons behind the disparity may explain why a certain set of rules is adopted in a certain region, why they fit in well with the context and whether they could also fit in well with a different legal, economic, political or cultural environment. This is valuable for legislators who are seeking inspiration.

This study aimed to provide businesses, consumers, academics and legislators in two jurisdictions, China and the EU, with an understanding of the counterpart's consumer contract law. It did so by answering five research questions: (1) In Chinese law and EU law, where can we find the rules regulating consumer contracts? (2) Which legislative rules regulate consumer contracts? (3) How are they applied by courts or other authorities? (4) What are the similarities and differences when we compare these rules and the ways of being enforced? (5) What are the possible reasons for these similarities and differences? Among the aforementioned five research questions, the first one requires looking at the sources of law. The remaining research questions require finding the relevant rules; describing the formulation, interpretation and enforcement of these rules; comparing them; summarising the similarities and differences; and providing possible explanations for these comparative findings. Four research hypotheses underlie the research conducted. These hypotheses are based on the presumption that the existence of differences in consumer contract rules can be primarily ascribed to the disparity of markets. These hypotheses were tested on the basis of the comparative outcome, where the relevant rules in Chinese law and EU law were described and compared. This study, however, did not address all issues regarding consumer contracts. It only dealt with one preliminary problem, how to define the concept of a consumer contract, and two substantive topics, unfair terms and withdrawal rights. In order to obtain a more complete picture, relevant rules in German law and English law were studied to show how EU rules are implemented on the national level.

This final chapter presents the main findings of this study. Section 6.2 addresses the aforementioned first research question. The sources of Chinese and EU consumer contract law that were looked at in this study are revisited. Section 6.3 deals with the remaining research questions. A more detailed description of the hypotheses is provided first. Then the formulation, interpretation and enforcement of the relevant consumer contract rules in China and the EU are described and compared. Finally, the comparative findings are used to verify the hypotheses. Some general remarks are made in Sect. 6.4. Section 6.5 discusses the limits of this study and the recommendations for future research.

6.2 Sources of Consumer Contract Law in China and the EU

6.2.1 Introduction

This section aims to answer the first research question: In Chinese law and EU law, where can we find the rules regulating consumer contracts? This question needs to be answered, because there are many rules that have an impact on consumer contracts, and it is necessary to find those that were the focus of this study. Specifically, in China, the content of a consumer contract might be influenced by national statutes, local regulations, industry practices, the parties' individual agreement, etc. In the EU, an important feature that has an impact upon the applicable law is the multilayered governance system. The EU legislator is not the only one who creates rules for the parties of consumer contracts. National legislators also play important roles. However, it was not possible for this study to take a close look at all these rules. This study only focused on the rules which set rights and obligations of the parties to consumer contracts at the Chinese national level and EU level. In this section, the Chinese sources (Sect. 6.2.2) and the EU sources (Sect. 6.2.3) are described, respectively, followed by a comparison (Sect. 6.2.4).

6.2.2 Sources of Consumer Contract Law in China

Many instruments can be seen as sources of consumer contract law in China, such as the Constitution,[1] the statutes enacted by the National People's Congress,[2] the administrative regulations promulgated by the State Council,[3] the judicial interpretations and cases published by the Supreme People's Court[4] and the policies made by the state government and by the Chinese Communist Party.[5] Besides, some scholars suggest that doctrines and customary law are legal sources as well. In China, scholars differ greatly on what are the sources of law in general. The different criteria they use lead some scholars to regard some instruments, such as policies of the state or of the Chinese Communist Party, as legal sources, while they are not in some other scholars' eyes. This study only focused on national legislation and judicial interpretations as relevant sources of consumer contract law. Not too much attention was paid to the Constitution in this study, because it does not provide any specific rule regarding consumer contracts. Furthermore, judges are not allowed to

[1] The Constitution of the People's Republic of China (2004 Amendment) (《中华人民共和国宪法(2004修正)》).

[2] National People's Congress of the People's Republic of China (中华人民共和国全国人民代表大会).

[3] State Council of the People's Republic of China (中华人民共和国国务院).

[4] Supreme People's Court of the People's Republic of China (中华人民共和国最高人民法院).

[5] Communist Party of China (中国共产党).

cite the Constitution, so it is not possible for it to set substantive rights and obligations of the parties to a consumer contract. Based on the same reason, policies, doctrine and customary law were touched upon only when they may help with the interpretation of the relevant legislation.

Only legislation and judicial interpretations were important in this study's context, because these are the instruments which can be cited in judicial decisions. Legislation in China refers to 'laws', 'administrative regulations', 'local regulations', 'autonomous regulations' and 'separate regulations'. This study focused on laws, because they provide the fundamental rules on consumer contracts at the national level. Among all the laws, the Contract Law 1999[6] provides the general rules on policing contracts, most of which are also applicable to consumer contracts, and the Consumer Protection Law 2013[7] offers special rules on consumer protection, so these two laws are the most important ones. Some other laws, such as the Insurance Law 2009,[8] the Product Quality Law 2009[9] and the Food Safety Law 2015,[10] were also touched upon, because some provisions contained in these statutes also regulate traders' obligations. Judicial interpretations are the legal documents published by the Supreme People's Court to interpret laws. They aim to improve legal certainty and ensure that similar cases are treated equally. Since judicial interpretations provide rules which are even more specific than laws and they can also be cited as the basis for a ruling, they are as important as laws themselves. In the areas of consumer contracts, there are two judicial interpretations on the Contract Law 1999.[11]

[6] Contract Law of the People's Republic of China (《中华人民共和国合同法》).

[7] Law of the People's Republic of China on the Protection of Consumer Rights and Interests (2013 Amendment) (《中华人民共和国消费者权益保护法(2013修正)》).

[8] Insurance Law of the People's Republic of China (2009 Revision) (《中华人民共和国保险法(2009修订)》).

[9] Product Quality Law of the People's Republic of China (2009 Amendment) (《中华人民共和国产品质量法(2009修正)》).

[10] Food Safety Law of the People's Republic of China (2015 Revision) (《中华人民共和国食品安全法(2015修订)》).

[11] They are the Interpretation I of the Supreme People's Court of Several Issues concerning the Application of the Contract Law of the People's Republic of China (《最高人民法院关于适用〈中华人民共和国合同法〉若干问题的解释(一)》) (Interpretation No. 19 [1999] of the Supreme People's Court (法释[1999]19号)) and the Interpretation II of the Supreme People's Court of Several Issues concerning the Application of the Contract Law of the People's Republic of China (《最高人民法院关于适用〈中华人民共和国合同法〉若干问题的解释(二)》) (Interpretation No. 5 [2009] of the Supreme People's Court (法释[2009]5号)).

6.2.3 Sources of Consumer Contract Law in the EU

Private law in the EU consists not only of EU legislation but also of national law and conventions adopted by the Member States. Although these rules also have an impact on consumer contracts, this study focused on the EU level.

At the EU level, law is composed of three categories of sources: primary law which refers to the treaties establishing the EU and its predecessors; secondary law which refers to the legal instruments based on the treaties, such as regulations and directives; and supplementary law including the case law of the Court of Justice of the European Union (hereinafter 'CJEU'), international law and the general principles of law. In the field of consumer contracts, directives are important, because they provide most of the substantive rules which may set rights and obligations for EU traders and consumers. Although directives leave it up to the Member States to choose the form and methods of implementation, the results that need to be achieved are the same.

In this study, the focus was mostly put on the Unfair Contract Terms Directive[12] and the Consumer Rights Directive,[13] because they are most relevant to the substantive topics addressed in this study: unfair terms and withdrawal rights. In order to obtain a better understanding of the rules, this study also looked into the directives repealed by the Consumer Rights Directive, which are the Doorstep Selling Directive[14] and the Distance Selling Directive.[15] In addition, some other directives, which regulate some specific types of consumer contracts but do not provide general rules, were mentioned as well, such as the Timeshare Directive,[16] the Package

---

[12] Council Directive 93/13/EEC of 5 April 1993 on unfair terms in consumer contracts [1993] OJ L95/29.

[13] Directive 2011/83/EU of the European Parliament and of the Council of 25 October 2011 on consumer rights, amending Council Directive 93/13/EEC and Directive 1999/44/EC of the European Parliament and of the Council and repealing Council Directive 85/577/EEC and Directive 97/7/EC of the European Parliament and of the Council [2011] OJ L304/64.

[14] Council Directive of 20 December 1985 to protect the consumer in respect of contracts negotiated away from business premises (85/577/EEC) [1985] OJ L 372/31.

[15] Directive 97/7/EC of the European Parliament and of the Council of 20 May 1997 on the protection of consumers in respect of distance contracts [1997] OJ L144/19.

[16] Directive 2008/122/EC of the European Parliament and of the Council of 14 January 2009 on the protection of consumers in respect of certain aspects of timeshare, long-term holiday product, resale and exchange contracts [2009] OJ L33/10.

Travel Directive,[17] the Insurance and Reinsurance Directive[18] and the Consumer Credit Directive.[19]

In addition to the directives, the case law of the CJEU was also looked into, because the CJEU fulfils the function of interpreting the law. If a national court is in doubt about the interpretation or validity of a rule, or whether a national rule or practice is compatible with EU law or not, it can consult the CJEU for clarification.

It should be noticed that the EU consumer contract law rules need to be implemented on the national level. Thus, German law and English law were selected for observing how EU rules are transposed into national law. For German law, this study focused on the German Civil Code[20]; for English law, the emphasis was on the statutory law for implementing the EU directives, such as the Unfair Terms in Consumer Contracts Regulations 1999, the Consumer Rights Act 2015 and the Consumer Contracts (Information, Cancellation and Additional Charges) Regulations 2013.

6.2.4 Comparison Between China and the EU

This section identified the selected legal sources that formed the basis of the analysis in this study.[21] It is pointed out that in China, statutes and their interpretations are the main sources that should be analysed. In the EU, the directives are the core sources. Although in both jurisdictions the courts play an essential role in terms of creating substantive rights and obligations and aim to form uniform interpretation over the whole jurisdiction, the Chinese Supreme People's Court usually aims to supplement the existing law which has been promulgated for a rather long period, while the CJEU, in many cases, acts at an earlier stage to provide clarifications for national legislators and judges based on a specific dispute.

[17] Directive (EU) 2015/2302 of the European Parliament and of the Council of 25 November 2015 on Package Travel and Linked Travel Arrangements, amending Regulation (EC) No 2006/2004 and Directive 2011/83/EU of the European Parliament and of the Council and Repealing Council Directive 90/314/EEC [2015] L326/1.

[18] Directive 2009/138/EC of the European Parliament and of the Council of 25 November 2009 on the taking-up and pursuit of the business of Insurance and Reinsurance (Solvency II) [2009] OJ L 335/1.

[19] Directive 2008/48/EC of the European Parliament and of the Council of 23 April 2008 on credit agreements for consumers and repealing Council Directive 87/102/EEC [2008] OJ L133/66.

[20] Bürgerliches Gesetzbuch (German Civil Code).

[21] For details, see Chap. 2 of this study.

6.3 Rules on Consumer Contracts: A Comparative and Explanatory Analysis

6.3.1 Introduction

This section aims to answer the remaining research questions. The second research question is which legislative rules regulate consumer contracts. It requires identifying the relevant rules and describing how they are formulated. The third research question concerns how these rules are applied by courts or other authorities. It requires studying the interpretation and enforcement of the relevant rules. The fourth research question is what are the similarities and differences if we compare these rules and the ways they are enforced. It requires comparing these rules and summarising the comparative findings for further analysis. The fifth research question is what are the possible reasons for these similarities and differences. This requires an analysis of the comparative findings and providing possible explanations.

In this section, these four research questions are answered by the verification of four research hypotheses. Specifically, this study presumes that differences in the rules on consumer contracts can be attributed to the difference in markets. They are further described in Sect. 6.3.2. Subsequently, these hypotheses are tested on the basis of the comparative findings (Sects. 6.3.3, 6.3.4, 6.3.5 and 6.3.6). At the end of the section, other findings obtained from this study are presented (Sect. 6.3.7).

6.3.2 Four Hypotheses

There are various types of markets in the world. This study suggests that markets can be divided into two main categories: more competitive ones and comparatively regulated ones. The primary difference between these two types of markets is the role of government. It can be observed from three perspectives: the extent to which the government participates in market transactions, which refers to the status of the state sector; the extent to which the government exercises control over the market, which includes the administrative burdens for market entry; and the tools generally used by the government.

The different roles of the government cause consumer law in different markets to be rather dissimilar. This can be observed from the following perspectives. Firstly, a regulated market usually does not have a high demand for consumer law, because administrative approaches are seen as more efficient and effective. Even if there are rules for consumer contracts, clarity and concreteness are not essential for the formulation, since openness or vagueness is conducive for further interpretation and administrative reaction. In contrast, a competitive market usually has a higher level of demand for consumer law, and it requires consumer law to be concrete and unequivocal. Secondly, the government of a regulated market usually has its own interests in the market, so the assessment of misconduct is a more substantive one. In a competitive market, although consumer law has the function of cracking down on the misconduct of traders, it usually does not touch upon the substantive contents of transactions in the market. Thirdly, the focus of consumer law in a regulated market is usually on consumer protection, while the provision of information usually occupies a position of great significance in a competitive market. Fourthly, compared with the emphasis on private enforcement in a competitive market, the enforcement of consumer law in a regulated market, to a large extent, depends on administrative bodies.[22]

For China and the EU, it can be observed that China's domestic market is a relatively regulated one, because in many core industries the state-controlled market participants play an essential role and the government frequently intervenes in the operation of the market. In contrast, the EU internal market is a more competitive one, because the running of the market is mostly left to non-governmental market participants and the barriers to market entry are comparatively fewer. If we apply the foregoing differences of consumer law to China and the EU, the following hypotheses were proposed in Sect. 1.3.5 of Chap. 1 and can now be verified by the comparative findings:

(1) With a more regulated market, China has a lower level of demand for consumer contract law rules, and the level of requirement for the clarity and concreteness of these rules is also lower. On the contrary, the demand for consumer contract law rules and their clarity and concreteness in the EU, which has a more competitive market, should be much higher.
(2) The criteria employed by Chinese consumer law on assessing misconduct are more substantive. In comparison, the assessment of misconduct in the EU context is a more procedural one.
(3) Chinese consumer law puts more emphasis on consumer protection in order to safeguard the property and personal rights and interests of consumers, whereas EU consumer law inclines to provide consumers with sufficient information in order to facilitate consumers to exert their party autonomy.
(4) The public enforcement of consumer law rules is more important in China than in the EU. The latter focuses more on the private enforcement.

6.3.3 *Verification of Hypothesis (1)*

6.3.3.1 Introduction

Hypothesis (1) suggests that 'With a more regulated market, China has a lower level of demand for consumer law rules and the level of requirement for the clarity and concreteness of the rules is also lower. On the contrary, the demand for consumer

[22] For details, see Chap. 1, Sects. 1.3.2, 1.3.3 and 1.3.4 of this study.

law rules and their clarity and concreteness in the EU, which has a more competitive market, should be much higher'.

This hypothesis may be verified by the comparative research on all three topics covered by this study. The rules in China and the EU on the definitions of consumer and trader, on the examples of terms which may be regarded as unfair and on the applicable scope of and exceptions to withdrawal rights, all reveal that Chinese consumer law is vaguer and more abstract, while EU consumer law is more precise and concrete. This is elaborated as follows.

6.3.3.2 The Concept of Consumer Contract

Firstly, hypothesis (1) may be verified since the Chinese definitions of 'consumer' and 'trader' are vaguer and more abstract, while the EU definitions are more concrete and precise.

In China, whether the special protection regulated by the Consumer Protection Law 2013 is applicable depends on two aspects: if the buyer in a transaction is not a 'consumer' or the seller is not a 'business operator' (trader), the Consumer Protection Law 2013 is not applicable. For the definition of consumer, Article 2 of the Consumer Protection Law 2013 provides: 'The rights and interests of consumers in purchasing and using commodities or receiving services for daily consumption shall be under the protection of the present Law'. Apparently, 'daily consumption' is the keyword to assess whether a private actor is a consumer. However, this concept is rather broad. It is not clear whether a legal person can be granted the status of consumer.

The definition of trader is given by Article 3 of the Consumer Protection Law 2013. It states: 'In providing commodities produced or sold by them or services to consumers, business operators shall comply with this Law'. This definition is also rather vague. One may ask whether hospitals and schools are traders, but the law fails to provide a clear answer. In fact, the legislator did not intend to provide a clear answer, because even in the legislative process it was not possible to achieve a common view. The drafters left this issue to future development.

In the EU, most EU directives provide the definitions of 'consumer' and 'trader' at the very beginning. In the past 20 years, the definition of consumer remained almost exactly the same: Article 2 of the Unfair Contract Terms Directive defines a 'consumer' as 'any natural person who, in contracts covered by this Directive, is acting outside his trade, business or profession', while Article 2(1) of the Consumer Rights Directive provides that consumer 'means any natural person who, in contracts covered by this Directive, is acting for purposes which are outside his trade, business, craft or profession'. With respect to the definition of trader, the Consumer Rights Directive combines all the elements identified in the previous directives and put them into one definition: 'trader' means 'any natural person or any legal person, irrespective of whether privately or publicly owned, who is acting, including through any other person acting in his name or on his behalf, for purposes relating to his trade, business, craft or profession in relation to contracts covered by this Directive'.

As for mixed situations, the CJEU held in the *Gruber* case that a natural person cannot be granted the status of consumer unless the link between the contract and the trade or profession of the person concerned was so slight as to be marginal and had only a negligible role. This viewpoint is reiterated by Recital 17 of the Consumer Rights Directive.

To sum up, for the definition of 'consumer', the EU definition clarifies that the consumer must be a natural person and he should act outside his trade, business or profession, while in China it is not clear whether only a natural person can be identified as a consumer. Chinese law simply provides that the consumption should be a daily one. For the definition of 'trader', the EU definition still focuses on 'trade, business and profession', while the Chinese one is much vaguer only mentioning providing commodities and services.[23]

6.3.3.3 Unfair Terms

Secondly, hypothesis (1) may be verified since the Chinese rules for assessing unfair terms are fewer in number and more abstract in formulation. It needs courts or other authorities to interpret and assess on a case-by-case basis. In contrast, the EU rules are more precise and easier for courts to apply.

For assessing unfair terms, the rules in both Chinese law and EU law consist of two parts: formal control, which focuses on the process of negotiation and the conclusion of the contract, and substantive control, which focuses on the definition of rights and obligations in substance. Substantive control includes two steps: the general criteria that can be applied to all circumstances and the lists that provide the examples of unfair terms. For the general criteria, Chinese law and EU law use abstract concepts or principles such as 'fairness' and 'good faith'. For the lists which provide examples of unfair terms, attention is paid to whether the allocation of rights and obligations creates an imbalance which is prohibited by law.

In China, Article 53 of the Contract Law 1999 prohibits two specific types of exemption clauses: a clause shall be null and void if it exempts liability for personal injury to the other party or property damage to the other party as a result of an intentional act or gross negligence. Besides, Articles 39 and 40 of the Contract Law 1999 and Article 26 of the Consumer Protection Law 2013 police the fairness of standard terms. Article 39 provides a general requirement that the user of the standard terms should abide by the principle of fairness when defining the rights and obligations. Nevertheless, Article 39 cannot be used as a sole basis for a ruling, because it does not provide specific criteria for assessing unfair terms. Article 40 of the Contract Law 1999 and Article 26 of the Consumer Protection Law 2013 provide three examples of terms regarded as unfair. On the basis of these two provisions, fairness requires that standard terms do not exempt or reduce the user's liability, increase the liability of the other party or deprive or restrict the other party of their material rights. It is noteworthy that the formulation of these two provisions is rather broad.

[23] For details, see Chap. 3 of this study.

For example, a standard term which exempts or reduces the user's liability is not always unfair. Thus, it needs further interpretation in individual cases.

In the EU, the Unfair Contract Terms Directive provides an annex with an indicative and non-exhaustive list of 17 model unfair terms. The formulation of these terms is rather unequivocal and concrete. For example, a term should not enable the seller or supplier to alter the terms of the contract unilaterally without a valid reason which is specified in the contract (example (j)). In many cases, this example can be simply applied. Generally speaking, the EU examples emphasise whether the term gives the user control over the terms or performance, whether the term determines the duration of the contract, whether the term restrains the counterparty from having the same rights as the user, etc. At the national level, the rules on exemption clauses are even more detailed. Besides, German law provides two types of lists: a black list which enumerates the contract terms that are prohibited without the possibility of evaluation and a grey list which enumerates the contract terms that may be regarded as unfair.

Comparing the examples provided by Chinese law and EU law, it can be observed that the Chinese examples are much fewer in number and much broader in formulation: only two types of exemption clauses regulated by Article 53 of the Contract Law 1999 can be directly applied by the courts, while for assessing standard terms, further interpretation is always necessary. In contrast, EU law provides more detailed and concrete examples for the assessment of fairness.[24]

6.3.3.4 Withdrawal Rights

Hypothesis (1) may be further verified by the comparison of the legal rules regarding withdrawal rights. Since withdrawal rights entitle the consumer to terminate the contractual relationship by his unilateral will, in most jurisdictions, withdrawal rights are only available in limited circumstances (the issue of applicable scope). Meanwhile, not all categories of commodities can be returned without reason (the issue of exceptions). On these two issues, the Chinese rules are vaguer and more open, and the EU rules are more precise and concrete.

In terms of the applicable scope, in China, Article 25 of the Consumer Protection Law 2013 states that 'consumers are granted the rights to return the commodities where business operators sell commodities on the Internet, on television, over telephone, or by mail order, etc.'. It can be observed that only specific patterns of distance contracts are regulated. To apply withdrawal rights to more situations, it is necessary to interpret a Chinese character with the meaning of 'etc.'.

As for exceptions, Article 25 of the Consumer Protection Law 2013 states that withdrawal rights are not applicable to the following commodities: '(1) Custom-made commodities; (2) Fresh, live, or perishable commodities; (3) Audio-visual recordings, computer software, and other digital commodities downloaded online or unpacked by consumers; (4) Newspapers or periodicals delivered'. These categories

[24] For details, see Chap. 4, Sect. 4.5 of this study.

are not the only exceptions. Article 25 also provides a fallback rule that withdrawal rights should not apply to other commodities unsuitable for return by their nature. However, no further interpretation of 'unsuitable for return by nature' is provided on the statutory level. This leaves room for traders to provide their own criteria for restricting consumers' withdrawal rights. To deal with this issue, the law requires that the trader has to inform the consumer that the commodity is nonreturnable at the time of the consumer's purchase and acquire his confirmation.

In EU law, withdrawal rights are regulated in the context of off-premises contracts, distance contracts, timeshare, life insurance, distance selling of financial services and consumer credit. The first two categories are focused on in this study. The Consumer Rights Directive provides the definition of these two concepts. The concept of a distance contract emphasises the lack of 'simultaneous physical presence'. The definition of an off-premises contract points out that, as long as the conclusion of the contract is away from the trader's business premises, the contract will fall into the applicable scope. The factor of simultaneous physical presence of both the trader and consumer is stressed. Besides, even if the contract was concluded inside the trader's business premises, if it is the immediately occurring result of the consumer being personally and individually addressed outside the business premises, it is still an 'off-premises contract'. German law and English law have implemented these EU rules on the national level. Apart from the contents which have already been regulated by the Consumer Rights Directive, national legislators further provide the enumeration of means of distance communication. For example, German law regulates that distance communication includes but is not limited to 'letters, catalogs, telephone calls, copies, e-mails sent via the mobile service messages (SMS) and broadcasting and telemedia'.

In terms of exceptions, Article 16 of the Consumer Rights Directive provides a list of 13 exceptions. German law and English law also have their lists of exceptions. On the basis of these three lists, it can be observed that EU, German and English legislators focus on:

1. The contract is a service contract, and the service has already begun prior to the consumer's withdrawal.
2. The price of the commodity is dependent on fluctuations in the financial market which cannot be controlled by the seller.
3. The commodity is nonreturnable due to the health protection or hygiene reasons.
4. The commodity is not suitable for return because it will be inseparably mixed with other goods according to its nature after delivery.
5. The contract is about urgent repair or maintenance.
6. The contract is concluded through an auction.
7. The contract is about betting or lottery.
8. The contract is relating to immovable property.

Among these categories, some of them are regulated by all three European jurisdictions studied, such as the circumstances where the price cannot be controlled by the seller, and some are only regulated by the Consumer Rights Directive or one of the national jurisdictions, for example, only the EU directive and German law provide that the right of withdrawal is not applicable to commodities which will be mixed with other goods after delivery.

Comparing the rules on applicable scope and exceptions, it can be observed that the EU rules are more precise and concrete. The EU applicable scope of withdrawal rights is determined by not only the abstract concepts, which are 'distance contract' and 'off-premises contract', but also the detailed definition of the concepts, which is also provided by the directive. These detailed and precise definitions offer national legislators a uniform standard to assess whether a type of transaction should fall into the applicable scope. In the Chinese context, neither abstract concepts nor definition is provided. The law only regulates several specific means of distance communication. Nevertheless, even if we only compare the enumerations provided by different jurisdictions, the number of means of distance communication listed in German law and English law is more than in Chinese law. Regarding the exceptions to withdrawal rights, a list of only four items is provided by the Chinese Consumer Protection Law 2013, while the assessment in other circumstances relies on a fall-back rule that other commodities can also be excluded if they are not suitable for return without reason due to their nature and the consumer has agreed with this. On the basis of this rule, e-commerce platforms have expanded the exception list to a great extent. Apart from the four items which are unequivocally written in law, multifarious types of commodities are declared to be nonreturnable in practice. In comparison, the EU legislator regulates a complete list of 13 items. There is no room for traders to add more commodities which they think are not applicable to withdrawal rights.[25]

6.3.4 *Verification of Hypothesis (2)*

6.3.4.1 Introduction

Hypothesis (2) presumes that 'The criteria employed by the Chinese consumer law on assessing misconduct are more substantive. In comparison, the assessment of misconduct in the EU context is a more procedural one'.

This hypothesis may be verified by the comparative research on the Chinese and EU rules regarding the fairness test, which is the central topic in the context of unfair terms control. This is elaborated as follows.

[25] For details, see Chap. 5, Sects. 5.2 and 5.3 of this study.

6.3.4.2 Unfair Terms

The rules on assessing unfair terms can be divided into two categories: formal control and substantive control. The former focuses on whether a real consent exists and how to establish the actual meaning of the term. The latter pays attention to the substantive distribution of rights and obligations.

In China, the distinction between formal control and substantive control is rather clear. Formal control is addressed by Articles 39 and 41 of the Contract Law 1999 and Article 26 of the Consumer Protection Law 2013. Article 39 of the Contract Law 1999 provides that the user of standard terms should draw the other party's attention to the terms whereby it excludes or limits its liability and the user should explain such terms upon the other party's request. If the user fails to comply with this obligation, the term is voidable. Article 26 of the Consumer Protection Law 2013 extends the scope of terms, which need to be brought to the consumer's attention, to 'every term which is related to consumers' vital interests'. Article 41 of the Contract Law 1999 provides the rule of interpretation *contra proferentem*. It states: 'Where there are two or more kinds of interpretation, an interpretation unfavourable to the party supplying the standard terms shall prevail'.

In terms of substantive control, firstly it should be noted that two specific types of exemption clauses are prohibited by Article 53 of the Contract Law 1999. Besides, Article 54 of the Contract Law 1999 provides that contract terms should not be 'obviously unfair'. If a contract term is obviously unfair, a party is entitled to request the people's court or an arbitration institution to modify or avoid the contract. However, what are the requirements for an obviously unfair term are not very clear. There is a heated debate among Chinese scholars on whether a subjective element of bad faith is necessary. From a descriptive perspective, the subjective element is not necessary because there is no room for such interpretation. The sole requirement for an obviously unfair term is the imbalance between the parties' rights and obligations. This assessment is purely a substantive one.

Whereas Articles 53 and 54 of the Contract Law 1999 apply to all contracts, Articles 39 and 40 of the Contract Law 1999 and Article 26 of the Consumer Protection Law 2013 provide the rules for assessing the fairness of standard terms. Article 39 regulates the general requirement that the user of the standard terms should comply with the principle of fairness when defining the rights and obligations. To implement this abstract principle, Article 40 of the Contract Law 1999 and Article 26 of the Consumer Protection Law 2013 provide the list of terms regarded as unfair. According to these provisions, fairness requires that standard terms should not exempt or reduce the user's liability, increase the liability of the other party or deprive or restrict the other party of their material rights. It can be observed that these provisions are also purely relevant to the substance of a contract. They do not touch upon the procedural questions such as how the contract is negotiated or concluded.

In the EU, formal control in the context of the Unfair Contract Terms Directive refers to the requirement of using plain and intelligible language and the rule of interpretation *contra proferentem*. The language requirement is also known as the requirement of transparency. It is regulated under the idea that the consumer should be given an opportunity to examine all the terms. The rule of interpretation *contra proferentem* is regulated following the language requirement. According to Article 5 of the Unfair Contract Terms Directive, 'where there is doubt about the meaning of a term, the interpretation most favourable to the consumer shall prevail'.

In terms of substantive control, the Unfair Contract Terms Directive provides two criteria for determining whether a contract term is unfair: good faith and a significant imbalance in the parties' rights and obligations. These two criteria constitute the EU fairness test. Specifically, 'good faith' implies that the assessment of a contract term is supplemented by an overall evaluation of the different interests involved, and the assessment of good faith includes whether the consumer had an inducement to agree to the terms and whether the goods and services meet the special requirements of the consumer. The second criterion of the fairness test, 'significant imbalance', focuses on the substance of the term. 'Good faith' and 'significant imbalance' are separate elements of a two-stage test, the latter being dominant. This means the first step of the fairness test is to find out whether a significant imbalance exists in the substance of the term, and then it becomes necessary to determine whether the requirement of good faith has been met. From this perspective, the function of good faith is only to supplement the test of significant imbalance. Since 'significant imbalance' puts emphasis on the substance, the requirement of good faith focuses more on the procedural elements. It deals with the defects in the negotiation and conclusion of the contract. This makes the boundary between the fairness test and the requirement of transparency vague. Example (i) of the Annex explicitly provides that a term may be regarded as unfair if it irrevocably binds the consumer to terms with which he had no real opportunity of being acquainted before the conclusion of the contract. This is not relevant to the substance of the term but only relevant to how it was concluded. This is also the reason why German law and English law further regulate that the requirement of transparency should constitute part of the fairness test.

From the foregoing introduction, it can be observed that the Chinese rules on assessing the 'fairness' of the standard terms are more substantive because the focus of the evaluation is always on the allocation of the parties' rights and interests. The examples regulated for the fairness test only concern the parties' substantive rights and obligations. Furthermore, one term can be policed as null and void simply because the comparison of the performance is 'obviously unfair'. In the EU context, the procedural elements play a more important role: when assessing the fairness of a contract term, how the contract was negotiated and concluded and whether it is drafted in plain and intelligible language should be taken into account as well.[26]

[26] For details, see Chap. 4, Sects. 4.4 and 4.5 of this study.

6.3.5 *Verification of Hypothesis (3)*

6.3.5.1 Introduction

Hypothesis (3) supposes that 'Chinese consumer law puts more emphasis on consumer protection and the EU consumer law inclines to provide consumers with sufficient information'.

This hypothesis may not be clearly verified by the comparative findings. Only the rules on the period of withdrawal rights demonstrate that EU law puts emphasis on the trader's information duty, whereas in Chinese law we cannot find a similar duty.

6.3.5.2 Withdrawal Rights

Most jurisdictions regulate that the consumer can only exercise the right of withdrawal in a set 'cooling-off period', so as to balance the interests of the consumer and the trader. Thus, how this period is calculated becomes important.

In China, Article 25 of the Consumer Protection Law 2013 regulates that consumers must have the right to return the commodities within 7 days of receipt without reason. In terms of the calculation of the period, it should start on the second day of the receipt of goods. If the last day of the cooling-off period is a Sunday or an official holiday, the day after the holiday should be taken as the last day. In the Chinese context, when the period starts to run is not relevant to the trader's information duty.

Pursuant to the Consumer Rights Directive, in the EU, the consumer should have a period of 14 days to withdraw from a distance or off-premises contract. In terms of the calculation of the period, it is regulated that the day of the conclusion of the service contract should be the start date of the period, while for a sales contract, the period should begin from the day on which the consumer or a third party other than the carrier and indicated by the consumer acquires physical possession of the goods. It should be noticed that the time when the period starts to run also depends on whether the trader has provided the consumer with the information which is relevant to the right of withdrawal. If not, the withdrawal period should expire 12 months from the end of the initial withdrawal period.

However, under the topics of unfair terms and withdrawal rights, the emphasis on providing consumers with sufficient information can only be found in the rules on the calculation of the cooling-off period. Considering that these rules do not play a central role in the context of withdrawal rights, hypothesis (3) may not be simply verified by the comparison of these rules.[27]

[27] For details, see Chap. 5, Sect. 5.5 of this study.

6.3.6 *Verification of Hypothesis (4)*

6.3.6.1 Introduction

Hypothesis (4) presumes that 'The public enforcement of consumer law rules is more important in China than in the EU. The latter focuses more on the private enforcement'.

To some extent, this hypothesis may be verified by the comparative research on the Chinese, German and English public mechanisms for enforcing the rules on unfair terms. However, it should be noticed that the conclusion may not be applied to all EU Member States. This is elaborated as follows.

6.3.6.2 Unfair Terms

In China, apart from allowing consumers to initiate litigation, some administrative organs and local governments provide alternative mechanisms to deal with unfair terms. The common feature of these approaches is the intervention of public authorities. Among these authorities, the State Administration for Industry and Commerce plays an important role. It provides more detailed criteria for examining the fairness of terms and authorises its local branches to give a warning or impose a fine where unfair terms are used. Some local administrations for industry and commerce have developed their own mechanisms, such as requiring business operators to register their standard terms for further examination or inviting business operators for an 'administrative talk' to persuade them to abandon or modify their standard terms. Apart from the intervention by these public authorities, consumer associations also help individual consumers to strike down unfair terms. They expose unfair terms, by publishing 'comments on unfair terms' on their website, to warn consumers as well as to put pressure on businesses.

In the EU, the Unfair Contract Terms Directive requires Member States to take adequate and effective measures to protect consumers from unfair terms. To meet this requirement, Member States use various methods to help consumers address a public body. In Germany, public bodies simply have supervisory tasks. Consumer organisations play the core role in the context of fighting unfair terms. German law relies on private organisations to seek injunctive relief against the use of unfair standard contract terms. In England, although the Competition and Markets Authority as a public authority takes the responsibility to protect consumers from unfair terms, its primary instrument is to apply for an injunction.

Comparing the enforcement of relevant rules in different jurisdictions, it can be observed that the Chinese administrative bodies play a more significant role than their European counterparts. The administrations for industry and commerce can be the final evaluator of the fairness test and use more powerful approaches to strike down unfair terms, such as the imposition of a fine and 'administrative talks'. In

Germany and England, the final decision needs to be made by the court, and administrative punishment does not play a dominant role in addressing unfair terms.[28]

6.3.7 *Other Findings of This Study*

Apart from the comparative findings which are used to test the hypotheses, this study gained some other findings which were not directly relevant to the hypotheses. This is elaborated as follows.

6.3.7.1 Different Orientations of Withdrawal Rights and the Possible Explanation

When we observe the legal rules on withdrawal rights in China and the EU, it can be first concluded that the Chinese rules are vaguer and more abstract, especially in the context of the applicable scope and exceptions, while the EU rules are more precise and concrete. In addition, there is another conspicuous difference, which is the rules' orientation.

Specifically, compared with their EU counterpart, the Chinese legislator is more inclined to protect traders' interests. This can be observed from the aforementioned first difference: the Chinese fallback rule on exceptions leaves great room for traders to regulate their own list, which may to a large extent restrict consumers' withdrawal rights. Secondly, the period for the consumer to decide whether he wants to cancel the contract is relatively short. Only 7 days is granted. If the trader does not voluntarily provide the consumer with another method to exercise the withdrawal right, such as sending a notification, the consumer has to send back the good within this 7-day period. In the EU, consumers have not only 14 days to decide to withdraw but another 14 days to send back the goods. Thirdly, regarding the amount of reimbursement, EU businesses are still required to bear the cost of transportation, while in China the trader is merely required to reimburse the payment for the goods. Fourthly, there is another difference with regard to the situation that the value of the good has diminished. In the EU, as long as the deduction of value is a consequence of the consumer's normal inspection and examination, he is not responsible for the diminution, and the exercise of the withdrawal right is not influenced. In contrast, the Chinese Consumer Protection Law 2013 regulates that for the commodity to be intact is a requirement of the exercise of withdrawal right. Consequently, the consumer may lose his statutory right if the commodity is damaged. Even if the damage is caused by the consumer's normal inspection, it makes no difference because the definition of 'intact' does not depend on the subjective intention of the consumer. Furthermore, 'intact' is again a concept that needs interpretation. Since there is no elaboration provided by law, the trader can regulate his own criteria which may have

[28] For details, see Chap. 4, Sect. 4.6 of this study.

great impact on the consumer's withdrawal right. To sum up, the Chinese withdrawal rights mechanism is more trader-oriented, while the EU mechanism is more consumer-oriented.

The reason for this difference could be that manufacturing and export constitute a significant part of Chinese economic growth, compared with its EU counterpart. Specifically, small- and medium-sized manufacturing enterprises play a rather important role in Chinese economic growth. Meanwhile, they are the traders who would be most affected by the newly promulgated rules on withdrawal rights. During the lawmaking process, many suggestions were submitted to the legislator mentioning the need to balance the interests between traders and consumers; otherwise these SMEs might not survive the new rules, which could negatively impact on the development of the economy. Thus, in the area of withdrawal rights, we can see that the law is inclined to balance the interest of traders and consumers, although the objective of the institution itself is to provide consumers with a set cooling-off period to rethink their decision. Furthermore, this difference could also be explained from a systematic perspective: if we observe the rules on consumer contracts as a whole, it could be the case that these rules are working alongside each other but are not running separately. Specifically, due to the reason that in the Chinese context the rules on unfair terms are more consumer-oriented, since the consumer can simply avoid the term through assessing the substantive allocation of the rights and interests, the need to provide the consumer with a powerful withdrawal right decreases.[29]

6.3.7.2 Similarities

The above differences are not the only findings of this study. Under the topics of unfair terms and withdrawal rights, Chinese law and EU law also regulate some rules in a similar manner.

With respect to the rules on unfair terms, this study revealed that both Chinese and EU legislators focus on non-individually negotiated terms (standard terms). Special rules have been designed to deal with this type of term. Secondly, for assessing unfair terms, Chinese and EU legislators both regulate two aspects: formal control which focuses on the process of negotiation and conclusion of the contract and substantive control which focuses on the substantive definition of rights and obligations. Rules that are relevant to formal control require the user of standard terms to provide the consumer with an actual opportunity to become acquainted with the terms and agree to them. Besides, judges and administrators are required to adopt the interpretation against the user when the term is ambiguous. Substantive control includes two parts: the general criteria that apply to all circumstances and the lists that provide the examples of unfair terms. For the general criteria, Chinese law and EU law both choose to use abstract concepts or principles such as 'fairness' and 'good faith'. For the lists which provide examples of

[29] For details, see Chap. 5, Sects. 5.3, 5.4, 5.5 and 5.6 of this study.

unfair terms, in both jurisdictions, attention is paid to whether the allocation of rights and obligations creates an imbalance which is prohibited by law. For example, it is concerned with whether the user of the terms is given the control over the terms or performance, whether the statutory rights of the consumer are restrained, etc. Thirdly, the consequences for unfairness are also similar: the unfair term cannot be enforced against the consumer.[30]

In the context of withdrawal rights, it is not difficult to observe that the fundamental structures of the rules in the two jurisdictions are relatively similar: if a rule is regulated in the EU directive, regardless of whether it is about the applicable scope, exceptions, lengths of periods, the specific requirements for exercising or the consequences of withdrawal rights, we can always find a Chinese counterpart. Indeed, this is not surprising, because when the Chinese withdrawal rights system was established, the EU legislation was specifically mentioned as a template to which the Chinese legislators had referred.[31]

6.4 General Remarks

On the basis of the foregoing analysis, a link between markets and their consumer law rules may be observed. The comparative study of Chinese and EU consumer law rules to some extent shows that a more regulated market, which refers to China in this study, tends to have more obscure and abstract rules; when assessing misconduct, these rules focus on the substance; and public authorities play a significant role in enforcing these rules. In a more competitive market, which refers to the EU in this study, consumer law rules are more precise and detailed; procedural elements are emphasised when assessing misconduct; and in some specific markets, for instance, Germany and England, the function of public authorities is limited compared to a regulated market.

Nevertheless, it should be noted that economic conditions do not remain the same for all the time. Apart from differences, some similarities can also be observed. This is not only because the EU law is used as a template for Chinese legislators to obtain inspiration. This phenomenon could be still ascribed to the economic background. China is moving towards a more competitive market. In many industries, mechanisms based on clear and precise legal rules are already considered as more effective approaches to deal with the problems brought by the development. For a competitive market, moderate government intervention is still necessary. In some special circumstances, for example, financial crisis, government intervention could be more required than usual. In these circumstances, the Chinese approaches introduced by this study could also be referred to. This is also in line with one presumption of this study: there is no best consumer law rule. There is only a consumer law rule which optimally fits the specific context.

---

[30] For details, see Chap. 4, Sects. 4.3, 4.4 and 4.5 of this study.

[31] For details, see Chap. 5, Sects. 5.2, 5.3, 5.4, 5.5 and 5.6 of this study.

6.5 Limits of This Study and Recommendations for Future Research

Although this study has provided a description of the legal institutions in terms of policing consumer contracts and tried to explain the reasons behind the differences, it is far from the end of research on this topic. This can be elaborated from the following perspectives.

Firstly, this study mainly describes the law from the doctrinal perspective. More empirical work is required to make the description more accurate. Although this study introduced many court decisions and provided some empirical evidence on the issue of the enforcement of relevant rules, it would be beneficial if the law in action could be more touched upon. The reason is not difficult to observe: sometimes the law in action differs from the law in the books. A rather detailed and well-designed rule could lose its significance simply because the enforcement is weak in practice.

Secondly, more interdisciplinary insights could be incorporated in the area of this research. This study aimed to find a direct link between markets and their consumer law, and this link can to some extent be observed on the basis of the comparative findings. However, this study primarily adopted a traditional legal approach. A closer observation of the markets and their consumer law rules from the economic perspective, no matter theoretical or empirical, would be appropriate.

Thirdly, this study has not touched upon normative questions. After the descriptive and explanatory introduction, no further analysis is given to assess questions such as 'which jurisdiction fits better with the market it serves' or even 'whether the consumer law has accomplished its tasks and how it should be improved'.

Fourthly, the application of the findings of this study is limited at this stage, since only China and the EU are selected to test the hypotheses. It is not clear so far whether the same idea also can be applied to other jurisdictions in the world. Furthermore, even in the context of Chinese law and EU law, limited topics and Member States were touched upon. This calls for further research on the link between markets and their consumer law.

Relevant Documents

Chinese Legislation

General Principles of the Civil Law 1987
中华人民共和国民法通则[General Principles of the Civil Law of the People's Republic of China]

Maritime Law 1992
中华人民共和国海商法[Maritime Law of the People's Republic of China]

Consumer Protection Law 1993
中华人民共和国消费者权益保护法[Law of the People's Republic of China on the Protection of Consumer Rights and Interests]

Contract Law 1999
中华人民共和国合同法[Contract Law of the People's Republic of China]

Judges Law 2001
中华人民共和国法官法(2001修正)[Judges Law of the People's Republic of China (2001 Amendment)]

Law on the Promotion of SMEs 2003
中华人民共和国中小企业促进法[Law of the People's Republic of China on the Promotion of Small and Medium-sized Enterprises]

Constitution 2004
中华人民共和国宪法(2004修正)[Constitution of the People's Republic of China (2004 Amendment)]

Organic Law of the People's Courts 2006
中华人民共和国人民法院组织法(2006修正)[Organic Law of the People's Courts of the People's Republic of China (2006 Amendment)]

J. Ge, *A Comparative Analysis of Policing Consumer Contracts in China and the EU*, https://doi.org/10.1007/978-981-13-2989-0

Property Law 2007
中华人民共和国物权法[Property Law of the People's Republic of China]

Tort Law 2009
中华人民共和国侵权责任法[Tort Law of the People's Republic of China]

Insurance Law 2009
中华人民共和国保险法(2009修订)[Insurance Law of the People's Republic of China (2009 Revision)]

Product Quality Law 2009
中华人民共和国产品质量法(2009修正)[Product Quality Law of the People's Republic of China (2009 Amendment)]

Food Safety Law 2009
中华人民共和国食品安全法[Food Safety Law of the People's Republic of China]

Consumer Protection Law 2013
中华人民共和国消费者权益保护法(2013修正)[Law of the People's Republic of China on the Protection of Consumer Rights and Interests (2013 Amendment)]

Law on Legislation 2015
中华人民共和国立法法(2015修正)[Legislation Law of the People's Republic of China (2015 Amendment)]

Insurance Law 2015
中华人民共和国保险法(2015修正)[Insurance Law of the People's Republic of China (2015 Amendment)]

Food Safety Law 2015
中华人民共和国食品安全法(2015修订)[Food Safety Law of the People's Republic of China (2015 Revision)]

Compulsory Education Law 2015
中华人民共和国义务教育法(2015修正)[Compulsory Education Law of the People's Republic of China (2015Amendment)]

General Provisions of the Civil Law 2017
中华人民共和国民法总则[General Provisions of the Civil Law of the People's Republic of China]

Chinese Judicial Interpretations

Interpretation No. 1 [1988] of the Supreme People's Court
《最高人民法院〈关于雇工合同应当严格执行劳动保护法规问题的批复〉》[The Official Rely of the Supreme People's Court Concerning Issues Employment Contract Shall Strictly Implement the Labor Protection Laws and

Regulations],[1988]民他字第1号[Interpretation No. 1 [1988] of the Supreme People's Court]。

Instrument No. 6 [1988] of the Supreme People's Court
《最高人民法院关于贯彻执行〈中华人民共和国民法通则〉若干问题的意见(试行)》[Opinions of the Supreme People's Court on Several Issues concerning the Implementation of the General Principles of the Civil Law of the People's Republic of China (For Trial Implementation)],法(办)发[1988]6号[Instrument No. 6 [1988] of the Supreme People's Court]。

Interpretation No. 19 [1999] of the Supreme People's Court
《最高人民法院关于适用〈中华人民共和国合同法〉若干问题的解释(一)》[Interpretation I of the Supreme People's Court of Several Issues concerning the Application of the Contract Law of the People's Republic of China],法释[1999]19号[Interpretation No. 19 [1999] of the Supreme People's Court]

Interpretation No. 25 [2001] of the Supreme People's Court
《最高人民法院关于以侵犯姓名权的手段侵犯宪法保护的公民受教育的基本权利是否应承担民事责任的批复》[Official Reply of the Supreme People's Court on Whether the Civil Liabilities Shall Be Borne for the Infringement upon a Citizen's Basic Right of Receiving Education],法释[2001]25号[Interpretation No. 25 [2001] of the Supreme People's Court]。

Instrument No.6 [2008] of the Supreme People's Court
《最高人民法院印发〈最高人民法院关于开展案件质量评估工作的指导意见(试行)〉的通知》[Notice of the Supreme People's Court on Issuing the Guiding Opinion of the Supreme People's Court on Carrying out the Case Quality Evaluation Work (for Trial Implementation)],法发[2008]6号[Instrument No.6 [2008] of the Supreme People's Court]。

Interpretation No. 15 [2008] of the Supreme People's Court
《最高人民法院关于废止2007年底以前发布的有关司法解释(第七批)的决定》[Decision of the Supreme People's Court on Abolishing the Relevant Judicial Interpretations (the Seventh Batch) Promulgated before the End of 2007],法释[2008]15号[Interpretation No. 15 [2008] of the Supreme People's Court]。

Interpretation No. 5 [2009] of the Supreme People's Court
《最高人民法院关于适用〈中华人民共和国合同法〉若干问题的解释(二)》[Interpretation II of the Supreme People's Court of Several Issues concerning the Application of the Contract Law of the People's Republic of China],法释[2009]5号[Interpretation No. 5 [2009] of the Supreme People's Court]

Interpretation No. 14 [2009] of the Supreme People's Court
《最高人民法院关于裁判文书引用法律、法规等规范性法律文件的规定》[Provisions of the Supreme People's Court on Citation of Such Normative Legal Documents as Laws and Regulations in the Judgments],法释[2009]第14号[Interpretation No. 14 [2009] of the Supreme People's Court]。

Instrument No. 51 [2010] of the Supreme People's Court
《最高人民法院印发〈关于案例指导工作的规定〉的通知》[Notice of the Supreme People's Court on Issuing the Provisions on Case Guidance],法发[2010]51号[Instrument No. 51 [2010] of the Supreme People's Court]。

Instrument No. 18 [2014] of the Supreme People's Court
《最高人民法院关于发布第六批指导性案例的通知》[Notice of the Supreme People's Court on Issuing the Sixth Group of Guiding Cases],法[2014]18号[Instrument No. 18 [2014] of the Supreme People's Court]。

Instrument No. 130 [2015] of the Supreme People's Court
《〈最高人民法院关于案例指导工作的规定〉实施细则》[Detailed Rules for the Implementation of the Provisions of the Supreme People's Court on Case Guidance],法[2015]130号[Instrument No. 130 [2015] of the Supreme People's Court]。

Interpretation No. 10 [2016] of the Supreme People's Court
《最高人民法院关于审理消费民事公益诉讼案件适用法律若干问题的解释》[Interpretation of the Supreme People's Court on Several Issues concerning the Application of Law in the Conduct of Consumer Civil Public Interest Litigations],法释[2016]10号[No. 10 [2016] of the Supreme People's Court]。

Letter No. 181 [2017] of the General Office of the Supreme People's Court
最高人民法院办公厅对十二届全国人大五次会议第5990号建议的答复意见[Reply of the General Office of the Supreme People's Court to Suggestion No. 5990 of the Fifth Session of the Twelfth National People's Congress],法办函[2017]181号[Letter No. 181 [2017] of the General Office of the Supreme People's Court]。

Chinese Administrative Regulations, Local Regulations and Department Regulations

Regulation on Direct Selling Administration 2005
《直销管理条例》[Regulations on Direct Selling Administration],国务院令第443号[Order of the State Council, No.443]。

Regulations on the Prohibition of Pyramid Selling 2005
《禁止传销条例》[Regulations on the Prohibition of Pyramid Selling],国务院令第444号[Order of the State Council, No. 444]。

Measures of Guangdong Province for Implementing the Law of the People's Republic of China on the Protection of Consumer Rights and Interests (Amended in 2012)
广东省实施《中华人民共和国消费者权益保护法》办法。

Regulations of Shanghai on the Protection of Consumer Rights and Interests 2015
《上海市消费者权益保护条例》(2015)。

Regulations of Shanghai on Supervision on Contractual Standard Terms
《上海市合同格式条款监督条例》。

Provisions of Zhejiang Province on Administration and Supervision on Contracts
《浙江省合同行为管理监督规定》。

Provisions of the State Administration for Industry and Commerce on Main Functions, Internal Bodies and Staffing
《国务院办公厅关于印发国家工商行政管理总局主要职责内设机构和人员编制规定的通知》[Provisions of the State Administration for Industry and Commerce on Main Functions, Internal Bodies and Staffing],国办发[2008]88号 [No. 81 [2009] of the State Administration for Industry and Commerce]。

Measures 2010
《合同违法行为监督处理办法》[Measures for the Supervision and Handling of Contract-related Violations],国家工商行政管理总局令(第51号)[Order No. 51 of the State Administration for Industry and Commerce]。

Notice on Life Insurance 2011
《关于规范人身保险业务经营有关问题的通知》[Notice on Relevant Matters concerning Regulating Issues of Life Insurance],保监发[2011]第36号[No. 36 [2011] of the China Insurance Regulatory Commission]。

Interim Measures 2017
《网络购买商品七日无理由退货暂行办法》[Interim Measures for the Return without Reasons of Commodities Purchased Online within Seven Days],国家工商行政管理总局令(第90号)[Order No. 90 of the State Administration for Industry and Commerce]。

Introduction for Use of Products of Consumer Interest – General Principles, GB 5296.1 – 1997
《消费品使用说明——总则》,中华人民共和国国家标准:GB 5296.1—1997。

Introduction for Use of Products of Consumer Interest – Part 1: General Principles, GB 5296.1 – 2012
《消费品使用说明——第一部分:总则》,中华人民共和国国家标准:GB 5296.1—2012。

Provisions of Shanghai on Public Hearing of Standard Terms
上海市工商行政管理局关于印发《上海市合同格式条款听证规定》的通知 [Provisions of Shanghai on Public Hearing of Standard Terms],沪工商合(2010)324号[No. 324 [2010] of the Shanghai Administration for Industry and Commerce]。

Notice of the Shanghai Administration for Industry and Commerce on Issuing the 'Discretionary Standards of the Shanghai Administration for Industry and Commerce for Administrative Penalties for Violations of the "Measures for the

Supervision and Handling of Contract-Related Violations" and the "Provisions of Shanghai Municipality on the Supervision of Standard Contract Clauses"'

上海市工商行政管理局关于印发《上海市工商行政管理局关于违反〈合同违法行为监督处理办法〉、〈上海市合同格式条款监督条例〉行政处罚裁量基准》的通知[Notice of the Shanghai Administration for Industry and Commerce on Issuing the 'Discretionary Standards of the Shanghai Administration for Industry and Commerce for Administrative Penalties for Violations of the "Measures for the Supervision and Handling of Contract-Related Violations" and the "Provisions of Shanghai Municipality on the Supervision of Standard Contract Clauses"'],沪工商合(2014)194号[No. 194 [2014] of the Shanghai Administration for Industry and Commerce]。

Chinese Cases

Guiding Case No. 1

指导案例1号[Guiding Case No. 1]:上海中原物业顾问有限公司诉陶德华居间合同纠纷案[Shanghai Zhongyuan Property Consultancy Co Ltd v Dehua Tao],《中华人民共和国最高人民法院公报》2012年第2期[Gazette of the Supreme People's Court of the People's Republic of China, 2012(2)]。

Guiding Case No. 23

指导案例23号[Guiding Case No. 23]:孙银山诉南京欧尚超市有限公司江宁店买卖合同纠纷案[Yinshan Sun v Jiangning Store of Nanjing Auchan Supermarket Co Ltd],江苏省南京市江宁区人民法院(2012)江宁开民初字第646号民事判决书[Civil Judgment (2012) Jiangning-Kai-Min-Chu-Zi No. 646 of the People's Court of Jiangning District of Nanjing City in Jiangsu Province]。

Yuling Qi v Xiaoqi Chen et al.

齐玉苓诉陈晓琪等以侵犯姓名权的手段侵犯宪法保护的公民受教育的基本权利纠纷案[Yuling Qi v Xiaoqi Chen et al.: Dispute over Infringement of a Citizen's Basic Right to receive Education Protected by Constitution Through infringement of Right of Name],《最高人民法院公报》2001年第5期[Gazette of the Supreme People's Court of the People's Republic of China, 2001(5)]。

Guangdong Zhitong Telecom Ltd Co v Fenming Hong

广东直通电讯有限公司诉洪分明电话费纠纷案[Guangdong Zhitong Telecom Ltd Co v Fenming Hong],《中华人民共和国最高人民法院公报》2001年第6期[Gazette of the Supreme People's Court of the People's Republic of China, 2001(6)]。

Yanhui Yan v China Southern Airlines Co Ltd and Minhui Company

杨艳辉诉南方航空公司、民惠公司客运合同纠纷案[Yanhui Yan v China Southern Airlines Co Ltd and Minhui Company],《中华人民共和国最高人民法院公报》2003年第5期[Gazette of the Supreme People's Court of the People's Republic of China, 2003(5)]。

Jun Gu v the Shanghai Branch of Bank of Communication
顾骏诉上海交行储蓄合同纠纷案[Jun Gu v the Shanghai Branch of Bank of Communication],《中华人民共和国最高人民法院公报》2005年第4期[Gazette of the Supreme People's Court of the People's Republic of China, 2005(4)]。

Shuling Yang v China Pingan Property Insurance Ltd Co Tianjin Baodi Branch
杨树岭诉中国平安财产保险股份有限公司天津市宝坻支公司保险合同纠纷案[Shuling Yang v China Pingan Property Insurance Ltd Co Tianjin Baodi Branch],《中华人民共和国最高人民法院公报》2007年第11期[Gazette of the Supreme People's Court of the People's Republic of China, 2007(11)]。

Hai Wang v Yong'an Company
王海诉天津市龙门大厦永安公司买卖纠纷案[Hai Wang v Yong'an Company],天津市河北区人民法院(1997)北民初字第2号民事判决书[Civil Judgment (1997) Bei-Min-Chu-Zi No. 2 of the People's Court of Hebei District of Tianjin City]。

Zhongkai Hu v Tianhua Mansion
胡仲凯诉新昌县天华商厦买卖金利来票夹索赔案[Zhongkai Hu v Tianhua Mansion], 浙江省绍兴市中级人民法院(1998)绍中法经终字第330号民事判决书[Civil Judgment (1998) Shao-Zhong-Fa-Jing-Zhong-Zi No. 330 of the Shaoxing Intermediate People's Court in Zhejiang Province]。

China Real Estate Development Zhengzhou Ltd Co v Minhe Chu
中国房地产开发郑州公司诉楚敏和等撤销商品房买卖合同纠纷案[China Real Estate Development Zhengzhou Ltd Co v Minhe Chu],河南省高级人民法院(2002)豫法民一终字第213号民事判决书[Civil Judgment (2002) Yu-Fa-Min-Yi-Zhong-Zi No. 213 of the Henan High People's Court]。

Nanjing Rixin Fat Chemical Plant Ltd Co v Jingtai Industry(Group) Ltd Co
南京日信油脂化工有限公司诉京泰实业(集团)有限公司等购销合同纠纷案[Nanjing Rixin Fat Chemical Plant Ltd Co v Jingtai Industry(Group) Ltd Co],山东省高级人民法院(2002)鲁民四终字第3号民事判决书[Civil Judgment (2002) Lu-Min-Si-Zhong-Zi No. 3 of the Shandong High People's Court]。

Fujian Sanmu Group Inc v Huangxing Real Estate Development Ltd Co
福建三木集团股份有限公司与福建省泉州市煌星房地产发展有限公司商品房预售合同纠纷案[Fujian Sanmu Group Inc v Huangxing Real Estate Development Ltd Co],中华人民共和国最高人民法院(2004)民一终字第104号民事判决书[Civil Judgment (2004) Min-Yi-Zhong-Zi No. 104 of the Supreme People's Court of the People's Republic of China]。

Guofeng Zheng, Guoqing Chen v Jiangsu People's Hospital
郑雪峰、陈国青诉江苏省人民医院医疗服务合同纠纷二审案[Guofeng Zheng, Guoqing Chen v Jiangsu People's Hospital],《中华人民共和国最高人民法院公报》2004年第8期[Gazette of the Supreme People's Court of the People's Republic of China, 2004(8)]。

Nanjing Zhiheng Technology Ltd Co v Shanghai Qisu Express Ltd Co
南京智恒科技有限公司诉上海奇速快递有限公司货物运输合同案[Nanjing Zhiheng Technology Ltd Co v Shanghai Qisu Express Ltd Co],上海市长宁区人民法院(2006)长民二(商)初字第811号民事判决书[Civil Judgment (2006) Chang-Min-Er-Shang-Chu-Zi No. 811 of the People's Court of Changning District of Shanghai City]。

Chunlin He v Kaiming Luo
何春霖与罗开明等房屋买卖合同纠纷上诉案[Chunlin He v Kaiming Luo],四川省成都市中级人民法院(2008)成民终字第2318号民事判决书[Civil Judgment (2008) Cheng-Min-Zhong-Zi No. 2318 of the Chengdu Intermediate People's Court in Sichuan Province]。

Henan Luozhoujie Highway Ltd Co v Beijing Shizhenger Construction Engineering Ltd Co
河南省漯周界高速公路有限责任公司与北京市市政二建设工程有限责任公司建设工程合同纠纷上诉案[Henan Luozhoujie Highway Ltd Co v Beijing Shizhenger Construction Engineering Ltd Co],河南省高级人民法院(2008)豫法民一终字第19号民事判决书[Civil Judgment (2008) Yu-Fa-Min-Yi-Zhong-Zi No. 19 of the Henan High People's Court]。

Hongjian Lin v China Mobile Fujian Ltd Co Changle Branch
林宏剑诉中国移动通信集团福建有限公司长乐分公司电信服务合同纠纷案[Hongjian Lin v China Mobile Fujian Ltd Co Changle Branch],福州市中级人民法院(2009)榕民终字第147号民事判决书[Civil Judgment (2009) Rong-Min-Zhong-Zi No. 147 of the Fuzhou Intermediate People's Court]。

Beijing Yahao Real Estate Broker Ltd Co v Beijing Badachu Real Estate Development Ltd Co
北京亚豪房地产经纪有限公司第五分公司与北京八大处房地产开发有限公司委托合同纠纷上诉案[Beijing Yahao Real Estate Broker Ltd Co v Beijing Badachu Real Estate Development Ltd Co],北京市高级人民法院(2009)高民终字第514号民事判决书[Civil Judgment (2009) Gao-Min-Zhong-Zi No. 514 of the Beijing High People's Court]。

Meiya Lu v Shaoxing Lutong Express Service Ltd Co
鲁梅雅与绍兴路通快递服务有限公司邮寄服务合同纠纷上诉案[Meiya Lu v Shaoxing Lutong Express Service Ltd Co],浙江省绍兴市中级人民法院(2010)浙绍民终字第833号民事判决书[Civil Judgment (2010) Zhe-Shao-Min-Zhong-Zi No. 833 of the Shaoxing Intermediate People's Court in Zhejiang Province]。

Shanghai Yuantong Express Ltd Co v Shanghai Dinghang Electric Engineering Ltd Co
上海圆通速递有限公司与上海鼎航电气工程有限公司运输合同纠纷上诉案[Shanghai Yuantong Express Ltd Co v Shanghai Dinghang Electric Engineering Ltd Co],上海市第二中级人民法院(2010)沪二中民四(商)终字第815号民事判决书[Civil Judgment (2010) Hu-Er-Zhong-Min-Si-Shang-Zhong-Zi No. 815 of the Shanghai No. 2 Intermediate People's Court]。

Tianan Insurance Ltd Co Rugao Branch v Yuanxing Sun
天安保险股份有限公司如皋支公司与孙元兴等保险合同纠纷上诉案[Tianan Insurance Ltd Co Rugao Branch v Yuanxing Sun],江苏省南通市中级人民法院(2010)通中民终字第1352号民事判决书[Civil Judgment (2010) Tong-Zhong-Min-Zhong-Zi No. 1352 of the Nantong Intermediate People's Court in Jiangsu Province]。

Dou etc v Dong
窦光某等与董某等房屋租赁合同纠纷上诉案[Dou etc v Dong],上海市第一中级人民法院(2010)沪一中民二(民)终字第3349号民事判决书[Civil Judgment (2010) Hu-Yi-Zhong-Min-Er-Min-Zhong-Zi No. 3349 of the Shanghai No. 1 Intermediate People's Court]。

Guangqiang Li v Guangzhou Fanyu Guibo Automatic Device Factory
李广强与广州市番禺桂博自动化设备制造厂劳动争议纠纷上诉案[Guangqiang Li v Guangzhou Fanyu Guibo Automatic Device Factory],广东省广州市中级人民法院(2010)穗中法民一终字第427、428号民事判决书[Civil Judgment (2010) Sui-Zhong-Fa-Min-Yi-Zhong-Zi No. 427, 428 of the Guangzhou Intermediate People's Court in Guangdong Province]。

China Dadi Property Insurance Ltd Co Chongqing Branch v Chongqing Jiafeng Industry Ltd Co
中国大地财产保险股份有限公司重庆分公司与重庆嘉峰实业(集团)有限公司财产损害赔偿纠纷上诉案[China Dadi Property Insurance Ltd Co Chongqing Branch v Chongqing Jiafeng Industry Ltd Co],重庆市第五中级人民法院(2011)渝五中法民终字第367号民事判决书[Civil Judgment (2011) Yu-Wu-Zhong-Fa-Min-Zhong-Zi No. 367 of the Chongqing No. 5 Intermediate People's Court]。

Guo v Shanghai Xinbang Logistic Ltd Co
过某某与上海新邦物流有限公司运输合同纠纷上诉案[Guo v Shanghai Xinbang Logistic Ltd Co],上海市第二中级人民法院(2011)沪二中民四(商)终字第320号民事判决书[Civil Judgment (2011) Hu-Er-Zhong-Min-Si-Shang-Zhong-Zi No. 320 of the Shanghai No. 2 Intermediate People's Court]。

Piyan Zhang v China Life Insurance Ltd Co Linli Branch
张丕岩与中国人寿保险股份有限公司临澧支公司意外伤害保险合同纠纷[Piyan Zhang v China Life Insurance Ltd Co Linli Branch],湖南省临澧县人民法院(2013)临民二初字第101号民事判决书[Civil Judgment (2013) Lin-Min-Er-Chu-Zi No. 101 of the People's Court of Linli County in Hunan Province]。

Jianhua Liu v Hainan Airline Ltd Co
刘建华与海南航空股份有限公司消费服务合同纠纷上诉案[Jianhua Liu v Hainan Airline Ltd Co],海南省海口市中级人民法院(2013)海中法民二终字第300号民事判决书[Civil Judgment (2013) Hai-Zhong-Fa-Min-Er-Zhong-Zi No. 300 of the Haikou Intermediate People's Court in Hainan Province]。

Shanghai Consumers' Association v Guangdong Oppo Mobile Communication Co Ltd
上海市消费者权益保护委员会诉广东欧珀移动通信有限公司侵权责任纠纷案[Shanghai Consumers' Association v Guangdong Oppo Mobile Communication Co Ltd],上海市第一中级人民法院(2015)沪一中民一(民)初字第10号民事裁定书[Civil Ruling [2015] No. 10 of the Shanghai No. 1 Intermediate People's Court]。

Shanghai Consumers' Association v Tianjin Samsung Communication Technology Co Ltd
上海市消费者权益保护委员会诉天津三星通信技术有限公司侵权责任纠纷案[Shanghai Consumers' Association v Tianjin Samsung Communication Technology Co Ltd],上海市第一中级人民法院(2015)沪一中民一(民)初字第10号民事裁定书[Civil Ruling [2015] No. 10 of the Shanghai No. 1 Intermediate People's Court]。

Ming Yan v Beijing Jingdong Century Information Technology Co Ltd
阎明诉北京京东世纪信息技术有限公司买卖合同纠纷案[Ming Yan v Beijing Jingdong Century Information Technology Co Ltd],北京市海淀区人民法院(2015)海民(商)初字第18179号民事判决书[Civil Judgment (2015) Hai-Min-Shang-Chu-Zi No. 18179 of the People's Court of Haidian District of Beijing City]。

Jianhua Cai v Shanghai Oriental TV Shopping Co Ltd
蔡建华诉上海东方电视购物有限公司电视购物合同纠纷案[Jianhua Cai v Shanghai Oriental TV Shopping Co Ltd],上海市杨浦区人民法院(2015)杨民一(民)初字第3098号民事判决书[Civil Judgment (2015) Yang-Min-Yi-Min-Chu-Zi No. 3098 of the People's Court of Yangpu District of Shanghai City]。

Yanshen Liao v Guangzhou Jingdong Trading Co Ltd
廖颜深与广州晶东贸易有限公司等买卖合同纠纷上诉案[Yanshen Liao v Guangzhou Jingdong Trading Co Ltd],广东省广州市中级人民法院(2015)穗中法民二终字第1064号民事判决书[Civil Judgment (2015) Sui-Zhong-Fa-Min-Er-Zhong-Zi No. 1064 of the Guangzhou Intermediate People's Court in Guangdong Province]。

Shaoqing Li v Guosen Securities Co Ltd Shenzhen Middle Shennan Road Securities Sales Department, Guosen Securities Co Ltd
李少清与国信证券股份有限公司深圳深南中路证券营业部、国信证券股份有限公司证券欺诈责任纠纷[Shaoqing Li v Guosen Securities Co Ltd Shenzhen Middle Shennan Road Securities Sales Department, Guosen Securities Co Ltd],深圳市中级人民法院(2016)粤03民终4548号民事判决书[Civil Judgment (2016) Yue-03-Min-Zhong No. 4548 of the Shenzhen Intermediate People's Court]。

Eu Treaties, Regulations and Directives

Treaty of Rome (TEC)
Treaty establishing the European Community

Brussels Convention
Convention on jurisdiction and the enforcement of judgments in civil and commercial matters, Convention adopted on 27 September 1968 [1972] OJ L299.

SEA
Single European Act

TFEU
Treaty on the Functioning of the European Union

Brussels I Regulation
Council Regulation (EC) No 44/2001 of 22 December 2000 on jurisdiction and the recognition and enforcement of judgments in civil and commercial matters.

Regulation on Consumer Protection Cooperation
Regulation (EC) No. 2006/2004 of the European Parliament and of the Council of 27 October 2004on cooperation between national authorities responsible for the enforcement of consumer protection laws (the Regulation on consumer protection cooperation).

Rome I Regulation
Regulation 593/2008 of the European Parliament and of the Council of 17 June 2008 on the law applicable to contractual obligations (Rome I)

Product Liability Directive
Council Directive 85/374/EEC of 25 July 1985 on the approximation of the laws, regulations and administrative provisions of the Member States concerning liability for defective products [1985] OJ L210/29.

Doorstep Selling Directive
Council Directive of 20 December 1985 to protect the consumer in respect of contracts negotiated away from business premises (85/577/EEC) [1985] OJ L 372/31.

Commercial Agents Directive
Council Directive 86/653/EEC of 18 December 1986 on the coordination of the laws of the Member States relating to self-employed commercial agents [1986] OJ L382/17.

Unfair Contract Terms Directive
Council Directive 93/13/EEC of 5 April 1993 on unfair terms in consumer contracts [1993] OJ L95/29.

Distance Selling Directive
Directive 97/7/EC of the European Parliament and of the Council of 20 May 1997 on the protection of consumers in respect of distance contracts [1997] OJ L144/19.

Electronic Signatures Directive
Directive 1999/93/EC of the European Parliament and of the Council of 13 December 1999 on a Community framework for electronic signatures [2000] OJ L13/12.

Consumer Sales Directive
Directive 1999/44/EC of the European Parliament and of the Council of 25 May 1999 on certain aspects of the sale of consumer goods and associated guarantees [1999] OJ L171/12.

Electronic Commerce Directive
Directive 2000/31/EC of the European Parliament and of the Council of 8 June 2000 on certain legal aspects of information society services, in particular electronic commerce, in the Internal Market [2000] OJ L178/1.

General Product Safety Directive
Directive 2001/95/EC of the European Parliament and of the Council of 3 December 2001 on general product safety [2002] OJ L11/4.

Distance Marketing Directive
Directive 2002/65/EC of the European Parliament and of the Council of 23 September 2002 concerning the distance marketing of consumer financial services and amending Council Directive 90/619/EEC and Directives 97/7/EC and 98/27/EC [2002] OJ L271/16.

Unfair Commercial Practices Directive
Directive 2005/29/EC of the European Parliament and of the Council of 11 May 2005 concerning unfair business-to-consumer commercial practices in the internal market and amending Council Directive 84/450/EEC, Directives 97/7/EC, 98/27/EC and 2002/65/EC of the European Parliament and of the Council and Regulation (EC) No 2006/2004 of the European Parliament and of the Council [2005] OJ L149/22.

Misleading and Comparative Advertising Directive
Directive 2006/114/EC of the European Parliament and of the Council of 12 December 2006 concerning misleading and comparative advertising [2006] OJ L376/21.

Consumer Credit Directive
Directive 2008/48/EC of the European Parliament and of the Council of 23 April 2008 on credit agreements for consumers and repealing Council Directive 87/102/EEC [2008] OJ L133/66.

Timeshare Directive
Directive 2008/122/EC of the European Parliament and of the Council of 14 January 2009 on the protection of consumers in respect of certain aspects of timeshare, long-term holiday product, resale and exchange contracts [2009] OJ L33/10.

Injunctions Directive
Directive 2009/22/EC of the European Parliament and of the Council of 23 April 2009 on injunctions for the protection of consumers' interests [2009] OJ L110/30.

Insurance and Reinsurance Directive
Directive 2009/138/EC of the European Parliament and of the Council of 25 November 2009 on the taking-up and pursuit of the business of Insurance and Reinsurance (Solvency II) [2009] OJ L 335/1.

Consumer Rights Directive
Directive 2011/83/EU of the European Parliament and of the Council of 25 October 2011 on consumer rights, amending Council Directive 93/13/EEC and Directive 1999/44/EC of the European Parliament and of the Council and repealing Council Directive 85/577/EEC and Directive 97/7/EC of the European Parliament and of the Council [2011] OJ L304/64.

Package Travel Directive 2015
Directive (EU) 2015/2302 of the European Parliament and of the Council of 25 November 2015 on Package Travel and Linked Travel Arrangements, amending Regulation (EC) No 2006/2004 and Directive 2011/83/EU of the European Parliament and of the Council and Repealing Council Directive 90/314/EEC [2015] OJ L326/1.

Eu Legislative Proposals, Decisions, Opinions, Recommendations, Resolutions and Policy Documents

COM(70) 600 final
Proposal for a Council Regulation embodying a Statute for European Company, COM(70) 600 final.

COM(85) 310 final
Commission of the European Communities, White Paper from the Commission to the European Council, COM(85) 310 final.

COM(90) 322 final
Proposal for a Council Directive on unfair terms in consumer contracts, COM(90) 322 final.

COM(92) 66 final
Amended proposal for a Council Directive on unfair terms in consumer contracts, COM(92) 66 final.

COM(2001) 398 final
Communication from the Commission to the Council and the European Parliament on Contract Law, COM(2001) 398 final.

COM(2004) 651 final
Communication from the Commission to the European Parliament and the Council, European Contract Law and the revision of the acquis: the way forward, COM(2004) 651 final.

COM(2006) 744 final
Green Paper on the Review of the Consumer Acquis (presented by the European Commission), COM(2006) 744 final.

COM(2008) 614 final
Proposal for a Directive of the European Parliament and of the Council on Consumer Rights, COM(2008) 614 final.

COM(2010) 348 final
Green Paper from the Commission of 1 July 2010 on policy options for progress towards a European Contract Law for consumers and businesses, COM(2010) 348 final.

COM(2011) 635 final
Proposal for a Regulation of the European Parliament and of the Council on a Common European Sales Law, COM(2011) 635 final.

COM(2012) 225 final
Communication from the Commission to the European Parliament, the Council, the Economic and Social Committee and the Committee of the Regions, A European Consumer Agenda – Boosting confidence and growth, COM(2012) 225 final.

COM(2012) 0573 final
Communication from the Commission to the European Parliament, the Council, the European Economic and Social Committee and the Committee of the Regions, Single Market Act II Together for new growth, COM(2012) 0573 final.

COM(2014) 910 final
Communication from the Commission to the European Parliament, the Council, the European Economic and Social Committee and the Committee of the Regions, Commission Work Programme 2015: A New Start, COM(2014) 910 final.

COM(2015) 634 final.
Proposal for a Directive of the European Parliament and of the Council on certain aspects concerning contracts for the supply of digital contents, COM(2015) 634 final.

COM(2015) 635 final.
Proposal for a Directive of the European Parliament and of the Council on certain aspects concerning contracts for the online and other distance sales of goods, COM(2015) 635 final.

Council Resolution of 14 April 1975 on a preliminary programme of the European Economic Community for a consumer protection and information policy, [1975] OJ C 92/1.

Commission Recommendation 2003/361/EC
Commission Recommendation of 6 May 2003 concerning the definition of micro, small and medium-sized enterprises (2003/361/EC), [2003] OJ L124/36.

Notification from the Commission concerning Article 4(3) of Directive 2009/22/EC of the European Parliament and of the Council on injunctions for the protection of consumers' interests, which codifies Directive 98/27/EC, concerning the entities qualified to bring an action under Article 2 of this Directive, [2016] OJ C 361/1.

Case Law of the Court of Justice of the European Union

Criminal proceedings against Patrice Di Pinto
Case C-361/89 [1991] ECR I-01206

Travel Vac SL v Manuel José Antelm Sanchi
Case C-423/97 [1999] ECR I-02195

Océano Grupo Editorial SA v Rocío Murciano Quintero (C-240/98) and Salvat Editores SA v José M. Sánchez Alcón Prades (C-241/98), José Luis Copano Badillo (C-242/98), Mohammed Berroane (C-243/98) and Emilio Viñas Feliu (C-244/98)
Joined Cases C-240/98 to C-244/98 [2000] ECR I-04941

Germany v European Parliament & Council
Case C-376/98 [2000] ECR I-08419

Cape Snc v Idealservice Srl
Case C-541/99 [2001] ECR I-09049

Georg Heininger and Helga Heininger v Bayerische Hypo-und Vereinsbank AG
Case C-481/99 [2001] ECR I-09945

Commission of the European Communities v Kingdom of Sweden
Case C-478/99 [2002] ECR I-04147

Cofidis SA v Jean-Louis Fredout
Case C-473/00 [2002] ECR I-10875.

Johann Gruber v Bay Wa AG
Case C-464/01 [2005] ECR I-00439

European Parliament v Council
Case C-436/03 [2006] ECR I-03733

Elisa María Mostaza Claro v Centro Móvil Milenium SL
Case C-168/05 [2006] ECR I-10421.

Annelore Hamilton v Volksbank Filder eG
Case C-412/06 [2008] ECR I-02383

Pannon GSM Zrt. v Erzsébet Sustikné Győrfi
Case C-243/08 [2009] ECLI:EU:C:2009:350

Jana Pereničová, Vladislav Perenič v SOS financ spol. s r. o.
Case C-453/10 [2012] ECLI:EU:C:2012:144

Banco Español de Crédito SA v Joaquín Calderón Camino
Case C-618/10 [2012] ECLI:EU:C:2012:349

Mohamed Aziz v Caixa d'Estalvis de Catalunya, Tarragona i Manresa (Catalunyacaixa)
Case C-415/11 [2013] ECLI:EU:C:2013:164

Dirk Frederik Asbeek Brusse, Katarina de Man Garabito v Jahani BV
C-488/11 [2013] ECLI:EU:C:2013:341

Constructora Principado SA v José Ignacio Menéndez Álvarez
Case C-226/12 [2014] ECLI:EU:C:2014:10

Sabrina Wathelet v Garage Bietheres & Fils SPRL
Case C-149/15 [2016] ECLI:EU:C:2016:840

German Legislation

German Civil Code
Bürgerliches Gesetzbuch

Foreign Investment Law 1969
Auslandsinvestmentgesetz

Act on General Conditions
Gesetz zur Regelung des Rechts der Allgemeinen Geschäftsbedingungen

German Act on Injunctions for the Protection of Consumers' Interests
Gesetz über Unterlassungsklagen bei Verbraucherrechts- und anderen Verstößen

Introductory Act to the Civil Code
Einführungsgesetzes zum Bürgerlichen Gesetzbuche

English Legislation and Cases

UCTA 1977
Unfair Contract Terms Act

Timeshare Act 1992
Timeshare Act

UTCCR 1999
Unfair Terms in Consumer Contracts Regulations

Regulations 2000
The Consumer Protection (Distance Selling) Regulations 2000

Enterprise Act 2002
Enterprise Act

Regulations 2008
The Cancellation of Contracts made in a Consumer's Home or Place of Work etc. Regulations 2008

Consumer Credit Regulations 2010
The Consumer Credit (Agreements) Regulations 2010

Timeshare Regulations 2010
The Timeshare, Holiday Products, Resale and Exchange Contracts Regulations 2010

Regulations 2013
The Consumer Contracts (Information, Cancellation and Additional Charges) Regulations 2013

CRA 2015
Consumer Rights Act 2015

George Mitchell (Chesterhall) Ltd v Finney Lock Seeds Ltd [1983] 2 A.C. 803.

Smith v Eric S Bush [1990] 1 A.C. 831.

Stewart Gill Ltd v Horatio Myer and Co Ltd [1992] Q.B. 600.

Bairstow Eves London Central Ltd v Smith [2004] EWHC 263 (QB).

Parker v The South Eastern Railway Company (1877) 2 C.P.D. 416.

Spurling Ltd v Bradshaw [1956] 1 W.L.R. 461.

Olley v Marlborough Court Ltd [1949] 1 K.B. 532.

L'Estrange v F Graucob Limited [1934] 2 K.B. 394.

Houghton v Trafalgar Insurance Co Ltd [1954] 1 Q.B. 247.

Alisa Craig Fishing Co Ltd v Malvern Fishing Co [1983] 1 All ER 92.

Interfoto Library Ltd v Stiletto Ltd [1988] 2 W.L.R. 615.

Director General of Fair Trading v First National Bank [2002] 1 A.C. 481.

Westminster Building Co Ltd v Beckingham [2004] EWHC 138 (TCC).

Scheme Ltd v West Bromwich Building Society [1998] 1 W.L.R. 896.

Bibliography

(Akerlof 1970) George A. Akerlof, 'The Market for "Lemons": Quality Uncertainty and the Market Mechanism', 84 *The Quarterly Journal of Economics* 3, 1970, p. 488–500.

(Bai (白江) 2014) 白江[Jiang Bai]:《对消费者撤回权立法模式的反思》[Rethinking the Legislative Mode of the Right of Withdrawal],《法学》2014年第4期[Law Science, 2014(4)], 第33—40页[p. 33–40]。

(Bar, Clive, Schulte-Nölke, Beale, Herre, Huet, Storme, Swann, Varul, Veneziano & Zoll 2009) Christian von Bar, Eric Clive, Hans Schulte-Nölke, Hugh Beale, Johnny Herre, Jérôme Huet, Matthias Storme, Stephen Swann, Paul Varul, Anna Veneziano and Fryderyk Zoll (eds.), *Principles, Definitions and Model Rules of European Private Law: Draft Common Frame of Reference (DCFR)*, Outline Edition, prepared by the Study Group on a European Civil Code and the Research Group on EC Private Law (Acquis Group) based in part on a revised version of the Principles of European Contract Law, Munich: sellier. european law publishers, 2009.

(Bar-Gill & Ben-Shahar 2013) Oren Bar-Gill & Omri Ben-Shahar, 'Regulatory Techniques in Consumer Protection: A Critique of European Consumer Contract Law', 50 *Common Market Law Review*, 2013, p. 109–126.

(Beale 1989) Hugh Beale, 'Unfair Contracts in Britain and Europe', 42 *Current Legal Problems* 1, 1989, p. 197–215.

(Beale 1999) Hugh Beale (ed.), *Chitty on Contracts, vol.1*, 28th edition, London: Sweet & Maxwell, 1999.

(Beale, Fauvarque-Cosson, Rutgers, Tallon & Vogenauer 2010) Hugh Beale, Bénédicte Fauvarque-Cosson, Jacobien Rutgers, Denis Tallon & Stefan Vogenauer, *Cases, Materials and Text on Contract Law*, 2nd edition, Portland: Hart Publishing, 2010.

(Beatson, Burrows & Cartwright 2016) Jack Beatson, Andrew Burrow & John Cartwright, *Anson's Law of Contract*, 30th edition, Oxford: Oxford University Press, 2016.

(Van den Bergh 2010) Roger Van den Bergh, 'Private Law in a Globalizing World: Economic Criteria for Choosing the Optimal Regulatory Level in a Multilevel Government System', in Michael Faure & André van der Walt (eds.), *Globalization and Private Law: The Way Forward*, Cheltenham: Edward Elgar Publishing, 2010, p. 57–96.

(Binding 2014) Jörg Binding, 'Consumer Protection Law in the People's Republic of China', *China-EU Law Journal* 3, 2014, p. 223–252.

(Brandner & Ulmer 1991) Hans Erich Brandner & Peter Ulmer, 'The Community Directive on Unfair Terms in Consumer Contracts: Some Critical Remarks on the Proposal Submitted by the EC Commission', 28 *Common Market Law Review*, 1991, p. 647–662.

(Bright 2000) Susan Bright, 'Winning the Battle against Unfair Contract Terms', 20 *Legal Studies* 3, 2000, p. 331–352.

(Bogdan 2013) Michael Bogdan, *Concise Introduction to Comparative Law*, Groningen: Europa Law Publishing, 2013.

J. Ge, *A Comparative Analysis of Policing Consumer Contracts in China and the EU*, https://doi.org/10.1007/978-981-13-2989-0

(Bu 2013) Yuanshi Bu (ed.), *Chinese Civil Law: A Handbook*, München: Beck, 2013.
(Bull 2016) William A. Bull, *Optional Instruments of the European Union: A Definitional, Normative and Explanatory Study*, Cambridge: Intersentia, 2016.
(Cao (曹士兵) 2006) 曹士兵[Shibing Cao]:《最高人民法院裁判、司法解释的法律地位》[The Status of Decisions and Judicial Interpretations of the Supreme People's Court],《中国法学》2006年第3期[China Legal Science, 2006(3)],第175—181页[p. 175–181]。
(Cauffman 2012) Caroline Cauffman, 'The Impact of EU Law on Belgian Consumer Law Terminology', 20 *European Review of Private Law* 5/6, 2012, p. 1325–1351.
(Chen 2003) Zhiwu Chen, 'Capital Markets and Legal Development: The China case', 14 *China Economic Review* 4, 2003, p. 451– 472.
(Chen (陈云良) 2006) 陈云良[Yunliang Chen]:"消费者概念之模糊性分析——模糊法学的一个应用"[The Fuzziness of the Concept of Consumer: an Application of Vague Legal Doctrine],《法学》2006年第10期[Law Science, 2006(10)],第83—88页[p. 83–88]。
(Chen 2010) Lei Chen, 'Private Property with Chinese Characteristics: A Critical Analysis of the Chinese Law on Property of 2007', 18 *European Review of Private Law* 5, 2010, p. 983–1004.
(Chen (陈芸) 2011) 陈芸[Yun Chen]:"快递行业限额赔偿格式条款的效力及损失赔偿"[On Effectiveness and Remedies of Standard Exemption Clauses Provided by Logistic Industries],《人民司法》2011年第24期[People's Judicature, 2011(24)],第71—74页[p. 71–74]。
(Chen (陈玺撼) 2014) 陈玺撼[Xihan Chen]:"网购可以后悔,具体如何落实"[You Can Regret in Online Shopping, But How to Materialize It],《解放日报》2014年3月1日第6版[Jiefang Daily, 2014/3/1, Page 6]。
(Cheng (成慧) 2014) 成慧[Hui Cheng]:"7天无理由退货怎么退"[How to Return the Goods through the Right of Withdrawal],《人民日报》2014年2月21日第4版[People's Daily, 2014/2/21, Page 4]。
(Cherednychenko 2015) Olha O. Cherednychenko, 'Public and Private Enforcement of European Private Law: Perspectives and Challenges', 23 *European Review of Private Law* 4, 2015, p. 481–489.
(Civil Law Office of the Legislative Affairs Commission of the Standing Committee of the National People's Congress (全国人大法制工作委员会民法室) 1999) 全国人大法制工作委员会民法室编著[Civil Law Office of the Legislative Affairs Commission of the Standing Committee of the National People's Congress (eds.)]:《〈中华人民共和国合同法〉立法资料选》[The Selection of Legislative Materials of the Contract Law of the People's Republic of China],法律出版社1999年版[Law Press, 1999]
(Civil Law Office of the Legislative Affairs Commission of the Standing Committee of the National People's Congress (全国人大常委会法制工作委员会民法室) 2013) 全国人大常委会法制工作委员会民法室编[Civil Law Office of the Legislative Affairs Commission of the Standing Committee of the National People's Congress (eds.)]:《消费者权益保护法立法背景与观点全集》[Legislative Backgrounds and Viewpoints on the Law on the Protection of Consumer Rights and Interests],法律出版社2013年版[Law Press, 2013]。
(Camerer, Issacharoff, Loewenstein, O'Donoghue & Rabin 2003) Colin Camerer, Samuel Issacharoff, George Loewenstein, Ted O'Donoghue & Matthew Rabin, 'Regulation for Conservatives: Behavioral Economics and the Case for "Asymmetric Paternalism"', 151 *University of Pennsylvania Law Review* 3, 2003, p. 1211–1254.
(Craig & Búrca 2011) Paul Craig & Gráinne de Búrca, *EU Law: Texts, Cases, and Materials*, 5th edition, Oxford: Oxford University Press, 2011.
(Cseres 2008) KJ Cseres, 'What Has Competition Done for Consumers in Liberalised Markets?', 4 *The Competition Law Review* 2, p. 77–121.
(Cui (崔建远) 2007) 崔建远主编[Jianyuan Cui (ed.)]:《合同法》[Contract Law],法律出版社2007年第4版[Law Press, 2007, 4th Edition]。
(Cui (崔建远) 2008) 崔建远[Jianyuan Cui]:《合同法总论》(上卷)[General Introduction to Contract Law (Vol. 1)],中国人民大学出版社2008年版[China Renmin University Press, 2008]。

(Cui (崔建远) 2014) 崔建远[Jianyuan Cui]:"编纂民法典必须摆正几对关系"[The Need For Straightening Several Relations When Enacting the Chinese Civil Code],《清华法学》2014年第6期[Tsinghua University Law Journal, 2014(6)],第43—53页[p. 43–53]。

(Dimatteo & Chen 2017) Larry A. DiMatteo and Lei Chen (eds.), *Chinese Contract Law: Civil and Common Law Perspectives*, Cambridge: Cambridge University Press, 2017.

(Durovic & Micklitz 2017) Mateja Durovic & Hans-W. Micklitz, *Internationalization of Consumer Law: A Game Changer*, Cham: Springer, 2017.

(Ebers 2010) Martin Ebers, 'ECJ (First Chamber) 6 October 2009, Case C-40/08, Asturcom Telecomunicaciones SL v. Cristina Rodríguez Nogueira – From Océano to Asturcom: Mandatory Consumer Law, Ex Officio Application of European Union Law and Res Judicata', 18 *European Review of Private Law* 4, 2010, p. 823–846.

(Fan (范子军) 2014) 范子军[Zijun Fan]:"'约谈执法'弹不动'霸王条款'"[Administrative Talk Cannot Deal with Unfair Terms],《人民法院报》2014年3月28日第02版[People's Court Daily, 2014/3/28, Page 02]。

(Fang(方流芳) 1996) 方流芳[Liufang Fang]:"中国法学教育观察"[Observations on Chinese Legal Education],《比较法研究》1996年第2期[Journal of Comparative Law, 1996(2)],第116—144页[p. 116–144]。

(Fang (方福建) 2002) 方福建[Fujian Fang]:"论'消费者'概念的法律界定"[On the Legal Definition of Consumer],《当代法学》2002年第2期[Contemporary Law Review, 2002(2)],第136—138页[p. 136–138]。

(Faure & Luth 2011) Michael G. Faure & Hanneke A. Luth, 'Behavioural Economics in Unfair Contract Terms: Cautions and Considerations', 34 *Journal of Consumer Policy* 3, 2011, p. 337–358.

(Fu 2011) Junwei Fu, *Modern European and Chinese Contract Law: A Comparative Study of Party Autonomy*, Alphen aan den Rijn: Kluwer Law International, 2011.

(Gao (高鸿业) 2014) 高鸿业主编[Hongye Gao (ed.)]:《西方经济学(微观部分)》[Western Economics: Microeconomics],中国人民大学出版社2014年第6版[China Renmin University Press, 6th edition]。

(Gao & He (高虹、何忠正) 1998) 高虹、何忠正[Hong Gao, Zhongzheng He]:"《消费者权益保护法》适用于处理医疗纠纷吗"[Is Consumer Protection Law Applicable to Medical Disputes?],《中国卫生事业管理》1998年第12期[Chinese Health Service Management, 1998(12)],第645—649页[p. 645–649]。

(Gavrilovic 2013) Nenad Gavrilovic, 'The Unfair Contract Terms Directive through the Practice of the Court of Justice of the European Union Interpretation or Something More', 9 *European Review of Contract Law* 2, 2013, p. 163–180.

(Ge (葛江虬) 2015) 葛江虬[Jiangqiu Ge],"论消费者无理由退货权——以适用《合同法》条文之解释论为中心"[On Consumers' Withdrawal Rights: A Focus on the Interpretation through the Application of the Contract Law],《清华法学》2015年第6期[Tsinghua University Law Journal, 2015(6)],第95—116 页[p. 95–116]。

(Geng, Yang & Janus 2009) Xiao Geng, Xiuke Yang & Anna Janus, 'State-owned Enterprises in China: Reform dynamics and impacts', in Ross Garnaut, Ligang Song & Wing Thye Woo (eds.), *China's New Place in a World in Crisis: Economic, Geopolitical and Environmental Dimensions*, Canberra: ANU E Press, 2009, p. 155–178.

(Goanta 2016) Catalina Goanta, *Convergence in European Consumer Sales Law: A Comparative and Numerical Approach*, Cambridge: Intersentia, 2016.

(Han (韩世远) 1994) 韩世远[Shiyuan Han]:"免责条款研究"[Research on Exemption Clauses],载梁慧星主编[Huixing Liang (ed.)]:《民商法论丛》(第2卷)[Civil and Commercial Law Review, Vol. 2],法律出版社1994年版[Law Press, 1994]。

(Han (韩世远) 2011a) 韩世远[Shiyuan Han]:"中国合同法与CISG"[Chinese Contract Law and the CISG],《暨南学报》2011年第2期[Journal of Jinan University (Philosophy and Social Sciences), 2011(2)],第7—13页[pp. 7–13]。

(Han (韩世远) 2011b) 韩世远[Shiyuan Han]:《合同法总论》[The Law of Contract],法律出版社2011年第3版[Law Press, 2011, 3rd Edition]。

(Han (韩世远) 2015) 韩世远[Shiyuan Han]:"消费者合同三题:知假买假、惩罚性赔偿与合同终了"[Three Problematic Issues in Consumer Contracts: Buying Fake on Purpose, Punitive Damage and the End of Contract],《法律适用》2015年第10期[Journal of Law Application, 2015(10)],第87—92页[p. 87–92]。

(Han 2017) Shiyuan Han, Consumer Sales Law in People's Republic of China, in Geraint Howells, Christian Twigg-Flesner, Hans-W. Micklitz, Chen Lei (eds.), *Comparative Consumer Sales Law*, Abingdon: Routledge, 2017.

(Hartkamp, Hesselink, Hondius, Mak & Perron 2011) Arthu Hartkamp, Martijn Hesselink, Ewoud Hondius, Chantal Mak, Edgar du Perron (eds.), *Towards a European Civil Code*, Fourth revised and expanded edition, Alphen aan den Rijn: Kluwer Law International, 2011.

(He (何春雷) 2009) 何春雷[Chunlei He]:"患者是不是消费者再引关注"['Whether Patients are Consumers' Attracts Attention Again],《中国消费者报》2009年4月17日第A2版[China Consumer News, 2009/4/17, Page A2]。

(Helleringer & Sibony 2017) Geneviève Helleringer & Anne-Lise Sibony, 'European Consumer Protection Through the Behavioral Lens', 23 *Columbia Journal of European Law* 3, 2017, p. 607–646.

(Hesselink 2011) Martijn W. Hesselink, 'The Concept of Good Faith', in Arthu Hartkamp, Martijn Hesselink, Ewoud Hondius, Chantal Mak, Edgar du Perron (eds.), *Towards a European Civil Code*, Fourth revised and expanded edition, Alphen aan den Rijn: Kluwer Law International, 2011.

(Hondius 1997) Ewoud Hondius, 'Non-implementation of the Directive on Unfair Contract Terms: the Dutch case', 5 *European Review of Private Law* 2, 1997, p. 193–196.

(Howell & Wilson 2016) Nicola Howell & Therese Wilson, 'The Limits of Competition: Reasserting a Role for Consumer Protection and Fair Trading Regulation in Competitive Markets', in Deborah Parry, Annette Nordhausen, Geraint Howells & Christian Twigg-Flesner (eds.), *The Yearbook of Consumer Law 2009*, New York: Routledge, 2016, p. 147–174.

(Hu & Yu (胡云腾、于同志) 2008) 胡云腾、于同志[Yunteng Hu & Tongzhi Yu]:"案例指导制度若干重大疑难争议问题研究"[On Several Significant and Difficult Issues Regarding the Case Guidance System],《法学研究》2008年第6期[Chinese Journal of Law, 2008(6)],第3—24页[p. 3–24]。

(Hu (胡康生) 2013) 胡康生主编[Kangsheng Hu (ed.)]:《中华人民共和国合同法释义》[Paraphrase on the Contract Law of the People's Republic of China],法律出版社2013年第3版[Law Press, 2013, 3rd edition]

(Huang (黄金荣) 2014) 黄金荣[Jinrong Huang]:"'规范性文件'的法律界定及其效力"[The Definition of 'Regulatory Documents' and Its Legal Effects],《法学》2014年第7期[Law Science, 2014(7)],第10-20页[p. 10–20]。

(Jansen & Zimmermann 2010) Nils Jansen & Reinhard Zimmermann, 'A European Civil Code in All But Name: Discussing the Nature and Purposes of the Draft Common Frame of Reference', 69 *The Cambridge Law Journal* 1, 2010, p. 98–112.

(Ji (冀祥德) 2010) 冀祥德[Xiangde Ji]:"对中国法学教育全面反思与展望"[The Difficulties and Prospects of the Current Legal Education in China],《中国政法大学学报》2010年第4期[Journal of CUPL, 2010(4)],第50—58页。

(Jia (贾东明) 2013) 贾东明主编[Dongming Jia (ed.)]:《中华人民共和国消费者权益保护法解读》[Understanding on the Law of the People's Republic of China on the Protection of Consumer Rights and Interests],中国法制出版社2013年版[China Legal Publishing House, 2013]。

(Jiang (强美英) 2010) 强美英[Meiying Jiang]:"关于医疗服务选择适用《消费者权益保护法》的思考"[Thoughts on Applying the Consumer Protection Law to Medical Services],《法律适用》2010年第5期[Journal of Law Application, 2010(5)],第28—32页[p. 28–32]。

(Jin (金可可) 2012) 金可可[Keke Jin]:"民法实证研究方法与民法教义学"[On Empirical Approach of Civil Law and Doctrinal Approcah of Civil Law],《法学研究》2012年第1期[Chinese Journal of Law],第48—50页[p. 48–50]。

(Jin (金可可) 2014) 金可可[Keke Jin]:"浅谈消费者无理由退货权的适用范围"[On the Applicable Scope of Consumers' Withdrawal Rights],《上海人大》2014年第8期[Shanghai Municipal People's Congress],第12页[p. 12]。

(Kawakami 2017) Mark T. Kawakami, *Flawed Strategies to Reducing Labor Exploitations: Reassessing the Role of Private Actors in the Global Supply Chain*, Maastricht: Universitaire Pers Maastricht, 2017.

(Kornet 2006) Nicole Kornet, *Contract Interpretation and Gap Filling: Comparative and Theoretical Perspectives*, Antwerpen: Intersentia, 2006.

(Lando & Beale 2000) Ole Lando & Hugh Beale (eds.), *Principles of European Contract Law, Parts I and II (Combined and Revised)*, prepared by the Commission of European Contract Law, the Hague: Kluwer Law International, 2000.

(Lando, Clive, Prüm & Zimmermann 2003) Ole Lando, Eric Clive, André Prüm & Reinhard Zimmermann (eds.), *Principles of European Contract Law, Part III*, prepared by the Commission on European Contract Law, the Hague: Kluwer Law International, 2003.

(Legal Department of Shanxi Administration for Industry and Commerce (山西省工商局法制处) 2013) 山西省工商局法制处[Legal Department of Shanxi Administration for Industry and Commerce]:"山西省工商系统查办的典型格式条款违法案件"[Typical Cases Regarding Violations by Standard Terms Handled by the Shanxi Administrative System for Industry and Commerce],《中国工商报》2013年7月4日第A03版[China Industry and Commerce News, 2013/7/4, Page A03]。

(Lei (雷磊) 2015) 雷磊[Lei Lei]:"指导性案例法源地位再反思"[Rethinking the Guiding Cases' Status of Legal Sources],《中国法学》2015年第1期[China Legal Science, 2015(1)],第272—290页[p. 272–290]。

(Li & Liu (李龙、刘诚) 2005) 李龙、刘诚[Long Li & Cheng Liu]:"论法律渊源——以法学方法和法律方法为视角"[On Sources of Law – From the Perspective of Legal and Jurisprudence Methodologies],《法律科学》2005年第2期[Law Science (Journal of Northwest University of Politics and Law), 2005(2)],第3-8页[p. 3–8]。

(Li (李华斌) 2008) 李华斌[Huabin Li]:"12点后退房,宾馆多收半天房费合法吗?"[Is It Lawful for Hotels to Charge Half Day's Fee When Check-out After 12.00?],《中国审判》2008年第8期[China Trial, 2008(8)],第94—98页[p. 94–98]。

(Li & Xu (李昌麒、许明月) 2012) 李昌麒、许明月[Changqi Li, Mingyue Xu]:《消费者保护法》[Consumer Protection Law],法律出版社2012年第3版[Law Press, 2012, 3rd edition]。

(Li (李适时) 2013) 李适时[Shishi Li]:"关于《中华人民共和国消费者权益保护法修正案(草案)》的说明"[Demonstrations on the Draft of the Amendment of the Law on the Protection of Consumer Rights and Interests],载贾东明主编[Dongming Jia (ed.)]:《中华人民共和国消费者权益保护法解读》[Understanding on the Law of the People's Republic of China on the Protection of Consumer Rights and Interests],中国法制出版社2013年版[China Legal Publishing House, 2013],第331页[p. 331]。

(Liang (梁慧星) 1993) 梁慧星[Huixing Liang]:《民法学说判例与立法研究》[Research on Civil Law's Theories, Cases and Legislation],中国政法大学出版社1993年版[China University of Political Science and Law Press, 1993]。

(Liang (梁慧星) 1995) 梁慧星[Huixing Liang]:《民法解释学》[Civil Law Hermeneutics],中国政法大学出版社1995年版[China University of Political Science and Law Press, 1995]。

(Liang (梁慧星) 1999) 梁慧星[Huixing Liang]:《民法学说判例与立法研究》(第2册)[Research on Civil Law's Theories, Cases and Legislation (Vol. 2)],国家行政学院出版社1999年版[China National School of Administration Press, 1999]。

(Liang (梁慧星) 2000) 梁慧星[Huixing Liang]:"中国的消费者政策和消费者立法"[On Chinese Consumer Policies and Consumer Legislation],《法学》2000 年第5期[Law Science, 2000(5)],第20—26页[p. 20–26]。

(Liang (梁慧星) 2001) 梁慧星[Huixing Liang]:"消费者权益保护法第49条的解释与适用"[On Interpretation and Application of Article 49 of the Consumer Protection Law],《人民法院报》2001年3月29日第3版[People's Court Daily, 2001/03/29, Page 3]

(Liang (梁慧星) 2002) 梁慧星[Huixing Liang]:《为中国民法典而斗争》[Fighting for China's Civil Code],法律出版社2002年版[Law Press, 2002]。

(Liang (梁慧星) 2007) 梁慧星[Huixing Liang]:《民法总论》[General Introduction to Civil Law],法律出版社2007年第3版[Law Press, 2007, 3rd Edition]。

(Liao (廖凡) 2012) 廖凡[Fan Liao]:"金融消费者的概念和范围: 一个比较法的视角"[Definition and Scope of the Concept of 'Financial Consumer': A Comparative Perspective],《环球法律评论》2012年第4期[Global Law Review, 2012(4)],第95—104页[pp. 95–104]。

(Ling 2002) Bing Ling, *Contract Law in China*, Hongkong: Sweet & Maxwell Asia, 2002.

(Liu (刘凯湘) 2008) 刘凯湘主编[Kaixiang Liu (ed.)]:《民法学》[Civil Law],中国法制出版社2008年第三版[China Legal Publishing House, 2008, 3rd Edition]。

(Liu, Ye & Yuan (刘建丽、叶树光、原磊) 2010) 刘建丽、叶树光、原磊[Jianli Liu, Shuguang Ye & Lei Yuan]:"'三鹿奶粉事件'对乳制品消费及食品安全控制的影响"[Sanlu Milk Powder Scandal's Impact on Dairy Consumption and Food Safety Control],《经济与管理研究》2010年第6期[Research on Economics and Management, 2010(6)],第26-31页[p. 26–31]。

(Liu (柳建龙) 2011) 柳建龙[Jianlong Liu]:"合宪性原则的本相与争论"[The Truth and Discussion of the Principle of Constitutionality],《清华法学》2011年第1期[Tsinghua University Law Journal, 2011(1)],第108—124页[p. 108–124]。

(Loos 2009) Marco Loos, 'Rights of Withdrawal', in Geraint Howells & Reiner Schulze (eds.), *Modernising and Harmonising Consumer Contract Law: With Reference to the Planned Horizontal Consumer Contract Directive*, Munich: sellier. european law publishers, 2009, p. 237–278.

(Loos & Samoy 2014) Marco B.M. Loos & Ilse Samoy, 'The Position of Small and Medium Sized Enterprises in European Contract Law: An Introduction', in Marco B.M. Loos & Ilse Samoy (eds.), *The Position of Small and Medium Sized Enterprises in European Contract Law*, Cambridge: Intersentia, 2014, p. 1–9.

(Luan & Luo (栾春娟、罗海山) 2009) 栾春娟、罗海山[Chunjuan Luan, Haishan Luo]:"中国民事法学研究现状的考察"[A Study on Chinese Civil Law Research],《哈尔滨工业大学学报(社会科学版)》2009年第4期[Journal of Harbin Institute of Technology(Social Sciences Edition), 2009(4)],第67—72页[p. 67–72]。

(Mankiw 2014) N. Gregory Mankiw, *Principles of Microeconomics*, 7th edition, Stamford: Cengage Learning, 2014.

(Markesinis, Unberath & Johnston 2006) Basil Markesinis, Hannes Unberath & Angus Johnston, *The German Law of Contract: A Comparative Treatise*, 2nd edition, Oxford: Hart Publishing, 2006.

(McKendrick 2016) Ewan McKendrick, *Contract Law: Text, Cases, and Materials*, 7th edition, Oxford: Oxford University Press, 2016.

(Meng (孟强龙) 2015) 孟强龙[Qianglong Meng]:"行政约谈法治化研究"[On the Institutionalisation of Administrative Talk],《行政法学研究》2015年第6期[Administrative Law Review, 2016(6)],第99—118页[p. 99–118]。

(Mi (米新丽) 2016) 米新丽[Xinli Mi]:"关于交易习惯的几点思考"[Several Thoughts About Transaction Customs],《政法论丛》2016年第2期[Journal of Political Science and Law, 2016(2)],第31—37页[p. 31–37]。

(Micklitz 2005) Hans-W. Micklitz, 'The Concept of Competitive Contract Law', 23 *Penn State International Law Review* 3, p. 549–585.

(Micklitz, Stuyck & Terryn 2010) Hans-W. Micklitz, Jules Stuyck, Evelyne Terryn (eds.), *Cases, Materials and Text on Consumer Law*, Portland: Hart Publishing, 2010.

(Micklitz & Reich 2014) Hans-W. Micklitz & Norbert Reich, 'The Court and Sleeping Beauty: The Revival of the Unfair Contract Terms Directive (UCTD)', 51 *Common Market Law Review* 3, 2014, p. 771–808.

(Micklitz 2015) Hans-W. Micklitz, 'The Transformation of Enforcement in European Private Law: Preliminary Considerations', 23 *European Review of Private Law* 4, 2015, p. 491–524.

(Müller-Graff 2004) Peter-Christian Müller-Graff, 'EC Directives as a Means of Private Law Unification', in Arthur Hartkamp, Martijn Hesselink, Ewoud Hondius, Carla Joustra, Edgar du Perron & Muriel Veldman (eds.), *Towards a European Civil Code*, 3rd fully revised and expanded edition, Nijmegen: Kluwer Law International, 2004, p. 77–100.

(Nebbia 2007) Paolisa Nebbia, *Unfair Contract Terms in European Law: A Study in Comparative and EC Law*, Portland: Hart Publishing, 2007.

(Nebbia 2010) Paolisa Nebbia, 'Unfair Contract Terms', in Christian Twigg-Flesner (ed.), *The Cambridge Companion to European Union Private Law*, New York: Cambridge University Press, 2010, p. 216–228.

(Novaretti 2010) Simona Novaretti, 'General Clauses and Practice: The Use of the Principle of Good Faith in Decisions of Chinese Courts', 18 *European Review of Private Law* 5, 2010, p. 953–981.

(Peel & Treitel 2007) Edwin Peel & G. H. Treitel, *Treitel on the Law of Contract*, 12th edition, London: Sweet & Maxwell, 2007.

(Poole 2012) Jill Poole, *Textbook on Contract Law*, 11th edition, Oxford: Oxford University Press, 2012.

(Qian (钱玉文) 2006) 钱玉文[Yuwen Qian]:"消费者概念的法律再界定"[The Re-identification of the Concept of Consumer],《法学杂志》2006年第1期[Law Science Magazine, 2006(1)], 第136—138页[p. 136–138]。

(Qu (屈文生) 2012) 屈文生[Wensheng Qu]:"和制汉语法律新名词在近代中国的翻译与传播——以清末民初若干法律辞书收录的词条为例"[The Translation and Dissemination of Modern Chinese Legal Concepts Coined in Japan – The Research on Entries Included by Several Legal Dictionaries in Late Qing and Early Republic],《学术研究》2012年第11期[Academic Research, 2012(11)],第122—129页[p. 122–129]。

(Reisch & Micklitz 2006) Lucia A. Reisch & Hans-W. Micklitz, Consumers and Deregulation of the Electricity Market in Germany, 29 *Journal of Consumer Policy* 4, 2006, p. 399–415.

(Ren (任震宇) 2009) 任震宇[Zhenyu Ren]:"中消协公布2009年消费维权十大举措"[The China Consumers' Association Publishes 10 Major Measures to Safeguard Consumers' Rights 2009],《中国消费者报》2009年3月20日第A02版[China Consumer News, 2009/3/20, Page A02]。

(Research Office of the Legislative Affairs Commission of the Standing Committee of the National People's Congress (全国人大法工委研究室编写组) 1999) 全国人大法工委研究室编写组[Research Office of the Legislative Affairs Commission of the Standing Committee of the National People's Congress]:《中华人民共和国合同法释义》[Paraphrase on Contract Law of People's Republic of China],人民法院出版社1999年版[People's Court Press, 1999]。

(Research Office of the Supreme People's Court (最高人民法院研究室) 2009) 最高人民法院研究室编著[Research Office of the Supreme People's Court (eds.)]:《最高人民法院关于合同法司法解释(二)理解与适用》[Interpretation and Application of the Interpretation II of the Supreme People's Court of Several Issues concerning the Application of the Contract Law of the People's Republic of China],人民法院出版社2009年版[People's Court Press, 2009]。

(Rott 2010) Peter Rott, 'Information Obligations and Withdrawal Rights', in Christian Twigg-Flesner (ed.), *The Cambridge Companion to European Union Private Law*, New York: Cambridge University Press, 2010, p. 187–200.

(Rougier-Brierre 2007) Guillaume Rougier-Brierre, 'The Particularities of Contractual Negotiation and Practice in China', 2007 *International Business Law Journal* 2, 2007, p. 151–170.

(Schmid 2005) Christoph U. Schmid, 'The Instrumentalist Conception of the Acquis Communautaire in Consumer Law and Its Implications on a European Contract Law Code', 1 *European Review of Contract Law* 2, 2005, p. 211–227.

(Schulte-Nölke 2008) Hans Schulte-Nölke, 'Right of Withdrawal', in Hans Schulte-Nölke, Christian Twigg-Flesner & Martin Ebers (eds.), *EC Consumer Law Compendium: The Consumer Acquis and its transposition in the Member States*, Munich: sellier. european law publishers, 2008, p. 471–481.

(Sibony & Helleringer 2015) Anne-Lise Sibony & Geneviève Helleringer, 'EU Consumer Protection and Behavioural Sciences: Revolution or Reform?', in Alberto Alemanno & Anne-

Lise Sibony (eds.), *Nudge and the Law: A European Perspective*, Oxford: Hart Publishing, 2015, p. 209–233.

(Smits 2006a) Jan Smits, 'Comparative Law and Its Influence on National Legal System', in Mathias Reimann & Reinhard Zimmermann (eds.), *The Oxford Handbook of Comparative Law*, Oxford: Oxford University Press, 2006, p. 477–512.

(Smits 2006b) Jan M. Smits, 'European Private Law: A Plea for A Spontaneous Legal Order', in Deirdre M. Curtin, Jan M. Smits, André Klip, Joseph A. McCahery, *European Integration and Law: Four Contributions on the Interplay between European Integration and European and National Law to Celebrate the 25th Anniversary of Maastricht University's Faculty of Law*, Antwerpen: Intersentia, 2006, p. 55–107.

(Smits 2007) Jan Smits, 'Law Making in the European Union: On Globalization and Contract Law in Divergent Legal Cultures', 67 *Louisiana Law Review*, 2007, p. 1181–1203.

(Smits 2012a) Jan Smits, 'Rethinking Methods in European Private Law', in Maurice Adams & Jacco Bomhoff (eds.), *Practice and Theory in Comparative Law*, Cambridge: Cambridge University Press, 2012, p. 170–185.

(Smits 2012b) Jan M. Smits, *The Mind and Method of the Legal Academic*, Cheltenham: Edward Elgar Publishing, 2012.

(Smits 2014a) Jan M. Smits, William Bull, Catalina Goanta & Mark Kawakami (eds.), *European Private Law(2014–2016)*, 4th Edition, Nijmegen: Ars Aequi Libri, 2014.

(Smits 2014b) Jan M. Smits, *Contract Law: A Comparative Introduction*, Cheltenham: Edward Elgar Publishing, 2014.

(Smits 2016) Jan M. Smits, 'New European Union Proposals for Distance Sales and Digital Contents Contracts: Fit for Purpose?', *Zeitschrift für europäisches Privatrecht* 2, 2016, p. 319–324.

(Smits (斯密茨) 2017) 【荷】扬·斯密茨[Jan Smits]:《法学的观念与方法》[The Mind and Method of the Legal Academic],魏磊杰、吴雅婷译[Translated by Leijie Wei and Yating Wu],法律出版社2017年版[Law Press, 2017]。

(Steennot 2015) Reinhard Steennot, 'Public and Private Enforcement in the Field of Unfair Contract Terms', 23 *European Review of Private Law* 4, 2015, p. 589–619.

(Su (苏号朋) 2004) 苏号朋[Haopeng Su]:《格式合同研究》[A Study on Standard Contract Clauses],中国人民大学出版社2004年版[China Renmin University Press, 2004]。

(Su (苏号朋) 2013) 苏号朋[Haopeng Su]:"《消费者权益保护法》修改中若干重大问题研究"[On Several Significant Issues in the Amendment of the Law on the Protection of Consumer Rights and Interests],《西部法学评论》2013年第2期[Western Law Review, 2013(2)],第1—7页[p. 1–7]。

(Suli (苏力) 2003) 苏力[Suli]:"司法解释、公共政策和最高法院——从最高法院有关'奸淫幼女'的司法解释切入"[Judicial Interpretation, Public Policy and the Supreme People's Court – Judicial Interpretation on the Crime of Fornication with an Underage Girl as Cutting Point],《法学》2003年第8期[Law Science, 2003(8)],第3—29页[p. 3–29]。

(Suli (苏力) 2004) 苏力[Suli]:《也许正在发生——转型中国的法学》[Maybe It is Happening – The Transformation of China's Legal Scholarship],法律出版社2004年版[Law Press, 2004]。

(Suli (苏力) 2006) 苏力[Suli]:"当代中国法学教育的挑战与机遇"[The Challenges and Opportunities of Chinese Modern Legal Education],《法学》2006年第2期[Law Science, 2006(2)],第3—21页[p. 3–21]。

(Sun (孙良国) 2011) 孙良国[Liangguo Sun]:"消费者何以有撤回权"[Why Consumers Are Entitled Withdrawal Rights],《当代法学》2011年第6期[Contemporary Law Review, 2011(6)],第105—112页[p. 105–112]。

(Sun (孙良国) 2012) 孙良国[Liangguo Sun]:"消费者撤回权中的利益衡量与规则设计"[Interest Balancing and Rule Design in Consumers' Right of Withdrawal],《浙江社会科学》2012年第7期[Zhejiang Social Sciences, 2012(7)],第58—64页[p. 58–64]。

(Sun (孙良国) 2014) 孙良国[Liangguo Sun]:"论新《消费者权益保护法》中的主要规制技术"[On New Regulatory Techniques in the New Consumer Protection Law],《当代法学》2014年第4期[Contemporary Law Review, 2014(4)],第79—85页[p. 79–85]。

(Swann 1979) Dennis Swann, *Competition and Consumer Protection*, New York: Penguin Books, 1979.

(Tan & Hu (谭振亚、胡建) 2012) 谭振亚、胡建[Zhenya Tan, Jian Hu]:"论格式条款之订入合同及其效力——以中国大陆与德国、中国台湾地区立法之比较为视角"[On Incorporation and Effectiveness of Standard Terms – On the basis of the Comparison among Mainland China, Germany and Chinese Taipei],《云南财经大学学报(社会科学版)》2012年第1期[Yunnan Finance & Economics University Journal of Economics & Management, 2012(1)],第137—142页[p. 137–142]。

(The Research Group of the Comprehensive Department of the National Bureau of Statistics of the People's Republic of China(国家统计局综合司课题组) 2014) 国家统计局综合司课题组[The Research Group of the Comprehensive Department of the National Bureau of Statistics of the People's Republic of China]:"我国经济增长动力及其转换"[The Driving Forces of the Domestic Economic Growth and Its Transformation],《调研世界》2014年第12期[The World of Survey and Research, 2014(12)],第3—8页[p. 3–8]。

(Trentmann 2016) Frank Trentmann, *Empire of Things: How We Became a World of Consumers, Fifteenth Century to the Twenty-First*, New York: HarperCollins, 2016.

(Twigg-Flesner 2010) Christian Twigg-Flesner, 'Introduction: Key Features of European Union Private Law', in Christian Twigg-Flesner (ed.), *The Cambridge Companion to European Union Private Law*, New York: Cambridge University Press, 2010, p. 1–19.

(Twigg-Flesner 2013) Christian Twigg- Flesner, *The Europeanisation of Contract Law: Current Controversies in Law*, 2nd edition, Abingdon: Routledge, 2013.

(Wang & Cui (王利明、崔建远) 2000) 王利明、崔建远[Liming Wang, Jianyuan Cui]:《合同法新论•总则》[New Theory on Contract Law: General Principles],中国政法大学出版社2000年修订版[China University of Political Science and Law Press, 2000, revised Edition]。

(Wang (王利明) 2002a) 王利明[Liming Wang]:"消费者的概念及消费者权益保护法的调整范围"[The Concept of Consumer and the Applicable Scope of the Consumer Protection Law],《政治与法律》2002年第2期[Political Science and Law, 2002(2)],第3—12页[p. 3–12]。

(Wang (王利明) 2002b) 王利明[Liming Wang]:《合同法研究》(第1卷)[Research on Contract Law (Book 1)],中国人民大学出版社2002年版[China Renmin University Press, 2002]。

(Wang et al. (王利明等) 2011a) 王利明等[Liming Wang et al.]:《民法学》[Civil Law],法律出版 社2011年第3版[Law Press, 2011, 3rd Edition]。

(Wang (王利明) 2011b) 王利明[Liming Wang]:《侵权责任法研究(上卷)》[Research on Tort Liability Law (Book 1)],中国人民大学出版社2011年版[China Renmin University Press, 2011]。

(Wang (王利明) 2012) 王利明[Liming Wang]:"我国案例指导制度若干问题研究"[On Chinese Case Guidance System],《法学》2012年第1期[Law Science, 2012(1)],第71—80页[p. 71–80]。

(Wang (王伟玲) 2002) 王伟玲[Weiling Wang]:"金融消费者权益及其保护初探"[On Protection of Rights and Interests of Financial Consumers],《重庆社会科学》2002年第5期[Chongqing Social Sciences, 2002(5)],第34—36页[pp. 34–36]。

(Wang (王晓雁) 2010) 王晓雁[Xiaoyan Wang]:"5到10年内'金融消费者'有望成为法律概念"['Financial Consumer' is Expected to Become a Legal Concept in 5 to 10 Years],《法制日报》2010年3月15日第6版[Legal Daily, 2010/3/15, Page 6]。

(Wang (汪世荣) 2000) 汪世荣[Shirong Wang]:"司法解释批复四题"[Four Problems on the Written Reply of Judicial Interpretation],《法律科学(西北政法学院学报)》2000年第4期[Law Science (Journal of Northwest Institute of Political Science and Law), 2000(4)],第16—28页[p. 16–28]。

(Wang (王洪亮) 2010) 王洪亮[Hongliang Wang]:"消费者撤回权的正当性基础"[On the Legal Bases of Withdrawal Rights],《法学》2010年第12期[Law Science, 2010(12)],第96—107页[p. 96–107]。

(Wang (王书成) 2012) 王书成[Shucheng Wang]:"论合宪性解释方法"[On the Interpretation of Constitutionality],《法学研究》2012年第5期[Chinese Journal of Law, 2012(5)],第50—68页[p. 50–68]。

(Weatherill 2010a) Stephen Weatherill, *Cases and Materials on EU Law*, 9th edition, Oxford: Oxford University Press, 2010.

(Weatherill 2010b) Stephen Weatherill, 'Competence and European Private Law', in Christian Twigg-Flesner (ed.), *The Cambridge Companion to European Union Private Law*, Cambridge: Cambridge University Press, 2010, p. 58–69.

(Weber & Faure 2015) Franziska Weber & Michael Faure, 'The Interplay between Public and Private Enforcement in European Private Law: Law and Economics Perspective', 23 European Review of Private Law 4, 2015, p. 525–549.

(Wilhelmsson 2011) Thomas Wilhelmsson, 'Standard Form Conditions', in Arthu Hartkamp, Martijn Hesselink, Ewoud Hondius, Chantal Mak & Edgar du Perron (eds.), *Towards a European Civil Code*, Fourth revised and expanded edition, Alphen aan den Rijn: Kluwer Law International, 2011, p. 571–586.

(Workers' Daily (工人日报) 2003) 工人日报[Workers' Daily]:"一场诉讼改变了民航规定"[A Lawsuit Change CAAC's Regulation],《工人日报》2003年6月14日[Workers' Daily, 2003/6/14]。

(Wu (吴志勇) 2004) 吴志勇[Zhiyong Wu]:"浅议合同格式条款的行政监管"[On the Administrative Supervision on Contractual Standard Terms],《工商行政管理》2004年第16期[Biweekly of Administration for Industry and Commerce, 2004(16)],第29—30页[p. 29–30]。

(Xu (徐卫东) 2008) 徐卫东[Weidong Xu]:"中国高等法学教育三十年发展回顾"[Thirty Years of Legal Education in Main Land of China],《当代法学》2008年第1期[Contemporary Law Review, 2008(1)],第3—10页[p. 3–10]。

(Yan (晏扬) 2016) 晏扬[Yang Yan]:"'消协起诉水务'堪称公益诉讼样本"[Consumers' Association sue Tap Water Company: A Template for Public Interest Litigation],《检察日报》2016年11月2日第5版[Procuratorate Daily, 2016/11/02, Page 5]。

(Yang (杨琴) 2011) 杨琴[Qin Yang]:"中日经济发展与消费者法制"[Sino-Japanese Economic Development and Consumer Law],《贵州大学学报(社会科学版)》2011年第6期[Journal of Guizhou University(Social Sciences), 2011(6)],第24—31页[p. 24–31]。

(Yang (杨立新) 2013) 杨立新[Lixin Yang]:"消法关于消费者概念的规定应当修改"[The Provision on the Concept of Consumer of the Consumer Protection Law Should be Amended],《中国审判》2013年第6期[China Trial, 2013(6)],第24—25页[p. 24–25]。

(Yang (杨立新) 2014) 杨立新[Lixin Yang]:"非传统销售方式购买商品的消费者反悔权及其适用"[On Consumers' Withdrawal Rights in the Non-traditional-sales Contexts and Their Application],《法学》2014年第2期[Law Science, 2014(2)],第30—38页[p. 30–38]。

(Yang (杨兆敏) 2009) 杨兆敏[Zhaomin Yang]:"只要损害了利益,就要挑战行规权威"[Industry's Authority Should be Challenged When Consumers' Interests Are Infringed],《工人日报》2009年9月9日第5版[Workers' Daily, 2009/09/09, Page 5]。

(Yao (姚敏) 2013) 姚敏[Min Yao]:"6种餐饮霸王条款被北京工商局叫停"[Six Types of Unfair Terms Are Prohibited by the Beijing Administration for Industry and Commerce],《中国消费者报》2013年12月16日第B01版[China Consumer News, 2013/12/16, Page B01]。

(Yin (尹田) 1995) 尹田[Tian Yin]:《法国现代合同法》[French Modern Contract Law],法律出版社1995年版[Law Press, 1995]。

(Yin (尹华广) 2005) 尹华广[Huaguang Yin]:《论我国格式条款立法规制的不足与完善》[Drawbacks of China's Legislative Regulation on Standard Terms and the Improvement],《黑龙江省政法管理干部学院学报》2005年第6期[Journal of Heilongjiang Administrative Cadre Institute of Politics and Law, 2005(6)],第48—50页[p. 48–50]。

(Yu 2017) Xiaowei Yu, *Preventing Medical Malpractice and Compensating Victimised Parents in China: A Law and Economics Perspective*, Cambridge: Intersentia, 2017.

(Zeng (曾锦) 2013) 曾锦[Jin Zeng]:"金融消费者的概念界定"[On the Definition of Financial Consumer],《经济界》2013年第4期[Economic Affairs, 2013(4)],第32—36页[p. 32–36]。
(Zhang & Lu (张红勤、陆立权) 2004), 张红勤、陆立权[Hongqin Zhang, Liquan Lu]:"加强格式条款行政监管,拓展合同执法新领域"[Enhancing Supervision on Standard Terms and Expanding Domains of Executing Contract Regulations],《工商行政管理》2004年第16期[Biweekly of Administration for Industry and Commerce, 2004(16)],第23—25页[p. 23–25]。
(Zhang 2006) Zhang Mo, *Chinese Contract Law*, Leiden: Koninklijke Brill NV, 2006.
(Zhang (张文显) 2007) 张文显主编[Wenxian Zhang (ed.)]:《法理学》[Jurisprudence],高等教育出版社2007年第3版[Higher Education Press, 2007, 3rd Edition]。
(Zhang (张文显) 2011) 张文显主编[Wenxian Zhang (ed.)]:《法理学》[Jurisprudence],高等教育出版社2011年第4版[Higher Education Press, 2011, 4th Edition]。
(Zhang (张学哲) 2009) 张学哲[Xuezhe Zhang]:"消费者撤回权制度与合同自由——以中国民法法典化为背景"[On Withdrawal Rights and the Freedom of Contract – In the Context of the Codification of Chinese Civil Law],《比较法研究》2009年第6期[Journal of Comparative Law, 2009(6)],第62—73页[p. 62–73]。
(Zhang (张学哲) 2011) 张学哲[Xuezhe Zhang]:"论消费者撤回权的构成与行使要件"[On Requirements and the Exercise of Withdrawal Rights],《华东政法大学学报》2011年第1期[Journal of the East China University of Political Science and Law, 2011(1)],第42—51页[p. 42–51]。
(Zhang (张明楷) 2011) 张明楷[Mingkai Zhang]:《刑法学》[Criminal Law],法律出版社2011年第四版[Law Press, 2011, 4th Edition]。
(Zhu (朱景文) 2007) 朱景文[Jingwen Zhu]:《中国法律发展报告》[Report on the Chinese Legal Development],中国人民大学出版社2007年版[[China Renmin University Press, 2007]。
(Zhou (周哲) 2013a) 周哲[Zhe Zhou]:"重庆整治'苹果'不公平合同格式条款——五十一家授权服务商经销商被要求整改"[Chongqing Cleans up Apple Inc's Unfair Standard Terms: 51 Authorised Service Providers and Franchisers are Required to Amend Their Terms],《中国工商报》2013年6月6日第A01版[China Industry and Commerce News, 2013/6/6, Page A01]。
(Zhou (周哲) 2013b) 周哲[Zhe Zhou]:"重庆整治苹果公司不公平条款有进展——三十四家授权服务商经销商承诺先行整改"[Chongqing is Making Progress in Cleaning up Apple Inc's Unfair Terms: 34 Authorized Service Providers and Franchisers Promised to Amend Their Terms],《中国工商报》2013年6月29日第A01版[China Industry and Commerce News, 2013/6/29, Page A01]。
(Zhu 2012) Xiaodong Zhu, 'Understanding China's Growth: Past, Present, and Future', 26 *Journal of Economic Perspectives* 4, 2012, p. 103–124.
(Zhu (朱岩) 2010) 朱岩[Yan Zhu]:"社会基础变迁与民法双重体系建构"[Transformation of the Social Foundation and Construction of a Dual System of Civil Law],《中国社会科学》2010年第6期[Social Sciences in China, 2010(6)],第151—168页[p. 151–168]。
(Zimmermann 2009) Reinhard Zimmermann, 'The Present State of European Private Law', 57 *American Journal of Comparative Law* 2, 2009, p. 479–512.
(Zweigert & Kötz 1998) Konrad Zweigert and Hein Kötz, *An Introduction to Comparative Law*, Translated by Tony Weir, Oxford: Oxford University Press, 1998.

Online Sources

News, Reports, Online Official Documents, Etc

Beijing Evening (北京晚报), 'Jingdong is Complained in terms of their Withdrawal Policies: Goods cannot be Returned Because They have been Opened' (《京东无理由退货遭投诉:拆开不能退》), 7 July 2013, available at: <http://tech.sina.com.cn/i/2013-07-07/17428515418.shtml>.

BMVJ, 'Tasks of the Federal Ministry of Justice and Consumer Protection', available at: <http://www.bmjv.de/EN/Ministry/StructureOrganisation/Tasks/tasks_node.html;jsessionid=D0EC846058CDF5B72045B8BD5C3EF4F8.1_cid324>.

Chris Buckley, 'Insight: China premier-in-waiting schooled in era of dissent', 28 October 2011, available at: <http://www.reuters.com/article/us-china-politcs-li-idUSTRE79R09O20111028>.

Kui Chen, 'How to Apply the Guiding Cases of the Supreme People's Court in Judicial Practice', China Guiding Cases Project, 22 April 2012, available at: <https://cgc.law.stanford.edu/commentaries/3-judge-chen>.

Eva Cheng, 'New Chinese property law protects robber barons', available at: <http://www.green-left.org.au/node/37269>.

China Consumers' Association (中国消费者协会), 'Comments on standard unfair terms' (《点评不公平格式条款》), available at: <http://www.cca.org.cn/web/dcjd/newsList.jsp?id=313>.

China Consumers' Association (中国消费者协会), 'Problem No. 1 of Comments on Apple Maintenance Terms: Old Component which has been Replaced Belongs to Apple Inc. but not Owner, published on 30 August 2012' (《再评苹果维修条款问题1:更换旧件归公司财产不容自处分》(2012年8月30日发布)), available at: <http://www.cca.org.cn/web/ztbd/news-Show.jsp?id=61840&cid=3581>.

China Consumers' Association (中国消费者协会), 'Special Report: Comments on Standard Unfair Terms in Apple Inc's Maintenance Contracts' (《专题报道:点评苹果维修不公平格式条款》), available at: <http://www.cca.org.cn/web/ztbd/newsList.jsp?id=3581>.

China Consumers' Association (中国消费者协会), 'Survey on the Implementation of Withdrawal Rights in E-Commerce Businesses' (《网购企业落实消费者"后悔权"调查报告》), available at: <http://www.cca.org.cn/web/dcjd/newsShow.jsp?id=67498>.

China Industries Information (中国产业信息网), 'Statistics of Alibaba: Dairy Products Sales Volume 2017' (《2017年全年奶粉母婴在阿里系电商上的销售情况统计》), available at: <http://www.chyxx.com/industry/201803/619274.html>.

China.org.cn, 'Contract Law of the People's Republic of China', available at: <http://www.china.org.cn/china/LegislationForm2001-2010/2011-02/12/content_21908031.htm>.

CNNIC (China Internet Network Information Center) (中国互联网络信息中心), 'Research on Chinese Online Shopping Market in 2012' (《2012年中国网络购物市场研究报告》), available at: <http://www.cnnic.cn/hlwfzyj/hlwxzbg/dzswbg/201304/P020130417543965742695.pdf>.

Congressional Executive Commission on China, 'Communique of the 6th Plenum of the 16th CPC Central Committee (Chinese and English Text)', available at: <http://www.cecc.gov/resources/legal-provisions/communique-of-the-sixth-plenum-of-the-16th-cpc-central-committee-chinese>.

Delegation of the European Union to China, 'EU_China T rade (11/03/2015)', available at: <http://eeas.europa.eu/delegations/china/press_corner/all_news/news/2015/20150311_en.htm>

Viktoria Dendrinou, 'Thousands to Protest in Brussels Against China Steel Trading: Calls to stop European Union granting market-economy status to world's largest steel producer', The Wall Street Journal, 14 February 2016, available at: <http://www.wsj.com/articles/thousands-to-protest-in-brussels-against-china-steel-trading-1455450843>.

European Commission, 'The European Single Market', available at: <http://ec.europa.eu/growth/single-market/index_en.htm>.

Gaoshan Legal (高杉Legal), 'A Collection of Judicial Viewpoints in Typical Cases on Transferring Guarantee' (让与担保典型案例裁判观点集成), available at: <http://www.360doc.com/content/15/0616/20/22513831_478599531.shtml>.

Jiangqiu Ge, 'The Comparative Contract Law Course in Maastricht seen through Chinese Eyes', available at: <http://www.mepli.eu/2013/01/the-comparative-contract-law-course-in-maastricht-seen-through-chinese-eyes>.

Institute for Chinese Social Sciences Research and Assessment of Nanjing University (南京大学中国社会科学研究评价中心), 'Public Notification Regarding Journals Selected by the Chinese Social Sciences Citation Index (2017–2018)' (《关于〈中文社会科学引文索引(CSSCI)来源期刊和收录集刊(2017–2018)目录〉的公示》), available at: <http://cssrac.nju.edu.cn/a/xwdt/zxdt/20170116/2805.html>.

jd.com (京东商城), 'After-sale Policies' (《售后政策》), available at: <http://help.jd.com/help/question-97.html>.

jd.com (京东商城), 'After-sale-service Policies' (《售后服务政策》), available at: <http://help.jd.com/help/question-149.html#help1709>.

jd.com (京东商城), 'General Rules on Return or Replace Goods' (《退换货总则》), available at: <http://help.jd.com/help/question-97.html>.

jd.com (京东商城), 'Nutrilon Jingdong Official Flagship Store' (诺优能京东官方旗舰店), available at: <https://mall.jd.com/index-1000002688.html>.

Lawbank, 'Civil Code of the Republic of China', available at: <http://db.lawbank.com.tw/Eng/FLAW/FLAWDAT0201.asp>.

Lingjun Kong (孔令君), 'Wang Hai's These Years as a Professional in Cracking down on counterfeits' (《职业打假人王海的这些年》), Jiefang Daily, 21 March 2012, available at: <http://focus.news.163.com/12/0321/01/7T361DLT00011SM9.html>.

Ministry of Industry and Information Technology of the People's Republic of China (中华人民共和国工业和信息化部), 'the Planning for Promoting the Development of the SMEs (2016–2020)' (《促进中小企业发展规划(2016—2020年)》), available at: http://www.miit.gov.cn/n1146295/n1652858/n1652930/n3757016/c5081157/content.html.

Vivian Ni, 'China Telecom, China Unicom Face Anti-Monopoly Probe', available at: <http://www.china-briefing.com/news/2011/11/10/china-telecom-china-unicom-face-anti-monopoly-probe.html>.

Christian Oliver and Michael Pooler, 'Europe split over whether to grant China market economy status', Financial Times, 28 December 2015, available at: <http://www.ft.com/cms/s/0/2f581276-a716-11e5-955c-1e1d6de94879.html#axzz40QA5bqxe>.

Pkulaw.cn, 'Dispute over Infringement of a Citizen's Basic Right to Receive Education Protected by Constitution Through Infringement of Right of Name', available at: <en.pkulaw.cn>, Reference Code of pkulaw.cn: CLI.C.66950(EN).

QS Top Universities, 'QS World University Rankings by Subject 2012: Law', available at: <www.topuniversities.com/university-rankings/world-university-rankings/2012/subject-rankings/social-science/law?page=1>.

Hans Dietmar Schweisgut, 'A word from the EU Ambassador', available at: <http://eeas.europa.eu/delegations/china/eu_china/40th_anniversary_of_eu_china_relations/index_en.htm>.

Nianci Sheng (盛念慈), 'The Initial Training Class for the Xinjiang Political and Legal Cadres Held by Tsinghua University is Brought to a Successful Close' (《首期清华大学新疆政法干部高级培训班圆满结束》), available at: <http://www.xjkunlun.cn/zzgz/gbgz/gbjy/2007/197331.htm>.

Sina Education (新浪教育), 'The Report of the Employment of the Undergraduate Students of Tsinghua Law School' (《清华大学法学院就业情况》), available at: <http://edu.sina.com.cn/gaokao/2012-06-07/2118341709.shtml>.

Stanford Law School | China Guiding Cases Project, 'Guiding Cases in Perspective', available at: <https://cgc.law.stanford.edu/guiding-cases/>.

S. R., 'Why China's Five-year Plans are so Important', The Economist, 26 October 2015, available at: <http://www.economist.com/blogs/economist-explains/2015/10/economist-explains-24>.

Taobao.com (淘宝网), 'Agreements on Returning Goods in 7 Days without Reasons' (《7天无理由退货服务协议》),available at: <http://service.taobao.com/support/knowledge-1121954.htm#>.

Taobao.com (淘宝网), 'Applicable Scope, Dealing Process and Conditions on "7-days-return"' (《"七天退货"支持范围、处理流程及条件》), available at: <http://service.taobao.com/support/seller/knowledge-5701303.htm>.

The National People's Congress of the People's Republic of China, 'Functions and Powers of the Standing Committee', available at: <http://www.npc.gov.cn/englishnpc/Organisation/2007-11/15/content_1373018.htm>.

The National People's Congress of the People's Republic of China (全国人民代表大会), 'Articles and Interpretations on the Draft of the Amendment of Law on the Protection of Consumer Rights and Interests' (《消费者权益保护法修正案(草案)条文及草案说明》), available at: <http://www.npc.gov.cn/npc/xinwen/lfgz/flca/2013-04/28/content_1793762.htm>.

The National People's Congress of the People's Republic of China (全国人民代表大会), 'Articles of The Second Draft of the Amendment of the Law on the Protection of Consumer Rights and Interests' (《消费者权益保护法修正案(草案二次审议稿)条文》), available at: <http://www.npc.gov.cn/npc/xinwen/lfgz/2013-09/06/content_1805745.htm>.

The National People's Congress of the People's Republic of China (全国人民代表大会), 'Articles and Interpretations on the Draft of the Amendment of Law on the Protection of Consumer Rights and Interests' (《消费者权益保护法修正案(草案)条文及草案说明》), available at: <http://www.npc.gov.cn/npc/xinwen/lfgz/flca/2013-04/28/content_1793762.htm>.

The Supreme People's Court of the People's Republic of China, 'Contract Law of the People's Republic of China', available at: <http://en.chinacourt.org/public/detail.php?id=97>.

The Supreme People's Court of the People's Republic of China (中华人民共和国最高人民法院), 'The Director of the Research Office of the Supreme People's Court Meets the Press on the Case Guidance System (《最高人民法院研究室负责人就案例指导制度答记者问》)', available at: <http://www.court.gov.cn/xwzx/jdjd/sdjd/201112/t20111220_168539.htm>.

Tmall.com (天猫), 'Nutrilon Official Flagship Store' (Nutrilon官方旗舰店), available at: <https://nutrilon.tmall.com/index.htm?spm=a1z10.3-b-s.w5001-14968957225.2.113b1853HImpV4&scene=taobao_shop>.

Verbraucherzentrale Bundesverband, 'Welcome to the VZBV', available at: <http://en.vzbv.de/>.

Verbraucherzentrale Bundesverband, 'What we do', available at: <http://en.vzbv.de/1578.htm>.

Wikipedia, '2008 Chinese milk scandal', available at: <https://en.wikipedia.org/wiki/2008_Chinese_milk_scandal>.

Wikipedia, 'Chinese economic reform', available at: <https://en.wikipedia.org/wiki/Chinese_economic_reform>.

World Trade Organization, 'China's WTO Accession Protocol', 11 December 2001, WT/L/432, available at: <https://www.wto.org/english/thewto_e/acc_e/completeacc_e.htm>.

Jingming Wu (吴景明), 'Regrets in the Amendatory Progress of Consumer Protection Law' (《中国政法大学副教授:消法修改遗憾》), available at: <http://finance.sina.com.cn/review/mspl/20131008/112116920314.shtml>.

www.china.com.cn (中国网), 'Bawang Tiaokuan Still Exist While the New Consumer Protection Law has been Come into Effect for One Month; E-commerce Platforms Set Doorsills for Return' (《新消法满月霸王条款不死,京东等电商设退货门槛》), available at: <http://tech.china.com.cn/internet/jjds/20140415/107532.shtml>.

Gao Xu, 'State-Owned Enterprises in China: How Big Are They', 19 January 2010, available at: <http://blogs.worldbank.org/eastasiapacific/state-owned-enterprises-in-china-how-big-are-they>.

Ji Zhao (赵霁), 'Discussion on the Binding Force of the Guiding Cases' (《指导性案例的拘束力问题探讨》), available at: <http://www.gy.yn.gov.cn/Article/spyf/dlq2010/fglt/201104/22595.html>.

Research Services, Working Papers, Etc

(Cafaggi and Micklitz 2007) Fabrizio Cafaggi and Hans-W. Micklitz, Administrative and Judicial Collective Enforcement of Consumer Law in the US and the European Community (August 2007), *EUI LAW Working Paper* No. 2007/22, available at SSRN: <http://ssrn.com/abstract=1024103>.

(Conway et al. 2010) Paul Conway et al., 'Product Market Regulation and Competition in China', OECD Economics Department Working Papers, No. 823, OECD Publishing, 2010, available at: <https://doi.org/10.1787/5km32vmgmfbx-en>.

(Evaluation and Fitness Check (FC) Roadmap 2015) European Commission, 'Evaluation and Fitness Check (FC) Roadmap', 12/2015, available at: <http://ec.europa.eu/smart-regulation/roadmaps/docs/2016_just_023_evaluation_consumer_law_en.pdf>.

(Koske et al. 2015) Isabell Koske et al., 'The 2013 update of the OECD's database on product market regulation: Policy insights for OECD and non-OECD countries', OECD Economics Department Working Papers, No. 1200, OECD Publishing, 2015, available at: <https://doi.org/10.1787/5js3f5d3n2vl-en>.

(OECD 2007) OECD: 'Roundtable on Economics for Consumer Policy', DSTI/CP(2007)1/FINAL, available at: < www.oecd.org/sti/consumer/39015963.pdf>.

(OECD 2008) OECD: 'The Interface between Competition and Consumer Policies', DAF/COMP/GF(2008)10, available at: <www.oecd.org/regreform/sectors/40898016.pdf>.

(OECD 2017) OECD: 'Use of Behaviour Insights in Consumer Policy', OECD Science, Technology and Innovation Policy Papers, No. 36, 2017, available at: <http://www.oecd-ilibrary.org/docserver/download/c2203c35-en.pdf?expires=1501141760&id=id&accname=guest&checksum=8B3B166E107839DBEEDCCF933EECD022>.

(Puccio 2015) Laura Puccio, 'Granting Market Economy Status to China: An Analysis of WTO Law and of Selected WTO Members' Policy', European Parliamentary Research Service, November 2015 – PE 571.325, available at: <http://www.europarl.europa.eu/RegData/etudes/IDAN/2015/571325/EPRS_IDA%282015%29571325_EN.pdf>.

(Morrison 2015) Wayne Morrison, 'China's Economic Rise: History, Trends, Challenges, and Implications for the United States', Congressional Research Service, 7-5700, www.crs.gov, RL 33534, 21 October 2015, available at: <https://www.fas.org/sgp/crs/row/RL33534.pdf>.

(Schulte-Nölke 2007) Hans Schulte-Nölke, Christian Twigg-Flesner & Martin Ebers (eds.), *EC Consumer Law Compendium – Comparative Analysis*, Prepared for the European Commission under Service Contract No. 17.020100/04/389299: 'Annotated Compendium including a comparative analysis of the Community consumer acquis', available at: <http://ec.europa.eu/consumers/archive/cons_int/safe_shop/acquis/comp_analysis_en.pdf>.

(Szamosszegi & Kyle 2011) Andrew Szamosszegi & Cole Kyle, 'An Analysis of State-owned Enterprises and State Capitalism in China', 26 October 2011, available at: <http://www.uscc.gov/sites/default/files/Research/10_26_11_CapitalTradeSOEStudy.pdf>.

(Twigg-Flesner 2007) Christian Twigg-Flesner, The Implementation of the Unfair Contract Terms Directive in the United Kingdom (November 30, 2007), *Contemporary Issues in Law*, 2006/2007, available at SSRN: <http://ssrn.com/abstract=1399631>.

FSC
www.fsc.org
MIX
Papier | Fördert
gute Waldnutzung
FSC® C083411

Kolibri 360 GmbH
Ferdinand-Jühlke-Straße 7
99095 Erfurt, Deutschland
produktsicherheit@kolibri360.de